D0342702

Praise for *The Telling*

"With a broad range of sources, deep insight, and true wisdom, Mark Gerson renews for his readers the enchantment of the Passover celebration."
—Rabbi David Wolpe, Sinai Temple of Los Angeles

"In *The Telling*, Mark Gerson brilliantly illuminates some of the big questions from the Haggadah whose answers can define what constitutes a meaningful life. By showing how the Haggadah enables its readers to deploy ancient Jewish wisdom to help answer the most contemporary questions, this book will help your Pesach to be what it can be: a life-guiding event, every year, for anyone who learns enough to give it the opportunity."
—Senator Joseph Lieberman

"I am not Jewish, but every Passover, I feel like I am. When I leave the Gersons' Seder, which my family and I have attended for many years, I am always left with an appreciation for Jewish familial and holiday traditions and with a desire to more deeply explore the story of Exodus and the characters that frame biblical history. *The Telling* is the perfect introduction for those desiring to explore this aspect of Jewish life. This book is full of knowledge and thought-provoking questions and answers to the many mysteries that surround this sacred Jewish day. While it may be difficult for you to actually attend a Gerson Seder, *The Telling* is the ideal surrogate."
—Tiki Barber, former running back for the NY Giants, radio host for CBS Sports Radio, and former cast member of *Kinky Boots* on Broadway

"Mark Gerson's *The Telling* is as broadly creative and inclusive as it is rigorous and intellectually deep. This book will reach, engage, and inspire countless lives whose families and communities will discover new meaning and purpose through the book's myriad insights. Mark Gerson invites readers (observant and secular, experienced and seekers, Jewish, and gentile) into a vast watered garden of Jewish wisdom that he makes accessible to all and nourishing to every soul."
—Rabbi Jonah Pesner, director of the Religious Action Center of Reform Judaism

"Transformative and compelling, Mark Gerson's inspired book *The Telling* invites all people of faith to understand the foundational realities of personal and communal identity and responsibility. In a day of vitriolic polarization, Gerson re-introduces us to the Haggadah as a living guide, given to the Jewish people, but a gift for all humanity, which provides rhythm to the beautiful and necessary dance between individualism and universalism. If you read this book and absorb its principles, your life will be fuller and richer." —Bishop Robert Stearns, pastor at the Full Gospel Tabernacle and founder of Eagles' Wings

"This beautifully written book is a fascinating guide for living a meaningful life. I highly recommend it." —Jon Gordon, author of *The Energy Bus*

"Once a year, shortly before Pesach (emphatically not Passover!), Mark Gerson steps out of his role as a world-class entrepreneur and becomes a teacher of Torah—or more precisely, of the Haggadah. Those sessions have become legendary, and this book helps explain why. Here is Gerson's inimitable voice—passionate, erudite, and most of all deeply in love with Jewish wisdom. Read this book to understand why the Haggadah has endured as a seminal Jewish text and why it remains no less relevant today than when it was first written." —Yossi Klein Halevi, author of *Letters to My Palestinian Neighbor* and *Like Dreamers*

"Mark Gerson draws on a diverse set of Jewish and secular wisdom to illuminate the Passover story in all its boundless depth. This book, which seamlessly transitions between rich storytelling, fascinating biblical interpretation, and deep historical context, is another reminder of why the Haggadah has been treasured by Jews for thousands of years. *The Telling* is a vital contribution to the Seder—it's a guide to the great Jewish guidebook." —Dan Senor, author of *Start-up Nation*

THE
TELLING

THE
TELLING

How Judaism's Essential Book Reveals the Meaning of Life

MARK GERSON

ST. MARTIN'S
ESSENTIALS
NEW YORK

First published in the United States by St. Martin's Essentials,
an imprint of St. Martin's Publishing Group

THE TELLING. Copyright © 2021 by Mark Gerson. All rights reserved.
Printed in the United States of America. For information, address
St. Martin's Publishing Group, 120 Broadway, New York, NY 10271.

www.stmartins.com

Designed by Steven Seighman

Library of Congress Cataloging-in-Publication Data

Names: Gerson, Mark, author.
Title: The telling : how Judaism's essential book reveals the meaning of
    life / Mark Gerson.
Identifiers: LCCN 2020042048 | ISBN 9781250624246 (hardcover) | ISBN
    9781250624253 (ebook)
Subjects: LCSH: Haggadah. | Seder. | Passover—Customs and practices. |
    Life—Religious aspects—Judaism.
Classification: LCC BM674.79 .G46 2021 | DDC 296.4/5371—dc23
LC record available at https://lccn.loc.gov/2020042048

Our books may be purchased in bulk for promotional, educational, or business use.
Please contact your local bookseller or the Macmillan Corporate and
Premium Sales Department at 1-800-221-7945, extension 5442,
or by email at MacmillanSpecialMarkets@macmillan.com.

10 9 8 7 6 5 4 3

CONTENTS

AUTHOR'S NOTE

Around fifteen years ago, I made a discovery. It was not the kind of discovery that a treasure hunter or medical researcher would make—where something presents in an instant and changes everything. It was more like the type of discovery described by the biblical Abraham in the book of Genesis. He had been married to Sarah for many years when, approaching Egypt to escape a famine, he declared, "Now I know you are a beautiful woman!"[1]

It was the discovery of something that had always been there but had escaped notice. It was not a discovery that concluded a process. It was one that began a journey.

My discovery was of the Haggadah, the book of the Jewish holiday of Pesach.

Like Sarah to Abraham, the Haggadah and Pesach had long been with me. I had, for as long as I could remember (and probably before that), participated in Pesach Seders and read from the Haggadah. Seders were the highlight of the Jewish year—the time when my family and friends gathered in a warm and welcoming environment to tell the story of the Jewish liberation from the Pharaoh's Egypt by reading the Haggadah, participating in beloved rituals (especially finding the afikoman and reading the Four Questions), and eating the special foods unique to the holiday. This kind of experience partially explains why American Jews are far likelier to attend a Seder than to fast on Yom Kippur, light Shabbat candles, or marry another Jew.[2]

These warm Pesach experiences prepared me for the discovery—which occurred a few weeks before a Pesach in the early 2000s. My friend Jeff Ballabon asked me to get together with him for a cigar in Manhattan to study the Haggadah. I had studied Jewish ideas with Jeff a few times before—so the prospect of enjoying a cigar and discussing a Jewish text with him was entirely welcome.

In that first session, we discussed one of the most familiar parts of the Pesach Seder—the Four Sons. Jeff, using a book by Rabbi Jonathan Sacks, showed me how the very familiar passage of the wicked son contained both the diagnosis of how the son became that way and how he could be redeemed. Jeff and I kept studying, and I started to do so on my own as well. And it became apparent that the Haggadah had enormous reserves of life-changing wisdom just beneath the passages that were familiar to me and most other Jews.

At the Seder that year, I shared some of what I had learned with my fellow attendees—and the discussions that these insights sparked showed how interesting this material was to so many people. I was hooked. It was around this time, for reasons I cannot explain, that I developed an exercise addiction. I physically *must* start the day by running at least 4.5 miles. I began to watch and listen to Haggadah and Torah commentaries every day on the treadmill—a process that takes a little longer each year. The more I learned, the more I realized how much more there was to learn and how much I wanted to study. I learned that the wisdom in the Haggadah is not only vast but literally infinite. I experienced how it teaches us how to think of life's biggest questions, guide us in the most frequent and most practical situations, and so much in between. I saw how unearthing the Haggadah's lessons and teachings, embedded in the passages and rituals familiar to everyone who has attended Seders, is enjoyable, instructive, and actionable—and also thrilling.

The only word that can adequately capture the relationship that I developed with the Haggadah is *love*. I wanted to share it. When I discussed what I was learning with both traditional and liberal Jews, I received the same reaction: genuine interest, even fascination, and always a desire to learn more.

I wanted to share this even more broadly. So in 2013, my wife (a rabbi) and I hosted our first Seder preparation session at our home in New York. The goal was for attendees to emerge with a few new ideas or discussion topics from the Haggadah that they would share at their Seders the following week. The apartment filled up, people took notes and stayed late with lots of questions and insights—and the reports came back a couple of weeks later that this night of learning made for the most meaningful discussions ever. I kept studying, and our Pesach preparation session became an annual event. Jews of all religious backgrounds, as well as interested gentiles, started coming. Within a few years, we were hosting multiple sessions a year in venues that could accommodate many more people than could our apartment.

After one of the sessions several years ago, one of the participants, Anna Phillips, came up to me and reminded me of something I had said—that the Haggadah is not a holiday manual but the Greatest Hits of Jewish Thought. Consequently, Anna said, can we continue this kind of study throughout the year? My and Erica's answer: Absolutely—we'll study the weekly Torah portion (the parsha) every week like we do the Haggadah every year.

So our weekly sessions of two hours of text study every Saturday morning began. There are now dozens of people who attend online and offline—including Jews of all religious observance, gentiles, adults, and children. These sessions have been a complete joy in so many different respects, especially as participants (most of all me) have come to see that perhaps *all* of life's consequential questions are asked and answered in the Torah. And I saw that the most important ideas that emanated from Torah study invariably tie back to a Haggadah passage, confirming that our sacred Pesach text is really a book for all seasons.

In 2015, having seen how universally interesting and simply *exciting* Torah ideas are—especially for people, like me, who have not had much experience with them—I decided to see if I could introduce the genius of the Haggadah to more than just the people I could meet. I decided to write a book for Seder leaders so that they could make their Seders what they should be: the most interesting, instructive, and meaningful evening of the Jewish year, with lessons and instructions to be learned, remembered, studied, and lived by in the year to come and beyond. That book was almost done in time for our Seder in 2018.

At the conclusion of our Seder, our friend Ken Mehlman turned to me and noted that it is remarkable how much practical wisdom, interesting ideas, and actionable insights were in the Haggadah. I said, "Thank you, yes." He said that I should share it with more people than were just at the Seder. I told him that I had nearly completed a guide for Seder leaders.

Ken said that was not the book I should have written. I asked Ken what he had in mind. He said that the Haggadah, as we had just learned at the

Seder, was the original guide for life—and that the book should be about how its lessons are accessible, actionable, and potentially transformative to Jews and gentiles, at the Seder and outside it.

Ken was, as ever, right. The rewriting process began. And here it is.

Since my first study session with Jeff, one of the main sources of enjoyment has been sharing and learning the Haggadah (and its source, the Torah) with many people. First and foremost are those who attend our weekly Torah study. There are also numerous other people whom I have been fortunate to be able to regularly turn to for everything ranging from biblical interpretations to parsing Hebrew words. The following (incomplete!) list is also a demonstration of how love of Torah can create and/or strengthen friendships. These people include Daniel Aminetzah, Jeff Ballabon, Yaron Carni, Eli Elefant, David Fox, Daniel Jeydel, Tal Keinan, Mati Kochavi, Professor Raphael Magarik, Ambassador Michael Oren, Judith Pieprz, Doron Spielman, Bishop Robert Stearns, Cantor Howard Stahl, and Rabbis Shmuley Boteach, Yechiel Eckstein (of blessed memory), Meni Even-Israel, David Fohrman, Matt Gewirtz, Moshe Gitler, Elie Kaunfer, Simcha Mirvis, Moshe Scheiner, Joe Schwartz, Meir Soloveichik, Steven Weil, Levi Welton, Mark Wildes, and David Wolpe.

I would also like to thank the remarkable editors whose deeply insightful, seasoned, and learned understanding helped me navigate through the abundance of ideas and learnings presented by the Haggadah and the book creation process: Richard Abate, Adam Bellow, Joel Fotinos, Rabbi Moshe Gitler, Gwen Hawkes, Mitch Horowitz, and Claire Wachtel.

At the end of the Pesach preparation session I led for Congregation Rodeph Shalom in 2020, I invited everyone to attend our weekly Torah study. Rhonda Kirschner has come each week since. In the midst of a discussion, I cited something from my forthcoming book. Rhonda emailed me that she would love to read and edit it. I sent her the manuscript—and she sent it back to me weeks later with the most incisive, intelligent, and detailed set of corrections and suggestions imaginable. I would also like to extend my deepest appreciation to another member of the Torah study group. Phil Getz read the manuscript, and showed me what remarkable editing can be done with such a combination of deep knowledge, profound insights, and careful attention. And Phil and Rhonda have both showed what great friendships can be made through a shared love of Torah.

I would also like to acknowledge the many people I have never met who made this book possible. That includes the many scholars and commentators cited in this book, but is not limited to them. I wrote my last book twenty-five years ago and spent an inordinate amount of time in libraries along the East Coast—with microfilm, card catalogs, directories, and as a daily consumer of interlibrary loan. I don't know if those things even exist anymore. If I could have told my younger self that I would write another book in a quarter century that would require vastly more research but no presence in any library, my younger self would think me insane.

I would like to thank everyone who developed the many mechanisms that enabled such an astonishing array of valuable knowledge to be easily accessible. Specifically (but by no means comprehensively!), I would like to thank those at Google who developed the search engine and cloud storage and those at Apple who deployed the tablet. Being able to call up a specific source or even a general idea and to be immediately gratified, being able to call up the manuscript anywhere and keep writing on a device that was just in my pocket, being able to check any of thousands of previous versions instantly: it's a miracle. These technologies easily collapsed fifteen years of work in half, and made it possible to learn better as well as faster. They enabled immediate, interesting, and serendipitous cross-referencing, which made this process vastly more efficient and enjoyable.

And God has blessed me with a wonderful family—who has been deeply integral in this process as in everything else meaningful. One could say that this book was in the works for most of my forty-seven years as the love of Pesach was instilled by my parents, Susan and Michael Gerson, before my conscious memory begins. My mother, as she has been for four decades, was a great editor in every respect—from suggesting clarifications on major ideas to catching spacing errors. My son Joshua, who is eleven, has been studying the Haggadah and the Torah with me for five years. He has shown me, by using passages from the Torah and Haggadah texts we have studied to make decisions and understand the world, how accessible and relevant these ancient texts are to addressing the most contemporary questions. And he has also illustrated, by all his actions, a major theme of the Haggadah— the role of the firstborn in setting an example—for Elijah, Talia, and Aviva. I am reminded of that each time I see his four-year-old sister, Aviva, sitting quietly at Torah study looking at him and taking it all in.

My ultimate expression of love and gratitude is to my wife, Rabbi Erica Gerson. Erica has created, and I use this term carefully and meaningfully, a perfect Jewish home. She has, through example, shown me what God intended and imagined when he said that it is not good for man to be alone and created a helpmate (or, more precisely, a "help against oneself"[3]) for the biblical Adam. She has led a Jewish family that comprehensively educates our four children (no Pesach connection, God just gave us that many) in the values, commitments, and practices that we have grown to cherish together. She has created a Jewish home that welcomes with love and respect lots of different people on Shabbat, Pesach, and every other major holiday and that is always warm, loving, and simply enjoyable to be in. Erica is the most valorous, trusted, and beloved wife in the history of marriage. I could say so much more, but the author of the "Eishes Chayil" song/prayer (from Proverbs 31) that Jewish husbands sing to our wives each Shabbat evening captures her essence with stunning accuracy. She has taught me, and everyone who knows her, what it means to craft life principles, put them into action, and have a great time doing so. This book, like every expression of love, gratitude, and Jewish yearning I can offer, is for her.

Next year in Graceland!

THE
TELLING

THE METHODOLOGY

The first step toward understanding anything thought or said, from a comedy routine to a user's guide, is always the same. It is to get one question right: What is its genre? The genre of this book is a guidebook. It is a guidebook to the Haggadah—which is the book we use to conduct the Pesach (or Passover) Seder. But the Haggadah, as we'll see, is not simply a holiday manual. It is the Greatest Hits of Jewish Thought. The purpose of this book, therefore, is to guide the reader through the Haggadah, showing the wisdom, insights, and highly practical guidance within every passage.

The establishment of the genre answers two questions about this book. First, when should this book be read? The answer: Anytime one is seeking what the Haggadah provides—the way to live a happier, more fulfilling, and better life. Just as a book about the animating ideas behind America's founding might be especially appreciated around July 4 but can be enjoyed anytime, this book will have special resonance at Pesach but is for all seasons.

Second, how should this book be experienced? It should be *used*—both to enable Jewish ideas and principles to enrich one's life and to make one's Seder what it should be: the most interesting, inspiring, and instructive night of the year. It is a book that can be, but by no means needs to be, read all the way through. A reader should feel comfortable opening to a chapter that seems like it might speak to her at that moment, and read only it. A Seder leader should, realizing that even the most robust Seder can only address a fraction of the topics enabled by the Haggadah, pick five or maybe ten of the ideas of this book and focus on them.

One of the teachings derived from the Haggadah, which will surface throughout this book, is that there can be multiple interpretations of the same thing that are all different, each true, none contradictory. I have applied this lesson in the writing and structure of the book. Particularly for a book as vast as the Haggadah, there are numerous—perhaps countless—ways to approach it effectively. I had to pick one. It is by no means the only way.

This book is divided into three sections. The first is about the background of the Pesach celebration and the Haggadah that is its animating text. This section covers four concepts. First, what Pesach is for the Jewish people. Second, what the Haggadah is for the Jewish people. Third, the purpose of Pesach and the Haggadah for God. Fourth, how God and his greatest of all prophets, Moses, decided to implement the vision that Pesach embodies.

The second section of this book is about the preparation for the Pesach Seder. It might seem odd that preparation should warrant such extensive attention. But the preparation for the Pesach celebration is, as prescribed in the Torah and done in Jewish homes today, so detailed, so meaningful, and so important that it is not really preparation at all. It is part of the event.

The third section of this book is about the Haggadah. With the exception of the last chapter, it will focus entirely on the Maggid (Telling) section of the Haggadah. This is the section of the Haggadah that contains the parts that are familiar to all Seder-goers—the Four Questions, the Four Sons, the song "Dayenu," and much more. But that is not why most of this book is about Maggid. Maggid is the part of the Haggadah that is directly responsive to the discussion and directives in Exodus 12 and 13. That alone earned the focus in this book.

This Maggid section constitutes most of this book. Each chapter discusses a passage in the Haggadah (which is quoted at the top of the chapter) or a theme raised directly by two or three passages. The Haggadah I used is the ArtScroll. Any variations from mainstream Haggadot will be small—so the reader can follow along with any Haggadah she has. I also used the ArtScroll edition for most of the biblical translations.

Readers may, and hopefully will, identify important aspects of the Haggadah and the Pesach holiday that are not mentioned in this book. This identification will lead thoughtful and engaged readers to ask: "Why isn't this passage or that idea—which I find interesting, instructive, or memorable—included?" There will be different specific answers, depending on the question. But there is one general answer: This book is incomplete.

This seems to be the inevitable state of a book about the Haggadah.

Every time—*every single time*—that I thought I concluded anything related to the Haggadah, I realized that I had just generated more questions. Every "discovery" turned out to open several new avenues of inquiry. This means, practically, that this book could never, in any meaningful sense, be complete. One of the lessons I learned in writing this book is that this state of incompletion describes any genuinely Jewish experience. This phenomenon, as applied to the Haggadah itself, will be explored in the chapter "The Unfinished."

Uses of language often embed a political, philosophical, or religious orientation inside a word choice. This is not the case with regard to my non-capitalization of the pronoun "he" when referring to God. This is simply in accordance with the *Chicago Manual of Style*. It *is* the case in this book in at least four instances. First, the term I use to describe the desert people whom God freed from Egypt is *Jews*. An argument could be made for calling us, at the time of the Exodus, *Hebrews* or *Israelites*. But we are named after the biblical character Judah, who lived hundreds of years before the Exodus. Moreover, one of the main purposes of the Pesach holiday is for Jews today to identify completely and even literally with our biblical ancestors. Calling us all by the same name—Jews—seems to be the best way to honor that commitment.

Second: I have used the term *Jew hatred* instead of anti-Semitism. Anti-Semitism is a term that was invented by nineteenth-century German pseudo-scientific race theorists who believed in the inferiority of the "Semitic" race (of which Jews were a part). According to the philologist Jonathan Hess, the term was used to distinguish "modern" forms of Jew hatred from previous forms. "Anti-Semitism" quickly became an expression that encompassed all forms of Jew hatred.[1]

The problems with the term "anti-Semitism" derive from its bizarre origin. First, as we'll see, there is remarkable consistency in the philosophy of Jew hatred from its very beginning to the present time. Second, Jew haters today routinely say that they are not "anti-Semitic" because this or that group they like is also Semitic.

The term that most clearly, honestly, and comprehensively describes antagonism against Jews is "Jew hatred"— and so that is what I use in this book.

Third: I use the terms "we" and "us" throughout the book. One of the lessons of Pesach is that the Jews are one people, through time and across geography, with no history (as defined as a chronicle of what happened to others in the past) but with a completely shared experience. I think that is correct. Accordingly, it would not be right to refer to Jews enslaved in Egypt as "they." As we'll see, the Haggadah places each Jew there. The Pesach spirit and message guide me, therefore, to an enthusiastic "me" and "us."

Fourth: One could argue, and probably correctly, that it does not really matter whether our ancestors at the time of the Exodus are called Hebrews, Israelites, or Jews—or what I call myself. But this does not extend to the authorship of the Torah, which consists of Genesis, Exodus, Leviticus, Numbers, and Deuteronomy, and is the canonical text of the Jews from which all commentaries, laws, customs, practices, and other sacred books (especially the Haggadah) derive. If God wrote the Torah, it is completely authoritative. If people wrote the Torah, it might still be authoritative (as the United States Constitution is)—but significantly less so.

So—who wrote it? Throughout this book, I use the term *author of the Torah*. One might say that this is an evasion—as *obviously* the author of the Torah wrote the Torah. That would be a fair criticism. But I use this term *author of the Torah* not because I want to avoid the question but because I want to answer it. Who wrote the Torah—God or people? I believe that it was probably both. *Probably* because that reflects the humility that is required with all questions whose answers cannot be known. *Both* because this is the logical conclusion of what we learn about God in the Torah. As we'll see, *everything* that God does after he creates people is in partnership with people. This is evident in the Torah itself, which contains several instances where God amends the Torah or changes its course because people (both prophets and ordinary citizens) convince him to do so.

Moreover, there is a force greater than logic that demonstrates co-authorship. The Torah and its great derivative work (the Haggadah) are simply too interesting; too relevant to everyone's challenges and opportunities; too persistently defining in the political, social, and psychological development of mankind; too accessible to people of all ages and at all stages at all points in thousands of years of Jewish history—they are, in a word, *too good*—to be written by a person alone.

No person or even people is that wise and talented.

As for human involvement? People make the choice to learn the Torah and Haggadah, to teach the Torah and Haggadah to our children, to devote Judaism's most important evening to understanding their lessons, and to try to live accordingly in the year that follows. The Torah is too good to be written without God, but it would have suffered the fate of a buried treasure were it not for our consistent commitment to understand and live by it. As God tells Moses in Deuteronomy, "Now write down this song and teach it to the Israelites and have them sing it!" We do so at each Seder.

THE REAL JEWISH NEW YEAR

An ancient people of the Bible, the Jews, have just endured years of brutal slavery in the claws of the most powerful country in the world, Egypt. The Jewish deity has had enough. He is determined to free the Jews and, in the process, show everyone (the Jews, the Egyptians, and, by extension, every people) that he is the *only* God. This victory would immediately invalidate not just the authority but the *existence* of all other gods. It would communicate that this God loves and cares for everyone, making him deserving of universal allegiance. It would establish his adopted "firstborn," the Jews, as the people whose example would carry his truth through the world. It would be a revolution that only God could imagine and execute.

The outcome of events often seem, at their completion, to have been inevitable. But in the process toward that completion, hardly predictable. This is certainly the case with the Exodus. By the time of the tenth plague, God's mission of taking the Jews out of Egypt and into the Promised Land seems far from an assured success. He has already made nine acts of spectacular intervention. All have failed. The Jews are still enslaved, and the Pharaoh is recalcitrant.

God has the tenth plague ready. It is the slaying of the Egyptian firstborn, to be executed just after midnight on the fifteenth day of the first month of the year. The previous plagues all contained the possibility of being followed by another that could concentrate the Pharaoh's mind further. Frogs could be followed by gnats, which could be followed by wild beasts, which could be followed by cattle disease. But what could come after the slaying of the firstborn? If the Egyptian regime were to survive this plague, the Jews would stay enslaved and ultimately be extinguished. God, if defeated in a world that admires only power, would be finished.

This is the most important moment the world would ever know. The major players understand this. God's beloved prophet, Moses, has just experienced an emotion he never had before—one that would subsequently be all but prohibited in Judaism.[1] He is in a state of "burning anger." The Pharaoh, who has aroused this emotion in Moses, refuses to let the Jews go. He is ready for the final showdown.

God, too, is ready. He acts . . . by declaring a holiday. This holiday, he ordains, is to be celebrated annually per Exodus 12:14 "throughout your generations, as an eternal decree."

It is the holiday we know as Pesach, or (unfortunately, for reasons we will discuss) Passover. Pesach is, by far, the most widely observed Jewish holiday. Even Jews who are otherwise completely nonobservant are likely to attend a Seder.[2] Pesach has also become *the* focal point for the astonishing Christian rediscovery of Jewish roots that is now occurring, as exemplified by the spontaneous launching of tens of thousands of Christian Seders and countless Christians attending those and Jewish Seders as well.

The growing influence of this Jewish holiday is having ramifications even beyond religious precincts. The Indian philosopher Vishal Mangalwadi writes, "Not many people realize that the Exodus story [which Pesach tells] is . . . the foundation of the modern world."[3] That, because of this unprecedented appreciation of Pesach, is rapidly changing. Both those who seek an ever-deeper relationship with God and those who think themselves exempt from divine influence are discovering that we all live in a world forged by Pesach. And it's all very exciting.

What exactly is this holiday that captures the imagination of almost every Jew, and is creating and strengthening this new and historic friendship between Jews and Christians? The Torah tells us precisely. Pesach, we learn in Exodus 12:2, should occur at "the head of months, the first month of the year." The Pesach Seder is, therefore, the Jewish New Year celebration.

Many people will say, "Stop! Rosh Hashanah is the Jewish New Year." This is a mistake. As Rabbi Meir Soloveichik says, "The most common statement made about this holiday, one which I habitually make as well, is actually incorrect. . . . Rosh Hashanah is known as the 'Jewish New Year' . . . [but] Rosh Hashanah is *not* the Jewish New Year."[4] Or, as the scholar Nehemia Gordon concludes, the designation of Rosh Hashanah as the Jewish New Year is "outright bizarre."[5]

Rosh Hashanah is not in the Torah and is barely mentioned in the Bible (which consists of the two dozen books that constitute the Torah, the

Prophets, and the Writings).[6] The holiday that it effectively replaced, the "Day of Loud Blasts" from Leviticus 23:24, was never a New Year. The most that can be said about Rosh Hashanah as a New Year is that it occurs *exactly* six months after the formal Pesach preparations begin, has long been celebrated as a New Year, and, most important, raises some of the same themes as Pesach.

Still, there is nothing wrong with following the Rabbinic tradition and celebrating Rosh Hashanah as a New Year. The concept of multiple New Years is both normal and purposeful. The Torah has multiple New Years, even though Rosh Hashanah is not one of them. In the United States, we celebrate January 1 (the calendrical New Year), July 4 (the national New Year), and our birthday (our personal New Year), and acknowledge various fiscal New Years. By instituting Rosh Hashanah as a New Year, the designers of the Jewish calendar institutionalized the belief that opportunities and responsibilities provided by Pesach are too consequential to be considered only annually.

With the Torah having established Pesach as the Jewish New Year, it immediately moves to how the holiday should be celebrated. And it does so with a level of detail accorded no other holiday in the Torah. The menu, the way the meat should be prepared, and the purpose of the dinner discussion are just a few of the instructions pertaining to Pesach that are required in Exodus. Why, we are drawn to ask, would the Torah include such detailed instructions regarding how Jews are to celebrate our New Year?

Perhaps the author of the Torah was sculpting Judaism, designing Jewish life, and *creating* Jews—and wanted our celebrations to reflect the kind of people we would ideally become. More than we design celebrations, they actually design us. This is something that is easily observable. The best single way to understand an individual or a community is to observe their celebrations. How does a community acknowledge Memorial Day? How does an individual celebrate his fortieth birthday? How does a family celebrate B'nai Mitzvah or a couple a wedding? Even a glimpse will enable an observer to reliably project the aspirations, priorities, and values of the celebrants. And by telling us *how* to celebrate, on the verge of our becoming a free people, the Torah leads us to consider just what kind of people celebrate this way and thus what kind of people we should become.

The first question we ask about any occasion is: When is it? Often, the answer is not meaningful. If George Washington and Abraham Lincoln were born in October instead of February, the significance of Presidents' Day would be the same. That is not the case with Pesach.

In Exodus 13:4, God decrees that Pesach shall occur "in the spring." That Judaism should have a spring festival is, by itself, unremarkable. The gratitude at having survived the winter and the feeling of renewal that the new season projects has inspired celebrations everywhere. There is the Songkran water festival in Thailand, Holi in northern India, Easter egg rolls on the White House lawn, the Festival of Scrambled Eggs in Bosnia, and Walpurgis Night in northern Europe.

But there is a problem for the Jewish spring celebration. The Jewish calendar is on a lunar schedule. This means that the year is approximately 354 days long—and that months are disassociated from seasons. The Islamic year also follows a lunar calendar—and, consequently, Ramadan has fallen in every month. It should be impossible, therefore, for a holiday on a lunar calendar to be tied to a particular season.

How, then, could Judaism have a holiday designed specifically for the spring?

The designers of the Jewish calendar answered by adding a leap month (Adar) seven times every nineteen years. This ensures that Pesach will always fall in the spring. But there is another problem: not all spring days are created equal. The only difference between the moment before and the moment after the spring equinox is the human designation of season. And the author of the Torah decreed that Pesach should fall in the spring for a substantive reason, not to satisfy a technical requirement. It is not as if any spring day would do.

The early twentieth-century Princeton professor and minister Henry van Dyke wrote, "The first day of spring is one thing, and the first spring day is another."[7] The ancient rabbis, who interpreted the Torah as they designed the calendar, would have agreed. The Jewish calendar is arranged so that Pesach always occurs when the barley is ripened and the trees abound with seasonal fruit. Pesach, therefore, does not occur when spring officially starts. It starts several weeks later, when it feels like spring.[8]

The ramifications of this calendrical workaround to place Pesach in the heart of spring are defining and pervasive. Yom Kippur occurs in the autumn, Hanukkah occurs in the winter, and Tisha B'av occurs in the summer *only* because Pesach occurs when it feels like spring. The Jewish calendar, and the Jewish life lived in it, revolves around the spring festival that is our New Year celebration.

It is not at all obvious that this should be the case. The biblical book of Ecclesiastes says, "To everything there is a season"—establishing that there is something special about each season. Therefore, there could be special qualities in other seasons that would have earned them Pesach. Why, then, would Jewish life be oriented around spring? There are at least two possibilities.

First, the emphasis on spring brings our attention outside. Pesach, as we will see, is a holiday that calls significantly upon the intellect—whose exercise primarily occurs indoors. The emphasis on a season, whose distinctions manifest only outside, reminds us that Pesach is not only or even primarily an experience of and for the mind. The centrality of a specific season reminds us that the ultimate purpose of Pesach is to bring us outside. This means going outside of who we are to evaluate what we should change and to imagine who we could be. This means going outside into the world, learning from its wisdom, and influencing it with our values and our conduct.

And it means going outside physically, where we are reminded that places, like people, are unique and appreciated in their distinctiveness. It is with this realization that we can appreciate why the Jewish heart has beaten so insistently, and especially on Pesach, toward one Land. There is something about one's mother that separates her from all other women; there is something about one's childhood home that distinguishes it from other homes of similar size; and there is something about the Land of Israel that has made it the object of yearning on every Pesach for thousands of years.

Second, the distinctive experience of spring is easily identifiable, and the significance of its identity is equally apparent. The ice melts, the leaves return, the days lengthen, animals mate, flowers bloom, and 500 million birds from more than five hundred species pass over southern Israel. Spring is the season of renewal, rebirth, and re-creation.[9]

With the *when* of the Jewish New Year settled, the next questions are: Where and with whom should we celebrate? The Torah has those answers as well. "[The Pesach meal] must be eaten," the Torah tells us in Exodus 12:46, "inside the house." The instructions specify the meat, the mandated carbohydrate and the prohibited carbohydrate, the timing, the attire . . .

and what to do about leftovers. "You shall not," the Torah stipulates in Exodus 12:10, "leave any of it until the morning."

Why are *leftovers* forbidden? The Torah plants the answer six verses previously, before we could know to ask the question. "If any household is too small for a whole lamb, they must share one with their nearest neighbor, having taken into account the number of people there are." Modern estimates, which cohere with ancient reports, suggest that the consumption of a lamb would require at least fifteen people and possibly many more, depending on the age of the lamb.[10] This means that multiple households had to join together to properly experience the Pesach meal. Embedded in this seemingly obscure directive is the initial lesson in freedom that God provides for the Jews.

The fundamental act of a free person, the Torah shows in Exodus 12:4, is to share. It is through this sharing—among individuals, within a household, and then among households—that the first community would form, and Jewish communal life would be created.

There is still one question remaining. With households gathered together in community to celebrate the Jewish New Year—what should they do besides eat dinner? There are many possibilities. The author of the Torah could have directed the attendees to have an outdoor prayer service, engage in an ancient equivalent of touch football, or participate in a communal dance. Instead, God orders something very different.

HAGGADAH:
WHEN A GREAT BOOK IS NOT MEANT TO BE READ

God's order, as communicated through his beloved prophet, Moses, is placed in Exodus 13:8. Moses says, "You shall tell your son on that day, 'It is because of what the Lord did for me when I came out of Egypt.'"

As everyone who has experienced a story knows, the instruction "to tell" does not explain itself. There are always many different ways to tell a story, let alone one as rich, complex, and dynamic as that of the Exodus. And the choice of what to include and emphasize in any telling can make for a very different story. Yet neither God nor his most beloved prophet offers any instruction about how the story should be told other than "tell your son." Moses provides the general direction and gives his descendants the choice of how to execute along with the responsibility to do so.

It is by no means clear how we would have chosen to fulfill this command. We could have decreed a special religious service. We could have developed an oral tradition. We could have required that our children memorize parts of Exodus 12 and 13. But more than two thousand years ago, our ancestors made a different choice.

They chose to interpret Exodus 13:8 as the *commissioning of a book*. The book is the Haggadah—which means, appropriate to its biblical source, "Telling." And it just might be the strangest, most instructive, and simply *best* book ever written.

Given the clear mandate in the Torah to tell the story of the Exodus, the structure of the book that enables us to do so should be clear enough. The story of the Exodus—about how the Jews were enslaved in Egypt for two hundred years before God, working with Moses, liberated us—is described in the biblical book of Exodus. One would presume, then, that the obligation to tell the story of the Exodus would be best discharged through a synopsis of Exodus. And, sure, the Haggadah does draw from Exodus. But it also draws from Genesis, Deuteronomy, Ezekiel, Joshua, Chronicles, Joel, Psalms, stories from a Seder held by five rabbis, songs from throughout Jewish history, Jewish prayer—and an invitation to use all those subjects as the basis to interpret and discuss contemporary concerns and questions.

We tell the story of the Exodus, therefore, through a book that essentially curates the Greatest Hits of Jewish Thought with sources long before and after the great event itself. This alone constitutes a radical interpretation of the Exodus. Constructing it this way, the authors of the Haggadah were saying that the Exodus was not an event that began and ended but one that previous Jewish experience was spent preparing for and all subsequent Jewish experience is still living.

As previously discussed, the key to understanding the Haggadah is the same as it is for every book. It is to get one question right: What is its genre? Usually, the answer is obvious. A Stephen King thriller is unlikely to be mistaken for an instruction manual and a Michael Oren history is unlikely to be considered a romantic comedy. But sometimes the identification of a genre is more complicated. If a listener interprets a joke as social commentary or science fiction as science, the result can be a serious misunderstanding. This is true with the Torah and the Haggadah.

A rabbi of the Talmud, Ben Bag-Bag, famously said of the Torah, "Turn it around and around, for everything is in it."[1] He could have said the same thing about the Torah's great derivative work, the Haggadah. The infinitude of the Torah and the Haggadah make the identification of their genre easy to mistake.

Moses seems to have anticipated this problem, and its potential severity. At the end of Deuteronomy, he is near death. He has a few final words to share with his people as they prepare to create a life as a free people in the Promised Land. The subject of his parting words: the genre of the Torah. The Torah, he explains in Deuteronomy 10:13, is provided "*for your benefit.*"

The Torah and the Haggadah are, therefore, *guidebooks*—intended to lead us through *all* the decisions, challenges, and opportunities in our lives. And it is certainly *all*, as the Torah and the Haggadah offer direct guidance for seemingly every activity, from the feeling we should have at breakfast to understanding our existential purpose.

If the question were posed, "What is one supposed to do with a book?" the answer would be obvious: Read it. But no one only reads the Haggadah, or recommends that it just be read. Reading the Haggadah is like reading the lyrics of a song. There is nothing wrong with doing so, but it will not produce anything of the intended experience.

One might suggest that we don't "read" the Haggadah because the Torah instructs us to "tell" the story. But no one speaks of telling the story either. Instead, we use the Haggadah to enable us to *retell* and *relive* the story. This is curious for two reasons. First, there is nothing about *living* (let alone *reliving*) in the Torah. And second, the Torah says nothing about *retelling*—only *telling*. Yet we insist, and always have, that the command to tell can only be realized through *retelling* and *reliving*.

In other words, we use the Haggadah to *retell* and *relive* the story. This arouses two questions. Why the *live*? And why the *re*?

As we'll see, the Torah's conceptions of remembering and knowing are always associated with action. The Talmud, the canonical text of third- and fourth-century Torah interpretation, interprets the biblical verse "That you may look upon it [the ritual fringes] and remember all the commandments of the Lord and do them" to mean "that looking at the ritual fringes leads to remembering the mitzvot, and remembering them leads to doing them."[2] If one "knows" something and does not *act* accordingly, the knowledge is considered void or even absent. Jews are the "people of the book" who both revere words and are acutely aware of their limits. Jewish telling requires living.

Why, then, do we insist on the *retelling* and *reliving*? *Re* indicates that the activity has been done *before*. If we reunite a group, renew a soul, or reread a book, it means we are doing the task *again*. But *re* is used infrequently. Adults rarely do a task for the first time, and we do not use *re* to describe most of them. No one says, "I rewent to the office," "I rewent to sleep," or "I rewent to the men's room"—regardless of how often we previously did those activities. Why, then, is *re* always deployed in the Pesach context?

One answer is suggested in the analysis of books by the Russian novelist Vladimir Nabokov. "A good reader, a major reader, an active and creative reader is a rereader."[3] When we read (or are told) something for the first time, we are consumed with grasping the plot, following the story, or comprehending the argument. For most content we consume, that is enough. But as the earliest designers of our Pesach celebration knew thousands of years before Nabokov, the genuine experience of a truly great work is in its *reconsideration.*

The acknowledgment in the Pesach *re* that we are living and telling the story again leads us to ask: With whom are we doing so? Two answers emerge, both of which reveal a central purpose of our Jewish New Year celebration.

First, we are retelling and reliving the story with our younger selves. This acknowledgment invites an existential accounting of oneself. How did I think of the wicked son when I was an adolescent compared to now, when my child is that age? How do I understand the gratitude expressed by "Dayenu" now, compared to when I was younger, when I did not know from life's complexities?

Any such question will likely lead to a revelatory sequence. First, I am in many ways a different person now from who I was then. One reason is that I made choices then that contributed significantly to who I am now. Consequently, I will be different in the future—and the choices I make now will significantly impact who I will be later. It is this realization—that the choices I make today determine the different person I will be in the future—that genuinely prepares us for the Jewish New Year celebration and positions us to be guided by the Haggadah.

The second answer derives from the fact that, as consistent with the dictates in Exodus 12, Seders are done among households joined in community. As our minds turn to our previous Jewish New Year celebrations, we invariably recall the second group with whom we are retelling and reliving the story. We think of the people who were at our previous Seders, and particularly those who have passed. We think of the ideas they shared, the perspectives they offered, the songs they sang, the food they ate, their idiosyncrasies that surfaced, and the feelings within us that they aroused. This leads to another revelatory sequence.

First, we imagine how they would fit into this year's Seder. How would they have related to my spouse and my children, my home, my guests, my customs, and my interpretations of the same text they used to celebrate Pesach? And we realize that they probably thought the same way, at the same time of year, about those who came before they did. As there have been more than one hundred generations before us who have had a Seder very much like ours, we can approach Pesach knowing that we are participating in the longest and greatest religious tradition in the world.

We then realize how (literally) unbelievable it is that we have been able to retell/relive a story for so long. A child's game of telephone loses a simple message before it gets to the end of a small line in a few moments. Yet if Jesus or even Moses were to walk into a Seder in Miami Beach and open the Haggadah, he would know exactly what was going on. A Jew from third-century Jerusalem, tenth-century Yemen, seventh-century Poland, nineteenth-century Cincinnati, twentieth-century Warsaw, or twenty-first-century Tel Aviv could sit down at any of the other Seders, comfortably participate, and fully contribute.

Equally stunning is that a Jew today from anywhere will find himself as comfortable at any Seder in the world as if he were a long-lost cousin surprising everyone with his presence. There may be language, cultural, or doctrinal differences—but they are immediately diminished by the welcome and the familiarity that such a traveler will experience.

This vertical continuity through the generations and horizontal continuity across the continents becomes possible when we realize just what the retelling and reliving are facilitating. The fundamental interaction with the Haggadah is, as discussed, not reading. It is a combination of activities: listening, speaking, being heard, and responding anew. Together, these constitute a familiar activity: a *conversation*. Indeed, by telling the story through a standard text—and using the fixed text to *retell*—we are able to have three separate conversations at the Jewish New Year celebration. We are conversing with those at our table, with those at Seders all over the world, and with those who relived and retold the story from the Haggadah for the past twenty-plus centuries.

One of the fundamental characteristics of every genuine conversation is its uniqueness. No two conversations are the same, and participants in a conversation cannot know in what direction it will head, where it will end up, and how it will change their relationship. A conversation is a highly volatile instrument.

Perhaps ironically, it is the dynamic and unpredictable vehicle of a conversation that has enabled the stability, durability, and continuity of the Jewish New Year celebration. The Haggadah has enabled Jews over thousands of years and across thousands of miles, in every cultural and socioeconomic climate, to participate in one conversation. It has been the Haggadah that has, literally and figuratively, kept all Jews on the same page everywhere and forever.

A short book that is not meant to be read, a conversation that extends through every geography and each generation. That is the foundation. But what is the Haggadah about? On one level, it is the guide to telling the story of our liberation from slavery in Egypt. However, the Jewish imagination (starting in the Torah) has always conceived of God's liberation of the Jews and the Jews' choice of how to exercise our freedom as inextricably linked. And there is nothing simple, easy, or conclusive about freedom. Indeed, the number and composition of subjects aroused in the Haggadah demonstrate just how pervasive, complicated, ambitious, and interesting the Jewish questions around freedom are.

The subjects addressed by the Haggadah include education, history, dreams, happiness, memory, parenthood, order, blessings, food, existential needs, hunger and wants, Jewish peoplehood, when to delegate, Jew hatred, curiosity, music, beginnings and endings, the meanings of why, the meaning of history, the time for brevity and for its opposite, wisdom and foolishness, why bad things happen to good people, evil and our responses to it, the relationship between the physical, emotional, and intellectual, individuality and community, idolatry in our day, family dysfunction, victimization, the politics of interpretation, forgiveness, the cultivation and expression of gratitude, habits, false humility, aging, the meaning of respect, the role of the imagination, the purpose and limits of political debate, analogies, the State of Israel, man's relationship with God, the Jewish relationship with gentiles, the purpose of freedom, the presentation of miracles—*and many more.*

GOD'S BUSINESS CARD

The Hebrew word for *face* is *panim*. This is probably familiar to most Jews over a certain age whose cheeks were squeezed by a grandmother who said, "Shayna Punim!" But this expression of affection hides a seminal teaching in the Hebrew language. *Panim* means *faces*. There is no Hebrew word for *face*. This is because no one has just one.

We intuitively understand this. No one presents the same way in her business profile, her online dating profile, at a funeral and a party, with strangers and with intimates, when making a commercial presentation, and when rooting for a team. And this is true internally as well. It might be unpredictable, but it is not remarkable, for one person to enjoy poetry, football, adventure travel, and romance novels. Walt Whitman, the quint-essential American poet, wrote, "I am large, I contain multitudes," and his Chilean counterpart Pablo Neruda titled a poem "We Are Many." It is about himself.

Despite our complexity, we have business cards with one title, online profiles that can be digested quickly, relatively short eulogies and obitu-aries, and will each reside beneath a gravestone with an epitaph that is the briefest of them all.

Why do we present to the world simple descriptions when only com-plexity exists? Why, in other words, do we so often describe things as having a "face" while understanding that only *panim* exist? The problem does not usually lie with the describer, who would speak more fully about himself if others would listen. The problem lies with the person to whom he is speaking. There are always so many things competing for our limited time, attention, and energy that we require a short and inevitably incomplete description. Toronto is a large and diverse city with a long and rich history. Yet when the British actor Peter Ustinov described Toronto as "New York run by the Swiss," presumably no one complained about all the attributes of that city that he did not address.[1] We live in a world only of faces but communicate in face.

As this problem derives from the listener, it is as significant for God as it is for us. Like the human beings he created, God wants to communicate with and for people. But he has a problem. As God, he is infinitely more complex than any person. But he is still communicating with the same people who, in our capacity as listeners, have limited focus and therefore generate the *panim* problem. Therefore, he needs to communicate using the methods that work for us as listeners.[2]

Yet the challenge posed by the *panim* problem is greater for God than for anyone else. And it is not just because God has so many more faces than any of us. It is because his work is more important. If a job candidate with two strengths emphasizes one when the employer is looking for the other and consequently does not get the job, there is a loss—but the wheels of global commerce will keep spinning.

If God presents himself suboptimally, then the moral direction of the world will be misaligned. The fate of humankind depends on God doing what no one has ever done—to have one description that will say it all.

What would God put on his business card?

Encapsulating *God* in one sentence fragment might seem impossible for anyone who communicates through language—including God. But God accepts this challenge, as soon as he begins a genuine relationship with the people he creates. After God promises Abraham, the first Jew and the first person with whom he has a genuine relationship, in Genesis 15:5 that his offspring will be like the stars of the sky, God defines himself.

How would he do so? Perhaps the most obvious would have been his greatest technical achievement: as the Creator of heaven and earth. Or, perhaps, he could have gone relationally—and identified himself, as Jewish liturgy subsequently would, as our father and our king or the God of our mothers and fathers. But God makes a very different choice.

"I am Hashem Your God who brought you out of Ur Kasdim to give you this Land."

Why would God say this? Abraham knows that he came from Ur Kasdim, that he is speaking with God, and is headed to the Land of Israel. But there is no redundancy. God is not allaying confusion or providing information. He is revealing a truth about himself and describing what he plans to do in the future.

God is declaring himself to be the one who takes us out of bad places and leads us to better places for a reason and with an expectation. He does not want to be understood as the God *of* history, who observes dispassionately. He wants to be understood as the God *in* history, who acts purposefully.

But there is a problem. No one else in the Torah—not even Isaac and Jacob (Abraham's son and grandson, respectively)—ever mentions Ur Kasdim. No one in the Torah cites Ur Kasdim as an inspiration to do anything. Ur Kasdim has barely ever had any resonance. God's first effort at self-description completely fails.

What does God do with such a failure? *He learns.* Specifically, he learns how to communicate strategically with people. This lesson is evident in what we, with the benefit of the whole Torah, easily recognize as missing from the Ur Kasdim sequence. There is no story around it. The Torah does not mention any of Ur Kasdim's people, events, culture, society, drama, or dynamics. We don't even know why Abraham left the place. With no story, Abraham's leaving Ur Kasdim never had a shot at inspiring anyone, let alone at introducing God to the world. God learns that people think in stories. He would put that lesson to work.

God goes through the rest of Genesis and the Exodus from Egypt without the opportunity to define himself again. Is he frustrated by his failure to define himself to the people he loves, especially when knowing him better would have helped them through many difficult and consequential times? Perhaps, but God's patience would be redeemed.

The Pesach story concludes with (as we'll see!) a scene that effectively consecrates a new world. With a free people devoted to God, and everyone else impressed by the divinely orchestrated slave revolt that freed them from the grip of the world's most powerful empire, God has the opportunity to define himself to a global audience. He does so within a month of the Jews being freed from Egypt in the context of a universal code that would become known as the Ten Commandments.

The First Commandment, which some regard as so fundamental that it is actually the introduction to the others, would serve as God's singular self-definition to the world. It has nothing to do with creating the heavens and the earth or giving the Torah to us at Mount Sinai. But it would be familiar to all fans of Ur Kasdim.

"I am Hashem Your God, who brought you out of the land of Egypt, out of slavery."

This short statement would introduce the daily prayers of Jews forever. It would power the dreams of freedom-loving people everywhere and forever. It answers the fundamental question of theology: Who is God? And through that answer, it helps us understand what God wants from us, what we should want from ourselves, and how we should operate in God's world. It would become the descriptive line on God's business card, his definition of what it means to be the God in history. And there are at least five existential lessons for us.

First, God's business card tells us what he regards as his most important attribute. He is not *primarily* the God who created the heavens and the earth or even gave us the Torah at Sinai—both acts performed *outside* history. He is *principally* the God who freed us from Egypt—an act performed *inside* history. When we think about the God in history, we might gravitate to events that are called "historical" and are reported in newspapers, recorded in books, and immortalized in museums. The Torah and Haggadah show that God does care about our grandest dreams, most audacious visions, and most notable accomplishments. These are part of who we are and the history we create. But that part rarely fills up an afternoon, and God gave us all of life.

God makes it very easy to figure out what it means for him to exist within history. Leviticus 25:36–37 decrees seemingly mundane regulations regarding the charging of interest and the price of food. God interrupts the issuing of these laws to present his business card: "I am Hashem Your God who brought you out of Egypt to give you the Land of Canaan and to be your God." He continues with regulations governing how we are to commercially engage with hired laborers. This interruption of laws governing everyday activity with a show of the business card would become a frequent part of the biblical narrative, situating all of God's laws in his identity as the God *in* history.

God, in ways described in the Torah, cares about the subjects covered by labor law, how we talk, if we enjoy our lunch (the manna in the desert, per Exodus 16:31, "tasted like honey wafers"), how we work and how we parent, how we pray and how we judge, how we treat those in need, how we love, how we hate, and how we spend our time. Living under the God in history means, as King Solomon decrees in Proverbs 3:6, that we are to "know God in all your ways."

Second, God's business card teaches us why he cares about "all your ways." If God had selected "Creator of the heavens and the earth" for his business card, his designation would have been *materially* comprehensive. But it would have been *spiritually* meaningless. "Great," we would have said, "you created the heavens and the earth—but *why*?"

By choosing for his business card the description as the one who freed us from Egypt, God answers that question without it being asked. He is saying, "I have a purpose. My purpose is what is most important to me. And that purpose is to make the world free."

What does God mean by *free*? This word does not come close to defining itself, as *freedom* is used to inspire and justify so many different things. But our God in history makes it easy to interpret. Most people are familiar with the line from the Torah "Let my people go"—even if just from its popularization in movies and songs. Indeed, that is the directive that God tells Moses to issue to the Pharaoh (the Egyptian monarch who would become the antagonist of God and Moses) many times. But God *always* includes with this command a variant of "so that they might serve Me." The point of freedom, the Torah teaches, is not liberation itself. It is for us to become, as God instructs in Exodus 19:6, "a kingdom of priests and a holy nation." For God and his people, freedom entails responsibility.

The third lesson from God's business card derives from what God puts on our business card. He hands it to us as soon as we are born, in Genesis 1:27—when he tells us that he "created mankind in his own image." If God has a defining purpose and each of us is created in his image, then each of us must have a driving purpose as well.

This realization leads one to ask: "What is my purpose?" It sounds like an intimidating question that will be difficult to answer. But that can't be. Our God, who defines himself as the liberator and cares about what we charge for food and money, is both highly aspirational and very practical. He would only give us a life-defining purpose if we could identify it easily and orient our lives accordingly.

Indeed, it is easy to identify. God created signs for us all over the place—internally and externally. The internal approach is personified by Gene Flewelling. He is a project manager with International Technical Electric & Construction, a Christian engineering firm that builds infrastructure in the poorest places in the world. In describing his work, Flewelling says,

> In the scripture . . . God asks Moses at the burning bush: "What is in your hand?" We all have something in our hand. . . . I am a lineman. I love being a lineman. I love my profession. For me, the revelation was that I . . . could do linework for God.[3]

Flewelling recognized that he had the skills to be an outstanding lineman, developed a love for the craft—and offers these gifts to God by improving the lives of God's often forgotten and ignored children.

Gene Flewelling speaks of something that the Haggadah will lead us to consider at length—the staff in Moses's hand. Before Moses is able to have the conversation with God at the burning bush that Flewelling references, Moses has to do something first. He has to notice that the bush, which is burning as bushes often do in the desert, is not being consumed. It is through his *paying attention*—it is by regarding something seemingly familiar in his environment as deserving of his wonder and appreciation—that God is able to deliver his purpose to Moses. And this leads to the external way in which we can identify our purpose.

The Torah, Rabbi Marc Gellman of Temple Beth Torah in New York writes, "is constantly confusing people with angels."[4] Abraham is home with his wife, Sarah, recovering from being circumcised at a very late age. Three men appear at their home, and Abraham and Sarah rush to provide these strangers with food, shelter, and comfort. These men, it turns out, are not just men. They are angels who deliver to Abraham the message from God that he and Sarah would have the child they yearned for, that his descendants would have the Land of Israel, and that these descendants would be blessed. In Hebrew, the word for *angel* and the word for *messenger* are the same—because their functions are the same.

The implications are existentially intriguing. If angels are regular people who carry messages from God, who—and where—are they? Rabbi Gellman notes:

> Perhaps it was the person who first gave you a book about science and sent you off on the road to becoming a scientist. Perhaps it was the person who told you that you would make a good lawyer or teacher or mother or friend or confidant at just the time when you had no intention of becoming anything like that. Perhaps it was the person who told you to watch out at just the time you needed to watch out.[5]

The realization that each of us has a readily identifiable, distinct, and divinely ordained purpose leads to the fourth teaching from God's business card: All other people do as well. This revelation guides us to at least two destinations. First, we have the opportunity to be God's angel for someone—and, perhaps, for lots of people. Each time we help another person to appreciate a capability she has or a contribution that she can make, we just might be helping that person discover her sacred purpose. This opportunity to be God's messenger exists in every word of gratitude, in each spark of encouragement, in every act of acknowledgment.

Second, if we identify another person living God's purpose, with or without our guidance, a feeling is immediately triggered and profoundly experienced. This is respect. If we see someone caring for a child, operating on a patient, trading stocks, designing an electrical system, teaching a class, shooting a basketball, leading a worship service, cleaning a church, fighting a fire, or driving a bus and think—*that person is doing God's work*—we will accord that person the kind of respect we would otherwise reserve for God. It is this divinely derived respect that constitutes the psychological basis for equality, the social basis for a flourishing society, and the religious basis for love.

That God has a purpose, and gives us a purpose with the ability to identify and fulfill it, leads to a fundamental question. If God is omnipotent and has a purpose he wants to achieve, wouldn't he just do it by himself? What does he want from me?

This question is answered in the fifth revelation from God's business card.

As we'll see in the chapters of this book on the plagues, every act that

God takes in accordance with the description on his business card is done in partnership with a person or multiple people. This is not unique to the Exodus. After the creation of the world, it describes almost everything he does—and, perhaps, *everything* he does that works out well.

And God seems to love this partnership.

Pursuant to the Jews worshipping the golden calf in Exodus 32, God plans to destroy his people but effectively asks Moses to argue with him—and changes his position when Moses does. God does not just want the partnership of prophets. In Numbers 9, God changes the rules of Pesach and consequently the Torah itself, at the request of several *ordinary* men. Eighteen chapters later, he changes the rules of inheritance, and consequently the Torah itself, at the request of five *ordinary* sisters.[6] In both cases, God changes his sacred text—*God transforms the way he wants the world to operate*—in response to regular people saying that they have a better way to implement God's principles than he does.

By acting in accordance with such partners, God is guiding us to a realization: I want you to be my partner—and there is no limit to what I want to do with you. How can each of us accept this sacred offer and become a partner for God? By starting, as God models, with the realization that each of us has *panim*—many faces. And someday we will be—as the Torah so hauntingly says of Abraham, Isaac, Jacob, Aaron, and Moses at the time of their passing—gathered to our people. At that point, there will be just one face presented on our gravestone and, eventually, in the memory of those who knew us. What will it be? Being free means that we can decide now, and act accordingly. We can have a business card whose description we can craft and earn, just as God did.

What should we put on our business card, and how should we act accordingly? For that, we have the Haggadah.

THE CRAZIEST DREAM
COMES TRUE: HOW WE LIVE
IN MOSES'S WORLD

It's Exodus 12:14. The tenth plague, the slaying of the firstborn of Egypt, is about to happen. The Jews, following centuries of slavery and witnessing nine brutal plagues, are about to be freed. As the Jews wait in the liminal space between slavery and freedom, God has an instruction for them: "You shall celebrate this day as an eternal decree through the generations!"

The extraordinary ambition of God's command (an *eternal* decree!) is evident with a consideration of the peoples mentioned in the Torah. There are lots of other peoples in the book of Exodus, all of whom were thriving when the Jews were just coalescing—the Perizzites, the Canaanites, the Jebusites, and the Hittites, among others.

Where are they now?

Gone. Their civilizations are dead. Their ideas are lost. Their memories are erased. Their great moments are forgotten. Their heroes are anonymous. Their sacred places have disappeared. They are only known because the Torah has preserved them.

Why is the Jewish story different? In Exodus, God articulates the vision for the Jewish people. We would be a "kingdom of priests and a holy nation," and in so being inspire the world to seek and know God. But this vision, even accompanied by the gift of the Pesach holiday, would not be enough. The entire human experience to this point, chronicled in Genesis, is one example after another of God's will being thwarted by human error, misconduct, weakness, and myopia. But God does not give up.

God, as he demonstrated since creating mankind by saying, "Let *us* make man," would work with a partner. The success or failure of this enterprise—the survival of the Jewish people, the story of the Exodus, God's ability to function in history—would depend on the actions of God's chosen partner, Moses.

How might Moses enable his people to fulfill God's command to celebrate Pesach as "an eternal decree"? He has several tactics to choose from.

The most easily available perpetuation tactic for Moses would have been architectural. He was reared in Egypt, where the structures built to preserve the names of Egyptian royalty are still among the world's great tourist attractions. The Jews, whose role as slaves in Egypt was to "build storage cities," had the skills to do something similar. And they had building materials, as they would soon construct items in the desert such as the tabernacle and the golden calf.

But Moses seems to have never considered it. As the Egyptian pyramids still demonstrate, buildings can last a long time. But the culture and civilization of ancient Egypt has long disappeared. We can see why. Every college campus has buildings that are named for the person who donated them. What did that person believe, dream of, live for, and want for those walking into the structure named for him? All people who pass the building will eventually know that he had a connection to the institution, was rich, and had an ego that was massaged by his name on a building. That's all. A problem of time cannot be solved with a solution in space.

Architecture was out.

Another obvious solution: Moses could have commanded the study of history. But he does not seem to have considered it. There are many reasons why Moses might have dismissed history as the way to remember the Exodus as an eternal decree. At least one, and perhaps the decisive one, is evidenced by looking around the Seder table. The Revolutions of 1848, the Springtime of Nations that transformed Europe, were likely referenced at many Seders in 1850. It is as likely that no one at a Seder today knows anything about them. One of the formative events for a grandfather at the Seder in the early twenty-first century would be the Vietnam War. But what does his sixteen-year-old grandson know about the self-immolation of Thich Quang Duc or the Gulf of Tonkin Resolution? Probably about as much as the grandfather knows, or ever knew, about the Second Battle of Ypres or the Zimmermann Telegram.

This is not a criticism of any priority, process, or culture. It is a statement about history. Events that are of monumental importance will only be vaguely recalled two generations later, with the emotion and meaning rapidly diminishing en route to being completely stripped out. They will have been replaced by something more recent. This is the problem with history: there is too much of it.

With history and architecture out, how could Moses fulfill God's command to keep the memory of the Exodus going forever? The memory of the Exodus and its future significance—the existence of the Jewish people, even the survival of our God *in* history—would depend on his answer. One imagines him, having dismissed history and architecture, thinking . . . and then realizing that he has the answer. It had been there all along, well before God gave him the assignment and aroused the question.

When Moses was still negotiating with the Pharaoh to free the Jews in Exodus 10:9, he said something subtle: "We will leave *with our young and with our old.*"

The young would come first. This might be the most radical and important idea in the history of the world. Moses's contemporary Gautama (later known as Buddha) pursued enlightenment by leaving his son, Rahula. Moses's contemporaries in China worshipped their ancestors. Filicide (the sacrificial killing of children) was prevalent in Greek and Roman mythology, the world around Moses (which is why the Torah issues so many prohibitions against it), and in relatively modern societies whose mass graves of sacrificed children are still being found.[1] This prioritization of adults in perhaps every other culture would continue, without apology or explanation, for thousands of years. The expression "Children should be seen but not heard" was first recorded in a fifteenth-century English book of religious Proverbs as an "Old English saying."[2] This is evident in the art of pre-Renaissance European masters such as Bonaventura Berlinghieri and Paolo Veneziano, where children are portrayed, in the words of the nineteenth-century art historian Mary Merrifield, as "little old men and women."[3]

And there is Moses, who commands his people to orient their religion and their philosophy—indeed, their *lives*—around the primacy and centrality of children. In the Talmud, the ancient sages say that the unnamed "anointed ones" referenced in the biblical book of Chronicles are schoolchildren, that the world "only exists because of the breath of schoolchildren," and children could not be interrupted from their studies even to build the Holy Temple.[4] When the Jews are in a bind during the Purim story, Mordecai does not call upon rabbis, leaders, or scholars to help. He calls upon 22,000 children to pray.[5]

The idea that children should come first was a radical innovation that became a standard feature of Jewish life and then global culture. How would that orientation perpetuate an embattled people and their God forever? By itself, it would not. Like all ideas, its success would lie in its execution. Moses, of course, knows that. He has identified a characteristic that all children share, and that would allow him to operationalize his ruling that children should come first. He reveals the characteristic in Exodus 12:26, "And when your children ask you, 'What does this ceremony mean to you?' Then tell them."

When your children ask you! Not *if* your children ask you or *should* your children ask you or any other way to indicate that they *might* ask you. Instead: *When* your children ask you. In other words, they *will* ask you. In a world whose most sophisticated cultures would, for thousands of years, consider childhood as something to be merely tolerated or effectively denied, Moses had identified the asset he would work with to make the Exodus remembered as an eternal decree. He had identified an asset more dependable than buildings and more durable than history: children—and specifically their *curiosity*.

The curiosity of a child, recognized by a society oriented around children, leads to a sure result. It is described by Rebbe Menachem Mendel Schneerson, the last hereditary leader of the Chabad movement: "When a child asks something of his parents, they immediately accept it and do everything they can with joy and gladness to fulfill the child's request."[6]

Indeed, a universal characteristic of parents is the desire to satisfy the curiosity of their children. If a child asks why this night is different from all other nights or what the meaning of this service is to you, the parent will want to respond comprehensively, intelligently, meaningfully, and memorably. And she will be delighted if her child follows her answer with more questions.

A youth-first society, a child's curiosity, the parental yearning to satisfy it—Moses is moving fast, showing how he will operationalize the divine command of *eternal decree*.

Immediately following Moses's telling the people of Israel what to do when their children ask them about the meaning of the Pesach ceremony, God delivers the tenth plague: the smiting of the firstborn. The Pharaoh, hearing the "great outcry,"[7] awakes and summons Moses and Aaron. He tells them that they can take the Jews out of Egypt, and even asks for a blessing.

That sounds like victory—but only out of context. The Pharaoh had agreed to free the Jews after several previous plagues, but had retracted his promise each time. The odds of him retracting his promise again are, therefore, uncomfortably high. This is understood by all the Jews, as Moses instructs them in Exodus 12:11 to conduct their final meal with "shoes on your feet, your loins girded, your staff in your hand."

This is an existential rush. Make it out of Egypt before the Pharaoh changes his mind, and the Jews will have a chance at being a free people in God's Promised Land. Don't make it out in time, and the slavery will presumably continue with even more brutality—with God having exhausted the most conceivably punishing plagues. The future of God on earth and of the Jewish people would be determined by a race against time.

Would the Jews get out in time?

If there was ever a curious question, it would be: "How fast should Jews leave?"

But not to Moses. He has an estimated three million people to evacuate ahead of the world's most powerful army. But he also has an idea to share. And he does so in Exodus 13:8: "And you shall explain to your son on that day, 'It is because of what the Lord did for me when I went from Egypt.'"

He is not done. Several verses later, he decides that his listeners need to consider his question from a different angle: "And it shall be when your son will ask you at some point in the future time, 'What is this,' you shall say to him."

At this most pivotal moment in world history, when the three million Jews that Moses is responsible for are either going to begin the journey to freedom or get slaughtered en route back to slavery, he stops to discuss . . . educational philosophy?

One imagines a listener saying: "Moses, with all due respect—if we get out of here, we will have a very long time to consider education and anything else you want. If we don't, there won't be anyone to educate! So how about we just get out of here now?"

Moses might have replied, "I know as well as anyone that the Pharaoh will likely try to keep us—after all, it was I who has had all the conversations with him about leaving and staying. But if we don't come to an agreement now about our commitment to educating our children, there is no point in going at all. So let me finish!"

Moses was conditioning the very survival of the people on their commitment to education. He was betting the future of the Jewish people on our ability and willingness to teach and learn.

This is worth a pause to consider just how counterintuitive, radical, and even insane education as a means of perpetuation is. It is trite nowadays to speak of the centrality of children and the importance of education. That does not mean that such proclamations are natural, normal, or inevitable. It just demonstrates how successful Moses's idea was.

Successful—and, from the perspective of the time, crazy. Education has none of the characteristics that should carry anything for eternity. Education is intangible and can be ignored. If built, as Moses insisted, on the basis of the curiosity of children, education will yield all kinds of questions that could easily lead students away from any religious system or established way of thinking. Moreover, if one generation (or a significant part of a generation) does not sufficiently educate its children—because of deprioritization, oppression, disinterest, or anything else—then the entire chain of memory, corpus of knowledge, and tradition is destroyed. It does not matter how long education would have worked until that point. Its success depends on the comprehensive and enthusiastic participation of almost everyone in every generation.

There is another challenge. Education in the form of a nice, quick, and uplifting story of Moses defeating the Pharaoh might not be subversive—but it would not be interesting, sustaining, or remotely true. The Exodus, properly understood as it is in the Haggadah, references and encompasses all the important ideas and stories in Judaism from Creation on. The stories are intricate, the details are crucial, the lessons are complicated, and even the best characters are deeply flawed and only sometimes redeemed. The Jewish story that God wants perpetuated forever is a *complicated* story. There is no way its transmission could be accomplished neatly—or orally.

Hence, Moses's instruction in Deuteronomy 6:7: "You shall repeatedly teach them to your children and speak of them when you sit in your house and when you walk around the road, when you lie down and when you rise up . . . *write them on the doorposts of your house and on your gates.*"

Repeatedly teach them—this was to be an important aspect of the Mosaic educational philosophy, and to which we will return. But *write them on your doorposts*? That presumes that everyone entering and exiting the home would know how to read and write. But the alphabet had barely been invented! Literacy was so marginal that there is no report of anyone in the Torah prior to Moses reading or writing *anything*. This includes Jacob and Joseph, both of whom were geniuses. Moreover, if anyone were reading and writing at the time of the Exodus story, it would not have been slaves like the Jews.

But it was not just the technical problem of how to create a text-based education system in an almost entirely illiterate society that Moses had to solve. As with the prioritization of children, the implementation of such an educaton system would require a philosophy completely misaligned with what would be prevailing thought for thousands of years. The alphabet might have started to emerge at the time of Moses, but it is not as though societal leaders outside of Israel wanted to spread its great new potential. In fact, it was the opposite.

Elites, for thousands of years after Moses, recognized that literacy provides access to new ideas. Consequently, elites everywhere aimed to make their societies mostly illiterate by either discouraging or criminalizing mass literacy. Socrates was put to death in 399 BCE for doing in Greece essentially what Moses required in Israel: the crime in Athens was "corrupting the youth." King Richard II and the British Parliament in 1391 passed a law stating, "No serf or villain . . . should put his children to school." Seventeen years later, the British clergy passed a law called the Constitutions of Oxford.[8] It classified the translation of the Bible into English as a crime of heresy. Just over a hundred years later, William Tyndale published a translation of the Bible in accordance with his goal to "interpret the sense of the scripture and the meaning of the spirit."[9] In 1536, he was convicted of the crime of heresy— and punished by being strangled and burned to death.[10] His last words were, "Lord! Open the King of England's Eyes."[11] That would eventually happen, as he was named the 26th Greatest Briton by the BBC in 2002.[12]

The daughters of the greatest master of the English language, William Shakespeare, lived a hundred years later. They were illiterate. This was not because the Bard was a sexist, a bad father, or could not afford schooling. The celebrated creator of Cordelia, Juliet, and Portia appreciated strong women. It was just the way of literacy in his time. A generation later, 40 percent of the men in the English diocese of Norwich were literate. None of the women were.[13]

The commitment to universal literacy is just the foundation of how Moses, in the Pesach sequence of Exodus 12 and 13, indicates that he plans to achieve perpetuation through education. As every philosophy needs an implementation strategy to be meaningful, every implementation strategy needs a philosophy to guide it. And Moses articulates in those verses what is essentially a three-part theory of education. His educational philosophy would be augmented and developed in the Torah and in all great venues of Jewish thought—including the Haggadah.

The first is shown by when he chooses to introduce the subject. By speaking of how his people should educate their children at the moment when the Pharaoh's army is gearing to pursue them, he is teaching them about the importance of prioritization. Everyone wants to do, see, and be more than is possible, but all that gets done is what we prioritize. And the logic of prioritizing, Moses shows us, means being willing to sacrifice valuable things. And when it comes to educating our children, everything else can be sacrificed.

Second, he shows how we should relate to what we learn. The specifics in his language, as ever, matter. In Exodus 13:8, he says, "On that day tell your son, 'I do this because of what the Lord did for me when I came out of Egypt.'" *What the Lord did for me.* There should be nothing abstract or impersonal, Moses directs, about Jewish education. There will be no you and they—only me and us. There will be no history, but instead memory. We will become, he is saying, what we learn—and we will learn who we are.

The third facet of his philosophy derives from the fact that the specific questions that the child asks in Exodus 12:26 and 13:8 are different. Moses, in the latter verse, does not rephrase or forget what he had said probably an hour earlier. This prophet knows exactly what he was doing. He is teaching us that genuine learning needs to be responsive to the uniqueness of each child.

We will continue to explore and expound upon these educational insights throughout this book.

In the meantime, especially since Moses's goal was longevity and we are living thousands of years later, we can ask: How did Moses's crazy idea do?

Rabbi Jonathan Sacks points out that in the book of Judges, Gideon stops a random boy whom he expects to write down the names of seventy-seven elders. The boy does so.[14] In Pirkei Avot ("Ethics of our Fathers," the canonical book of early Jewish ethical teachings), Rabbi Yehuda ben Teima goes through the ideal life cycle of a person, ending with death at one hundred. It starts at age five, when the child begins "the study of Scripture."[15]

Much of what we know about early Jewish history comes from the author Josephus, who died in 100 C.E. He writes: "Should anyone of our nation be asked about our laws, he will repeat them as readily as his own name. The result of our thorough education in our laws from the very dawn of intelligence is that they are, as it were, engraved on our souls."[16]

By the time of Josephus, education was compulsory for Jewish children by the age of six and a town without children in school was excommunicated from the Jewish community. This discipline is reflected in an exchange recorded in the Talmud. One person asks: What is one to do when, because of a perforation, one is not sure whether a letter is a vav or a nun? The answer, provided by the early Rabbi Zeira: "Ask a child of average intelligence."[17] A child specifically of average intelligence was expected to know the alphabet and able to interpret it with authority! Moreover, students were not to be beaten with a stick or cane, older students were instructed to help younger ones, class sizes were limited to twenty-five, children could not miss school to perform other duties (even to "build the Holy Temple"), and students who were fast readers were paired with students who were slower so the latter would be encouraged to learn.[18]

A thousand years later, an Egyptian Jewish woman anticipating her impending death wrote a letter to her sister:

> My greatest wish is that you should take care of my little daughter and make an effort for her to study. Indeed I know that I am imposing a heavy burden on you. We do not have the means for her upkeep, let alone the cost of tuition. But we have an example from our mother and teacher, a servant of God.[19]

Across the world, at the same time, gentile observers were noting this strange Jewish commitment. A Christian monk in France wrote: "A Jew, however poor, if he had ten sons, would put them all to letters, not for gain, as the Christians do, but for the understanding of God's law; and not only his sons but his daughters too."[20] Seemingly all histories of eastern European Jewish life in the centuries that follow report how Jewish parents would sacrifice everything, even food, to provide schooling for their children.[21]

The success of education as memory, sometimes using the exact language of Moses, has enabled Jewish survival in times of plenty and times of famine. Rabbi Yisrael Spira, the Bluzhever Rebbe of Poland, was one of the great rabbis of Europe in the early to mid-twentieth century. His family was murdered by the Nazis, and he was enslaved in Bergen-Belsen. Because of a strange turn of events, Rabbi Spira got a small amount of matzah before Pesach in the Nazi concentration camp.

Another prisoner asked him who should get, essentially, the matzah rations. The rabbi said that it should be split among some of the adults so that they could fulfill their obligation to celebrate Pesach. Then a voice emerged. It was of an emaciated woman, whose family had also been slaughtered by the Nazis.

Bi'naarenu ubi'zkenenu!—"With our young and with our old."

The rabbi was immediately convinced by her application of Exodus 10:9, and gave the matzah to the children. Upon liberation, he married the woman—Bronia Melchior. They became two of the great Jewish leaders of postwar New York City.[22]

The Jewish mission, starting with Abraham and exemplified in the Pesach story, was always intended to be the story that would inspire and guide the world. On this most important of ancient Jewish priorities, how have the Jews done? It was not looking good in the time of Shakespeare. But Massachusetts became the first U.S. state to require universal education in 1852 and Mississippi the last state, in 1918. France required universal schooling in 1959, as did England in 1996. In 2017, a United Nations report castigated member states for having "missed . . . the goal" of increasing literacy—emphasizing that improving it would require "drastic measures." The global literacy rate was 86 percent, and 91 percent among youth.[23]

Meanwhile, Jews have achieved well in all academic pursuits. According to the Pew Research Forum, Jews are "the most highly educated of the world's religious groups," with Jewish women being better educated than Jewish men. Moreover, Jews have outperformed non-Jews in winning Nobel Prizes by 11,250 percent.[24] In 2018, the Canadian Broadcasting Corporation ran a segment asking a familiar question: "What's with the Jews? Their Contribution to Humanity Is Enormous, Unique, and Exceedingly Difficult to Explain."[25]

Maybe not. Maybe it is what happens when a people, from its founding, bets its perpetuation on the education of children. Maybe it is what flows from the description we put on Moses's business card. We don't call him our leader or our prophet or our founder—we call him Moses *Rabbeinu*, our teacher.

GETTING READY:
WHEN THE PREPARATION
IS PART OF THE EVENT

We always prepare for a new year. The preparations for January 1 and July 4 involve similar activities: deciding on the guests to invite or the invitation to accept, getting the food and drink, planning for the ball to drop or the fireworks to go off.

The preparation for the original and biblical Jewish New Year, Pesach, also involves food, drink, guest lists, and the accoutrements of ritual. But that is where the similarities end. The Pesach preparations originate in the Torah. On the first day of the first month (which became known as Nisan, when Hebrew months were named long after the Torah), God provides the Jews with detailed instructions about what to do on the tenth and fourteenth days. As will be discussed throughout this book, these instructions cover the food that would be served (a lamb, bitter herbs, and matzah), how the meat should be eaten (roasted, not cooked), the size of each gathering (enough people to consume a full lamb with no leftovers), the attire for the evening (shoes on the feet, staff in the hand), and much more.[1] Our preparations for Pesach today follow the instructions that God, in the Torah, provided the initial celebrants in Egypt.

In describing preparation generally, the twelfth-century Spanish Jewish philosopher and poet Judah Halevi said: "Preparing for a pleasure and looking forward to it . . . doubles the feeling of enjoyment."[2] The author of the Torah, intending for us to make this the most meaningful and instructive night of the Jewish year, seems to have incorporated this insight into Pesach preparations. There is no other holiday in the Torah that calls for anything close to this amount of preparation—not Yom Kippur, not the Day of Loud Blasts (what we now call Rosh Hashanah), not Sukkot, not Shabbat, nothing. The preparation for Pesach, in the Torah and today, ignites each aspect of the participant—the material, the social, the intellectual, and the spiritual. In fact, the preparation is so integral to the Pesach experience that it is perhaps better understood as part of the event itself. The focus here will be on three aspects of the preparation, all of which come directly from the Torah: the guest list, the food, and the topics of conversation.

THE GUEST LIST

The first aspect of preparation: Who should come to the Seder? As Rabbi Jonathan Sacks writes, there are only two times in the Torah when things are said to be "not good." One is in Genesis 2:18, when God says that it is "not good" for man to be alone. The other is in Exodus, when Moses's father-in-law, Yitro, tells him that it is "not good" to lead alone.[3] Solitude, the Torah is telling us, is not our proper state. Pesach, because it is the Jewish New Year celebration and because of what the Torah specifically says about it, calls for a heightened awareness about the problem of solitude and the communal obligations that we have developed to alleviate it.

In Exodus 12:47, the Torah says that the Pesach meal shall be experienced by "the whole community of Israel." The attendant obligations for us are clear and profound. It is incumbent upon *everyone* in a Jewish community to ensure that *every* Jew is welcomed at a Seder. This means identifying Jews in one's community who do not have a place to go for the Pesach celebration and welcoming them enthusiastically to our Seder. It also means acknowledging that putting on a Seder is an expensive responsibility, beyond the financial capability of many Jews. Consequently, Jewish communities have established Pesach relief funds for thousands of years. They were referenced in the Talmud and exist in every Jewish community today—and can be found with an Internet search or a call to probably any rabbi or Jewish leader.[4]

It is deeply appropriate that contributing to Pesach relief is both an essential and universal part of the preparation for our new year's commemoration. It is not only the first action one does in the Jewish New Year. It, and other actions like it, just might be the most important activities of the entire year. That begs the question: What kind of activity is contributing to a Pesach relief fund?

One thing it cannot be is charity, defined as giving voluntarily out of one's goodwill. There is no Hebrew word for charity, and no Jewish concept of it. Instead, we have *tzedakah*, which means "righteousness" or "justice." It is morally obligatory. The fourth-century Rabbi Assi, in a statement in the Talmud that seemingly every authority agrees with and amplifies whenever given the opportunity, says, "Tzedakah is as important as all the other commandments put together." As such, even recipients of tzedakah—whether the priests or the poor—are required to support others in need.[5] A purpose of tzedakah is, thus, to lift up the poor—but not only that. It is to define the Jewish community not as one group of givers and another of receivers but by one group of contributors—and thus to affirm the dignity of every member.

By divine providence or otherwise, the specific function that this tzedakah enabled—the ability of every Jew to experience Judaism's most important (and expensive) evening in a home—probably saved Judaism. After the centers of Jewish life, the first and second Temples, were destroyed (in 586 B.C.E. and 70 C.E.), any rational analysis would have predicted the end of Judaism. But Exodus 12 had also religiously ordained the holiness of the home, the family within, and the community that would be created when households joined together in homes. When the temples were destroyed, Judaism had a distributed alternative infused by the Torah with holiness all ready to go.

As we seek to fulfill our obligation to re-create the original Pesach celebration by joining with other households, a question automatically arises. Whom should we invite? This is, as anyone who has put together an invitation list knows, a potentially difficult task—and for many possible reasons. As pertains to the Seder, the Torah and derivative Jewish teaching are ready to guide.

First, the easy part. The Torah tells us, in Exodus 12:38, that we left Egypt after the proto-Seder with *"mixed multitude"*—gentiles who wanted to align their destiny with that of the Jewish people. Given that the gentiles had tied their fates to ours, it makes sense that we would have shared our final meal in Egypt with them. Accordingly, we should have gentiles on the night when we "relive" the experience of our biblical ancestors.

A possibly even more profound reason to include gentiles at the Seder derives from Numbers 10. After two difficult years of wandering in the desert following the Exodus, Moses is visited by his beloved father-in-law, Yitro. Yitro, whom the Torah identifies in Exodus 2:16 as a "Priest of Midian," is a gentile. Moses pleads with Yitro to stay with him, saying: "You have been as eyes for us."[6]

Why would Moses have identified as his "eyes" those of a gentile priest? For the same reason that the most insightful analysis of America was written by a young Frenchman (Alexis de Tocqueville): that psychological counseling can be so valuable. The outsider can often see things that closeness and familiarity obscure. Gentile guests, particularly if encouraged, will inevitably participate with a spirit of *newness* that will enliven and enrich the Seder experience.

It is entirely possible that the choice of which gentile friends to invite will be the easy part of the guest list. It is the contemplation of which relatives to invite that might be complicated, painful, and fraught. A host might recall someone who always invigorated Seders but died in the past year. Or, perhaps even more painfully, the invitation process will remind the host of his estrangement from a friend, a sibling, a parent, or a child.

And it could be worse even if everyone invited can come. If a host perceives that an acquaintance with alternatives will ruin or degrade the Seder, he can just not invite that person. That luxury does not exist with family. There could be the daughter who once sang the Four Questions so enthusiastically but now rejects everything about Judaism, the son who knows he has an alcohol problem but will surely drink the four cups of wine anyway, the nephew who used to ask so many innocent yet probing questions but is now likely to be on his phone all through the Seder, the brothers who are suing each other over stakes in a business their parents started, the uncle who is likely to loudly incite a political argument that an in-law will surely engage . . . and countless others.

We now know, with scientific certitude, just how painful these rifts can be—whether presented in absence or attendance. As the neuroscientist Dr. Mary Heinricher shows, the expressions *broken heart* and *hurt my feelings* exist in many languages. This is because they are universal and scientifically based descriptions. A broken heart and a broken leg, she writes, are "much the same to our brains."[7] The same pain receptors in the brain are activated by physical pain and by the feeling of social exclusion. The pain of broken relationships is explained by how our brains developed in evolution. For much of our evolutionary development, an interpersonal rupture could effectively deny an individual the protection that a community offers—and imperil the person's life. So it makes evolutionary sense that relational ruptures are painful in very much the same way that physical injuries are.

The ancient rabbis who designed the Pesach celebration did not have the benefit of twenty-first-century science on family rupture. But they had the Talmud's wisdom, which says: "A prisoner cannot free himself from prison, but depends on others to free him from his shackles."[8] And in the decision of what to do in synagogue on the Saturday morning before Pesach, they handed the Seder-goer feeling this pain the key he needs to unlock those shackles.

The haftarah is a reading from the prophetic books of the Bible (not the Torah) done on Shabbat at synagogue. It always serves as either a commentary on the Torah portion being read in synagogue that day or on a coming holiday. For instance, the haftarah on Shabbat Shuvah (between Rosh Hashanah and Yom Kippur) is the "Repentance to Bring Blessing" from Hosea. One of the haftarahs on Yom Kippur is the book of Jonah, the great meditation on forgiveness.

The Shabbat before Pesach is known as *Shabbat HaGadol*—the Great Shabbat. When selecting the haftarah for the Great Shabbat—the last service before Jews usher in the New Year celebration at home—the sages had an abundance to choose from. Any reading related to the glory of Israel, the responsibilities of freedom, the sanctity of the household, or the constancy of God's love would have been fitting.

But the sages chose something very different.

The haftarah read in synagogue on the Shabbat morning before Pesach is from Malachi. "Now I am sending to you Elijah the prophet. Before the day the Lord comes . . . He will turn the hearts of fathers to sons, and the hearts of sons to fathers."[9]

What does this have to do with Pesach? On its face, nothing at all. But it must be to Pesach what the Jonah story is to Yom Kippur. What about the harbinger of the Messiah reuniting families could be a commentary on Pesach, where we tell the story of the Exodus from Egypt?

By choosing this haftarah, the sages are telling us that they know that we might not be approaching Pesach with the joyful anticipation that Judah Halevi writes of. They are acknowledging that we might not be thinking about the Exodus at all, but about the guest list for Seder night. They are allowing the real possibility that our contemplation of who might attend or not attend will overwhelm us with dread, grief, and regret. If all, or even any, of those possibilities are true, then we will not be able to derive the meaning, guidance, and joy from the Seder that the author of the Torah wants us to have.

In the deployment of this passage of Malachi for Shabbat HaGadol, they are also telling us how to confront such pain, and enable ourselves to genuinely celebrate the Pesach holiday. The haftarah is the Jewish tradition putting its arm around such a Seder participant and saying the only thing that can help: You are not alone. Your pain now, which seems to you unique, personal, and perhaps shameful, is so widely shared that it is what we all discuss and pray about as we approach our most important holiday. Your pain, along with its cause, is so *human* that it will exist until the end of time. And your pain is so important and so real that assuaging it will be the prophet Elijah's crowning task before he ushers in the Messiah.

The reading of Shabbat HaGadol offers one who is experiencing a family rift ahead of Pesach the comfort that he is neither suffering alone nor uniquely. But that does not eliminate or even diminish the problem. It just might make him feel a little better. It treats the symptoms but not the underlying cause. The family problems are still there, in full force, ready to present at the Seder and elsewhere.

Judaism has, as well, a solution for the cause: *Ask for forgiveness.* This might sound elementary, but it is quite radical. Forgiveness is like mass education—it is an idea that is now universally admired but was conceived and introduced to the world in the Torah.[10] And it is always ready, along with the lessons from the reading from Malachi, to help ease the problem that we often confront on Shabbat HaGadol.

It is logical, and even expected, for one told to apologize on Shabbat HaGadol to respond by saying: "You don't even know the facts behind the problem! How can you be telling me to apologize?"

There are two Jewish responses to this that can be applied to almost any family dispute—without regard to the underlying issues. One is that it does not matter if it is just to issue the apology. The other is that it is almost always just to do so.

First, how could the justice of an apology be irrelevant? Why should one issue an apology if doing so would be undeserved or even untruthful?

The child-centered orientation of Judaism provides a very intriguing answer. Psalm 8:2 says, "Out of the mouths of babes and sucklings, you have established strength." This seems counterintuitive. Aren't adults supposed to give strength to children? Rabbi Menachem Mendel Schneerson, the eighteenth-century rabbi who was the third rebbe of Chabad, explained how adults can learn from children how to solve one of the most persistent sources of pain in seemingly every community:

> We see that children will become angry at each other, and immediately in a second they are finished [fighting] and there will be love and friendship between them, as if there was never any separation at all. On the other hand, with older men, if they come to an argument and anger, it is a very hard matter for them to come to true love and friendship.[11]

Children, in other words, intuit a great Jewish truth that their parents might have abandoned. This truth is revealed in one of the foundational stories of the Torah—the story that enables the creation of the first Jewish child, and thus the all-important chain of transmission.

In Genesis 18, Sarah and Abraham are very old and, to their great disappointment, childless. An angel comes to them and reveals that Sarah will have a child. Sarah "laughed," saying that her husband was too old.

Sarah's response presents God with a dilemma. This dilemma, and God's reaction to it, teaches us about the nature of genuine moral choices and about how to live through one common and particular time. If God tells Abraham that Sarah said that Abraham is "too old," God would have told the truth. But God would have emasculated Abraham and potentially damaged the marital relationship. If God tells Abraham that Sarah had said anything else, God would have lied.

Which would he choose?

There is nothing in the text to indicate that it is a difficult decision for God. He tells Abraham that Sarah said: "Will I really have a child, now that I am old?"

God, in this sequence, illustrates the nature of genuine moral dilemmas. They are not between right and wrong. They are between right and right.[12] And when it comes to this example of right versus right—telling the truth versus preserving a relationship—God's direction for us is clear. Maimonides, the twelfth-century rabbi widely regarded as the greatest of all rabbinic authorities, captures this: "The Torah was given only to bring peace to the world."[13]

So anyone contemplating a rift around Shabbat HaGadol can, comfortably and with the religious integrity that comes with sacrificing truth to mend a relationship, apologize.

However, it is usually unnecessary to go as far as God shows us that we can—and lie in order to sustain a relationship. It is almost always possible to offer an apology and be truthful. In any relationship rift, both parties are likely to be at fault. This does not mean that they are *equally* at fault. But it does mean that, in almost all instances, both parties to a rift *owe* the other an apology. Sure, each party believes that the other owes an apology first and more. One of them is probably right.

So what? If one party to a rift is one percent at fault, he still owes an apology. If he withholds it, he is not paying what he owes. That he, too, is owed an apology is irrelevant. He can offer his apology comfortably, and see if the person with whom he has a rift reciprocates.[14]

What will happen if, perhaps after contemplating the message from Shabbat HaGadol, a Seder participant sincerely apologizes? A 2013 study from Harvard University and the University of Pennsylvania is illustrative. The psychologists conducting the study had an actor ask strangers at a train station if he could borrow the stranger's cell phone. Nine percent of strangers gave him a phone.

The actor then revised his question. He said: "I'm sorry about the rain! Can I borrow your cell phone?" Almost half the people who received this "apology" complied. The researchers explained: "The apologizer communicates that he has taken the victim's perspective, acknowledges adversity and expresses regret."[15] If a slight and ridiculous apology—the actor is "sorry" about the rain?—is so effective in creating a moment of giving and sharing with a stranger, how much more so a genuine one, especially in the context of the most important night of the Jewish year.

THE BANISHED FOOD (AND ITS REPLACEMENT)

The second aspect of Pesach preparation begins with another Torah requirement. Exodus 12:15: "For a seven day period shall you eat matzah but on the previous day you shall banish the leaven from your homes; for anyone who eats leavened food—that soul shall be cut off from Israel, from the first day to the seventh day."

Banished, with the soul cut off! These are terms one would expect to be associated with idolatry, murder, adultery. But eating bread?

That food should be important to Pesach is not surprising. Judaism often attributes *religious* significance to food. As the eighteenth-century Russian sage (and founder of Chabad) Rabbi Schneur Zalman writes in his classic work *Tanya,* "Each item of food and drink that one ingests immediately becomes blood and flesh of his flesh."[16]

This is manifested in God's first instruction to people, which regards what fruit they can and cannot eat. It continues through the laws of kashrut, which attributes religious significance to everything a Jew eats. We are, the Torah implies, what we eat.

So it should be expected that Jewish holidays have ritual foods that help to define the occasion. We have dairy delicacies on Shavuot, we eat oil-drenched desserts on Hanukkah, we dip apples in honey on Rosh Hashanah, and we don't eat anything on Yom Kippur. We eat round foods during times of birth and mourning to remind ourselves of the circular nature of life—but we don't ban, banish, or otherwise discourage triangular pizza slices.

And therein lies the difference. It is not the existence of special foods that are distinctive to Pesach. It is the emphasis. If fifty-nine sixtieths of an item are kosher, the item is kosher. If any tiny increment of an item is chametz (a leavened food product), it is forbidden during Pesach.[17] There are instances when a Jew can be in the nonkosher food business, but he can have nothing to do with chametz during Pesach.[18]

In banishing chametz during the holiday, the Torah introduces matzah. The matzah referenced in Exodus 12 is not just a kosher for Pesach carb substitute. In fact, a biblical nickname of the holiday, as declared in Exodus 23:15, is "the Festival of Matzah." For now, why is the most important Jewish holiday, our New Year, named for a food—and a distinctly unappetizing one? Why, as Rabbi Meir Soloveichik asks, would we "actually give this wafer the honor of being affiliated eternally with freedom?"[19]

The most common explanation, that the Jews were planning on making bread for their final meal in Egypt but had to leave before it could rise, cannot be right. Per Exodus 12:39, the Jews do rush out of Egypt, with our matzah. But the menu for the Pesach meal was determined, by God per Exodus 12:14, two weeks earlier—on the first of the month. Matzah was on the menu and bread was not. Moreover, this menu requirement was to last "forever." The purpose of matzah must have been strategic, and its meaning eternal.

The directive to use matzah instead of bread precedes the night when we rushed out of Egypt—and, in a different context, follows it as well. In Leviticus 2, God instructs the Jews to build a Temple for him. The rules of the sacred Temple include a prohibition on leavened bread, an acceptance of unleavened bread, and a requirement that all offerings be salted.

There must be a moral significance to leavened and unleavened bread that first presents in the Pesach sequence and extends into the broad Jewish experience. And that answer can be found in the substance that is required for all offerings in the temple—salt.

We do not think of salt as anything special now, but that was not the experience of our ancient forebears. Salt was the main currency of the ancient world. The first city in Europe, which existed six thousand years ago before it was destroyed by an earthquake, was Solnitsata (Bulgarian for "Salt-works"). The original meaning of *salary* is "salt-money, a soldier's allowance for the purchase of salt."[20] The identification of salt with value continues to this day through the expression that someone is "worth his weight in salt."

Salt was not a currency like dollars or gold, which has value unrelated to any functional use. First, we enjoy salt so much that it might be at the level of need. With a few exceptions, the only foods that we do not add salt to are those that come heavily salted. Given how often we eat and how important the enjoyment of food is to human happiness, it is understandable that cities and societies would make it so central.

And salt has an even more important use. Salt absorbs water from food, creating a dry environment that is inhospitable to mold and bacteria. Before there was refrigeration, there was salt. Salt, unique among things in the ancient world, could not be destroyed by fire, time, or anything else.[21] Salt is the original preservative.

This property of salt was so important and universally regarded in the ancient world that it became an easy symbol for the original audience of the Torah. Biblical agreements specifically intended to last forever are often called a "covenant of salt."[22]

The opposite of salt, in its function as a preservative, is yeast. Joseph Hertz, the chief rabbi of Great Britain in the early to mid-twentieth century, writes: "Salt prevents putrefaction [the process of decay] while leaven and honey produce it."[23] A bagel, a roll, or a doughnut that has been left on the table for a few days cannot be safely consumed. A heavily salted item will last much longer. If one wants to symbolically fight yeast, perhaps for the decay it represents, the website of the Red Star Yeast Company provides the weapon: "Too much salt in dough can slow down or even inhibit yeast activity."[24] The application of salt prevents yeast from rising, thus creating matzah literally and a triumph of permanence over impermanence symbolically.

It makes sense that the authors of the Torah and the Haggadah would have wanted, for a holiday specifically designed to last *forever*, a central food that symbolizes permanence. Salt comes close, but does not work because it is not a food rather a seasoning that improves and sustains other foods. But there is a ready substitute. Salt, as previously mentioned, fights the process of decay wrought by leaven. Hence, the central Pesach food is unleavened bread—or matzah.

The role of leavened and unleavened bread in focusing us on permanent things starts before lit candles usher in the Seder. It is not only that chametz must be out of our homes before the holiday begins. The method of removing it, prior to the Seder, is integral to the spiritual purpose of its deletion.

The definitive code of Jewish Law, the Shulchan Aruch (which was compiled by the Safed rabbi Joseph Karo in the sixteenth century), instructs that we are specifically to *search* for the chametz.[25] The importance of searching, with the care and attention that such a process suggests and embodies, is articulated in Proverbs 2:3–5: "If you call out for insight and cry aloud for understanding and you look for it as for silver and search for it as a hidden treasure, then you will understand the fear of the Lord."

Moreover, the specifics of how we search for it are prescribed. We search for chametz by candlelight with a feather and a spoon. We use the feather to scoop the chametz crumbs into the spoon. Why candlelight rather than the light of the sun or the moon?

The answer is provided in Proverbs 20:27: "The spirit of man is the candle of the Lord, searching all of his innermost parts."[26] As we rid our homes of chametz, we search our "innermost parts." We dedicate ourselves to that which we want to preserve and make permanent, we identify the things that are temporary, and we mark what we should dispense with. We do so at night, by candlelight, to create an aura of dramatic seriousness, an air of carefulness, a sense of meticulousness, a feeling of serenity.

And we do so in a way that requires maximum human agency and accentuates human responsibility. If we relied on sunlight or moonlight, the light would be entirely God's. But we do so with man-made products. Taking an account of our innermost parts is a responsibility we must assume ourselves.

Given how important it is to rid one's home of chametz—completely and properly—there is an interesting qualification. Jewish law decrees that one should only search in places where one would have brought chametz.[27] The eighteenth-century rabbi Yisroel Hopstein, known as the Kozhnitzer Maggid, explains why. While searching for one's own chametz is required, searching for someone else's is just as strictly forbidden.[28] The challenge of Pesach is to rid *ourselves* of what does not belong. This is not the time to criticize others or to think about how anyone but oneself should be different.

The morning after the search mission is complete, we burn the chametz. Given that our charge is to rid our homes of chametz in the most dramatic fashion, burning it is appropriate. Along with the chametz, we also burn the feather, the spoon, and the candle. The feather and the spoon have been contaminated by the chametz, so that makes sense. But why do we burn the candle?

The explanation was given by Yehudah Aryeh Leib Alter, the nineteenth-century master known by his great work *Sfas Emes*. The only purpose of the candle, he taught, is to search for chametz. Because its sole function is to look for negativity, it must be destroyed.[29]

There is a common practice of "selling" one's chametz to a gentile while it stays in the home. There are even websites where one can download a contract to "sell" one's chametz. Ownership is mentioned many times in the Torah, but never in relation to ridding one's home of chametz. And why would it be? The act of removing the chametz from our homes and purging it from our lives during this week is a substantive act. It is the original spring cleaning for the Jewish soul. The practice of keeping the chametz in the home but "selling" it to a gentile violates the plain instruction and meaning of the text, destroys its purpose, and insults the significance of this ritual.

This is not the time or the place for technical workarounds. This is a moment for dramatic acts of union with the Torah and its life-affirming guidance for each of us. The chametz, the ultimate symbol of impermanence, must be found by candlelight—and then removed, destroyed, donated, or burned and banned for the remainder of the week. Chametz must be out of our lives during this holiday whose nickname, *in the Torah,* is the Festival of Matzah.

THE TOPICS

That leaves the third and final subject to prepare for the Seder: what should be discussed from the Haggadah. Given that the wisdom in the Haggadah is inexhaustible, the investigation of one question always leads to several more, and the time of a Seder evening is limited, a prepared Seder leader must first realize what her role is for the evening: a Jewish freedom educator who has to make some tragic choices. She will always have vastly more ideas to share, questions to raise, and insights to elicit than can be aired. Important, inspiring, provocative, and actionable passages and ideas will have to wait until next year.

Some solace might come from the wisdom of the nineteenth-century Polish rabbi Menachem Mendel of Kotzk, known as the Kotzker Rebbe. A visitor told the rebbe that he had gone through the entire Talmud three times. "That truly is something," the rebbe responded, "but more important . . . is the number of times the Talmud has gone through you."[30]

The Seder leader should not be concerned with how much of the Haggadah her guests go through but how much of the Haggadah goes through them. And more comfort will come from the fact that, as we will explore more deeply, an experience can only be genuinely Jewish if it concludes in a state of being existentially *unfinished*.

With literally dozens or hundreds of choices of questions to ask and points to emphasize, how should the Seder leader choose?

One of the names that Moses has for God is "God of the Spirits of All Flesh."[31] Moses uses this name to refer to God in his ability to know the uniqueness, distinctiveness, and special qualities of each individual. We cannot know anyone nearly to the extent that God can know everyone but, as has been mentioned previously (and will be again!), we are created in his image. The Seder leader can consider the specific people in the room and try to project what will resonate most profoundly with each person individually and with the group generally.

Accordingly, the Seder leader can ask: What might each person at the Seder be struggling with? What can each person aspire toward? What Jewish wisdom embedded in the Haggadah will help each person ask a needed question, clarify an important dilemma, or set a direction for the new year? This act of preparing for the Seder also trains the leader in perhaps the most fundamental principle of Jewish education—that learning succeeds to the extent that the teaching is specifically responsive to the individual student.

As the Seder leader contemplates that responsibility, she can draw inspiration and ideas from an insight by the sixteenth-century Safed rabbi Mordechai HaKohen, as developed by the twentieth-century American rabbi Norman Lamm. In Leviticus 16, God provides instructions to Aaron (the first high priest) regarding the conduct of the Yom Kippur service. Aaron, God says, shall "remove his linen garments which he wore when he came to the sanctuary, and he shall leave them there." He was never to wear these garments again. This is particularly interesting, as these garments—to be worn on Judaism's holiest day—are presumed to be expensive.[32]

Why could Aaron not wear these garments on the following Yom Kippur? To symbolize and emphasize what Rabbi Lamm identifies as "a new spirit, a new insight, a new intuition in what we are doing."[33] In this spirit, the Seder leader should realize, regardless of whether all the attendees are the same as those who attended last year: This is a *new* group. Every person will bring with them a year's worth of new experiences, encounters, learnings, and perspectives. Every person, therefore, is different than he or she was last year—and this year's topics and discussion can reflect that sacred growth.

The practical application of this orientation will entail selecting five to ten parts of the Haggadah that will most profoundly resonate with the specific people at the Seder, and prepare those for discussion—and be delightfully ready for the unexpected.

THE PROMISE

Regardless of what is discussed, there is one Jewish principle that should be constant across every New Year celebration. This relates to the importance of words. In 1862, an article in *The Christian Recorder* contained the first known published reference to what it called an "old adage": "Sticks and Stones will break my bones but words will never hurt."[34]

By contrast, Jews have a Yiddish expression: "A slap goes away, a word is here to stay."

The most authoritative biblical translation (from Hebrew to Aramaic) is written by Onkelos, a first-century convert to Judaism. This version is so respected that the Talmud contains a section of rabbis conjecturing on its greatness, with it being stated that "Onkelos revealed the translation of the Torah." In Genesis 2:7 in the Onkelos Torah, God forms man from the dust of the ground, blows into his nostrils the soul of life—and man becomes "a speaking spirit."

As man expresses his divine spark by speaking, the morning prayer emphasizes how God chose to create the world. "Blessed is the One who *spoke* and brought the world into creation." Indeed, it was through nine *God said*s in Genesis that God created everything from light to birds. The idea that words contain the ability to create and destroy continued, undiluted, into the world once it was settled and its fate would be determined by people and the exercise of our free will. Proverbs 18:21: "The tongue has the power of life and death."

It is for this reason that Moses commands in his parting speech in Deuteronomy 23:24: "You shall observe and carry out what emerges from your lips."

You shall observe and carry out what emerges from your lips. This should inspire what we can deem the Onkelos Rule, to be applied on Seder night: Tonight, we will *mean* everything we say.

Its announcement may be likelier to generate confused laughs than objections. But this confusion can be easily elucidated. As we'll see, the Haggadah contains phrases such as "All who are hungry, come and eat," "Next year in the Land of Israel," and "All who speak at length shall be praised." Abiding by the Onkelos Rule means that one should only say those passages (or anything else) if she can do so with *genuine* conviction. This discipline will have multiple results.

First, it will lead one to ask: How hard is this? The extent to which meaning everything we say is a challenge on Seder night will educate us about our relationships with language and with truth more generally. It will also lead to a deeper and more honest Seder discussion, as every participant will be able to trust the conviction of everyone else on all that is said.

A genuine execution of this policy will result in some participants at least pausing before reading a passage from the Haggadah—and perhaps refusing to say it at all. A Seder-goer who hesitates or refuses, on the principle of needing to mean everything she says, should know that she is in the best of company. Rabbi Schneur Zalman refused to say the words of the Haggadah [presumably he said other words from the Haggadah] "The order of the Pesach is concluded!" as he held that a Seder should never conclude but instead continue to inspire throughout the year.[35]

If a Seder-goer refuses to say a specific passage, what will follow? The others at the table will certainly be surprised, then intrigued, and ultimately inspired by the seriousness with which their fellow celebrant appreciates the Haggadah. The gates of discussion will burst wide open, and this will lead to one of two outcomes for the (non)speaker. The ensuing discussion may help the (non)speaker to understand the passage, enabling her to say the passage with conviction. Or the ensuing discussion may enrich the understanding of the (non)speaker, but she still may not be able to say it.

Both are admirable outcomes, true to a people and a tradition that has always accorded words with seriousness and sanctity.

THE CONTEXT

There are so many disparate aspects of the Pesach preparation that one can easily become immersed in one or many aspects of it—from the charoset recipe to the topics for discussion. The great nineteenth-century Lithuanian rabbi Yisrael Salanter was asked by his students about which law to be especially mindful of in their Pesach preparations. He answered, "An elderly woman works at the bakery. Be careful not to hurt her feelings."[36]

The laws that derive from God's business card always prevail.

SINGING THE TABLE OF CONTENTS: WHY HIGHLY RELIGIOUS MARRIED WOMEN ARE SO SEXUALLY SATISFIED

Pesach is sometimes, very accurately, called the *Festival of Freedom*. And yet the evening meal designed to commemorate it is called *Seder*—which means "order." This is interesting and paradoxical, as freedom and order are generally thought to be exact opposites.

Indeed, much of the early book of Genesis can be interpreted as a battleground for these two ideas. Judaism does not have original sin, but it has an original tension: order versus freedom.

In Bereshit, the first parsha (Torah portion, of which there is typically one read in synagogues per week), God creates the world. By the end of this parsha, God, who has just created light and people, animals, the sea, and rest, is disgusted. People had begun to increase—and what did they do? Men notice only the beauty in women, "and they took themselves wives from whomever they chose."[1]

Whomever they chose—with no reference to those choices being governed or structured. This is pure freedom.

This pure freedom leads to great "wickedness," as every "product of the thoughts of his heart was but evil always."[2] God develops "heartfelt sadness" to the point where he believes that he has only one option: to destroy the world. He would begin again, with the one man who had found "grace in His eyes"—Noah.

So God destroys the world with a "great flood," and Noah and his family are the only human survivors. They re-create the world but soon enough, God is profoundly disappointed. "Everyone on earth had the same language and the same words"—with the presumption being that everyone thought the same way. First, there is too much freedom. Then, too much order. Both are, for God in the book of Genesis, catastrophes.

After the flood, God vows that he will never destroy the world again. Instead of destroying the world, God gives the people different languages and scatters them throughout the earth. In other words, he destroys the order that man had created. But this does not solve the problem of freedom and order for humankind.

On the contrary, this tension is very much with us. Should teachers encourage children to memorize facts or to express themselves creatively? Should coaches make players do drills or allow them to scrimmage? Should employers provide employees with a set number of vacation days or leave it to their discretion? Should universities impose, suggest, or reject a core curriculum?

It may seem like this tension, as it has bedeviled everyone from God in Genesis to surely every parent at the Seder table, will be with us always and forever. Perhaps. But the Haggadah, in its very structure, presents its resolution. And it does so right at the beginning of the Seder, as if to use the resolution of this tension to frame our thinking for the new year ahead.

We start the Seder by opening to the table of contents in the Haggadah. This consists of the fifteen steps from Kaddesh to Nirtzah. A table of contents is, of course, the *order* of a book. Most readers glance at the table of contents of a book and then move on quickly. This is not what happens with the Haggadah at the Seder. We sing it—yes, we *sing the table of contents.* On this Festival of Freedom, we are so insistent on order that we sing the table of contents. It is almost weird.

Singing the table of contents is not even the first example of how order is emphasized during the Pesach celebration. Before we arrive at the Seder table, we will have cleansed our homes of all vestiges of chametz with a fastidiousness that is unique to Pesach. The table itself will have the same items, probably arranged in the same way, as it has for generations. We conduct the Seder according to a fifteen-step formula that never changes. And we use a Haggadah that has changed remarkably little through the millennia and, barring a concerted effort to make it something different, does not differ significantly between versions today.

The Seder is named order, it looks like order, it is structured like order—and then it begins. As the scholar Erica Brown points out, the evening incorporates planned and unplanned spills. Its fundamental food will crack into crumbs. Seder participants drink four cups of wine. There is singing, reclining, hiding, seeking, and finding, doors opening and closing. And there is conversation, lots of it—*from* a set text but designed to lead in new, different, and original directions that speak to where each of us is today and would like to be later.[3]

The disorder is so sprawling that one wonders if whoever named the event *Seder* did so with a sense of humor. But of course the name *Seder* cannot be explained as a joke. Instead, it yields one of Judaism's most serious truths. This truth is revealed through the realization that the freedom that is so productively discussed and so enjoyably lived at the Seder could only exist within the kind of structure the Haggadah provides. Freedom, we learn, flourishes only within order.

This Jewish teaching is, appropriately for the Pesach holiday, expressed experientially. What Seder attendee believes that the evening would be enhanced if there were no text to guide, no rules to follow, no familiar songs to sing, and no prescribed foods to eat? Perhaps none. The ideas that inspire, the teachings that enlighten, the conversations that surprise, and the memories that are created at the Seder only happen because of the order imposed by the Haggadah and the traditions around it.

As with everything Pesach related, these lessons are not for the Seder but for the year ahead. Manifestations of this Pesach teaching occur everywhere. Basketball is a sport where players become great by putting creativity, innovation, and improvisation to physical form. Yet at the beginning of each season, the great UCLA coach John Wooden, who instructed some of the most creative players of all time (including Lew Alcindor, Gail Goodrich, and Bill Walton), implemented the same tactic. He instructed his players how to put on their socks and tie their sneakers.[4]

The institution best known for order is the military—with its uniforms, formations, training, and strict rules governing all aspects of service. Yet one of the most quoted ideas in military thought is: "No plan survives contact with the enemy"—and the term *snafu* was invented in the United States Marine Corps during World War II: "Situation Normal, All Fucked

Up." It is the adherence to the most strict order that prepares soldiers to flourish in its complete absence.

The order/freedom dynamic that is so elegantly reconciled at the Seder explains a question (which is sometimes a criticism) of Judaism. Why is Judaism, which commands the *love* of God, so full of laws governing *everything* from what kind of fish we can eat to when married couples can have sex?

This era is the first when we are able to scientifically assess ancient truth claims. We can now ask, and scientifically answer, the question of whether people are better off living within or outside of social structures. The arenas of faith and love provide a fertile ground for discovery, as marriage and religious institutions are ubiquitous, interesting, and important. Consequently, the institutions of marriage and faith have been frequently studied by social scientists—providing us with an abundance of data regarding human behavior and happiness within highly ordered systems.

Professor Tyler VanderWeele, an epidemiologist and biostatistician at the Harvard T. H. Chan School of Public Health, reviewed years of studies on family happiness. Among his findings are that a couple whose family regularly attends religious services together reduces its risk of divorce by almost 50 percent—and will live, on average, seven years longer than their secular counterparts. He concludes: "[The evidence suggests a] protective effect of religious participation, especially religious service attendance, on health, for outcomes as diverse as all-cause mortality, depression, suicide, cancer survival and subjective well-being."[5]

The Framingham Offspring Study, an offshoot of the Framingham Heart Study (which is an ongoing analysis of cardiovascular health since 1948), studied over 3,000 men during a ten-year period. The study, as analyzed by Harvard Medical School, concludes that even after controlling for age, body fat, smoking, blood pressure, diabetes, and cholesterol, married men have a 46 percent lower rate of death than unmarried men over a ten-year period.[6] A University of Miami study of 145,000 men with prostate cancer showed that married men survive vastly longer than unmarried men (whether never married or widowed). Another Harvard Medical School study determined that married men have a significantly better survival rate from bladder cancer because of the impact of marital "psychosocial support" on immune function.[7] A Japanese study concluded that unmarried men have a 300 percent greater chance of dying of cardiovascular disease than married men.[8]

An important part of marriage is, of course, sex. It is, from an evolutionary perspective, predictable that sex would have all kinds of positive health effects that extend life. Now, we know specifically how. Among other things, sex triggers the release of neurohypophysial hormones—which relieves stress, crystallizes emotional memories, reduces drug cravings, improves social skills, fosters generosity, and induces sleep.[9] Sex also, well into the next day, reduces the amount of cortisol and adrenaline (which are associated with stress). The quantity of sexual activity is positively correlated with decreased heart disease in men, while the quality of sex (but not the quantity) is associated with decreased heart disease in women. This might at least partially explain why the ketubah (the Jewish wedding contract) requires a husband to give his wife not just sex but to satisfy her "conjugal needs"—in other words, sexual pleasure.[10]

Single people can, without much social constraint these days, have as much sex as they want. One might think, therefore, that single people would benefit more from the adaptive qualities of sex than their married counterparts. The data, though, suggests otherwise. A large study from Indiana University in 2012 showed that 72 percent of married people and 39 percent of single people had sex in the previous year, and that married people between the ages of twenty-five and fifty-nine are five times likelier than single people to have sex more than once a week.[11] The even larger General Social Survey, produced by the University of Chicago and the National Science Foundation in 2017, showed that married people are vastly likelier to have sex consistently than those who have never married or are divorced, separated, or widowed.[12]

So we know that married people have more sex and better health outcomes than people who are "free" to sleep with whomever they want. What happens when an additional layer of order is added—that of religiosity? A 2019 study reported in *The New York Times* shows that married couples who are either secular, "less religious," or "religiously mixed" have the same level of sexual satisfaction. The level of sexual satisfaction increases 50 percent when a couple is "highly religious." The most sexually satisfied type of person in the eleven countries surveyed is the highly religious married woman.[13]

This is genuine free love, as organized at the Seder and embedded in the Pesach celebration.

We are now ready for the Seder.

MUSIC AND FOOD: THE THEOLOGY AND SCIENCE OF REMEMBERING

Why we sing the table of contents of the Haggadah is one question. Why we sing anything at the Seder is an even more fundamental one. The authors of the Haggadah had only one night in which to distill the entire Jewish corpus of freedom, to imprint the story of the Exodus into the Jewish memory of our children. So much to cover—dozens of topics, hundreds of questions—and the authors of the Haggadah decided to have us sing the table of contents, "Dayenu," the Four Questions, and others?

Similarly, one observing Pesach from afar might think it is a religiously themed cooking show. The Seder leader ensures the presence of special foods, arranges them thoughtfully, points to them, and discusses them. Yes, clearly, the Jewish New Year celebration commands a good meal. So do other Jewish events. Yet only on Pesach, when we have dozens of the most fundamental questions to discuss in one short evening, do we devote so much time to preparing and talking about the food.

What is going on?

First, music. One of the seminal themes and functions of the Pesach experience is the constructing and strengthening of Jewish community. This purpose is evident from when the Torah establishes that the Pesach meal would be constituted by households joining together—and, as we will see, rises to maximal importance in the Haggadah text. From military fight songs to chants at protest marches, from national anthems to school cheers, from the Four Questions to "Dayenu" at the Seder, groups of people often express their fidelity to each other and build their shared commitments to each other by singing together. Why? Again, twenty-first-century science explains the logic informing an ancient Jewish practice. Oxytocin is the neuropeptide that is produced by the most profound activities of human bonding—sexual intercourse and breastfeeding. Hence its nickname: the "love hormone." Experiments in the 2000s have shown that there is another activity that induces the release of oxytocin: singing together.[1]

Another deeply important purpose of the Seder is to strengthen and instill Jewish memory. The Haggadah guides us to consider Jewish life from the Torah as a continuous story, and the enslavement of our ancestors as part of our experience rather than our history. And the Seder itself is designed, in ways that we will see, to create lasting Jewish memories for our children.

In 2018, the *Journal of Prevention of Alzheimer's Disease* published a paper about the autonomous sensory meridian response (ASMR)—which is the brain function that is aroused by music. Even as Alzheimer's and other forms of dementia destroy the memory, the ASMR generally remains unaffected.[2] Music, modern science instructs us, is the most durable part of the memory.

A 2013 study by the Cornell University psychologist Carol Lynne Krumhansl shows how the music of one's youth and even of one's parents' youth produces both lucid memories and a powerful emotional response. She concludes,

> Music transmitted from generation to generation shapes autobiographical memories, preferences and emotional responses, a phenomenon we call cascading "reminiscence bumps." These new findings point to the impact of music in childhood and likely reflect the prevalence of music in the home environment.[3]

A night devoted to the cultivation of memory, as the Seder in large part is, would *need* music. Long before social science, the authors of the Haggadah seemed to know that and acted accordingly.

We know, from just after the worst time in Jewish history, how early these memories form and of what lasting importance they can be. During the Holocaust, there were Jewish children who escaped Nazi murderers by living in Catholic monasteries. Some entered as early as 1939. When the war ended, Jewish representatives went to these monasteries to find the Jewish children. A French Catholic directive approved by Pope Pius XII prohibited church institutions from returning any children who had been baptized to anyone who would not ensure their Christian upbringing. The implementation of this directive was complicated and varied, and often hinged upon a child identifying himself as Jewish, after his family had been murdered and he had lived most of his short life in a monastery. How would a child, who might have entered the monastery well before he could articulate anything, identify the religion of his birth? The Jewish authorities, sometimes accompanied by American soldiers, figured out a way. They sang the Shema—and saw which children would either cry for their mothers or softly sing along to a song they could not forget.[4]

As Shakespeare wrote in *Twelfth Night,* "If music be the food of love, play on." Now, food.

Marcel Proust's classic *Remembrance of Things Past* begins when the narrator tastes a madeleine dipped in tea. Prior to that taste, he had only one memory of his childhood home—but the culinary experience unleashes years of memory that constitute one of the great literary works of the twentieth century. Proust describes this experience in a term he invented: *involuntary memory.* He might have invented the term, but the connection between food and memory was deep in the New Year tradition of his Jewish mother.

The neuroanthropologist John Allen published *The Omnivorous Mind* in 2012. Allen writes that there is a part of the brain called the hippocampus that is crucial in the formation of "long-term, declarative memories—those that can be consciously recalled and which contribute to the autobiographies we all carry around in our heads." The hippocampus he writes, has "direct links to the digestive system. Many of the hormones that regulate appetite, digestion and eating behavior also have receptors in the hippocampus. Finding food is so important to survival that it is clear that the hippocampus is primed to form memories about and around food."[5]

So the human brain has evolved to connect food with memory. Those who wrote the Haggadah would not have known what is meant by a "reminiscence bump" or "evolutionary neuroscience," but they somehow knew that sustaining a memory would be best carried by matzah and maror (bitter herbs), dipping and dessert, and lots of singing.

WHAT WE CAN LEARN FROM AN EGG: THE LOGIC OF THE SEDER PLATE

The designers of the Seder—from the author of the Torah to the ancient rabbis—knew that food would have to be an integral part of an evening devoted to memory. And everyone who has been to a Seder is familiar with these foods: maror, charoset, the roasted bone, the roasted egg, karpas, and matzah. These foods are far from customary. Indeed, most appear on our tables only on Seder night. As everything in the Haggadah is designed to teach us something or guide us somewhere, we are led to ask: Why these foods? What can we learn from them specifically?

We can begin with the egg. The twelfth-century Spanish authority Ibn Ezra said that the egg is a rebuke to the slave masters of Egypt. Egypt prohibited the consumption of eggs and meat together, and so we symbolically defy them by doing so.[1] The nineteenth-century Polish rabbi Yaakov Leiner wrote that the egg looks like a final product—but its essence (the animal within) has not even presented itself yet. This, he said, symbolizes the Exodus from Egypt. Our liberation might seem like a glorious end, but it is just the beginning.

According to the sixteenth-century Polish rabbi Moses Isserles, the egg symbolizes mourning.[2] Indeed, the egg is the staple food at Seudat Havra'ah, the Meal of Condolence—the first a family has following a loss. The egg, because of its circular shape, serves to remind that life always goes on. Why would we incorporate mourning at a Pesach celebration? For the same reason that a groom breaks a glass under the chuppah (wedding canopy) at his wedding, and that we don't sit shiva (formally mourn) on Shabbat or during holidays. We ritually experience sadness at times of joy, and joy at times of sadness to remind ourselves that neither should ever constitute the entirety of one's expectations.[3]

The twentieth-century Polish rabbi Meir Shapiro, known as the Lubliner Rav, said that the egg exemplifies the learning from Exodus 1:12: "The more [the Jews] were oppressed, the more they multiplied and spread."[4] Just as Jews respond to even existential challenges by getting stronger, the egg becomes harder the longer it is boiled.

Charoset is a unique concoction of apples, nuts, spices, and red wine. This food only appears at Pesach. Rabbi Akiva, who lived in the second century and is on everyone's list of possible GOAT (greatest of all time) rabbis, said that the charoset represents "the deeds of righteous women." These are the Jewish slave women who insisted that, despite the brutal slavery, their husbands make love to them under apple trees to perpetuate their people. His proof text is the Song of Songs, the biblical book that is devoted to sexual expression. Chapter 8, verse 5, of the Song of Songs is: "Under the apple tree, I aroused you. There your mother conceived you."[5] Among the items mentioned in the Song of Songs are apples, figs, pomegranates, grapes, walnuts, dates, saffron, and cinnamon—the ingredients of a charoset recipe.

A contemporary of Rabbi Akiva, Rabbi Yochanan, said that the charoset symbolizes the clay used to make bricks during the slave experience.[6] Indeed, the word *charoset* derives from the Hebrew word for clay—*cheres*. Maimonides agreed with this interpretation and included in his recipe for charoset spices that resembled the straw that the Jews used to make the bricks.[7]

So which commentator is right, with either the eggs or the charoset? All of them. There is no suggestion that any of the aforementioned rabbis ever said that any alternative belief is wrong. Instead, this mutual regard is a manifestation of the Jewish conviction that "there are seventy facets to Torah."[8] There can, and often are, multiple correct interpretations of the same thing—each of which summons a different *truth*.

It is deeply instructive that Pesach should be the moment when we consider the fact that multiple interpretations of the same thing can be right. Rabbi Elie Kaunfer of Mechon Hadar writes, "Understanding something as having multiple meanings is one of the deepest expressions of freedom."[9] The ability to recognize multiple truths, demonstrated by the egg and the charoset on the Seder plate, does more than enable us to derive the deepest guidance from the Haggadah and the Torah. It just might provide the basis for good citizenship, especially in an easily divided society.

INVITE *THAT* SELF

Whoever is hungry—let him come and eat!
Whoever is needy—let him come and celebrate Pesach!

The Seder is ready to begin. The doors close. Everyone is seated. The Seder leader takes three matzahs and breaks the middle matzah. The smaller broken piece stays with the whole pieces. The larger broken piece is "stolen" by a child and hidden. Later, the child will redeem the matzah and return it to the Seder leader in exchange for a gift. The matzah is called the *afikoman*. We often focus on the redeemed piece, as we develop such fond memories of the *afikoman*. But what happens with the broken piece, as we'll see, is much more important. Its purpose will be revealed by, and after, the words that immediately follow its creation.

After breaking the matzah, the Seder leader issues what sounds like an invitation: "Whoever is hungry—let him come and eat! Whoever is needy—let him come and celebrate Pesach!"

What kind of an invitation is this? Who, in planning any kind of social event, issues invitations after the event has begun and in the privacy of the event space? Moreover, a conventional invitation and RSVP process is specifically required for the earliest Pesach commemorations that our Seders follow. An attendee, the Mishnah tells us, "must be registered for it." The registration period ended when the sacrificial lamb was slaughtered, in the afternoon preceding the evening Seder.[1]

It is so strange to invite someone to an event after it has begun that one wonders: Is this actually an invitation? It certainly sounds like an invitation—even a highly enthusiastic one. So why would such a lively invitation be issued after the event has begun?

The answer lies in the Hebrew word for *panim*. *Panim* is, as we have discussed, plural. There is no Jewish way to speak about someone having "a" face because no one has only one. Human beings, who are created in the image of the infinite God, all have multiple identities. The invitation, therefore, is not being extended to the individual who is at the Seder table. It is being issued to a particular "face" of the individual. The specifics of the invitation—the hungry, the needy—describe exactly which face is being invited.

It is one who doesn't get out much, as his controller is usually hiding him or disguising him with other faces. But it is always there—and, ironically, it is the one sought throughout the Jewish tradition. It is the face most beloved by God.

It is the face of broken self, the treasured soul of the Jewish imagination.

Shortly after being liberated from Egypt, Moses ascends the mountain to commune with God. He spends forty days and nights on the mountain and comes down with two tablets—which we identify as the Ten Commandments. Upon the mountain, God tells Moses that the Jews (in his absence) have constructed a golden calf and are worshipping it. As Moses descends from the mountain, his "anger burned." He smashes the tablets in Exodus 32:19, "breaking them to pieces at the foot of the mountain."

Moses punishes the people by, among other things, making them melt the calf and drink it. God then calls Moses back to the mountain. "Chisel out two stone tablets like the first ones, and I will write on them the words that were on the first tablets, *which you broke*."

The clause *which you broke* seems unnecessary. Moses knows which tablets God was referring to—the only tablets are the ones he broke! Moreover, a principle of Jewish psychology is captured in the Mishnah, the canonical compilation of the Jewish oral tradition: "If one had repented, another should not say to him, 'Remember your earlier deeds.'"[2] For instance, if a child comes to his parent and offers a sincere apology for sneaking an extra dessert, the parent should not respond by criticizing the child for gluttony.

So why would God, especially at this moment of reconciliation, bring up the fact that Moses broke the tablets?

The answer had been waiting. In the preceding chapter, God commissions the artisan Bezalel to construct the ark in which the tablets would be housed. This is not an ordinary container. It is, per Numbers 10:33, the "Ark of the Lord's Covenant"—which resided in the Temple's Holy of Holies. What is in this most sacred of places? Per Deuteronomy 10:2, God explains to Moses: "I will write on the tablets the words that were on the first tablets, which you broke, and you shall put *them* [in the ark]."

Which you broke—again! And *them*—plural!

What is "them"? The ancient rabbis, in a rare moment of seeming unanimity, explain that "them" refers to both the new tablets and the pieces of the broken tablets. The rightful home of the broken tablets is, God instructs, in the holiest place in the world. More than that, the holiest place itself is made of broken pieces. The sixteenth-century rabbi from Prague, Shlomo Luntschitz, known as the *Kli Yakar* (his great work), notes the specifications for the Temple as recorded in Exodus 25:10. The specifications for the altar and the table are given in whole numbers, but the specifications of the ark are delivered in fractions. This is not, the *Kli Yakar* explains, a matter of architectural convention. It is a point of moral instruction. "Every person should imagine himself as if he is lacking some element of wholeness of wisdom, and he must still measure out some more to fill in his deficiencies."[3]

The broken tablets, and all they represent, continued to occupy the holy places (actual and metaphorical) in Judaism. The canonical eleventh-century French Torah commentator Shlomo Yitzchaki, known by an acronym for his name, Rashi, analyzed the final words of the Torah:

> Never again has there arisen in Israel a prophet like Moses, whom Hashem had known face to face, as evidenced by all the signs and wonders that Hashem sent him to perform in the land of Egypt, against Pharaoh and all his courtiers and all his land, and by all the strong hand and awesome power that Moses performed before the eyes of all Israel.

It is not surprising that the final words of the Torah would incorporate the ultimate praise of Moses or refer to God by the description on his business card. But what is the act that Moses performed before all Israel? Rashi identifies that the only act that the Torah referred as having been done "in the eyes of all Israel" was breaking the tablets. God's parting words in the Torah, Rashi concludes, are effectively a message to Moses: "Thank you for breaking the tablets."[4]

This interpretation is entirely consistent with previous and subsequent Jewish thought. Rabbi Alexandri, the first-century sage of the Talmud, traces the Jewish philosophy of brokenness to biblical verses written after the Torah: "If an ordinary person makes use of a broken vessel, it is a shameful thing. But the Blessed Holy One only makes use of broken vessels, as it is written: 'Adonai is close to the broken-hearted' (Psalms 34:19), 'He heals the brokenhearted and binds up their wounds' (Psalms 147:3), and 'With the lofty and the holy ones I dwell, and with the crushed and humble in spirit' (Isaiah 57:15)."

Or, as the Kotzker Rebbe says, "There is nothing so whole as a broken heart."

Back, now, to the broken piece of matzah—the twin sibling of the afikoman. The Talmud stipulates that eating without a blessing is considered stealing from God.[5] A Jewish blessing, as the eighteenth-century Rabbi Chaim of Volozhin says, is not just a nice sentiment. It indicates a desire that the thing being blessed be increased. God blesses a womb and the result is a multitude of children; God blesses the earth and the result is abundant food.[6]

When it comes time to bless God over the matzah, one might think that we would either say the blessing over all the matzah or remove the broken piece to sanctify God in an environment of wholeness. Instead, we do the opposite. We remove the bottom (whole) matzah and bless God over one whole matzah and over one broken matzah. As with the tablets in the ark, the broken and the whole are inseparable. We bless the whole and the broken, and we ask for *both* to be increased.

It is the self represented by *this* matzah—our incomplete, disappointed, confused, insecure, scared, scarred, vulnerable, and *broken* self—that is being invited to participate in the Seder. It is the self whose child decided not to attend the Seder, the self who believes himself "not a good Jew" because his Jewish knowledge and practice are so limited, the self who is so full of regrets that he regards himself as unworthy of participating in the Jewish New Year celebration and even of God's love, the self who wants to participate fully as a Jew but considers himself a hypocrite, the self for whom the memory of Seders past floods with recollections of relationships broken, commitments not kept, and opportunities missed, the self who is full of insecurities and vulnerabilities whom the authors of the Haggadah want at the Seder.

Given how sacred brokenness is in the Jewish imagination, why did the authors of the Haggadah not just say, "All who are broken, come and eat?" Because, perhaps, specifying need and hunger guides us to the two indispensable ways to understand and mend our broken selves.

That the authors of the Haggadah considered neediness a key to *wholeness* (as the opposite of brokenness) is, at least in the modern sensibility, puzzling. The one idea that people of very different philosophical dispositions seem to agree on is the value of independence. A late twentieth-century feminist slogan is, "A woman needs a man like a fish needs a bicycle." The libertarian alternative from Ayn Rand is, "Freedom (n.): To ask nothing. To expect nothing. To depend on nothing." The apolitical self-help literature agrees, as is evidenced in articles like "11 Reasons Why You Need to Be More Independent" and "8 Important Reasons Why You Should Be More Independent."[7]

There is no Jewish prayer equivalent to these secular expressions of yearning for independence. Instead, there is the complete opposite. We have: "Blessed are you, Lord our God, King of the universe, Creator of numerous living beings *and their needs*." We ask God to bless our brokenness, and thank him for creating our needs.

Even more stunning is that this prayer for need is a quintessential example of our desire to "walk in His ways"—to emulate God. In Numbers 27:16, Moses (acknowledging his advancing age) turns his focus to a successor. Moses calls upon God in God's capacity as the one who knows everyone intimately and asks God to appoint a successor. God selects Joshua and assures Moses that God would guide the new leader in his military challenges. The Jews would need God in the new Land, and God assures Moses that he, God, would be there for them.

Then God tells Moses to ensure that the people make offerings to him twice a day and additionally on every Jewish holiday. In other words, Moses tells God that the Jews need him—and God responds by telling Moses that God needs the Jews.[8] This seems counterintuitive. All needs, one might presume, flow from a lack of capability or a lack of knowledge. How could God—who is all powerful and all knowing—*need* anyone or anything?

Because, as Rabbi Angela Buchdahl says, "We are unconditionally loved by God." One might think that love *satisfies* needs—to alleviate loneliness, to give of oneself, to become better in the way that only a loving relationship can enable. And it does. But love also *creates* needs.

Every parent experiences this. Two people create a child. Though this child did not exist previously, the parents' most painful thought immediately becomes contemplating life without her. It is not the pain caused by losing something the parent likes, values, or even only loves. It is the pain caused by losing what she absolutely needs. And the love a parent has for a child only causes this need to deepen over time. A young adult child might wonder why his parent insists that he call home all the time. The answer is simple: the parent just needs him to, because love creates need.[9]

The emergence of need as the indispensable product of love presents in all of love's forms. One young man tells his intended that he loves her but, truthfully, would be fine without her. Another tells his intended that he simply cannot imagine life without her—as she completes him. Which young man would we want our daughter to marry? Which young man would we prefer our son to be?

To live fully and well, in the Jewish context, is within a system where we need and are needed. When we proclaim that we are needy, we reject the forced dependence of the slave and the sad independence of the narcissist in favor of the multifaceted system of obligations, responsibilities, and genuine love that constitutes interdependence.

Of all the needs that each of us has and should want to have, the Haggadah only directly discusses one. And that might just mean that this need is the most important—or, certainly, the most encompassing. It is hunger.

The idea that hunger is a need is counterintuitive. It would seem that *alleviating* hunger is the need. Again, the book of Numbers explains. We are in the desert, with God having provided everything for us—including a steady ration of food that tastes "like wafers made with honey." Yet we complain that we want to go back to Egypt!

Why are we so unhappy that we yearn for a return to Egyptian enslavement? The Torah, in Numbers 11:4, tells us. Because God unilaterally provides for all of our needs in the desert, we "craved a craving." And we are immediately given an example. God gives us the perfect food, manna. And what do we do? We "grind, pound and cook it"—we *work* it. It was not like we could make it better, but we craved a craving.

This is not a phenomenon of the Jews as freed slaves in the desert, but of Jews as human beings. "Man," Moses says in Deuteronomy 8:3, "does not live by bread alone." *Live* here is not qualified—it does not say live spiritually, live well, or live meaningfully. The Torah just says *live*. To *live*, we need sustenance other than bread as much as we need the most universal staple of the body.

Rabbi Y. Y. Jacobson, drawing from early letters of the Lubavitcher Rebbe, shows how this message is embedded into the Pesach sequence itself. In Exodus 12:9, God instructs regarding the Pesach meal: "You shall not eat it partially roasted or cooked in fire, only roasted over fire." This instruction is the only place in the Torah when there are dietary laws governing how food is prepared. Elsewhere, God offers no instruction or preference about whether we eat meat rare or well done, roasted or broiled, or prepared with or without a pot. But on Pesach evening, God is very clear: There shall be no water; there shall be no pot. Just meat and fire.

Why is God so insistent that, uniquely on Pesach, we ingest food made only with fire? Fire, Rabbi Jacobson says, never relaxes—it represents "striving, yearning, thirst, passion, tension [and] restlessness." While some religious traditions seek to provide stillness, calmness, serenity, and peace of mind, Judaism does the opposite. As God is infinite and we are created in his image, we understand that there is always something more significant that we should be hungry for.[10]

It is this conviction that sustained us through the most broken moments in the Jewish story. Hugo Gryn was born in Czechoslovakia in 1930. He and his parents were taken to Auschwitz in 1944, where his two brothers were murdered immediately. While in the camp, Hugo's father saved a tiny ration of margarine until Hanukkah—when he used it to make a light for the holiday. Hugo asked his father why he used the margarine for a Hanukkah light rather than to alleviate their extreme hunger. His father responded, "My child, we know you can live three days without water. You can live three weeks without food. But you cannot live for three minutes without hope."[11] Hugo Gryn died in 1996, a widely respected British rabbi.

Carl Jung was perhaps the greatest psychoanalyst of the twentieth century. At the age of fifty-seven, he published *Modern Man in Search of a Soul*. At the conclusion of the book, he writes,

> During the past thirty years, people from all the civilized countries of the earth have consulted me. . . . Among all my patients in the second half of life—that is to say, over thirty-five—there has not been one

whose problem in the last resort was not that of finding a religious outlook on life.

It is this sense of ultimate purpose and existential meaning that people *need* to sustain their mental health.[12]

Dr. Viktor Frankl, an Austrian doctor, had the opportunity to escape the Holocaust but stayed to care for his elderly parents. He spent four years in three slave labor camps—Theresienstadt, Auschwitz, and Dachau. His family was murdered. He survived and went on to write perhaps the most important book of the twentieth century, *Man's Search for Meaning.* It is in this book that Dr. Frankl, quoting Friedrich Nietzsche, encapsulates what he learned from the experience of slaves in the concentration camps: "Those who have a 'why' to live can bear almost any 'how.'"[13]

To live, Jewish teaching from the Torah to Viktor Frankl tells us we *need* a *why*. And embedded in every why is an insatiable hunger to deliver its answer to the world. This is the person to whom the Haggadah's Seder invitation is being addressed. The authors of the Haggadah want us to show up as our hungry self—the one who wants to grow more, know more, contribute more, and ultimately *be* more. And the Haggadah is there to show us how.

THE GREATEST PRINCIPLE
OF THE TORAH

Whoever is hungry—let him come and eat!
Whoever is needy—let him come and celebrate Pesach!

As discussed with reference to the meanings of Pesach foods, a genuinely Jewish interpretation can yield multiple meanings that can be very different and all true. This Haggadah passage calls forth our broken selves—while being issued in a way that also leads us to consider what is perhaps the most important idea in Judaism. And it is issued in a way that reminds us of what is perhaps the most important idea in Judaism.

In November 2018, the missionary John Allen Chau decided to proselytize among the people of North Sentinel Island in the Bay of Bengal, a protected area of India. The islanders are among the last people to be untouched by anything modern—from technology to ideas. Chau, against Indian law, reached the island—and was promptly killed. The islanders were not punished because the authorities recognized that they were a premodern people—and, consequently, could be expected to treat a stranger as they did John Allen Chau.

This notion of the stranger is embedded in our language. The term "barbarian" debuted in Greece at around the same time as the Exodus took place. Professor Luis Garcia Alonso of the University of Salamanca explains, "In the Pylos clay tablet collection we do find the word simply applied, apparently, to people from out of town." Yet, the meaning of the word is the same for us as it was for the ancient Greeks (and Romans, who adopted it from them).[1] The difference is that ancient people viewed all strangers like the North Sentinel Islanders still do: as barbarians.

It is ironic that we would classify the attitude of the Greeks, the Romans, and the North Sentinel Islanders as barbaric. Their attitude toward strangers may be barbaric, but it is also *natural*. We see this with babies, who resist being held by people they are not very familiar with. And we see it with toddlers who have to be reminded, "don't be shy," even with people who have earned their trust. And we see it with eating habits. By age two to two and a half, children develop what culinary scientists call *food neophobia*—children only "like" foods that they consider very familiar. Within a few months, even the parental fake "Yum" ceases to work. Toddlers can't be tricked out of their food neophobia.[2]

What does food neophobia have to do with the Jewish response to Egyptian slavery? Perhaps everything—as food neophobia is just the culinary application of generalized neophobia. We are conditioned through evolutionary psychology to view new things in our environment as threats. And the threats, from those posed by foods that may be poisonous to people who may be murderous, could be fatal. Even in modern society, we instinctively know this. As soon as children outgrow their pediatric neophobia, their parents bring it right back—and warn them never to talk to strangers. We are all, and sometimes with good reason, at least situational neophobes.

There is a class of strangers that no one fears. These are the strangers who are far away and will never come close. If the natural reaction to strangers in one's environment is fear, the natural reaction to strangers outside of the environment is apathy. The Scottish philosopher Adam Smith describes this phenomenon with the parable of the "man of humanity in Europe" who hears that the "great empire of China . . . was suddenly swallowed up by an earthquake."

> He would, I imagine, first of all, express very strong his sorrow for the misfortune of that unhappy people [and] he would make melancholy reflections upon the precariousness of human life. . . . And when all this fine philosophy was over, when all these humane sentiments had been once fairly expressed, he would pursue his business or his pleasure, take his repose or his diversion, with the same ease and tranquility, as if no such accident had happened. . . . If he was to lose his little finger tomorrow, he would not sleep tonight; but provided he never saw them, he will snore with the most profound security over the ruin

of a hundred million of his brethren, and the destruction of that immense multitude seems plain an object less interesting to him than this paltry misfortune of his own.[3]

It is against the backdrop of viewing the stranger as a source of fear or apathy that the author of the Torah presents a different idea. It is an idea so fundamental to Judaism that Rabbi Akiva calls it "the greatest principle of the Torah."[4] It is an idea so important in Judaism that the authors of the Haggadah clearly allude to it as the Seder begins. And it is so consequential that it is mentioned, in various forms, more often in the Torah than any other—including the commandment to love God.[5]

This idea, this commandment, is *to love the stranger.*

The Torah never instructs us to love our children, presumably for the same reason that no doctor ever told a patient to be sure to go to the bathroom tomorrow. We do not need to be told to do what we will do uninstructed. But we are instructed dozens of times in the Torah to love the stranger. Indeed, this commandment is so startling and counterintuitive that the author of the Torah does not come out and just tell us to love the stranger. It is as though it would be too novel and non-intuitive for us to do without significant preparation.

The conditioning begins in a story, well before any instruction or directive is provided. In Genesis, God is having a conversation with Abraham when three strangers appear at the gate. Abraham bolts from his discussion with God to take care of them. How does God react to being interrupted in this way? God announces that he has "chosen" Abraham to be "a great and powerful nation, and all nations of the earth will be blessed through him." It is as though Abraham's interrupting a conversation with God to greet strangers is what qualifies Abraham for this greatest of all blessings.

In Exodus, the commandments regarding the stranger begin—and, as Rabbi Shai Held shows, soon escalate.[6] The commandment is provided only in the negative, through an instruction of how *not* to treat the stranger.

In Exodus 23:9, the commandment is delivered only as an instruction of what not to do. "You shall not oppress a stranger, for you know the feelings of the stranger, having yourselves been strangers in the land of Egypt."

In Leviticus 19:34, it switches to positive: "The stranger who dwells with you shall be like a native among you, and you shall love him like yourself, for you were aliens in the land of Egypt—I am Hashem, your God." Later in Leviticus, the stranger becomes a "brother," in the context of prohibiting the charging of interest to an impoverished person whether he is a Jew or a "proselyte or resident [gentile]."[7]

By Deuteronomy, we are ready for the ultimate commandment. It is provided with the grandest rationale—that keeping it is what enables us to be like God.

> For the Lord your God is God supreme and Lord supreme, the great, the mighty and the awesome God, who shows no favor and takes no bribe, but upholds the cause of the fatherless and the widow, and loves the stranger, providing him with food and clothing. You too must love the stranger, for you were strangers in the land of Egypt.

The emphasis placed on this commandment leads us to consider an earlier commitment regarding the Seder: We will mean every word we say tonight. The operative word here is not "stranger," as he/she is easy to iden tify. The word, or really the concept, that requires purposeful understanding is love. In order to figure out what it means to love the stranger—in order to comply with what Rabbi Akiva said is the greatest principle of the Torah—we must first answer: What does it mean to love?

The dictionary definition of love is "an intense feeling of deep affection."[8] And that certainly captures how a groom feels about his bride, a mother about her child, or a patriot about his country. But then there is the report from the National Domestic Violence Hotline: "We hear from many people who are in abusive relationships, even those who left relationships, but say that they love their abusive partner."[9]

Can a battered woman have "an intense feeling of deep affection" for her husband? Apparently, yes. But can she love him? The question itself is hideous.

By contrast, it is easy to identify genuine love. It is the kind of behavior that makes observers remark admiringly: "That's love." We don't say that when we observe an act of domestic violence—or even a romantic gesture like a whirlwind date to Tuscany or a gift of birthday chocolates. We say it when we see a soldier run through fire to rescue an injured comrade, a boy staying up all night to comfort his frightened sister, a young man who drives for hours to give encouragement to his intended before a major test, a woman who visits her husband in the hospital each day for decades following a devastating brain injury.

This phenomenon is elucidated by Rashi's commentary on Deuteronomy 6:5. He explains that to "love God" means to "*perform* his commandments out of love." The *performative* conception of love is reflected in the Hebrew language, where two words that share a common root are understood to have a profound connection. The Hebrew words for *love* and *give* share the same root, *ahav*—which means "to give." Love, we learn, does not live in feelings but in *acts* of mutual giving. Thus, a man who hits his wife does not love her regardless of what he says or any "affection" he might *feel*. Loving one's child, friend, spouse, or parent requires actions worthy of love—and so does loving the stranger. This experience of love is embedded in the Hebrew language.

As Rabbi David Wolpe points out, the word *korban* ("sacrifice") shares a root with the word *karov* ("draw close").[10] We "draw close" to others through sacrifice, and it is through this process that love is marinated. That, perhaps, is why the most profound love is between a mother and her child. Every time a woman gets pregnant, she risks death to give life to her child.

The Jewish insistence that love be robust, genuine, and lived contains a paradox. The paradox is described, and criticized, in the New Testament's book of Matthew: "You have heard that it was said, 'Love your neighbor and hate your enemy.' But I tell you, love your enemies and pray for those who persecute you."[11]

Is Matthew right? Are Jews, for whom love of the stranger is a religious imperative, allowed to hate?

Matthew is correct. In fact, he is more correct than that statement allows—as the Torah permits hatred of even more than just "your enemy" as described by Matthew. The Torah, ever mindful of and instructive about the challenges of the moral life, suggests three kinds of hatred—half of which are acceptable.

The first kind of hatred is that directed to "your brother." It is described in Leviticus 19:17, when God commands: "You shall not hate your brother in your heart." Does this mean, Rabbi David Fohrman asks, that it is acceptable to hate outside of your heart? Apparently! The logic of articulating one's hatred—taking it out of the privacy of one's heart—shows why.[12]

If a person expresses his hatred to his "brother," what might happen? There are three possibilities. First, the process of articulating his hatred might make him realize his hatred is unreasonable and indefensible. The hatred ends there. Second, he might believe that his hatred is justified and the "brother" might agree and genuinely apologize. The hatred ends there. Third, he might believe that his hatred is reasonable and justified—and the "brother" might disagree. In the first two instances, the relationship is repaired—and a love, cleansed and perhaps stronger than ever, can begin again. In the third instance, the hatred persists—but after having given peace a chance. In all cases, there is no ambiguity.

The second kind of hatred regards not any kind of "brother" but our enemy. In Exodus 23:5, the donkey of "someone you hate [is] crouching under its burden." What should one do? One might expect a religious text to say: "Help him!" The Torah does say that, but with a critical nuance. "You shall repeatedly help *with him*." One should not, therefore, help *without him*. If "the one you hate" is unwilling to work with you, then there is no chance for reconciliation and it should not be fruitlessly pursued. We are to do all we can to turn hatred into love, but no more.

The third kind of hatred regards a different kind of enemy. He is exemplified by Amalek, a people in the book of Exodus who attack us when we are hungry, weak, and mutinous. Amalek, the Torah tells us ominously, will be with us "from generation to generation." This is not the enemy with whom we might collaborate in lifting a fallen donkey and transform a relationship. This is an enemy who murderously attacks the weak. The question then becomes: How should one engage with such an enemy?

One way would be that described by Bishop Desmond Tutu: "An enemy is a friend waiting to happen."[13] In the Torah's world, that response would be appropriate for a "*brother*" whom one "hates"—two-thirds of the time. It would not apply to the KKK members who killed four girls when they bombed the 16th Street Baptist Church in Birmingham, Alabama, in 1963,[14] the Nazi officers who beat, gang-raped, and killed women they considered "spies,"[15] the Spanish inquisitors who burned "heretics" at the stake, or those in the regime of Saddam Hussein who gouged out the eyes of children to use as leverage against their parents.[16] Such people are not only *our* enemy. They are God's enemy—the people who, in the words of King David in Psalm 139: 21-22, "hate you God . . . and rise against you." They are not ours to forgive.

For people like that, the Bible provides a clear, consistent, and comprehensive answer. King David tells us in Psalm 97:10, "The fear of the Lord is to hate evil," and declares in the aforementioned Psalm 139 that he will "hate those who hate you God . . . with the utmost hatred I will hate them." This is not a matter of, per Saint Augustine and Mahatma Gandhi, hating the sin and loving the sinner. This is a matter of hating both.[17] There is, as the book of Ecclesiastes instructs, "a time to love and a time to hate." And hatred, like love, requires action. Leviticus 26 offers the blessings that we will receive if we follow God's words. One of them is "peace in the Land." This blessing will not come because our enemies will have decided to love us—but because, per Leviticus 26:7, "you will chase down your enemies and slaughter them with your swords."

Why does Judaism make such nuanced distinctions about hatred—governing how we can hate a brother and then how we can hate an enemy—rather than, perhaps, just forbidding it altogether? The first-century sage Rabbi Elazar explains: "Anyone who becomes merciful upon the cruel," he says, "will end up being cruel to the merciful."[18] And being cruel to the merciful is the opposite of what is commanded by Rabbi Akiva's greatest principle of the Torah—to love the stranger. In order to *genuinely* love—in order to express love not as a vague sentiment but as a life-defining conviction—one needs to know when and how to hate.

JUST WHO ARE YOU CALLING A STRANGER?

Whoever is hungry—let him come and eat!
Whoever is needy—let him come and celebrate Pesach!

Wait! We just quoted God, reiterated throughout the Torah, commanding us to love the stranger because "you were strangers in the land of Egypt."

If the commandment to love the stranger is unnatural and counterintuitive, the reason to do so—because "you were strangers in the land of Egypt"—is ahistorical and even offensive.

Why?

A dispassionate Jew, empowered by the examples of Abraham and Moses to argue with God, might have responded:

"Did you just say that I was a *stranger*? I was a *slave*. In fact, *God*, maybe you need a reminder as to what exactly it meant to be a slave. Let me read to you from a contemporaneous Egyptian account—the Satire of the Trades, a document that describes slavery in the Middle Kingdom, which as you know is when we were enslaved there:

"He is dirtier than vines or pigs from treading under his mud. His clothes are stiff with clay; his leather belt is going to ruin. Entering into the wind, he is miserable . . . his sides ache, since he must be outside in a treacherous wind . . . his arms are destroyed with technical work. What he eats is the bread of his fingers, and he washes himself only once a season. He is simply wretched through and through.[1]

"You, God, call *that* being a stranger? A stranger is the new kid in the playground, a stranger is the person who just sat next to me on the subway. As for my experience in Egypt: My experience as a 'stranger' was only in the brief time before the Pharaoh enslaved us. I was a *slave* . . ."

We can hear the thundering voice of God saying, "Stop! Remember what I told you way back in Genesis: 'I myself will go down with you to Egypt.' I know exactly your experience, as I watched you the entire time and I freed you from slavery. I'll leave you now with two words: Remember Joseph!"

Remember Joseph? Yes. Joseph's brothers throw him into a pit and he is saved only by being sold to a passing tribe. Through a wild string of events, Joseph ends up as the second most powerful man in Egypt. He is in control of the world's food supply in a time of famine when his brothers come to him for food. They do not recognize Joseph until he reveals himself.

He tells them that he is "your brother, Joseph, whom you sold into Egypt." He anticipates that they will be "distressed or reproach yourselves" but he urges them otherwise, as he has interpreted his situation differently. "God sent me before you to preserve life. . . . So it was not you who sent me here, but God." By interpreting his experience as that of a divine messenger, rather than the victim of an attempted fratricide, Joseph is able to reconcile with his brothers and feed a starving world.

God's imagined interlocutor would now understand. Interpretation is a choice. God, or anyone else, could have focused the Jewish experience in Egypt on our being strangers or slaves. Why would God have insisted on the *stranger* interpretation? For a reason that perfectly illustrates why Moses says in Dueteronomy that the Torah exists "for [our] benefit."

If we define ourselves by our slave experience, we will risk considering ourselves to be perpetual victims. We will risk developing an inadequacy that will govern all our approaches, a sense of negative inevitability that will lead us to conclude that positive change is impossible, and a persistent feeling of powerlessness that will deprive us of the agency that freedom promises.

One who identifies as a slave will be vulnerable to what the psychologist Martin Seligman has termed "learned helplessness," which he defines as "the giving up reaction . . . that follows from the belief that whatever you do doesn't matter." Psychologists who have studied learned helplessness have associated it with depression, anxiety, phobias, and the inability to effect positive change.[2]

If we define our formative experience as that of a stranger, we will be inclined to reach out with empathic obligation to those who are alone in a world that requires companionship, to be filled with gratitude for the freedom and fellowship that we now have, and will treasure the dignity and agency that come with helping and giving. We will prepare ourselves to fulfill the Torah commandment to love the stranger.

By teaching us to choose our interpretations, God is not only steering us from victimhood and the helplessness and hopelessness that it produces. He is offering a profound lesson in freedom. Why do we experience anger, happiness, humor, offense, exasperation, or joy? One view, which is perhaps the default, is that the event moves through our reservoir of experiences, values, and expectations and a response is produced. But that sequence removes all agency from the decision. And what notion of freedom would hold that we cannot choose our reactions, responses, and attitudes? Without these choices, there is not enough of life available for freedom to be meaningful. When we recognize that we can choose our interpretations, we understand the potential of freedom to transform how we experience so much of life. This can even apply to, as Professor Tovah Leah Nachmani shows us, traffic.

Professor Nachmani tells the story of her teacher's teacher, Rav Tzvi Yehuda Kook. Rav Kook and a student were stuck in traffic on a busy Jerusalem street. The student was annoyed, as most people are when they are delayed in traffic. Perhaps the rabbi was as well, but he chose to interpret it differently. "This is the fulfillment of the promise that God made to the prophet Zechariah!" The prophecy, made after the destruction of the First Temple in 587 B.C.E., was that there would once again be children playing in the streets of Jerusalem.[3] The student and his rabbi both were delayed and knew the text—but one chose to see it as an annoyance and the other as a moment of profound spiritual encounter.

This kind of choice is even more common than the traffic that can, among other things, produce it.

Is an unfortunate comment a cause for anger or an innocent malapropism? Is an unreturned phone call or rejected meeting request a blow to our self-conception or a mistake of a disorganized person? Is being rejected a meaningful setback or an educational moment?

We can make a good case, from the facts, for any of those choices—just as Rav Kook and the student each could have. Which, though, would make us happier, healthier, and better prepared to advance through a complicated world?

LOVE AND RESPONSIBILITY: ISRAEL

Now, we are here; next year may we be in the Land of Israel!

This is another moment to recall our commitment at the outset of the Seder: to mean everything that we say. In that spirit, we contemplate last year's Seder, in Melbourne or New York, Los Angeles or Paris, when we also said, "Next year may we be in the Land of Israel." Here we are, again. Given that we hope to be having the Seder next year in the same place we are now, should we say this passage now?

Absolutely—in the context of the previously discussed vertical and horizontal conversations that we have on Pesach.

First, the vertical conversation. At this moment, we should imagine our ancestors—in India and Yemen, Germany and Greece, New York or places that have been lost to history and survive on no maps. These people spoke in any of hundreds of languages. Some were rich and some were poor, some were secure and some were persecuted, some were deeply learned and some did not engage intellectually, some experienced Pesach while it was still cold and some were basking in the Mediterranean spring. They all began and concluded their Seders by expressing a yearning for Israel and its holy city.

When we say, "Next year in the Land of Israel," we are speaking to them. We are acknowledging their yearning and telling them, "Great-great-grandma and -grandpa, your greatest dream, your deepest yearning, the subject of your daily prayers that you turned east for every day—it worked, it happened, *Israel*—it came true!"

We are celebrating with them, with the enthusiasm of one who is delivering the most unbelievably great news to a loved one.

This act of vertical celebration leads one to ask: Why did our ancestors, wherever they were, yearn for a country they could not have reasonably imagined existing? The first observation, whose implications will be explored in a later chapter, is that *they imagined*! The answer to why they imagined Israel brings us to the source of the Jewish imagination itself.

The Jewish *need* for Israel is exactly as ancient as the Jewish people. The first Jew was the biblical Abraham, and God promises him three things: blessings, descendants, and the Land of Israel. This promise is repeated to Abraham's son Isaac and again to Isaac's son Jacob.[1] There must be something so important about the Land, there must be something so sacred about Israel, that explains its centrality to the divine project on earth. The reasons will bring us to the core of Zionism, from Abraham to today.

First, there is a misconception about Zionism that needs to be clarified.

In his book *The Will to Live On,* the American Jewish author Herman Wouk discusses a dinner that he had with David Ben-Gurion in 1955 following the Tel Aviv production of *The Caine Mutiny* (adapted from Wouk's book). Wouk had to take the trip from Tel Aviv to Ben-Gurion's home in Sde Boker in an army vehicle with military escorts. As the meal concluded, Ben-Gurion said to him, "You must return to live here, this is the only place for a Jew like you. Here you will be free."

Wouk replied, "Free? With enemy armies ringing you, with their leaders publicly threatening to wipe out the Zionist entity, with your roads impassable by sundown—free?"

"I did not say safe," Ben-Gurion replied. "I said free."[2]

In this exchange, Wouk and Ben-Gurion were essentially discussing two theories of Zionism. Wouk's theory, at least until the meeting in Sde Boker, was that Israel exists to serve as a safe haven for Jews. When Jews are persecuted, the existence of Israel guarantees us a home—a place where we are always welcome and will be protected. This function of Zionism is completely absent in the Torah. It only only emerged in the late nineteenth century when Theodor Herzl saw, through the Dreyfus trial in France, how virulent Jew hatred could overtake a liberal population in the birthplace of the Enlightenment. As Jews in the twentieth century from Germany to the Soviet Union to Iraq experienced, this is a deeply unfortunate and important function of Israel. But it is not its purpose.

The purpose of Israel is not to escape Jew haters. It is to serve God.

What does it mean to serve God? The ultimate answer to this existential Jewish question is provided in Exodus 19:6. We are to become a "kingdom of priests and a holy nation." This is not a vague sentiment. It is a divine command.

Indeed, Jewish life, as prescribed in the Torah, is a comprehensive experience. It involves, among other things, the administration of judicial functions, the conduct of statecraft, the imposition of criminal law, the development of an economy, care for the poor and dispossessed, and setting an example for other nations. And these are in addition to the dozens of Torah commandments that can *only* be performed in the Land of Israel.[3]

None of these tasks can be discharged virtually. They require the authority to tax and spend, to wage war and make peace, to set rules and penalize rule breakers, to respect private property and provide public goods, to collectively and comprehensively recognize the dignity of the poor and dispossessed, and to have an immigration policy that welcomes Jews from the most diverse cultures and brings them together with the depth that reflects one people coming together after thousands of years of exile. These Jewish tasks require a state. And the Torah is exceptionally clear that this state is to be one with a special mission.

In his parting words in Deuteronomy, Moses says:

> You should preserve and perform [the commandments in the Land]. For this is your wisdom and understanding in the eyes of the nations, who will hear all these laws and say, "only this great nation is a wise and understanding people." Which nation is so great as to have such righteous decrees and laws?

Or, as the prophet Isaiah famously interpreted, this nation-state is to become a "light unto the nations." The purpose of this state is to inspire all other states, leading people everywhere toward the source that ordained it.

The Torah often instructs people to act with their "heart and soul." But there is only one time in the Bible when God does something with his heart and soul.[4] That is in Jeremiah 32:41, when God vows to "assuredly plant them in this Land with all my heart and all my soul."

How do we respond? With analogies that speak to what we depend on most. The prophet Isaiah refers to Jerusalem as "heart-Jerusalem" in one passage and prophesies that the Jews would be nursed "at her comforting breasts" in another. The prophet Jeremiah writes: "If I forget you, Jerusalem, may my right hand forget its skill. May my tongue cling to the roof of my mouth if I do not remember you, if I do not consider my Jerusalem my greatest joy."[5]

What kind of people uses terms of romantic endearment (heart-Jerusalem) to describe a city? What kind of people, in its holy text, compares a city to a right hand and a tongue—and leaves the impression that the fullness of feeling is still incompletely expressed? What kind of people has sustained this love, in all its intensity, through thousands of years, hundreds of places, and the best and worst experiences that a people can have?

A people in love—in love with God and with the Land where that love can blossom in sacred action and inspire the entire world.

The unique love between the Jewish people and Israel is the first way that we fulfill our obligation to be a "light unto the nations." By loving Israel, we teach ourselves and all observers about love itself. In the Jewish love for Israel and its capital, we see love's obligations, durability, adaptability, and sustainability. We see the persistent longing that a lover has for his beloved and the appreciation that the lover has once united with his intended. We see the intense physicality and the tender emotions that love inspires and how it needs to be expressed in so many ways: song, praises, poems, prayers, and *action*. We see that genuine love means accepting demanding responsibilities, embracing the opportunities they create, working hard, and sacrificing accordingly.

It is with *love*—of the deepest and most abiding kind—that we say, "Next year in the Land of Israel." With the devotion of love and the commitment to mean everything we say on Pesach, a logical question emerges. When we say the words *Next year in the Land of Israel!*, are we committing ourselves to living in Israel next year?

The Haggadah passage does not say: "Next year *may we live* in the Land of Israel"—but "Next year in the Land of Israel." This distinction creates the opportunity and responsibility for all Jews—those in Israel, those who are planning to move to Israel, those who plan on staying in the diaspora—to be *in* the Land of Israel and to share in the responsibility to make that country a kingdom of priests and a holy nation.

Those in the diaspora who intend to stay can conceive of this passage with the realization that the practice of Jews electing to live outside the Land is as old as the Torah. In Numbers 32, the tribes of Reuben and Gad ask Moses for permission to settle, for economic reasons, outside the Land. Moses is at first taken aback and accuses them of wanting to "sit back" while their fellow Israelites fight for the Land. The two tribes assure Moses that they will not only fight for the Land but that they will be the "vanguard" of the army. Moses grants their wish. The Gaddites and the Reubenites would not live in the Land of Israel, but our greatest prophet welcomed them as full members of the Jewish community so long as their contributions would be sacrificial, substantive, and constant.

Those settled in the diaspora can say, "Next year in the Land of Israel," in the spirit of the Gaddites and the Reubenites. Many of us can go to Israel. It is a miracle that we can actually say this—we can go to Israel, the Jewish state! A Jew should want to at least visit Israel with the same urgency and enthusiasm as he would visit any place or person he loves. And in this case, visits to Israel have all kinds of benefits in addition to the enjoyment of the traveler—those of biblical understanding, of social bonds, of Jewish cohesion, of economics.

Putting one's body in Israel—permanently or as a traveler—is an important way of discharging the Pesach obligation to be in Israel next year. But it is not the only way. There are Israeli organizations to support, products to buy, investments to make, friendships to form, and facts to publicize. These and others are all ways that one can "be" in Israel—and thus genuinely partake in this aspect of the great Pesach conversation with our ancestors and with Jews and other Zionists around the world today.

JUDAISM IN A WORD:
NEWNESS

Now, we are slaves; next year may we be free men!

This statement is stunning. We are sitting at a beautiful Seder, contemplating great ideas in the first generation when almost every Jew in the world is able to freely practice his faith. Yet we are calling ourselves slaves. Slaves! The Jews under the Pharaoh were slaves; Blacks under Southern plantation owners were slaves; so were Jews in Nazi concentration camps and Yazidis under Islamists in Iraq. And so are sex slaves in American cities now.

But today's Jews? In New York, Berlin, Sydney, Montreal? In Tel Aviv?

As previously discussed, understanding a text first requires identifying its genre. The same discipline can be applied to understanding part of a text. The line "Now, we are slaves" is not a legal determination, a sociological insight, or a normative statement. It is a metaphor, and recognizing its literary purpose is crucial to understanding the Torah and the Haggadah.

We are well equipped to do so. According to the linguist James Geary, we use one metaphor every ten to twenty-five words, which equates to six metaphors a minute. We use metaphors far more frequently than we use the word *I*.[1]

The Torah is also full of metaphors. Rabbi Andrea Weiss points out that just the "Song of Moses" in Deuteronomy 32 portrays God as a father, an eyelid, an eagle, a mother who has gone through labor, a nursing mother, and a protective rock.[2] These metaphors are, tellingly, mutually exclusive. One cannot be a mother and a father—or an eagle and a rock. But we don't use metaphors to make precise comparisons. Instead, we use them to highlight what the philosopher Max Black calls the *associated commonplaces* between the two things.[3] If we call God a "rock," we are not saying that he is actually a rock. We are highlighting what God shares with a rock: strength, dependability, and permanence.

And we are doing something else as well. The Christian theologian Sallie McFague explains that metaphors highlight what the two things have in common—and, in so doing, how they are different as well. The very purpose of a metaphor can be seen, at least partially, through its inexactitude. Professor McFague writes, "Metaphorical statements . . . always contain the whisper, 'it is *and it is not.*"[4] A basketball writer, for instance, who says that a college shooting guard is the "next Michael Jordan" calls our attention to how the player is—and is not—like the Chicago Bulls great.

It is with Professor McFague's insight in mind that we approach this section of the Haggadah. The authors of the Haggadah, by having us declare that we are slaves, are inviting us to simultaneously ask two questions: How *are* we slaves? And how are we *not* slaves?

First, how we are *not* slaves. We can consider the aforementioned description of Egyptian slavery from *The Satire of the Trades,* and amplify it from the historical record. The ancient Greek historian Herodotus, writing after the Exodus, describes how the ancient slave masters would regularly blind their slaves. In Numbers 16, Moses is dealing with the greatest internal threat to his regime. The rebels tell him that they will not accede to him, even if he "gouges out the eyes of those men." Moses had never blinded anyone or threatened to—but their concern reflects just how ubiquitous the blinding of both slaves and vanquished opponents was in the ancient world.[5]

Other techniques, used as punishments for breaking even minor items, included cutting off hands, fingers, thumbs, and big toes. The Code of Hammurabi stipulates that a slave who says "You are not my master" is to have his ear cut off. Male slaves were often castrated so that thoughts of women would not make them less productive. Knocking out a slave's teeth was another technique to limit the amount of food a slave would consume. Cicero wrote of how the Romans would cut off the tongues of slaves to stop them from testifying.[6]

Readers of this book do not live like this at all. One of the functions of declaring "Now we are slaves" is to realize just how free we are. This is true individually, communally, and nationally. Professor McFague's whisper is, blessedly, as insistent as it could be.

But as we reflect on how we are not slaves, we are also drawn to consider how many people are slaves today. Slavery, for a variety of reasons, is much more profitable for slave masters than ever before. The consequence of this, and the lack of effort against it, is hideous.

There are now more slaves in the world than there ever have been.[7]

This includes bonded labor in India, chattel slaves in Mauritania (where slaves are officially considered "the full property of their masters"), fishing slaves on Lake Volta in Ghana, construction slaves in North Korea, road-building slaves in Laos, cotton-picking slaves in Uzbekistan, domestic slaves in China, mining slaves in the Congo, tea- and rice-farming slaves in South Asia, the slaves who built the stadiums for the 2022 World Cup in Qatar, child soldier slavery in Iran (a regional hub for human trafficking, where enslavement is punished very lightly and where the diminished weight given to women testifying in court makes it hard to convict slave masters), and many others.[8]

If one is attending a Seder in an American city, it is *certain* that there is slavery within walking distance. Tens of thousands of slaves live in the United States. These are often young girls, lured into sex slavery and addicted to drugs by pimps who require them to have sex with dozens of men each day. These girls are often branded with tattoos signifying which slave master they belong to, and they are kept in slavery through physical violence and the threat of murder.

As we will see, Jewish "knowledge" always assumes commensurate action. In stating that we know that there is slavery, each of us is committing to do something to (in the fullest spirit of Pesach) stop this evil.

We have heard the whisper that we are not slaves. But we, reading from the Haggadah, did just say: "We are slaves." That requires figuring out what associated commonplaces we have with slaves and then working to liberate ourselves.

The Torah provides us with at least two ways in which we can consider ourselves slaves.

The first explanation exists in the Hebrew word for Egypt itself—*Mitzrayim*. Mitzrayim derives from the root *tzar*, which refers to a narrow, tight, or constraining place. Anyone who has felt constrained by obligations to the point where it seems as though life consists of going from one responsibility to the next without any ability to decide how to spend an hour has been to this place. This experience is not slavery, but it certainly does not feel like freedom. This is because it shares an "associated commonplace" with slavery—which is the lack of control over one's time. And this means that decisions about time are the essence of what it means to be a free person.

Judaism's philosophy of time is revealed at the beginning of the Pesach story. In Exodus 12:2, right before the Pesach sequence begins, God declares the first Jewish holiday and the first mitzvah. The holiday is Rosh Chodesh, and the mitzvah is to inaugurate this monthly holiday by declaring the new moon.

The commandment to declare the new moon constituted an existential challenge to how everyone else in the ancient world thought of time. Before Exodus 12:2, the standard by which people evaluated time was the sun. The sun, which always rises in the east and sets in the west on a predictable schedule, embodies constancy. In comes Exodus 12:2, with God directing the Jewish people to evaluate time not by the sun but by the moon. This declaration is not a matter of astronomy but of philosophy. Time, God is telling us, is not cyclical and instead can progress. The opportunities to begin again are frequent, beckoning, and divinely ordained. Through Rosh Chodesh, the author of the Torah provides the permission to improve and places it within the regular course of time.

The author of the Torah was just getting started. Rosh Chodesh is constructed to have a deeply personal significance. This is revealed in two crucial words. "This month is the beginning of months *for you*." Why *for you*? Those words seem superfluous. "This month is the beginning of months" would have seemingly explained what Rosh Chodesh is.

The sixteenth-century Italian rabbi Obadiah Sforno offered an explanation. The *for you*, he writes, is God's way of saying, "From now these months will be yours, to do with as you like. This is by way of contrast to the years when you were enslaved and had no control over your time or timetable at all."[9]

The *for you*, Sforno interprets, leads us to understand what it means to be free. To be a slave means to have no control over one's time. A slave's time is owned, controlled, and directed by his master. To be free is to have control over one's time—to be able to decide how to allocate the hours, days, and years that constitute our lives. The measure, therefore, of how we live as free people is largely a function of how we choose to spend our time.

With so many opportunities available to the free person, and time being necessarily constrained, how can we rightly perform this task? Judaism answers this question in the way that Rosh Chodesh was declared by the ancient Jewish courts in Temple times. When the sighting of the new moon was confirmed, the head of the Beit Din (the Jewish court) would declare, "Sanctified!" and all Jews in attendance would respond: "Sanctified! Sanctified!"[10]

This is the Jewish expression of freedom. The fundamental act of a free person is to *sanctify* time. The Hebrew word for *time* has the same root as the word for *invitation—z'man.* This illustrates the Jewish conception of time—it is an invitation. The English language provides the perfect way to think about how we can respond to this invitation. When we speak of "spending time," we acknowledge that time is a valuable and finite resource. We can spend time wisely, waste it, or worst of all, kill it. We glorify freedom when we spend time wisely, with the goal of sanctifying it.

These choices—the opportunities of the "for you" of Exodus 12:2—are present all the time. A father can choose to regard a meal with his daughter as the five hundredth of its kind or the first he has had, and the only one he will ever have, with her at this unique stage in her life. An employee can drive to work dreading the monotony ahead—or he can think about how his work can best improve the lives of his clients, customers, and colleagues. A board member can regard a committee meeting as a boring requirement or as the sacred work of building something meaningful with others. A Jew can choose to regard the Torah as an ancient chronicle of an era long past or as his "portable homeland" that has an inexhaustible supply of lessons and learnings ready to help him live a happier, truer, and more fulfilling life today.[11] A husband can choose to regard dinner with his wife as a trip to the stomach's filling station or as an evening filled with the anticipation of all the things that renewed love and commitment might bring.

The opportunity to sanctify time, however, is too great for the Torah—our great guidebook—to have left it at that. The Torah guides us toward one crucial way in which we can always sanctify time. It is embedded in the name of the holiday Rosh Chodesh itself. The word *rosh* means head and the word *chodesh* shares a root with the word *chidush,* which means "newness." Thus, *Rosh Chodesh* means, in addition to the head of months, "the head of newness."[12]

We sanctify time, thus, by seeking newness. Judaism has thrived through five millennia by finding, celebrating, and commanding newness *everywhere*. The first blessing a congregation says over the Torah is: "Blessed are you, God . . . /Who has chosen us from all peoples and given us Your Torah./ Blessed are You, God, who gives Torah to us." The use of past tense for the first verb signifying "giving" is easily explicable. God *gave* us the Torah at Mount Sinai. But it is immediately followed by the present tense—"who *gives* us the Torah." God gave us the Torah long ago and continues to give it to us—meaning that the Torah is endlessly generative, with new lessons to be derived with each encounter.[13]

In Deuteronomy, which is Moses's great summary/interpretation of the experience of the Jews from the Exodus on, he says, "And these words that I command you *today* shall be upon your heart." Why does he include *today*? These words had been commanded previously—and everyone who says anything does so on the day she says it! The inclusion of the word can be best comprehended in the context of Moses's dream that the words of Torah would be spoken forever. The rabbis of the Midrash explain that "*I command you today*" means "they should not appear to you as an antiquated edict which no one cares about but as a *new* one, which everyone hastens to read."[14]

Psalm 96 calls us to sing a song to the Lord. What kind of song? A beautiful song, a heartfelt song, a pious song? No—"Sing a *new* song to the Lord." It is with newness—with its freshness, enthusiasm, curiosity, and desire to do more—that Moses, the Psalmist, and God are asking for our commitment.

The Torah's presentation of newness just might be the answer to the question that all adults have, wistfully, asked at some point. "Where did all the time go? It seems like yesterday when . . ." And it really does seem like yesterday.

This is not a new phenomenon. It is described by the nineteenth-century French philosopher Paul Janet in his *Revue Philosophique*. He writes, "Let anyone remember his last eight or ten school years: It is the space of a century. Compare them with the last eight or ten years of life: It is the space of an hour."[15]

Why does our perception of time, the very measure of the length of our lives, seem to pass so much faster now than it did when we were younger? The frequently provided reason is that each moment becomes a smaller percentage of our life as we get older. The time in a semester seemed long when it was 2 percent of our life (and more of the life we can remember), but less so when it is .5 percent.

But if it were just a matter of a larger denominator, we would experience time similarly during different parts of the same year. We know that is not the case. The geologist Albert von St. Gallen Heim wrote in the *1892 Yearbook of the Swiss Alpine Club* that 95 percent of climbers who had suffered an accidental fall reported that "time became greatly expanded."[16] And it is not only the most dramatic moments that prolong time. We know that a week spent in an entirely new environment feels much longer than the same time spent doing our normal routine.

There must be something different about the way that adults *generally* experience time as we get older that accounts for why time speeds up. If we can get that right, we might be able to adjust how we experience time—and *effectively* lengthen our lives.

The nineteenth-century psychologist William James offers an explanation. "The foreshortening of the years as we grow older is due to the monotony of memory's content. . . . In youth we may have an absolutely new experience, subjective or objective, every hour of the day." Young people experience time slowly not because of their age, but because they constantly encounter new things. Older people, by contrast, develop routines—which James classifies as "monotony."[17] This, James writes, accounts for time seeming to move faster.

Modern science has shown that James was exactly right. The Stanford neuroscientist David Eagleman conducted an experiment where he flashed an image of a brown shoe on a computer screen many times—and interrupted it with an image of a flower. The subject reported that the flower was on screen for "much longer," even though the images were all presented in the same amount of time.[18] Professor Eagleman explains, "Time is this rubbery thing. It stretches out when you really turn your brain resources on, and when you say, 'Oh, I got this, everything is as expected,' it shrinks up."[19]

This insight has been abundantly confirmed by social science, and even has a name: "the oddball effect." Professors Rolf Ulrich and Karin Bausenhart define it as the phenomenon whereby: "people overestimate the duration of rare events."[20] Generating this "overestimation," therefore, is the key to prolonging the experience of living. All one has to do is add more rare events to one's life.

The lessons of the oddball effect for Pesach are profound. To prolong time, to appreciate time, to *sanctify* time, the guidance from the Torah and modern social science is clear. We should pursue new experiences and form new relationships; we should find what is special and distinctive in familiar things; we should allow ourselves to "begin again." It is by experiencing newness that we make life both longer and better.[21]

The "restriction" we might face with time is one "associated commonplace" that we could experience with slaves. The "restriction" we might face with decision-making is another—and, again, the Torah guides us toward liberation. If a juridical slave is told to do something by his master, he must do it or risk a severe penalty. We free people can *theoretically* decide not to do what we are told. If a boss, a spouse, a parent, or even a rabbi tells us to do something that we know is wrong, how easy is it to do the right thing? If a choice is between receiving a major benefit by doing the wrong thing (when the odds of getting caught are remote or nonexistent) or doing the right thing, what chance does the right thing have?

The Torah provides the ultimate assistance.

In Leviticus 25:55, God describes how the Jews should live as a *free people*: "For the Children of Israel are slaves to me, they are my slaves."

To be truly free, then, one needs to be a *slave*? The Reverend Dr. Martin Luther King Jr., who was intentionally reliving the Exodus story, thought so. From his final speech, delivered on April 3, 1968:

Well, I don't know what will happen now. We've got some difficult days ahead. But it really doesn't matter with me now, because I've been to the mountaintop. And I don't mind. Like anybody, I would like to live a long life; longevity has its place. But I'm not concerned about that now. I just want to do God's will. And He's allowed me to go up the mountain. And I've looked over. And I've seen the Promised Land. I may not get there with you. But I want you to know tonight, that we, as a people, will get to the Promised Land. So I'm happy, tonight. I'm not worried about anything. I'm not fearing any man. Mine eyes have seen the glory of the coming of the Lord![22]

The fear that Dr. King spoke of is so ubiquitous that the expression "fear not" is, as Rabbi Dov Greenberg points out, the most frequent instruction in the Torah.[23] Its ubiquity must be a consequence of its prevalence and importance. But Dr. King had conquered it in the way the Torah suggests and everyone can emulate: through complete commitment to God. When one is acting in accordance with God, there is no need—as Dr. King said—to fear any man.

How can an observant Jew, who knows that he needs to lose weight but just can't win any battles with food, not even be tempted by bacon, cheeseburgers, lobster, or ice cream soon after meat? Because, as it pertains to kosher food, he is a slave to God. How can a man who genuinely believes that he took his marriage vow before God observe the beauty of another woman and not be tempted by her? By regarding himself as a slave to God. When can a person put in the position to win an illegitimate advantage in business for which he will never be caught confidently pursue the path of honesty? When he is a slave to God.

We are either slaves to God or slaves otherwise.

If we are tempted by greed, lust, or the favor of another person to perform an act that we know is wrong, the easiest way to stay on the right path is to believe and say: I am a slave to God, and therefore I have to do what God requires of me.

THERE IS SUCH A THING AS A BAD QUESTION—AND SOMETIMES A GOOD REASON FOR IT

Why is this night different from all other nights?

The Mah Nishtanah—the Four Questions—is perhaps the best-known part of the Seder. Its purpose is to have children notice something different about this night from all other nights—that, for instance, on all other nights we eat many vegetables but on this night only maror. The children, surprised to find no chametz, only one vegetable, multiple dippings, and people reclining, are thus impelled to ask a question. It is from these questions that the adults begin to tell the story of Pesach.

But there are some problems. First, one does not express surprise by reading from a script—and the questions are all in the Haggadah. Second, the children have all heard these questions before—and familiar things are not surprising. Why, then, did the authors of the Haggadah choose reciting the Four Questions as the way to stimulate the interest of Jewish children forever?

The answer lies in a third curious fact about these questions. They are not interesting.

Our children, who are used to dipping their fries in ketchup and their chips in salsa, will not respond in wonder at the multiple dippings referenced in the Four Questions. We can reply that dipping was once a luxury, something indulged in only once during the appetizer course and once during the main course. They are unlikely to be interested, let alone awed. Realistically, they won't care. And the other three questions are no better.

This is not a modern phenomenon; it is not like "kids these days" are missing something that their ancestors appreciated. The Four Questions were not good enough for Rabbi Akiva, who distributed nuts and roasted grain to the children to arouse their interest.[1] They were not good enough for Maimonides, who said, "[The Seder leader] should make changes on this night so the children will see and be motivated to ask, 'Why is this night different from all other nights?' . . . What changes should be made? He should give them roasted seed and nuts, the table should be taken away before they eat."[2] And they weren't good enough for the thirteenth-century Roman rabbi Zedekiah ben Abraham, who said that the Seder plate should contain "toasted grains, types of sweets and fruits to entice the children and drive away their sleepiness so that they will see the change and ask questions."[3]

It seems that the Four Questions never sufficed. So why, in this text that emphasizes the need for consistent improvement, were they never changed? To impart, as the Seder begins, three Jewish insights about education.

First, we educate by encouraging our children to ask questions. But not, as the inadequacy of these four demonstrates, (only) these questions! Which questions, then, should we encourage children to ask?

The second insight, which answers that question, is best articulated in Proverbs 22:6: "Teach a child according to his way and even when he is old he will not depart from it." The person most capable of understanding a child—of knowing "his way"—is the parent. The Haggadah is not supposed to teach our children. It is supposed to guide us as we do so. The responsibility of teaching a child belongs to the person who knows the child best: the parent.

The implications for the Seder are easy to conceive and implement, as the examples of the aforementioned rabbis demonstrate. Does one of our children love chocolate? Then put a piece of chocolate on her plate at the beginning of the meal. Does another love to sing? Then start the Seder with a song and be sure that the Seder is sufficiently musical. Does another love baseball? Then give him a pack of baseball cards if he asks good questions. Is another mischievous? Whoopee cushions are kosher for Pesach.

This imperative of individuated education, which has been embedded in the Haggadah for millennia, is being recognized now as the most effective educational philosophy. In the twenty-first century, the ideal of individual education has been recommended by UNICEF, encouraged by the U.S. Department of State, and described by the Hall of Fame NFL coach Bill

Parcells as the reason for his success: "I'm consistent in that I treat them all differently."[4]

The third insight into Jewish education from the Four Questions is revealed through how the aforementioned rabbis taught their children. They all used foods that, presumably, their children liked the most. Jewish education, they were demonstrating, is done with joy and transparent love—for the students and for the subject. In fact, the first-century sage Hillel the Elder ruled that a "strict tempered" person was disqualified from teaching.[5] A custom in the Jewish community of the Atlas Mountains in Morocco was to bring a five-year-old child in a ritual walk to the synagogue. There was a board with the Aleph-Bet on it, and the letters would be covered in honey. The child would then lick the letters, making his first educational experience one of sweetness that would linger in his memory.[6]

Does this ancient Jewish technique work? In the book *Chicken Soup for the Soul*, Eric Butterworth tells of a college professor who sent his students to inner-city Baltimore to evaluate two hundred boys. The college students wrote a pessimistic report. A quarter century later, another professor found the study and decided to see how those boys had done. Twenty of the two hundred had moved away. All but four of the remaining 180 were doing exceptionally well. The professor found these now middle-aged men and asked them how they had become so successful. They said, "There was a teacher," and named her. The professor then tracked down the teacher, and asked her for the techniques that worked so well. Her eyes sparkled—and she replied: "I loved those boys."[7]

When the passage from the Haggadah concludes, we come to an important realization about the Four Questions. *They are not answered*.

Why?

In the early 1970s, a man from Baltimore, Rabbi Tzvi Hersh Weinreb, was going through what he later identified as an early midlife crisis of sorts. He had all kinds of existential questions—about his career, about his family, about his Jewish purpose. So he did what many Jews did at that time—he called the number for 770 Eastern Parkway in Brooklyn to seek an appointment with the Rebbe Menachem Mendel Schneerson.

He reached the Rebbe's secretary and identified himself as a "yid from Baltimore" with a need for direction from the Rebbe. The secretary put down the phone and told the Rebbe what the call was about. Rabbi Weinreb heard the Rebbe say, "Tell him that there is a Jew who lives in Maryland that he can speak to. *Der yid hayst Veinreb* [His name is Weinreb]."

A stunned Rabbi Weinreb said to the secretary, "Tell the Rebbe that I am Weinreb!"

The Rebbe replied, through his secretary, "If that's the case, then he should know that sometimes one needs to speak to himself."

Rabbi Weinreb later called this a "life-changing moment." He explained:

I believe I understood what the Rebbe was trying to tell me. If I could put words in his mouth, he was saying, "You're looking for answers outside yourself. You're not a kid anymore; you're a man. You are thirty years old, you are a father, you are a teacher of Torah. You have to have more self-confidence. It's time to grow up and listen to yourself. Don't be so dependent on others. Trust yourself. . . ." I think up to that time I had a tendency to be very ambivalent. I was not a risk-taker; I was a procrastinator when it came to making decisions. From that point on, I became decisive.[8]

The Rebbe and the authors of the Haggadah were teaching the same lesson: Jewish freedom means seeking wisdom, incorporating it into one's own thinking, and then confidently deciding for oneself. The Haggadah might be the ultimate guidebook, but there always remains a distinction between guidance and instruction. And identifying and living in accordance with that distinction is the responsibility of a free person.

THE GREAT JEWISH PERMISSION

We were slaves to Pharaoh in Egypt.
Our ancestors were idol worshippers.

The way that people usually tell their origin story is through a god, a demigod, or an exalted and sometimes perfect man. Jews do the opposite. We act in accordance with the instructions provided in the ancient texts, among them, the Mishnah, and "begin with the shame, and conclude with the praise."[1] In the Haggadah, we do this by declaring ourselves to be slaves and idolaters, one being the lowest materially and the other the lowest spiritually. We were, we tell ourselves, as low as possible in every way.

As we look around our own Seder tables and consider the state of the Jewish people, we will inevitably consider just how far we have come since our days as slaves and idolaters. There are many ways to think about this—from the remarkable and varied achievements of the State of Israel to the overrepresentation of Jews at the top of just about every field of human endeavor except painting. We can be proud of these achievements, but carefully. Pride can easily lead to satisfaction, which (as will be discussed later) is a cardinal Jewish vice.

Instead, there is another reason to track our progress from being slaves and idol worshippers. If, we should tell ourselves, we can get to where we are now from where we were then, imagine where we can go from here. Our progress, from this perspective, is not a cause for satisfaction. It is one of expectation and ultimately obligation.

This declaration that we were slaves and idolaters is actually the second time during the Seder evening when we recognize the progression from shame to praise. We begin the event, as we do every Jewish holiday, by lighting candles—*in the evening*. This is because a Jewish day, contrary to how we usually experience a day, begins at night. This was established by God in Genesis 1:5. "And there was evening, and morning, one day." The evening comes first.

Why is the Jewish day structured so counterintuitively? In the preceding verse, God had created the light and the darkness. The light, God said, is "good." He does not praise the darkness. God, then, considers the light to be superior to the darkness. To get to the light, the choreography of the Jewish day instructs, we have to first go through the darkness.

By so insistently starting the Jewish story in darkness, the authors of the Haggadah are sending a clear message. We all have challenges, failures, and disappointments. Left to their own logic, they will win a crushing victory and infuse us with regret, sadness, and bitterness. In comes the Pesach celebration—telling us that the only way to access the light is through the darkness and that the Jewish experience is one of starting as slaves and idolaters and ascending from there.

If the authors of the Haggadah determined that both slavery and idolatry (our material and spiritual starts) need to be represented on our night of national redefinition, they could have been included together. The Haggadah, probably the most efficient book ever written, would have been even more concise if it read: "In the beginning, our ancestors were slaves and idol worshippers." Instead, we begin telling the Jewish story following the Four Questions with, "We were slaves to Pharaoh in Egypt." After the Four Sons (who come later in the text), we *begin again* with, "Our ancestors were idol worshippers." Rabbi Meir Schweiger of Pardes identifies two additional times when the Haggadah begins again.[2]

This is curious. The natural number of times for a story to start is *one*. A person has one birth, a basketball game has one tip-off, a romance has one moment when the boy meets the girl. As it pertains to stories: Aristotle observed that a "whole" story has a beginning, a middle, and an end.[3]

Yet imagine if a fifth grader, asked to describe the components of a story, wrote that a story should have multiple beginnings and no endings and therefore the concept of a middle makes no sense. In Jewish terms, she would earn an A+. In the Haggadah, where we fulfill our formal obligation to tell the story of the Exodus, we begin, and then we begin again—and perhaps again and again. We will return to the part about no endings.

Why, in the Haggadah, do we begin again so insistently? Because the Haggadah is the great text of Jewish recommitment, and beginning again just might be the most important idea in Judaism. The Holocaust survivor and Jewish philosopher Elie Wiesel spoke of how Adam and Eve suffer the worst experience for a parent: one son murders another. This couple, who had previously been expelled from the Garden of Eden for violating the one law God provided, have plenty of reasons to lose themselves in despair, guilt, and incapacitating sorrow. Instead, they have another child, Seth. Wiesel explains, "When He created man, God gave him a secret—and that secret was not how to begin but how to begin again."[4]

The secret of the Torah?

Adam and Eve actually begin again twice: after being expelled from the Garden and again after Cain murders Abel. Ten generations later, the world is full of people—but, we learn in Genesis 6:5, "the wickedness of Man was great upon the earth, and every product of the thoughts of his heart was but evil always."

God destroys the world and begins again with Noah and his family. The results there are also catastrophic but God, after dispersing the people and changing their languages, allows people to begin again.

In Genesis 28, Jacob goes into exile to escape the murderous wrath of his brother, Esau, whose birthright and blessing he had at least arguably stolen. Decades later, God comes to Jacob in a dream and tells him to leave the land of his treacherous father-in-law (Laban) and return home. Jacob secures the agreement of his wives (Rachel and Leah), and they embark on the journey. But before even fulfilling God's command, Jacob has something he must do first: he must make amends with his estranged brother. Jacob, with good information that the reunion will end in his violent death, separates from his family and spends the night before it alone.

That night, he engages in an all-night wrestling match with an angel or a man (the text is tantalizingly ambiguous). At dawn, he is about to win the match. But he has a condition for his victory: "I will not let you go without a blessing." The fight ends, and the angel changes Jacob's name to Israel, explaining, "Your name will no longer be Jacob, but Israel, because you have struggled with God and with humans and have overcome."[5]

The defining quality of a Jew, we learn, is to emerge from a struggle with a blessing—to allow oneself to begin again, having extracted a blessing from the struggle.

There is, as Rabbi David Wolpe identifies, one problem. Jacob lets his opponent go, but without the angel/man blessing him. But that could not be: the deal was release in exchange for a blessing! And indeed, there is. It is given in the angel's changing Jacob's name to Israel. It is the blessing of self-transformation.[6] Subsequently, we are called the Children of Israel—establishing our foundational blessing as the ability to begin again.

The deep incorporation of beginning again into the Pesach celebration is emulated throughout the Jewish year. Many nations have a festival of trees. The United States celebrates Arbor Day on the last Friday in April. The Spanish tree festival is in late March, the Filipino tree festival is in late June, New Zealand's Arbor Day is on June 5, the Mexican National Tree Day is in July, and the Korean Tree Loving Week is in early April.[7] The Jewish Tu B'shevat (New Year of the Trees) is on the fifteenth of Shevat—in January/February, when trees seem dead! But something is about to happen. The fifteenth of Shevat is the midpoint between fall and spring. This significance, according to the thirteenth-century Spanish rabbi Menachem Meiri, is that it is the date the budding process begins. It is in the moment when trees seem dead but are poised to begin again that Jews celebrate them.[8]

We conclude the annual cycle of reading the Torah on Simchat Torah with the parsha Vezot HaBerachah from Deuteronomy. We would normally wait a week before reading the next parsha. Instead, we immediately follow the last passage in Deuteronomy with the first part of the first passage in Genesis. The opportunity to begin the Torah again is too good to pass up.

We finish a tractate in the Talmud with a unique prayer: "We will return to you, Tractate___, and you will return to us." We do not celebrate the dedication of the Second Temple in 586 B.C.E. Instead, we celebrate its *rededication* on Hanukkah. And at Pesach, we relive and retell, beginning the story again each year.

All this leads to the question: Why is *beginning again* "the secret of the Torah," and a theme that emerges in seemingly everything Jewish? For, perhaps, the same reason that we are invited to the Seder in our capacity as broken. Our world is composed of broken individuals, relationships, and communities. This brokenness does not happen at the beginning of a relationship. The permission to begin again is the only way that the broken can be made whole.

This is so with broken people. A person may have damaged himself in any of an infinite number of ways. In the process, he certainly will have disappointed and hurt many people—including those he loves and possibly profoundly. How, reflecting on the damage that he has done and caused, can he have the self-respect needed to live productively and fully? How can he continue? By knowing that the eternal and insistent invitation from God and through Judaism is to begin again.

An ongoing conversation of almost three thousand years shows just what Judaism thinks of the person who accepts this invitation. The prophet Isaiah says, "Peace to him who is far [from God] and to whom is near."[9] Rabbi Abbahu of the Talmud notes that Isaiah lists the one who is far before the one who is near. Why, the sage asks, does Isaiah prioritize the one who is far from God over the one who is near? He concludes, "In a place where the penitent stands, the completely righteous are unable to stand."[10] It is he who begins again who earns the highest place in the rabbinic estimation.

This is curious. It is, of course, better to be a penitent than a persistent sinner—but why would Isaiah and Rabbi Abbahu prioritize him over someone who did not sin? Seventeen centuries later, Rabbi Schneur Zalman explained why.[11] It takes courage, strength, and determination to acknowledge that change is needed, to decide to change, and to actually transform oneself. It is the one who has gone through difficulty and emerged transformed who will understand the darkness and appreciate the light. It is the one who was broken, has begun again, and will be able to inspire others to do so whom Isaiah places closest to God.

Very few things in Judaism happen in private, and beginning again—though it requires soulful introspection and existential moral yearning—is not one of them. The permission to begin again can revive a broken person, and it can, as well, repair a broken relationship. This is exemplified in the words *I'm sorry*. These are not just words, to the extent that any are. These have, *literally*, magical power. One could have done years of harm, causing untold pain—and a simple "I'm sorry" can function as a reset button. This does not seem possible, especially as the embodiment of truth is that every action generates an equal and opposite reaction. Years of inflicting pain, and two words reset everything—how is that equal and opposite? Yet these two words often work that way.

The power of these words issues from what one who apologizes is really doing. He is acknowledging that he damaged the relationship. He is confessing that his action put the relationship in a state of unhealthy disequilibrium. And he is asking the person wronged one question: Can we begin again?

What will the person receiving the apology think? Every parent whose child ever pleaded "I'm sorry!" knows. It depends on how the recipient of the apology assesses the following: Do those words reflect a genuine change, one that indicates a true desire to begin again? If the answer is yes, then the relationship can immediately begin again—and with more depth and meaning than if the wrong had not been committed.[12]

The power of beginning again is evident in its presence and also in its absence. If there is no option to begin again, what fills the void? A good subject for Pesach discussion.

THE GREATEST SEDER OF ALL

*Had the Holy One, Blessed is he, not taken our fathers out of
Egypt, then we, our children, and our children's children would
have remained subservient to Pharaoh in Egypt.*

Read literally, this passage is insane. The Egypt of the Torah does not exist
and has not for thousands of years. Yes, of course there is a country today
called Egypt in the same place. But everything about Egypt is completely
different, from the political system to the religion. There has been no continuity of anything. The other peoples in the Torah, from the Hittites to
the Jebusites, are all gone as well. Given that there are no Pharaohs, and no
other ancient people from the Bible, how, but for the Exodus, would we still
be subservient to the Pharaoh in Egypt?

As we'll soon see, the purpose of the Exodus was never only to free the
Jews. It was always to educate the nations of the world about God and the
freedom he envisioned for mankind. Consequently, the "we" in this Haggadah passage applies to all people who have yearned for freedom.

In early 1960, a young Michael Walzer traveled to the American South to
write about what turned out to be the beginning of the civil rights movement.

In Montgomery, Alabama, he found himself in a small Baptist church
and "listened to the most extraordinary sermon that I have ever heard—on
the Book of Exodus and the political struggle of southern blacks. There
on his pulpit, the preacher . . . acted out the 'going out' from Egypt and ex-
pounded its contemporary analogies: he cringed under the lash, challenged
the Pharaoh, hesitated fearfully at the sea, accepted the covenant and the
law at the foot of the mountain."

In 1985, Professor Walzer published *Exodus and Revolution,* chronicling how he "found the Exodus almost everywhere, often in unexpected places." This includes the Italian monk Girolamo Savonarola, who gave twenty-two sermons on the Book of Exodus before he was executed in 1498, the German peasants' revolt in 1524, the Scottish Reformation in the 1500s, the Protestant Reformation in the 1500s, the British revolutionary Oliver Cromwell in the 1600s, the Puritans in the House of Commons in 1640, the Massachusetts Constitution of 1780, the Boer nationalists fighting the British in 1900, the Black nationalists in South Africa in the 1980s, liberation theology in Argentina, Peru, and Colombia in the 1970s, and many others.[1]

But there is one nation that had a foundational, special, and sustaining relationship with the Exodus story. Alexis de Tocqueville writes in *Democracy in America*, "On my arrival in the United States, the religious aspect of the country was the first thing that struck my attention."[2] A lot of time has passed, and a lot of things have changed since Tocqueville's observation. But the religious character of the United States, despite the secularization of the rest of the West, has remained.[3] It is often said that the United States is a Christian nation, a Judeo-Christian nation, and/or a religious nation that cultivates pluralism and respects the many faiths of its citizens. Each of those is correct, but there is a more accurate characterization of American religion, one that is responsive to its history, its aspirations, and its theology.

The United States is a Moses nation.

In the early seventeenth century, a group of English Calvinists determined that the practice of their religious freedom required them to be in a new land. They called themselves Pilgrims and initially went to Holland—where they freed themselves from King James and considered themselves to be fulfilling God's plan as a chosen people. William Bradford, William Brewster, and a hundred other people departed from England to the New World on their ship—the *Mayflower*. Their mission, Bradford said, would be as important as that of "Moses and the Israelites when they went out of Egypt." Upon arriving at Cape Cod on November 11, 1620, they thanked God for letting them pass through the Red Sea and then, "solemnly and mutually in the presence of God and one another," the leaders of every household, signed the Mayflower Compact. A covenant made between God and a nation, with an explicit affirmation of the consent of the governed, was a unique idea in 1620—but was modeled exactly upon Moses, God, and the Jewish people at Sinai.[4]

A century and a half later, the colonists stirred with the desire to create their own nation. They had their inspiration and the guiding principles for the new nation at hand. The great pamphleteer Thomas Paine despised religion and hated Moses. Yet he could not escape the uniting reference that would convince the public to free themselves from British rule. In *Common Sense*, he called upon his fellow colonists to join him in rejecting "the hardened, sullen tempered Pharaoh of England forever."[5]

The seal that Benjamin Franklin designed for the United States was of Moses parting the Red Sea. Franklin explained the inspiration behind his design: "Moses standing on the shore, and extending His hand over the sea, thereby causing the same to overwhelm Pharaoh, who is sitting in an open chariot. . . . Rays from a pillar of fire in the clouds reaching to Moses, to express that he acts by the command of the deity."[6] Thomas Jefferson, who also wanted the seal to be an illustration of the Exodus, adopted what would have been Franklin's motto for the United States as his personal motto: "Rebellion to tyrants is obedience to God."[7]

In 1969, Marquette University professor Robert Hay analyzed the post–Revolutionary War descriptions of George Washington. He writes that it was commonplace to refer to revolution as "our miraculous deliverance from a second Egypt—another house of bondage," to liken the Fourth of July to the day the Jews "came out of Egypt," and to insist that "God [had] raised up a Washington" just as he had earlier "qualified and raised up Moses."[8] In his chronicle of the influence of Moses on the United States, Bruce Feiler calculates that two-thirds of the eulogies at Washington's death compared the "leader and father of the American nation" to the "first conductor of the Jewish nation."[9]

Absalom Jones was born a slave in 1746. A remarkable entrepreneur, Jones bought his freedom and became a church leader in Philadelphia. His sermons assumed a form that would become common in the Black church. There would be a title and below the title a passage from Exodus—indicating that what was to follow (the sermon) would be a commentary on the biblical passage. This was following a standard convention. As with commentaries generally, the linkage between the sermon text and the Exodus passage was sometimes direct and sometimes more subtle—but in many instances the pastors explicitly structured their sermons as a commentary on Exodus.[10]

Absalom Jones's most famous sermon was given on January 1, 1808. Titled "A Thanksgiving Sermon," it was given in acknowledgment of the abolition of the slave trade, which happened that day. The sermon is framed, explicitly, as a commentary on Exodus 3:7–8—which also forms the basis for a section in the Haggadah. It is the part of the Exodus story where God declares that he has seen the affliction of his people—and is about to rescue us from Egypt and bring us to the Promised Land.

In this sermon, which is delivered on its anniversary in African American churches across the United States to this day, Pastor Jones speaks of the brutality, horrors, and evil of American slavery. He wonders why God would have let it continue for so long and if any good might come from this hideous situation. He does not have answers to those questions, but he has a historical precedent that gives him hope, inspiration, and spiritual guidance.

> The history of the world shows us, that the deliverance of the Children of Israel from their bondage, is not the only instance, in which it has pleased God to appear in behalf of oppressed and distressed nations, as the deliverer of the innocent, and of those who call upon his name. He is as unchangeable in his nature and character, as he is in his wisdom and power. . . . The God of heaven and earth *is the same, yesterday, and to-day, and for ever* [emphasis in original].[11]

The slave trade was abolished but slavery continued to rage. Its victims had the same inspiration as Pastor Jones. Whereas his primary medium was sermons, theirs was music, and their songs became known as *slave spirituals*. This canon includes the song "Wade in the Water," with the lyrics: "Who's that young girl dressed in red / Wade in the Water / Must be the children that Moses led / God's gonna trouble that water." It includes "Go Down Moses," with the lyrics: "Go down Moses / Way down in Egypt land / Tell all Pharaohs to / Let my people go!" I recommend the Blind Boys of Alabama's rendition of "Wade in the Water" and the Paul Robeson version of "Go Down Moses"—but there are many stirring versions.

Yale professor Yolanda Smith writes of the "slave [musical] canon," "As enslaved Africans looked to the Bible, they identified with the plight of the Hebrew children of God and appropriated their story of bondage and liberation."[12] Correct—but with one caveat: they did not appropriate the

Exodus story. The story was theirs all along. It was created for them—and all others who are oppressed, persecuted, and yearning for the freedom that God declares it is his purpose to create on earth.

The abolitionist publisher William Lloyd Garrison had a nickname for Harriet Tubman, the legendary leader of the Underground Railroad who rescued slaves and brought them to freedom. It was "Moses."[13] The renowned leader and ex-slave Frederick Douglass described the "spontaneous feeling of [his] heart" when hearing Garrison speak at Liberty Hall in Massachusetts. "You are the man," Douglas reports thinking of Garrison, "the Moses, raised up by God, to deliver his modern Israel from bondage."[14]

During the Civil War, it was common for Northerners to compare President Abraham Lincoln to Moses and for Southerners to describe him as a Pharaoh.[15] President Lincoln was shot on the Friday night during the week of Pesach. Seemingly all Shabbat sermons the next day mourned the president, who the rabbis said was a modern-day Moses—the great liberator who was not to enter the Promised Land. This made President Lincoln, in the words of historian Harold Holzer, "a Jewish martyr before he became a Christian martyr."[16]

The Jews were soon joined in comparing President Lincoln to Moses. The Black abolitionist and early civil rights leader Philip Alexander Bell eulogized the president as the "Moses of his age," while Black and white preachers made the same comparison the rabbis had. They said that President Lincoln, like Moses, was a liberator who was not to enter the Promised Land with those he liberated.[17] The great journalist of the Civil War era Charles Carleton Coffin wrote in his 1893 biography of Lincoln: "The millions whom Abraham Lincoln delivered from slavery will ever liken him to Moses, the deliverer of Israel."[18]

Several years after the Civil War, former slave states enacted racist "Black Codes." The freed slaves were terrorized by the White League, the KKK, and countless vigilantes. The former slave Benjamin "Pap" Singleton determined that there was no future for Blacks in these states—and led around fifty thousand former slaves to the "promised land" of Kansas, as well as a few other states. The name of the movement: the Exodusters.[19]

Most Blacks did not move to this "promised land." While their vision for how change would be implemented differed, their ideas had a familiar common basis. Frances Ellen Watkins Harper titled her epic poem "Moses,

A Story of the Nile." She shared it with Black and white audiences, an experience she considered "building the Promised Land."[20] The pastor John Jasper taunted the former Confederacy with Moses's song of the Jubilee, "The Lord God Is a Man of War, the Lord Is His Name."[21]

Almost a century later, the work of liberation was still far from done. In 1954, a young preacher took to the pulpit of the Dexter Avenue Baptist Church in Montgomery, Alabama. The Reverend Dr. Martin Luther King Jr. proceeded to give a sermon so good, so moving, and so consequential that he would give it often—including, famously, at the Cathedral Church of St. John the Divine in New York City in 1956. The title of the sermon: "The Death of Evil by the Sands of the Seashore." The sermon is presented explicitly as a commentary on Exodus 14:30.

> The Hebraic Christian tradition is clear that in affirming the long struggle between good and evil, good eventually emerges as the victor. . . . A graphic example of this is found in the early history of the Hebrew people. You will remember that in a very early stage of her history the Children of Israel were reduced to the bondage of physical slavery under the gripping yoke of Egyptian rule.[22]

Dr. King used the Exodus as the guide for his freedom journey. He relied on the Exodus to get through challenges: "You don't get to the Promised Land without going through the wilderness." He referenced it to motivate his people: "We've got to keep going. . . . The Red Sea has opened for us, we have crossed the banks, we are moving now, and as we look back we see the Egyptian system of segregation drowned upon the seashore." Well before he was assassinated in 1968, he had fully adopted the persona of Moses. The title of his final speech: "I've Been to the Mountaintop!"[23] That is where Moses concluded his life, looking at the Promised Land he would never enter.

Following the assassination of Dr. King, the Black Power movement became ascendant. Its intellectual leader, Jaramogi Abebe Agyeman (who was previously known as Bishop Albert Cleage), disagreed with Dr. King on many things—but had the same hero and source of inspiration. Agyeman's 1972 book *Black Christian Nationalism* proclaimed Jesus "the Black Messiah"— but had much to say about a more ancient Jew:

Moses took more than two million disorganized Black people out of Africa, kept them together for more than forty years in the wilderness, and finally brought them to the Promised Land. The King of Moab looked down in fear at the Nation Israel and said, "A people has come out of Egypt." No greater feat of sheer organization has been achieved anywhere in the annals of human history.[24]

Cleage/Agyeman's message of Black Christian Nationalism was articulated in his sermons. They bore titles such as "But God Hardened Pharaoh's Heart," "The Promised Land," and "Coming In out of the Wilderness."

On December 31 of each year, Black American churches fill with parishioners. They do not go to celebrate New Year's Eve but instead to relive and remember the greatest moment in American history. At the stroke of midnight on January 1, 1863, the Emancipation Proclamation went into effect—freeing the slaves. Each year, Black Americans congregate to relive and remember the night that their ancestors went from slavery to freedom—on the anniversary of that night. The name of the occasion: *Watch Night*.

Why is it called *Watch Night*? Because the last meal in Egypt was consumed on what God calls, in Exodus 12:42, *leil shimurim,* "the night of watching." The idea of watching is of extraordinary significance toward the understanding of the Pesach story, and a subsequent chapter of this book will be devoted to it. We Jews, unfortunately, have largely lost the reference to watching in discussing Pesach. Black Americans, in celebrating their exodus from slavery to freedom on the anniversary of its pivotal day, have kept it alive.

In 1949/50, the House chamber in the U.S. Capitol was remodeled. The result: there are twenty-three marble relief portraits over the gallery doors—depicting (according to the office of the Architect of the Capitol) "historical figures noted for their work in establishing the principles that underlie American law." The eleven profiles in the eastern half face left and the eleven in the western half face right. They all look sideways toward one portrait in the middle, the only one facing forward—the portrait of Moses.[25]

In 1923, a movie producer became the first person to spend a million dollars producing a film. The producer was Jewish in the same way that Elvis Presley was. He had a Christian father and was raised as such. But his mother was Jewish—making him, according to traditional Jewish law, fully and irrevocably Jewish. It is unclear what, if any, influence his Jewish heritage had upon Cecil B. DeMille. It is much more clear what influence Cecil B. DeMille had on the Jewish heritage of the United States.

DeMille's million-dollar film in 1923, *The Ten Commandments*, was a silent movie, as sound did not come into movies until several years later. The extras were hundreds of new Jewish immigrants who had recently escaped the pogroms of eastern Europe for Los Angeles. A gentile actress, Leatrice Joy, said of these Jewish extras, "They were living the time, these people. They weren't acting." A Jewish actor explained why: "We know the script. Our fathers studied it long before there were movies. This is a tale of our beginnings. It is deep in our hearts."[26]

The journalist Rita Kissin wrote of the reaction of the Jewish extras to the ocean scene, "Tears trembled on wrinkled cheeks, sobs came from husky throats. For many, the world had moved back 3,000 years, and they stood once more on the shores of the Red Sea, viewing the good omen of deliverance."[27] This was a familiar experience for these Jewish immigrants they were reliving and retelling the story of the Exodus, as they had done at the beginning of every spring.

In 1956, DeMille remade the movie—this time with sound so good that *The Ten Commandments* won the Academy Award for Best Special Effects in 1957. The movie was so long that it contained an intermission. Coming out in the most intense days of the Cold War, DeMille introduced the movie with a short monologue that connected the main issue of the day to his subject:

> Ladies and gentlemen, young and old . . . The theme of this picture
> is whether man ought to be ruled by God's law or by the whims of a
> dictator like Ramses. Are men the property of the state or are they free
> souls under God? This same battle continues throughout the world
> today. Our intention was not to create a story but to be worthy of the
> divinely inspired story created 3,000 years ago.[28]

The 1956 *The Ten Commandments* went on to be (to this day, inflation adjusted) a top-ten-grossing movie of all time. When DeMille died in 1959, five billion people had watched his films—twice the population of the world at the time. His two most popular films, by a significant margin, were the remake of *The Ten Commandments* and the original (in that order).[29]

The Ten Commandments was not even the most popular American media rendition of the Moses story. In the early 1930s, two children of Jewish immigrants, Jerry Siegel and Joe Shuster, became friends at Glenville High School in Cleveland, Ohio. With Jerry as the writer and Joe as the illustrator, they came up with a concept for a comic. It was rejected by several publishers but eventually caught on.

It was about a baby, Kal El (Hebrew for "Voice of God") who is born to parents from another world. Because of an impending catastrophe, the parents cannot protect him but are determined that the boy live. They place him in a spaceship and send him to Earth. The spaceship lands in the town of Smallville, where the infant is found on a farm and adopted by its owners, Jonathan and Martha Kent. They give him a new name: Clark. The boy discovers who he really is—a defender of justice and a fighter of evil. We know him, of course, as Superman. His story is, as the Pesach commandment to relive and retell the story of the Exodus, an enduring (and very faithful) *retelling* of the story of Moses.[30]

In his memoir *A Charge to Keep,* President George W. Bush discusses the moment when he felt called to the presidency. He was the governor of Texas, attending a church service when the pastor summarized Moses's reaction to being called by God to free the Jews: "Sorry, God. I'm busy. I got sheep to tend. Who am I that I should go to Pharaoh, and bring the sons of Israel out of Egypt?" God, of course, insists that Moses accept the call to leadership—which Moses does. Similarly, the pastor continued, America is "starved for leaders who have ethical and moral courage"—and that these would-be leaders should realize that "even Moses had doubts."

Governor Bush spoke of this to his mother, who told him: "He was talking to you."[31]

Senator Barack Obama's most important early speech was given on March 4, 2007, at the Brown Chapel AME Church in Selma, Alabama. He framed his philosophy as follows:

I just want to talk a little about Moses and Aaron and Joshua, because we're in the presence today of a lot of Moseses. . . . Like Moses, they challenged Pharaoh. . . . They took them across the sea that folks thought could not be parted. They wandered through a desert but always knowing that God was with them and that, if they maintained their trust in God, that they would be all right.[32]

Much of the rest of the speech focused on the opportunities and responsibilities of his generation (which he called the *Joshua Generation*)—continuing the work of the "Moses generation" that "pointed the way" but could not get "all the way there."

From Bradford to Jones, from Lincoln to King, from Paine to Obama, from DeMille to Superman, from Tubman to Bush, from Franklin to the Architect of the Capitol—these Americans show us just what the authors of the Haggadah meant when they said that the Exodus story is the reason that we are not subservient to a Pharaoh today. The Exodus story has given us the language, the vision, the direction, and the moral ambition to resist any Pharaoh and to construct a glorious alternative to him.

They, and everyone else who has helped conduct or participate in the American story, has answered another question. It is a question that has been asked by schoolchildren and philosophers, by politicians and artists, by soldiers and clergymen: What is America? The answer is very clear. American history is an exercise in reliving and retelling the story of the Exodus.

The United States of America is, simply, the greatest Seder ever conducted.

FEELING GOD'S PLEASURE

*Even if we were all men of wisdom, understanding, experience,
and knowledge of the Torah—it would still be an obligation upon
us to tell about the Exodus from Egypt.*

This passage reads like the response to someone who said, "The obligation to tell the story of the Exodus does not apply to people who are learned." But no one ever said such a thing. There is nothing in Jewish text, literature, or thought that would suggest that anyone is exempt from the Pesach obligations.

So what is this passage doing here—or anywhere?

The dispositive clue is in the word *tell*—as in "*tell* about the Exodus . . ." The distinction between telling and saying is subtle and easy to overlook. But it is crucial for the author of the Torah and the authors of the Haggadah. The question of the wise son is from Exodus 13:8: "And you shall *tell* your child." The question of the wicked son is from Exodus 12:26: "And when your children *say* to you."

What is the difference between *say* and *tell*? If a newspaper reports, "Senator Smith said," the reader can expect that the quote will be precisely recorded. But if a mother says to her child, "Tell me about your day," she will be disappointed to hear a strict recitation of the facts. She wants emotion and interpretation, opinions, and conclusions. The act of telling a story *requires* creativity; it encourages discussion, analysis, input from experience, a mixture of new and old interpretations. The outcome of telling a story is unpredictable—the one surety is that it will be new, creative, and original.

Who would oppose that?

A lot of people. As previously discussed, traditionalists in many religious and philosophical systems fear or simply oppose interpretation, creativity, and newness—particularly with sacred texts. Plato, for instance, wanted preachers but not poets in his ideal city. The preacher would directly convey divine instructions while the poet could be emotional, original—and subversive. The Talmud, by contrast, speaks of two rabbis who go to visit their teacher, Rabbi Joshua. They tell him that they came "to drink from your waters." He demurs, telling them that "it is not possible for there to be a *Beit Midrash* [place of Jewish study] without a new insight."[1]

Given that *telling* is so integral to everything Jewish, why would the Haggadah provide this instruction to the Jews who are specifically distinguished for their knowledge, wisdom, and understanding? There are at least four reasons.

First, they might *know* about the importance of telling—but this does not mean that they always *act like they know it.* The bridge between knowing that one should do something and actually doing it is notoriously long, winding, and unstable—even for the most revered people in a society. We will soon see how the Pesach story tells us how to shorten the bridge. In this passage, the authors of the Haggadah are showing us how to strengthen it. It is through *reminding.*

The eleventh-century Spanish master Abraham ben Meir Ibn Ezra said, "The core of all the commandments is the improvement of character—and the majority of them are essentially reminders."[2] These include the festivals of Pesach and Sukkot, hearing the shofar, affixing mezuzot (on every doorpost in one's home), and wearing tzitzit—the ritual fringes that observant Jews affix to clothing.

The commandment to wear tzitzit is so important that it becomes one of the few times when a reason for a commandment is explicitly given in the Torah. The Torah commands us in Numbers to put "tzitzit on the corners of their clothing throughout their generations . . . *so that you will remember all of the Lord's commandments and do them and not follow after your heart and after your eyes which lead you astray.*"[3] Why might wearing ritual fringes on one's clothes, as a reminder, be of such moral significance?

"Go and learn," Rabbi Natan instructs in the Talmud, "from the following incident concerning the mitzvah of ritual fringes."[4]

A man, the story in the Talmud recounts, travels overseas to visit a prostitute. He sends the payment ahead—four hundred gold coins. He arrives at the prostitute's abode and sees that she is the most beautiful woman he has ever met. There are seven beds, apparently in a bunk bed format. They are made of silver and gold, with silver ladders between them. When the man arrives at the top, the woman is naked—and he is as well. Except, apparently, for one thing: his ritual fringes. His fringes brush against him, and he is reminded of the verse from the Torah regarding the tzitzit.

The young man recalls that this verse says, "I am Hashem, your God" twice.[5] This doubling, he explains to the prostitute, is God telling us that we will be rewarded for keeping his commandments and punished for violating them. Reminded by the tzitzit and by the double mention of God, the young man tells the prostitute that he cannot continue. This most beautiful of women is so impressed that she gives a third of her possessions to the government, a third to the poor—and finds a "study hall" where she can begin the process of converting to Judaism. As for the young man? The Talmud tells us: "Those beds that she arranged for him in a prohibited fashion she now arranged for him in a permitted fashion."[6]

As we consider the moral decisions we make, it becomes apparent that they do not usually involve knowing what is right. It is about doing what we know is right. We know that we should be patient with our children, appreciative of our spouse, charitable with our resources, kind to the stranger—and that we should honor our parents, eat responsibly, look both ways before we cross the street, and pick up the laundry from the bedroom floor.

Why, then, do we so often fail at these and other basic tasks? That is a complex question that we need not try to answer—because the solution is so simple. Every observant Jew knows that gossip is a grave sin. If we, as some observant Jews do, put an anti-gossip sticker on our phones that stares at us during each conversation, will we gossip more, less, or the same? If we put a memento of our beloved grandmother on our desk, will we be likelier to be honest in business? If we see a photograph of our toddler by the dashboard, will we be likelier to drive more safely? Does, in other words, reminding work?

It is the twenty-first century, and that means that we don't need to wonder. We can scientifically verify.

In 2015, MIT professor Erik Duhaime studied how Moroccan merchants allocated money they were just given as part of his experiment. He found that merchants varied in their decisions about whether to keep the money or have a larger sum allocated to charity. The outlier: when the Muslim call to prayer was audible, *everyone* surveyed gave *all* the money to charity.[7] Harvard Business School professor Deepak Malhotra found that Christians are much likelier to participate generously in a charity auction on Sunday than any other day. He calls this the *Sunday effect*.[8]

The second reason is articulated by the Talmudic dictum "One cannot compare someone who learns something 100 times to someone who learns it 101 times."[9] Why would learning something for the 101st time be that transformative? Because of what the inventor and technological visionary Ray Kurzweil calls "The law of accelerating returns."

Pursuant to Kurzweil's Law, the rate of learning about a subject and consequently the amount we can know about it does not grow in a linear fashion. It grows in an exponential fashion, as the knowledge we have acquired previously makes it easier to acquire new knowledge. As Kurzweil wrote in 2001, "We won't experience 100 years of progress in the twenty first century—it will be more like 20,000 years of progress (at today's rate)."[10]

We have seen demonstrable applications of Kurzweil's Law in fields such as medicine and electronics, where there has been more progress in the twenty-first century than in thousands of years of previous history. More learning, as the authors of the Haggadah and the compilers of the Talmud knew, makes it easier to learn more. Possessing a base of knowledge makes it possible to affiliate new learnings with existing knowledge. The more one knows, therefore, the more he should participate in the Seder—as the knowledgeable person is best positioned to learn and grow the most.

The third reason that even the wisest people would want to attend a Seder relates to the fundamental conception of personhood. We all know that we change as we age, but often note the change only long after it occurred. One of the gifts of freedom is being reminded that we are changing, and to be able to thoughtfully direct the changes. These changes, and the moral opportunities to direct them, apply to everyone—from the youngest children to the most learned rabbis. Consequently, even the wisest attendee was a different person last year. And he'll be a different person next year—based at least somewhat, hopefully, on what she experiences at the Seder. Even the wisest person, therefore, can appreciate the Seder as if it were the only one he ever attended. Because, in the most substantial and meaningful way, it is.

The fourth reason why those with wisdom, understanding, and knowledge should participate in the Seder is described in the 1981 movie *Chariots of Fire*. The movie is not about Pesach, but about the 1924 Olympics. The Christian missionary and Olympic runner Eric Liddell defends his participation in the sport to his sister, who wants him to devote himself completely and directly to religious service. "I believe God made me for a purpose, but he also made me fast! And when I run, I feel his pleasure."[11]

When we tell the Pesach story among ourselves and to our children—anytime, but especially as part of a Seder—we should feel God's pleasure. Mining the treasures of the Torah through study and discussion and seeing them ignite the minds of our children, in service of perpetuating Judaism, is what we do at the Seder. Why would a person of wisdom, understanding, experience, and knowledge want to miss this opportunity?

He wouldn't.

THE STORY IS YOURS: WHERE ARE MOSES, JOSEPH, AND THE WOMEN OF THE EXODUS?

The more one tells about the discussion of the Exodus,
the more he is praiseworthy.

The Haggadah tells us that the more we discuss the story, the more praise-worthy we will be. But the biblical book of Ecclesiastes suggests a different approach: "God is in Heaven and you're on the earth; therefore, let your words be few."[1]

Ecclesiastes is in line with other discussions of brevity in the Bible, all of which regard it as a virtue. Why is the Haggadah, which gives more praise for more discussion, different?

First, an extended discussion about the Exodus enables us to fulfill our responsibility to *relive* the last meal in Egypt— the proto-Seder in the liminal space between slavery and freedom. The historic importance of this meal, even before it started, was clear. Exodus 12:42: "It is a night of watching for Hashem to take them out of the land of Egypt; this was the night for Hashem; a protection for all the Children of Israel *for their generations.*"

How would our ancestors have acted that night? Would the participants have concluded the meal early and gone to sleep shortly thereafter? Or would they have stayed up all night, fueled by nervous energy, discussing their experiences in Egypt, preparing for the imminent departure, and dreaming about new experiences as a free people in their own Land?

We might not stay up all Seder night. But we relive their experience, when they presumably did, by telling the story at length.

It is in this encouragement that we can, perhaps, find the answer to one of the most ancient and intriguing sets of questions about the Haggadah. Why isn't Moses in the Haggadah? Why aren't Joseph and the women of the Exodus—Miriam, Shifra, Puah, and the Pharaoh's daughter—mentioned in the Haggadah?

Is it even possible to tell the story of the Exodus without Moses, Joseph, and the women of the Exodus?

No. It's impossible. Doing otherwise is akin to telling the story of the American founding without mentioning Washington, Adams, Jefferson, Franklin, Madison, or Hamilton. Or telling the story of '90s basketball without Jordan, Malone, Pippen, Olajuwon, Stockton, or Barkley. If a teacher told her students to tell the story of the Exodus and the paper was returned without mentioning Moses, Joseph, Miriam, Shifra, Puah, Jochebed, or the Pharaoh's daughter (any of them!)—the teacher would have two choices. One is to simply fail the student. The other is to wonder if the student is actually thinking in an entirely different way.

The authors of the Haggadah obviously did not fail in telling the story of the Exodus. Yet they are in a seeming quandary: We are commanded by the Torah, on what became Seder night, to tell the story to our children. We use the Haggadah, but it does not contain most of the main characters in the story. The Haggadah is now commanding us to tell the story at length—which is really impossible without mentioning its main characters.

There is a resolution to this dynamic that seems like a riddle. The Haggadah requires us to tell the story by reaching outside the Haggadah! A guide—even a genuinely great book like the Haggadah or its human equivalent in a wise mentor—is only that: a guide. The Haggadah is significantly, purposefully, and strategically incomplete. The responsibility for something genuinely important, particularly the combination of parenting and Jewish perpetuation that the Pesach celebration embodies, must be insourced.

LIVING BY PRINCIPLES

It happened that Rabbi Eliezer, Rabbi Joshua,
Rabbi Elazar ben Azariah Rabbi Akiva, and . . .

We were just instructed by the Haggadah that lengthy discussions about the Exodus are to be praised. Now the Haggadah provides an example of such a discussion—with a twist that leads to one of the most important Jewish teachings.

The structure of this section of the Haggadah is astonishing, and thus deeply instructive. It starts by listing the attendees—Rabbis Eliezer, Joshua, Elazar ben Azariah, Akiva, and Tarfon. These are five of the greatest rabbis of all time. Then it tells us where the Seder was—in Bnei Brak, near what is now Tel Aviv. This Seder is for Judaism as the 1992 United States men's Olympic basketball team is for sport and the American Constitutional Convention is for political thought. There will never again be such a collection of talent in one place and at one time, doing their craft together.

So far, the Haggadah offers a conventional introduction for what promises to be an exceptional evening. A reader expects, now, to learn what these masters say at the Seder. But that is not what follows. Instead, we are told how the Seder ends. This strange structure invites us to wonder: What is so instructive about the way the Seder ends that it should be prioritized over everything that happens during the event itself?

This Seder, the Haggadah says, concludes when the rabbis' students come to them and say, "'Our teachers, the time has come for the reading of the morning Shema.'" In other words, the students burst into the room, unannounced and seemingly uninvited, to interrupt the discussion and tell their teachers that their Seder is over because it is time for their morning prayers.

This intervention would be jarring in any culture. It is especially jarring in Judaism, which is structured around education—and, hence, the sanctity of the student-teacher relationship. "The reverence for a teacher," the Talmud stipulates, "should be as for the reverence of heaven."[1]

And yet here the students burst into the Seder of their rabbis and command them to stop. Moreover, the students are nameless. They are not, so far as anyone knows, prodigies who would become great Jewish leaders. Nor are they notorious rebels. They are not exceptionally good or exceptionally bad. They are ordinary students, imbued in a culture of reverence for teachers. Yet they believe it perfectly appropriate to burst into the Seder of their teachers and tell them to end it. And their story is retold in the Haggadah, with unambiguous admiration.

Why?

We will discuss, in the context of the wicked son, the Jewish philosophy and practice of rebuking. For now, we can call forth a single incident in the Talmud where the sages wrestle with the concept of "rebuke," as derived from Leviticus 19:17, which says: "Rebuke your fellow so you will not share in his guilt." Suffice it to say that this statement has nothing to do with education. Yet the rabbis who discuss it in the Talmud find in it the obligation of teachers to rebuke students—and students to rebuke teachers![2]

What is so important about a student rebuking a teacher that it would inform the Talmudic interpretation of a seemingly unrelated Torah passage and constitute a passage in the Haggadah? Where, in other words, are we being guided? There are at least three destinations.

First is the example set by God in Numbers 9 and again in Numbers 27. As previously discussed, in two instances God changes his rules—he literally changes the Torah—to accommodate arguments made by ordinary people. These concern ritually unclean men who want to celebrate Pesach and five sisters who want to inherit in the Land. Neither the men nor the women are people of renown. Their ability to convince God to change the Torah is entirely attributable to the truth of their arguments. God, we learn, does not care about the status of who presents an argument. He wants us to be a nation not of men but of principles, and subjects himself to its logic. If God needs the assistance of ordinary people to live up to his principles, then all of us do as well.

This idea is so important for Judaism, and so revolutionary in human thought, that it would have to be taught on the Jewish New Year celebration. Given the emphasis that Judaism places on education, and the respect it accords teachers, the best conceivable illustration at Pesach would be by showing how students can successfully challenge their teachers regarding a Seder. And that is what the Haggadah provides here.

The second lesson from this Haggadah passage derives from *how* the students rebuke their teachers. As with the men and the women in Numbers, the students' rebuke comes from *within* the Jewish system. It reflects knowledge of and respect for Jewish practices, prayers, and obligations. It is with that knowledge, which the students must have worked hard and thoughtfully to accumulate, that they are able to develop and articulate the conviction that their rabbis are not acting in accord with the highest principles of the faith.

The third lesson derives from a silence in the Hebrew language. There is no Hebrew word for *obey*.[3] The absence of a word signifies the absence of a concept that a word would describe. This applies especially to the Fifth Commandment. While the child is commanded to always honor his parents, the absence of the concept of obedience means that it is possible (and sometimes necessary) to honor one's parents by disobeying them. This happens when the child can tell the parent that he respects their principles so much that he will always abide by them—even if that means disobeying them.

Jewish teaching has many examples of how this can happen. A child can move to another place to study even if the parent forbids it, even out of concern for idolatry, attend a synagogue against his parents' wishes, marry a (Jewish) person over his parents' disapproval, move to Israel over parental objection, and disobey his parents if the parent asks the child to transgress any commandment.[4]

If any parent believes that he deserves to be obeyed, the Torah has a ready answer. God does not even want to be obeyed. Abraham, Moses, the contaminated men who want to celebrate Pesach, and the five sisters who want to settle the Land all argue with God—*and they all win*. Why does God so often seek these challenges? And why does he change in response to them—rather than, being God, get it right the first time? In order to teach and guide us. What can we learn from the success of these challenges?

First, as discussed, God is teaching us that everyone—starting with God—lives under principles. If God himself can be challenged, then anyone can be. Second, this divine rejection of obedience is one way of God revealing himself. God learns and changes in accordance with what he learns. This is an essential part of what makes God perfect. Changing does not suggest a flaw. Not changing does—for God and then of course for people.

The students, who burst into the Seder to tell their rabbis to end the Seder because they have a responsibility to fulfill (to say the morning prayers), are acting in the tradition of Moses and Abraham arguing with God. How do the teachers respond? The Haggadah does not tell us because it does not need to. Their delight leaps off the page.

HUMILITY CAN BE A SIN

*Rabbi Elazar ben Azariah said "I am like a
seventy-year-old man . . ."*

It must have been quite a Seder in Bnei Brak, with these five rabbis telling the story with such fervor that they had to be interrupted in the morning by their students! The ideas, the perspectives, the wisdom, the analysis, the connections, the dreams, the predictions that must have filled the Seder! One wonders, what did they talk about?

We are only given one subject that they discussed. It is not about any of the great men and women of the Exodus or their precursors in Genesis. It is not about freedom, slavery, and liberation; it does not contain anything of ritual significance; it does not address any of the obligations or questions that are aroused on this Jewish New Year; it does not reference anything from the Torah.

We don't even get to it right away, and that's not only because the discussion of its conclusion comes first. First, we learn who brings up the subject—Elazar ben Azariah. He is known as "the young man who became gray overnight"—a distinction manifested by his being put on the Sanhedrin, the ancient Jewish court, as a teenager.[1] He was likely a teenager at the time of this Seder at Bnei Brak that is immortalized in the Haggadah.

We also learn how Rabbi Elazar ben Azariah introduces the subject of discussion. He says, "I am like a seventy-year-old man." This is interesting and instructive for multiple reasons, which build on the fact that this self-reference is regarded positively.

Indeed, the fact that this young man presents himself as "like seventy" should trigger a pause. The myth of a Fountain of Youth existed for thousands of years in cultures from ancient Greece to the sixteenth-century Caribbean. We might not believe in that anymore, but we have replaced it in the United States with an antiaging market that is estimated to be $60 billion a year.[2] Moreover, media outlets and research houses are full of reports and studies on the ideas, actions, and trends of young people. About the elderly? Not so much.

As previously discussed, Judaism invents the idea of prioritizing the young when Moses tells the Pharaoh, "We will go with our young and with our old." But there is no contradiction with having the young come first and the dictate in Leviticus 19:32: "You shall rise before the gray headed and honor the presence of an old man." This was never a matter of politeness. Twice, Moses is instructed to get advisers—once by Yitro (his mentor/father-in-law) and once by God. Both Yitro and God tell him to recruit exclusively from "the elders of Israel." As for the Fountain of Youth and antiaging creams? The Talmud tells multiple stories of Abraham praying to look old, and being rewarded by God through being recorded in the Torah as "advanced in age."[3]

That Rabbi Elazar ben Azariah would so positively describe himself as being like an old person is just one of the striking things about his introduction. The even more striking thing is that he describes himself so positively at all. We have a word for publicly describing oneself positively, and it does not have a positive connotation. It is: *bragging*. If this young rabbi really had the wisdom of a seventy-year-old, wouldn't he just make his point and let others marvel at his being wise beyond his years? Why would a great rabbi be immortalized for bragging, an act for which he suffers no criticism—at the Seder or subsequently?

The inclusion of such a mystery in the Haggadah can only exist to teach *us* something, to lead *us* to consider something that will help *us* in the new year, to guide *us* in some way. And sure enough, it does.

As God creates the world in Genesis 1, he stops six times to admire his work by calling it "good"—and at the end of the workweek praises himself even more by calling the finished product "very good." Much later, in Numbers 5:23, God enables his name to be erased in order to save a marriage. It is in this juxtaposition—between declaring one's work "very good" and sacrificing one's honor for a greater principle—where God defines humility.

The Torah almost never uses adjectives to describe people. Instead, the Torah presents its characters in stories and allows readers to come to their own conclusions. There is an exception, illustrating the importance of the quality it wants to establish with perfect clarity. In Numbers 12:3, God calls Moses "a very humble man, more than any man on the face of the earth." Yet Moses single-handedly takes on a gang that is harassing women, flares with anger at the Pharaoh, confidently leads a maddening people through wars and rebellions in the desert, and defiantly confronts God multiple times.

This is the humblest of all men?

There is more. Moses acquiesces when the artisan of the Torah, Bezalel, effectively tells him that there is a better way to design the Tabernacle. Moses tells God to "blot me out of your Torah" if God abandons the Jewish people. Moses is delighted when two other people, Eldad and Medad, are "prophesying in the camp"—an act that even his protege, Joshua, thought should be reserved for Moses. When Moses is insulted by his sister and she falls ill, he prays for her.

Like God who praises his own creation and allows his name to be erased to save a marriage, Moses fully acknowledges his accomplishments and the abilities that enable them—and always sublimates himself to the principles that he stands for. At seemingly every opportunity, he demonstrates his willingness and even eagerness to sacrifice his honor in order to benefit his family, his people, his faith, or his mission. It is *only* because of his robust self-assuredness that Moses is able to appreciate where others are better than him, brush off slights (and focus on genuine threats), and always sacrifice his personal interests for the principles that he is devoted to serving. The humble person, the Christian writer C. S. Lewis says, "will not be thinking about himself at all."[4]

How can the lesson in humility be best understood and lived by those at the Seder? Perhaps by starting with the question: Is life a gift from God? Most people, from every faith, would answer: "Yes, of course." However, Rabbi Moshe Scheiner suggests another approach—which begins by understanding the nature of a gift.[5]

A gift is something valuable that is given with nothing expected in return. In fact, any reciprocal obligation negates its status as a gift. A recipient of a gift may want to reciprocate, but he has no need to do so.

Life, unlike a gift, comes with substantial obligations to the giver. Life is not a gift but a loan. And every loan comes with a detailed agreement, full of detailed obligations (sometimes called *covenants*). God's side of the agreement contains the unique and substantial abilities he has given each of us. Our side of the agreement—our loan covenants—are the products of these abilities, deployed in service of making the world a dwelling place for God.

If one does not read the loan agreement, he is not being humble. He is being irresponsible. One who does not acknowledge and appreciate his special abilities will not be able to do the work God intends for him. For a scientist to advance human knowledge, a doctor to ameliorate human suffering, a lineman to install electrical systems, a parent to raise children, a businessperson to create jobs and donate to sacred causes, a teacher to inspire students, a firefighter to save families, that individual must be fully aware of her significant talents. With that confidence, she can work to develop and deploy them. A falsely humble person will be incapable of participating in that process to the detriment of people and the disappointment of God.

There is a Talmudic teaching that "all Israel are guarantors for each other."[6] This informs the fundamental principle of Jewish obligation: Each Jew is responsible for the actions and well-being of others in the community. That sounds like a nice idea, but Judaism is not a religion of inactive sentimentality. Instead, this teaching leads to a fundamental question of responsibility: How is one qualified to guarantee the well-being of another? Everyone who has guaranteed the rent on a child's apartment knows: the guarantor must be wealthier than the person whose obligation he is guaranteeing. As Rebbe Menachem Mendel Schneerson said, "if the Talmud says that all Jews serve as guarantors to each other, this means that in every Jew there is a quality in which he or she is superior to all others."[7]

This robust self-conception is, per the Rebbe, what we need to fulfill our obligations to each other. It may also be what we need to build the character to fulfill those obligations. Civilization depends upon people resisting actions that are enjoyable, profitable—and wrong. How can people carry this out? There are three general ways. The first, as discussed, is when the person believes that he is a "slave to God"—and thus simply cannot contravene God's rule. That might be ideal. The second is that the act is prohibited, with consequences that are enforced by an effective deterrence system. The third is when the person believes that he is "above it" or is "better than that."

Which of the latter two is more durable? The psychologist and rabbi Abraham Twerski recounts how his father would criticize him. His father would tell him, in Yiddish, "That is beneath your dignity."[8] It is by believing oneself to have an elevated dignity, by conceiving of oneself as better than an alternative self who would engage in a prohibited activity, and by regarding oneself as deserving of high expectations and capable of meeting them that one can avoid all kinds of temptations and pressures. A dependable way to avoid doing the wrong thing is to consider oneself too good to do it.

The authors of the Haggadah could have taught this lesson by having any rabbi brag about anything. It is instructive that the authors of the Haggadah sought to teach us this lesson using age. Age is often thought to be determinative, in that there are distinct qualities of the young and the old. There is obviously some truth to this—an old person will never play in the NBA. But how widely determinative is age? The Haggadah challenges conventional assumptions about age by highlighting that a teenager can have the wisdom of a revered elder. And this leads to another question: What surprising qualities might old people have? The Torah, and subsequent commentators, have something to say about that as well.

In Genesis 23, Sarah is described as having died at "one hundred years and twenty years and seven years." Not 127—but one hundred years and twenty years and seven years.

Why, Rashi asks, would the author of the Torah choose such a cumbersome way to describe her age? Because of her personality and character. Rabbi David Fohrman, citing Rabbi Joseph Soloveitchik, notes that everyone goes through stages of life.[9] Some people leave the characteristics of their previous stages behind when they enter the next one. Others, like Sarah, take the best qualities of one stage and bring it with them to the next stage. This kind of person, for instance, does not abandon the enthusiasm of a child as she gets older. She brings it with her, and in so doing exemplifies what it means to be a full Jewish person. At least one Jew seems to have been directly inspired by her example. At the end of the Torah, we are told that Moses dies at 120—with "his eyes undimmed and his vigor unabated."

What an inspiration to the young and the old at the Seder! A young person can achieve the wisdom of the elder and warrant a space at the table with the sages of the era. And a 120-year-old person can have the vitality of a youth whose eyes are undimmed. And to everyone: God has extended us an enormous loan—and in his role as the divine credit officer would only have done so if he had the confidence that we had the resources to make good on it.

WHEN TO FIND GOD

The phrase "the days of your life" would have indicated only the days; the addition of the word "all" includes the nights as well.

When Rabbi Elazar ben Azariah finishes bragging about his wisdom, what does he talk about? He states that, even though he is so wise, he could not figure out why we are commanded to mention the Exodus from Egypt "every night." This changes, he reports, when he hears Ben Zoma say: "In order that you may remember the day you left Egypt *all* the days of your life." In saying "all," he determines that the obligation to remember is during the day and also the night.

This is what is vexing our prodigy? He has the attention of the greatest rabbis of all time—and he is wondering about whether the description of a day also encompasses the night?

Rabbi Elazar ben Azariah is not making an obscure and legalistic argument. He is guiding us toward a reckoning with the central question of faith—the one asked by the confused Jews who had just been liberated in the desert and were beginning their long journey to the Promised Land: "Is God in our midst or not?"

As with so many of the most important questions in the Torah and in our lives, the answer is already there. It is waiting to be discovered.

As soon as the Exodus begins, God guides us out of Egypt and into the desert. He does so, per Exodus 13:21, with a pillar of cloud and a pillar of fire "so that they [the Jews] could travel day and night." The cloud would shield us from the heat of the sun during the day, and the fire would provide heat and light at night.

Later in Jewish history, the prayer schedule was invented. In both the morning and evening prayers, Jews specifically remember the Exodus. We do not do so in the afternoon prayer. The special distinctiveness of night and day would be embedded into the way that Jews communicate with God every day.

This is where the young Rabbi Elazar ben Azariah is guiding us at the Seder at Bnei Brak: to consider our faith, in the context of the day and the night.

Many have an easy time with faith in the proverbial nighttime of our lives. This is reflected in the World War I expression that "there are no atheists in foxholes." Even the most secular people often become very observant in their darkest moments—when a livelihood is threatened, when freedom is at risk, when death approaches. This observation, which has often been reported by clergy, has been verified by modern social science.

In 2012, New Zealand psychologists conducted a study of how people respond religiously when primed with concepts related to their death.

"The data show that . . . believers strengthen their beliefs [and] nonbelievers waver from their disbelief. . . . The results again revealed that . . . believers more readily judged religious concepts as real, while non-believers found it more difficult to judge religious concepts as imaginary."[1] This approach to faith is so common that it now has a name and a psychological literature around it.[2]

In good times, the relationship that nighttime believers have to faith is different. This was predicted by Moses. In his farewell speech in Deuteronomy, he says, "When I have brought them into the Land flowing with milk and honey . . . and they eat their fill and thrive, they will turn to other gods and worship them, rejecting me and breaking my covenant."

As Moses predicts and Rabbi Elazar ben Azariah surfaces in the Haggadah, people often deemphasize or even abandon God during the daytimes of their lives. The American Enterprise Institute scholar Tyler Castle has analyzed data that shows that people in less developed countries are far more religious than those in wealthy nations.

He concludes, "As people become more prosperous, they become more comfortable with their lives. . . . Perhaps they think they've figured life out on their own. *Life is great. I'm in control. Why do I need God?* I have found this to be true in my life, especially during certain seasons. . . . When my life seems to be going well, I am less likely to look to God for my provision. Instead, it is during the painful, lonely times that I cling desperately to God."[3]

One of the problems with nighttime belief is instability. Nighttime believers, Moses predicts in Deuteronomy 31:20, will come around to some "other god and worship them." In the past several decades, large numbers of Americans have declared themselves to be of "no religion." Does this mean that they are now moral connoisseurs, operating in the world in accordance with a self-directed philosophy equipped to guide them through their challenges, opportunities, responsibilities, and expectations? No. Roughly half of Americans who profess to believe in "no religion in particular" believe in astrology and the power of psychics.[4] Thirty years ago, very few Americans believed in witches. Now there are more than one million American Wiccans (pagans who claim to be witches)—making it, according to a *New York Times* report, the "fastest growing religion in America."[5] As the English philosopher G. K. Chesterton is reputed to have said, "When a man stops believing in God, he doesn't believe nothing. He'll believe anything."[6]

By complete contrast with nighttime believers, some people have an easier relationship with God during the day. Daytime believers have an easy time sharing the glory with God when things are going well. Their faith is challenged in darkness. They effectively believe that God has disappointed them, and express that with the conviction that God is absent or—in the words of the famous 1966 *Time* cover—even dead.

Rabbi Elazar ben Azariah, drawing upon what he learned from Ben Zoma, teaches us about the kind of relationship that God seeks with us. It is not just the kind of relationship that God wants—it is the only kind that makes sense. A relationship with God is not one for tactical use. He is not the doctor we call when we get sick or the event planner we call when we want to celebrate. He is not a nocturnal terror manager or an afternoon cheerleader. He is the pillar of cloud who cools the day and the pillar of fire who warms the night. He is our God whose deepest yearning, as described in Leviticus 26:10, is that "My Sanctuary [be] among you" and in Deuteronomy 26:11–12, "I will walk among you."[7]

Our God in history wants to live with us: The sanctuary is "among" us, and he wants to "walk among" us always. As with a parent and a ruler, different aspects of the relationship can surface at different times. But like every comprehensive relationship, it must be always on—during times of mournful seeking, joyful gratitude, and everything in between. He is always in our midst. We just have to open ourselves to him.

COMMITMENT

*But the Sages declare that "the days of your life" would
mean only the present world; the addition of "all"
includes the era of the Messiah.*

The sages continue with another seemingly obscure statement: that the word *all* in this passage refers to the era of the Messiah. They are saying that we are to remember the Exodus—we are to do a Seder—even when the Messiah comes. However, the Torah says nothing about a Messiah or an afterlife. Later biblical books reference a Messiah, but only abstractly. Subsequent Jewish teaching generally discusses the Messiah in the context of our obligation to prepare the world so that it is the kind of place where he would be comfortable. Why do the authors of the Haggadah and the "sages" they reference seemingly break from this tradition (the tradition that they created) to speak of the Messiah in such concrete terms?

Given that the Haggadah is a guidebook and the Pesach celebration is designed to enable us to live better in the coming year, there must be practical significance to this reference. The question must not be about how the Messiah will celebrate a Jewish holiday when he arrives—but about something that can help us.

As previously discussed, historical memory fades very quickly. Events that convulse the world are often forgotten two generations later. This is no one's fault. In fact, we experience it every day! Events that are very important, even consuming, eventually diminish in our estimation as more things happen. The argument that we had with a friend, our son's mischief that ignited our parental anger, the illness we suffered, the girl who broke our heart, the championship game our high school team lost, the election that our candidate won probably seemed like *everything* at the time. But after a surprisingly short time, it likely remains only as a fading memory. This is just what happens, as events always accumulate and the human mind has only limited focus.

How, then, to preserve the memory of an event for all eternity? With a commitment that will persist regardless of what happens subsequently, a resolution to arrest the memory's natural process of erosion and to maintain the preeminence of the event even if everything else changes. By turning history into memory and imbuing memory with the most important event of our Jewish year. The rabbis of Bnei Brak, and we following them, can achieve this with the Exodus by testifying that our commitment to it will persist even after *the* event of supreme importance (the coming of the Messiah). The Messiah may reset everything in the world, but not our commitment to telling the story of the Exodus in the way that we do. And if even the coming of the Messiah does not supersede our telling of the Exodus story, we should be sure that nothing before his arrival will either.

There is a curious and brilliant subtlety in the discussion of the rabbis—the proverbial dog that did not bark. There is one relatively rare characteristic that all these Jews had in common: None of their direct ancestors would have been enslaved. Either Rabbi Akiva or his father was a convert. And the other rabbis were Levites, whom the ancient rabbis do not believe to have been enslaved because Aaron (a Levite) was free to join his brother, Moses, without any mention of his being enslaved.[1]

But none of that was at all relevant at this great Seder in Bnei Brak. They said "We were slaves" in Bnei Brak, just as we do in New York. We make this statement as a nation, and that defines us personally. It does not matter if a Jew's ancestors were gentiles, Levites, or slaves in Egypt—we are all Jews, and that means that we were all slaves in Egypt.

THE JEWISH SECRET OF PARENTING

Concerning four sons does the Torah speak—one wise one, one wicked one, one simple one, and one who is unable to ask.

We discussed how the Haggadah reflects what is perhaps the most audacious idea ever: Moses's decision to bet the perpetuation of the Jewish people on our adoption of mass education and universal literacy. Moses, throughout the Torah, is not just an educational philosopher. He is also a tactician. The absolute importance of education in the Jewish imagination, particularly with regard to its implementation, is a principle that the authors of the remarkably brief Haggadah take multiple opportunities to emphasize. The very presentation of the four sons—before any of them say anything—reflect at least five of Moses's beliefs about education that would define Jewish life forever.

First, the Haggadah does not say, as one might expect, *a* or *the* wise son. It says *one* to introduce each child. The word *echad* ("one") has an unmistakable association in Judaism. As referenced from Deuteronomy to Zacharia to Job, this refers to the oneness unique to God.[1] The authors of the Haggadah are reminding—or instructing—us that each child has a spark of *echad* (Hashem) in her. Each child is a full person who should be considered as the "one" that she is—a full person created in God's image.

Second, the educational process takes place in the home. The earliest Jewish communities had a robust educational system thousands of years before anyone else in the world believed in having one. Still, education was never a function that could be outsourced. The questions in the Haggadah are asked by children, but they are not answered by teachers, rabbis, or anyone else. They are answered by parents. This seminal moment of Jewish education occurs in the home, with the parent providing instruction to his child.

Third, the education is done through questions. This is far from the only way that education could have been conducted. It is not even the predictable way. As previously discussed, questioning invites the conceiving, articulation, and development of subversive ideas that are seemingly not conducive to the perpetuation of a way of being. Still, the authors of the Haggadah have each son ask a question. With this choice, they are responding to the prompting of Moses, whose discussion in Exodus and Deuteronomy of what and how children would ask about the Exodus serves as the basis for these questions. They are responding to the logic of the entire Torah. The middle two words of the Torah—the words that the late chief rabbi of South Africa Louis Rabinowitz called "the dividing line between the words"[2]—are *darosh darash*: *Inquire Inquire*. Judaism, as literally as possible, hinges upon questioning.

The questions of the four sons are unprompted, surprising, and reflective of the specific personality of each child. Of course, knowledge matters—the children and adults at the Seder will appreciate the Haggadah more to the extent that they are familiar with the stories, passages, and references throughout it. The questions reflect different amounts and kinds of knowledge, and they are all welcome. But questioning, with all the risks it embodies, is the heart of the educational process.

Fourth, there are multiple kinds of children. It is not important that there are exactly four sons. What is important is that there are more than two sons. This demonstrates the Jewish belief that child-rearing is not singular (treat every child the same) or binary (there is a right and a wrong way to parent) but *complex*. Starting with the learning from *echad,* we are *reminded* that every child is unique—and so four is just a representation of an infinite number of children. As each child receives a different answer, responsive not just to the question but to the child, the authors of the Haggadah reveal the most important fact of Jewish education. Each child is being taught, as Proverbs 22:6 indicates, "according to his way."

The children are very different, but they are sitting at one table as Jews celebrating the same New Year. The Jewish philosophy of individuated child-rearing and education is ultimately, thus, in service of community.

The Jewish way to create a sacred and enduring community with common values and a shared vision is by respecting the uniqueness of each participant. It is by enabling each member to identify and develop what he can uniquely contribute that the community becomes stronger.

The fifth belief about education reflected in the four questions derives from a different interpretation of them. The children are not different people, but the same person at different stages of life. Accordingly, the same child goes from not knowing how to ask to being simple to being wicked (probably in adolescence) and finally wise.[3]

The interpretation might seem banal—yes, children grow and mature. But children don't always mature, and not at a predictable rate or in the same way. Moreover, there is no indication that the Four Sons are children. They are sons of a living father, but that could put them well past the ages when we often assume that people naturally change. The conception of the Four Sons as one son who might be any age, progressing, is a reminder of what is perhaps the quintessential Jewish idea—that we each can, at any age, transform ourselves and begin again. And one of the great functions of education, which can and should happen at any and every age, is to provide that avenue of transformation.

HOW INTELLECTUAL INQUIRY
IS OF LIMITED VALUE:
CONSIDERING THE WISE SON

The authors of the Haggadah could have picked any types of son to show-case. The wicked son would have to be chosen, at least in some variety. L. Frank Baum, the creator of *The Wizard of Oz,* also chose this archetype in the Wicked Witch of the West. But he countered her with the *Good* Witch of the North.

The Haggadah, in contrast, does not have a good son. Why do the authors of the Haggadah, unlike Frank Baum, choose wisdom over good-ness? There are several possibilities—none of which contradict each other and all of which can be simultaneously true and instructive.

As with many questions, that one triggers another: What is a good per-son? This might seem like a simple question, but it is surprisingly hard to answer. For Judaism, it is probably impossible to answer. This is due to the conviction that everyone always has a *yetzer hara* (an evil inclination) and a *yetzer tov* (a good inclination).

This may seem depressing: Everyone always has an evil inclination, and it can never be extinguished! But Judaism answers with an analysis from the Mishnah. The Mishnah considers Deuteronomy 6:5: "Love the Lord your God with all your heart and with all your soul and with all your strength." "All your heart," the Mishnah says, means "with your two im-pulses, the evil impulse and the good impulse."[1]

How does one love God with his evil impulse? Judaism posits two ways: by channeling to create good or structuring to prevent bad.

First, the channeling. The fourth-century sage Rabbi Nachman says that it is the evil inclination that provides man the impetus to build houses and to beget children.[2] His contemporary Rav Ashi says that certain people are born under the "nature of Mars" and need to spill blood. That sounds foreboding—and, indeed, Rav Ashi states that such a person might become a murderer or a thief. But, Rav Ashi continues, he also might take those same characteristics and become a butcher, a surgeon, or a mohel (the person who conducts circumcisions).[3] In three out of four instances, the person routes his *yetzer hara* for productive means and even divine purpose—just as the person who channels his ambition into building a house and the person who channels his lust into marriage and family do.

The rogue of the Talmud is Resh Lakish. As a young man, he was enormously strong—and used this physical capability to become a thief and gladiator. Under the influence of Rabbi Yochanan, Resh Lakish transforms himself. A changed man, he uses his past to become one of the great Jewish commentators on repentance. But his transformation does not mean that he became a scholar holed up in a yeshiva. When a great rabbi of the age, Rav Ivi, is captured by bandits and is in mortal danger, Rabbi Yochanan says that nothing could be done to save him. Resh Lakish disagrees. "Even if I am killed or I kill someone, I will go and I will save him with strength."[4]

Resh Lakish, Rav Ashi, and Rabbi Nachman all show how one can love God with the *yetzer hara*. At times, there is no opportunity to direct the *yetzer hara* positively. In these cases, the Jewish solution is to create structures to prevent it from causing harm.

This is exemplified in Deuteronomy 21, when a question emerges: What should the Jewish military victor do with a beautiful captive woman whom he desires? One might predict that a religious authority would respond: What kind of question is that? You can't do anything with her!

But the Torah instead says in Deuteronomy 21:10 that you "may take her to yourself as a wife." A Jewish soldier can take a captive woman for his wife? Sure—but, the Torah specifies, only after she comes into the home for a month, shaves her head, lets her nails grow, changes from the garment in which the soldier found her attractive, and cries constantly for her parents. If this process diminishes his desire, he must set her free. How is such a process likely to conclude?

In Leviticus, we are told that a Kohen (a priest) is forbidden to marry a divorcée—and the Kohen Gadol (the high priest) is forbidden to marry a divorcée or a widow. Why? In the first case, the priest may observe a married couple in strife and be attracted to the woman. Rather than "forbid" his lust, the Torah just stipulates that he can't do anything with it. In the second case, the high priest may be attracted to a woman and seek to have her husband killed so that he might sleep with her. That sounds like a remote possibility. But in the Book of Samuel, King David does it when he dispatches his soldier Uriah to certain death so that David can marry Uriah's wife, Bathsheba. Rather than "forbid" the lust of the Kohen Gadol, the Torah just prohibits him from marrying a widow.[5]

This is not to say that the evil inclination is easy to manage. In the channeling of bloodlust and structuring around sexual lust in Deuteronomy and Leviticus, the evil inclination is defeated. But these stories, and other similar ones, could easily have turned out differently and with devastating consequences. Channeling and structuring are tactics, not magic potions. The evil inclination, always ready for a tough fight, often wins.

The evil inclination, or at least just evil, has another way to win. This is by losing. Just as qualities associated with the *yetzer hara* like the desire to spill blood can have sacred manifestations, qualities associated with the *yetzer tov* can be morally devastating.

For instance: Is being "merciful" a good quality? One is tempted to say: Of course! And if the world were fully constituted with small children and sweet adults, it certainly would be. But the world is full of cruel people. As previously discussed, Rabbi Elazar of the Talmud says whoever is merciful to the cruel will end up being cruel to the merciful. Rav Ivi, when kidnapped, did not need a merciful person to issue wise words of Torah to his captors. He needed Resh Lakish, the sage who was once a gladiator, to be ready and capable of exercising violence on his behalf.

And it is not only with regard to the cruel that being merciful (or nice) can serve ill ends. Nice people often have a hard time saying no and engaging in any kind of conversation whose result might disappoint the other person. But everything done well in the world, from raising good children to building good companies, requires plenty of nos and a lot of disappointing people. Given the inevitable frequency with which "no" is required, he who cannot easily offer it will end up saying "yes" far more often than is deserved. He will, therefore, inadvertently reinforce behavior that should be changed. He will also end up agreeing to things that he cannot deliver on, as too many yeses end up contradicting each other. A "nice" person who cannot say no, therefore, will be unable to keep his word. Consequently, he will be unworthy of being trusted or even taken seriously—and will be deprived of the social capital he needs to build relationships and create anything meaningful.

If everyone has evil inclinations that could yield good results and good inclinations that could yield evil results, what is a good or evil quality? Perhaps there is no such thing—perhaps the value of a characteristic always depends on how it is applied. With the very existence of good and evil qualities called into question—how does one become a good person?

The answer, perhaps, is provided in the Talmud—through a conversation that Alexander the Great has with the Jewish sages. Alexander the Great asks the Jewish sages, "Who is called a wise man?" They respond, "The person who sees the consequence of his action."[6]

The characteristics of someone who can see the consequences of his actions—those of being learned, calibrated, judicious, thoughtful—are those needed to avert the evil inclination's temptations and rationalizations. It is the capacity to see the consequences of one's actions that gives an individual the chance to effectively govern all his inclinations.

There is an easily identifiable logic that accompanies the sages' definition. One who cheats in business is always going to be worried that the next call will be from someone telling him that he has been caught. One who commits adultery may not care about his relationship with his wife, but will set a bad example for his sons, teach his daughters not to trust men, and damage many important relationships with family and friends. By contrast, one who habitually gives to help those in need will likely see, when he is an old man, that his children and grandchildren do as well. A person who can see all of those things in the moment will be the most likely type of person to make good decisions.

The wise son has one additional advantage over the good son. One child will have to lead the others. Whom would we rather spend an evening with—a person who is wise or a person who is good? The Nobel Prize–winning fiction writer Isaac Bashevis Singer had a perspective on the subject: "Even good people don't like reading novels about good people."[7]

Now introducing the wise son.

The wise son asks, "What are the testimonies, decrees, and ordinances which Hashem, our God, has commanded you?" This question comes from

Deuteronomy 6:20 and is prefaced in the Torah by, "In the days to come." His future orientation will lead him to consider the consequences of his actions, and thus his good inclination holds a significant advantage.

In asking about testimonies, decrees, and ordinances, the wise son is demonstrating his expansive curiosity. He separates them and wants to know about *each* of them. This is an important Jewish act, as the Hebrew word *kadosh* has two meanings: holy and separate. It is only by separating things that we can accord each item its integrity—and understand and appreciate them.

The wise son then says, "our God." This is not linguistically necessary. If he had not said, "our God," his question could still be understood and answered. But that is not how the wise son asks questions. His acceptance of God ("our") is a core part of what defines him and how he thinks. His relationship with God is tender, loving, abiding—and defining.

The wise son loves God, he is curious, he has absorbed the Jewish teaching about distinctions, he thinks about these issues in the future. Where does all this lead? He finishes his question by asking his parent what has been commanded *to you*—not *to us*! So does he accept the testimonies, decrees, and ordinances or not?

The father never asks and so we never find out. What notion of wisdom is unconcerned with where someone ends up on the most important issues? The pursuit of wisdom might be a journey, but isn't the destination important?

Of course. As we will soon see, the father regards the destination as very important. He'll get there. But he also knows that how and when a question is addressed can be as educative as the answer itself. The question of whether his son *abstractly* accepts Judaism does not seem to concern him.

It is because the father of the wise son has so much faith in the child and in Judaism that he does not command or even suggest a particular approach. This father probably believes that a child who learns rigorously and comprehensively in the spirit of a loving relationship with God will come to an acceptable conclusion.

What will be the wise son's conclusion? The father knows that there is little chance that his son, who says *you* instead of *us*, will conclude that the father's theory and practice of Judaism is exactly right for him. The child's world is a different one, with new challenges, possibilities, perspectives, and realities. So it is only reasonable that the child's conclusions and practices, even if based on the same fundamental premises, will be different. As Moses says in Deuteronomy 31:19, in one of his parting messages: "And now write *for yourselves* this song!" Why does Moses call the Torah a "song"? Because every rendition of a song, while sharing the same melody and lyrics, is done in the unique voice, style, and interpretation of the singer. An adherent of the religion that designs its calendar around the changing moon rather than the steady sun should hope that his son's conclusions will not be the same as his.

The father, accordingly, does not answer the son with a plea toward piety. He starts, instead, by teaching him the "laws of Pesach." That is a reasonable response to the question asked at the Seder table about testimonies, decrees, and ordinances. However, that "answer" is immediately summarized by: "One may not eat dessert after the final taste of the Pesach offering."

Dessert is a familiar topic for parents, who often use it as leverage in negotiations about dinner, bedtimes, housework, and homework. But as an answer to a child's existential question about Judaism?

Yes. And for two very distinct and differently instructive reasons.

First, the father does not answer according to what the son asks but instead according to what he needs to know. In this, he is following an example that God sets several times in the Torah. In Exodus 3:11, Moses says to God, "Who am I that I should go to Pharaoh, and that I should take the Children of Israel out of Egypt?" God does not respond by telling Moses anything about himself. Instead, he says, "I will be with you." God knows that, contrary to the question, Moses is not really trying to understand himself. Moses is wondering how he could complete the mission. God answers *that* question, and Moses is satisfied.

Why do God in the Torah and the father in the Haggadah respond by answering so nonresponsively? Why is this strange way of engaging a question (a question is asked and a non-responsive answer is recorded) immortalized, for our benefit, in the Haggadah?

Let's imagine a child who, uncharacteristically, storms from the dinner table because the food is not to her liking. The father would, on one level, be justified in expressing disappointment. But what if the child had just experienced a major academic disappointment, been dumped by her boyfriend, or been excluded by her friends? It would show the love, compassion, and the insight that can only come from concerned intimacy if the father ignores the specific complaint and instead addresses the real problem rather than the child's imprecise expression of it.

The father wisely addresses the son's question indirectly. But why is his answer about *dessert*? The reason is revealed in the fundamental thing that one does with dessert—eat it. But one eats all foods, and the father speaks only of dessert. What is the distinguishing feature of dessert? Its taste.

The idea of tasting appears in the Bible. Psalm 34:8 says, "Taste and see the Lord is good." Taste *and* see—with tasting coming *before* seeing. To "scc"—to understand—whether something is good, the Psalmist is telling us that we must taste it. We must assess its practical applications before we can judge it.

This concern is familiar to anyone who has known bright, passionate, and engaged young intellectuals. The great twentieth-century intellectual Irving Kristol told the story of how his friend Saul Bellow would, as a young man, stay up all night with his friends engaged in conversation fueled by the tea and cakes supplied by Saul's aunt. When the evenings concluded, Saul's aunt would remark, "Your friends, they are so smart, so smart. But stupid!"[8] In other words: The ideas of very smart people can be inventive and interesting, clever and informed—and impractical, unworkable, and unjust.

The taste, the father in the Haggadah and Saul Bellow's aunt were saying, is what the young man is missing. The wise son of the Haggadah wants to know testimonies, decrees, and ordinances. Good. But he should also be interested in feelings, culture, actions, and consequences. The Seder might be (should be!) a spectacular intellectual endeavor. But that is not its purpose. Its purpose is to renew, educate, and deepen our commitment to freedom, en route to becoming a kingdom of priests and a holy nation. This requires thoughts and feelings, ideas and actions, the intellectual and also the physical, and most of all how things *taste*. The father, who seems unconcerned about the son's lack of using *us* in references to the acceptance of Judaism's laws, shows no such leniency when it comes to taste. The father is telling the son, "Whatever you believe at any moment—just be sure it *tastes* right. Judaism allows for an intellectual, spiritual, and religious journey, and I encourage you to go on it! Just always know: There are real people along the way, including yourself. Be sure that your beliefs, practices, and actions always pass the taste test."

And it is through this reminder that the father carries his wise son to the heart of their faith. With its emphasis on the importance of education, Judaism has become, in the words of the historian Paul Johnson, "an ancient and highly efficient social machine for the production of intellectuals."[9] This is fine and good. Indeed, Rabbi Akiva even says in a discussion recorded in the Talmud that study is greater than action. But *why* is study greater than action? Because: "Study is greater, but not as an independent value; rather, it is greater as study leads to action."[10] If study does not lead to action—or leads to the wrong action—its value can be wiped out or become negative. The Jewish book of ethics, Pirkei Avot teaches that one whose "wisdom exceeds his deeds" is like a tree that has many branches and few roots and will be uprooted by the wind.[11]

Jewish wisdom, the father is teaching his son, requires retelling *and* reliving, seeing *and* tasting, thinking *and* acting.

THE FUNDAMENTAL PRINCIPLE
OF JUDAISM: CONSIDERING
THE WICKED SON

Peer pressure is a modern, secular term. But it has an ancient and very Jewish provenance. In Numbers 1, military service is required for Jews. But Deuteronomy 20:3 offers a few exemptions. One is for a man who is "fainthearted and afraid." The Torah instructs, "Let him go and return to his house, lest he not cause the heart of his brothers to melt."

To the biblical author, peer pressure is such a significant—and apparently unsolvable—phenomenon that it justifies exempting someone from a fundamental commitment of democratic citizenship. This evaluation of peer pressure would continue as a major Jewish concern. King Solomon writes in Proverbs 13:20, "He who walks with the wise will become wise; he who walks with the foolish will be destroyed."

Much later, Maimonides observes,

It is natural for a man's character and actions to be influenced by his friends and associates and for him to follow the local norms of behavior. Therefore, he should associate with the righteous and be constantly in the company of the wise, so as to learn from their deeds. Conversely, he should keep away from the wicked who walk in darkness, so as not to learn from their deeds.[1]

Modern social science has validated this consistent Jewish concern. We now know that peer pressure affects or even determines what songs we like, what risks we take when driving, how often we exercise, what we eat, and the likelihood of young people to use condoms, drink, use drugs, smoke cigarettes, and graduate from high school. Social scientists (and not just them!) have often asked why so many adolescents engage in such destructive behaviors. The prevailing theory used to be that adolescents have insufficiently developed prefrontal cortexes (the part of the brain that governs impulse control). However, subsequent research has shown that adolescents make the same kinds of decisions as adults when in a state of emotional stability. The prevailing theory about adolescent misbehavior now focuses on the reward centers of the brain that, according to Beatriz Luna of the University of Pittsburgh Medical Center, appear to get triggered by peer influence. The peer pressure sets off an emotional response in the brain—and it is this response that is so difficult for adolescents, given the development of their brains at that stage, to govern.[2]

So it would seem that Maimonides's concern to "keep away from the wicked" would be especially applicable to the Seder. The Seder discussion could easily be hijacked, and the wicked son could easily corrupt the others. But everyone agrees that the wicked son should be included in the Jewish New Year celebration.

Why is the wicked son always invited? Because he is a son, and his parents do the inviting. A parent will always want his child at the Seder. It is easy to imagine a wicked son—he might be sullen, dismissive, or even angry, checking his phone in the midst of a blessing, making comments that are more contrarian than truth-seeking, or demonstrating in some other way his belief that this whole exercise is a waste of time. However, he is his parents' child, and his parents want him there.

This does not mean that the concerns about peer pressure are alleviated, or can be ignored. Quite the opposite. It just means that they have to be addressed—conceptually and practically. The moral development of all the children at the Seder, to say nothing of the integrity of the Seder, just might depend upon it.

How, then, can the parent balance her need to have her wicked son at the Seder with her concern that he might corrupt the other children and diminish this most important of Jewish nights for everyone? The Torah is there to help—with, per Numbers 19:2, "a red heifer without spot, wherein is no blemish, and upon which never came yoke." The pure red heifer is sacrificed and thrown into a fire with a lot of other things. The priest uses the concoction to purify someone who has been contaminated. The priest becomes contaminated and then must go through a cleansing process himself.

This story is sometimes discussed as the quintessential example of how the Torah can be inscrutable. But that can't be. The Torah is a guidebook "for [our] benefit," and therefore everything in it must be easily comprehensible and eternally relevant. This story, as interpreted by the great twentieth-century American rabbi Joseph Soloveitchik is not about an obscure ritual. It is about a great religious question: Should the religious person maintain his purity or defile himself to purify another?[3]

The teaching, from what the priest does with the pure red cow, is clear. It is a Jewish obligation to engage with—carefully, compassionately, strategically, but maximally—even the most wayward Jews. We are to sacrifice our purity to help purify another. As we will soon see, what the authors of the Haggadah identify as "the fundamental principle of Judaism" depends on it.

However: before we get to the response—the question from the wicked son.

The wicked son says, "Of what purpose is this work to you?" Perhaps the first thing we notice about his question is that he says, "to you." This is the same phrase as that of the wise son! It is as though the authors of the Haggadah were anticipating, and teaching, what the author John Updike observed in his essay about the Red Sox great Ted Williams, "There is a tissue thin difference between a thing done well and a thing done ill."[4]

The wicked son has something else in common with his wise brother. *He asks a question.* He is engaged! In his own way, to be sure—but the question is at least a potential lifeline to the Jewish tradition.

But he is the wicked son, and his question shows why. The first problem: He is questioning whether the Seder has a purpose at all![5] The wicked son has (perhaps) gone through Seder preparation, heard children sing the Four Questions, discussed the slavery of our people in Egypt and how it relates to us today, contemplated the significance of the Land of Israel, considered existential needs and hunger—and he is questioning whether the Seder has a purpose?

The question gets worse. The wicked son refers to Seder night as "work." Hebrew has two words for *work*—one that describes the slavery in Egypt and one that describes building God's sanctuary in the desert. The wicked son uses the former, equating participating in the Seder with being a slave.

And then he says *to you.* The wise son said *to you* as well. But the same word can have different meanings when said by different people in even slightly different contexts. The wise son wants to learn everything from his father. He has effectively declared his intent to decide, *after* careful study and respectful engagement, what he believes.

The wicked son's *to you* is entirely different. There is a question, but its meaning is not inquisitive but accusatory. As the Haggadah says, the wicked son's *to you* purposely "excludes himself." The existential problem that it embodies is immediately thereafter described in the Haggadah: "By excluding himself from the community of believers, he is denying the fundamental principle of Judaism."

This short statement is unique in the Haggadah for two reasons. First, it is not a response to the question. No one, let alone the wicked son, asks about the fundamental principle of Judaism. The father is instead offering a general commentary on the question to the entire group at the Seder. Second, Jewish teaching is based on the prioritization of questions over answers. As Rabbi Abraham Joshua Heschel says, "We are closer to God when we are asking questions than when we think we have the answers."[6]

But here, perhaps unique in Jewish thought, the authors of the great text could not resist definitively settling one question. What is the fundamental principle of Judaism? It is *the community*: full stop. In this, the authors of the Haggadah were not issuing a creative interpretation or otherwise freelancing. In Hosea 4:17, we are told, "Ephraim is joined to idols; leave him alone!" Why leave him alone—when, at other times, idolatry (the most prohibited activity in the Torah) is punished with extraordinary severity? Because, explains Rabbi Eliezer Hakapor in the Talmud, there must have been unity among the people—for God will tolerate even idolatry for the sake of unity.[7]

We have discussed that the first Jewish holiday is Rosh Chodesh, the holiday of the new moon. The moon is visible and arrives predictably. Consequently, one would not assume that "declaring" it would be a big deal, or that there would even need to be a practice of formally doing so. Yet the mitzvah of Rosh Chodesh is only fulfilled when two people independently witness the new moon and report it simultaneously to the rabbinical court. The great decisor of the Talmud, Rabbi Gamliel, ruled that even a likely mistaken identification of the new moon by two Jews should be considered valid.[8] Even an error in the calendar—an error in time itself—is considered a price worth paying to establish another principle: Jewish time can only progress within Jewish community.

It is no wonder, therefore, that the ancient Midrash states, "Israel will not be redeemed until they are all one society."[9] As the Seder is the night of Jewish redemption, this truth would have to find its way into the Haggadah. And this is an instructive place in the evening to place it.

The Seder is well under way, with plenty of questioning and discussion having occurred already—and considerably more to come. This is as it should be—Judaism generally, and its New Year commemoration specifically, encourage and celebrate the vibrancy and even the volatility of such engagement.

Yet here the authors of the Haggadah remind us that even this blessing comes with a potential cost. Discussions can become debates, debates can become arguments, arguments can become personal, and relationships can rupture. This can happen, quickly, even from a starting point of an idea that seems abstract or a principle that appears ancient. There is nothing in the Haggadah, or at the Seder, that is immune from this threat.

The Haggadah steps in to issue a reminder: The vibrant discussions you are having *must* strengthen the Jewish community across geographies, across time, at each Seder table. Allowing any Seder discussion to weaken the community is wicked.

If unity is so important, then it is not enough only to protect against disunity. A person concerned with his health will do things to avoid weakening his systems *and* to actively strengthen them. Seder-goers who want the "basic principle of Judaism" to thrive should want to do more than protect it from harm. They should want to strengthen it.

And this process can begin at every Seder table. Looking around the room, it will likely be apparent that the Seder-goers are primarily traditional or liberal. This is fine and inevitable; families are typically one or the other, and Pesach is the great holiday of the home. But Jews from both traditions should acknowledge that their Seder does not represent the full community of believers.

Acknowledgment of the inevitability of difference within Judaism can lead in one of two directions. One is toward tribalism, which will likely present as participants confirming the behaviors and beliefs of their side and condemning (often by caricaturing) those of the other. There is another option.

Leviticus 19:17 commands us to "rebuke, rebuke your fellow." Why is the word *rebuke* used twice? According to the Hasidic tradition, it is to emphasize that we must first rebuke ourselves before rebuking others.[10]

As Rabbi Yitz Greenberg said, "I don't care what denomination you are—so long as you are ashamed of it."[11]

In this spirit, liberal and traditional Seder leaders could encourage their attendees to list several deficiencies in their communities that could be improved as a result of having adopted attitudes, customs, and practices of the other. In so doing, we wouldn't be conceding or even sacrificing anything—but learning and improving in accordance with what the authors of the Haggadah tell us is the fundamental principle of Judaism.

It would also be in accordance with the customary Jewish greeting. The greeting, "Shalom Aleichem" (Peace unto you), is met with the response "Aleichem Shalom" (Unto you peace). This is as strange as responding to "Good morning" with "Morning good." Why do we return the most common pleasantry so strangely? Rabbi Moshe Scheiner explains what two Jews are really saying to each other through this strange sequence: "Even if we don't see eye to eye, I bless you and you [bless me]."[12]

Our goal, as either a liberal Jew or a traditional Jew, should not be to convince the other but to bless him. Blessing those who are different—especially as a Jewish blessing means asking that the blessed be *increased*—might be the ultimate expression of respect. It would be one Jewish community (or approach) saying to another: Even though we are very different, I am asking God to increase you! And from that we see that respect and not agreement (and certainly not uniformity) is the secret to Jewish redemption.

THE RESPONSE

Before seeing how the father in the Haggadah answers the question of the wicked son, we should acknowledge that he is in a difficult position. He already made one difficult decision by including the wicked son. Now he has another: should he answer the son? This challenge—and its difficulty—is illustrated in Proverbs 26:4–5: "Do not answer a fool according to his folly, or you yourself will be like him. Answer a fool according to his folly, lest he become wise in his own eyes."

Which is it? Should we answer a fool and challenge him or not answer a fool and avoid participating in a meaningless and possibly counterproductive exercise? The proverb does not even try to answer. Instead, the author of that proverb, King Solomon, identifies the likely risks on each side and leaves the application to each of us.

How should the proverb guide the father of the wicked son? In addition to the wicked son, the father must be concerned about how his response will influence the other children. If he answers the wicked son, he will likely receive a seemingly clever or sarcastic retort that could win the hearts of the other children. If the father does not answer, the others could reasonably conclude that he has no good argument. Or they could just as reasonably decide that the father is being rude and therefore that the behavior of the wicked son is justifiable.

The father, the authors of the Haggadah believe, must engage the wicked son. There could be lots of ways to do so, from kicking him out to appeasing him. But the father wants to do something else. He wants to help his wicked son improve.

We addressed earlier the imperative of rebuking, in service of denominational improvement and Jewish community. Both concern one's most general approach to Judaism, which is unlikely to involve anything personal or emotionally charged. Yet it is still difficult to carry out that rebuke. And now, as the father answers the wicked son specifically and directly, he must carry out a rebuke that is entirely personal and completely charged with emotion.

Anyone in this situation might be tempted to avoid it. But the Torah, and the Jewish interpretive tradition around it, insists otherwise. After God creates Adam, God notices that there is something wrong. "It is not good," God says, "for man to be alone." The badness that God identifies in being alone is evident in what he creates to solve this problem. God says, "I will make a help against himself," as he creates Eve from Adam's rib. Loneliness, the Torah shows, is not having someone to improve you.

How should people in relationships improve each other? The third-century rabbi Yosi bar Hanina explains: "Love unaccompanied by rebuke is not love."[13] He opined, to the agreement of many other rabbis that the reason that Jerusalem was destroyed several hundred years earlier was that people did not rebuke one another.

His near contemporary Resh Lakish says, "Peace unaccompanied by rebuke is not peace." And Proverbs 9:8 tells us that if we "rebuke the wise, he will love you."[14] Those who are wise seek continuous self-improvement, and know that rebuking is indispensable to it. This conviction reverberated through the millennia to where a legendary rabbi of the nineteenth century, Yehudah Aryeh Leib, was known as "the Mochiach [Rebuker] of Polonnoye." We might expect to see a rabbi venerated for his wisdom, kindness, courage, knowledge, leadership. But rebuking? In Judaism, of course.

So rebuking is indispensable for moral progress on a national, communal, and individual level. If there is ever a case where success lies in the execution, it is here. Rebuke can be considered surgery for the character. If not administered, the patient will continue to worsen. If administered improperly, the patient will react adversely and resent the surgeon. If administered with proper care, the rebuke can save or significantly improve the patient.

So how should rebuke be administered? Judaism has a three-part strategy, which is illustrated in the response to the wicked son.

Step 1: The rebuker should, if at all possible, rebuke himself first. As previously discussed in a different context, Leviticus 19:17 commands us to "rebuke, rebuke your fellow"—indicating that a rebuke of another must be preceded by a rebuke of oneself. This is what the father of the wicked child is doing when he is, through the blunting-the-teeth metaphor, criticizing himself.

Step 2: The rebuker should open the conversation with love. We see this modeled in Genesis 29:7 by Jacob. Jacob is exiled from his home and travels to find his uncle Laban in Haran. He arrives at the destination and sees men working in the field. "My brothers," he says, "The day is still long; it is not yet time to bring the livestock in; water the flock and go on grazing."

Jacob has barely met these strangers and immediately rebukes them on doing their jobs poorly! Yet the men accept the criticism from this stranger and respond with a calm and coherent explanation for why they were not working.

Why do these men so willingly accept this criticism from a stranger? Because of the way Jacob frames his criticism. The first thing he says to them is, "*My brothers.*" It is Jacob's connecting so deeply with them—using a term of both love and shared destiny—that enables the men to accept the criticism so gracefully and respond so productively.

We saw this biblical guidance put into action by the American who most intentionally and effectively lived the Torah. How did Reverend Dr. Martin Luther King Jr. convince much of the nation, including enemies, to adjust its philosophy and change its ways? By learning from Jacob. "If physical death is the price that I must pay to free my white *brothers and sisters* from a permanent death of the spirit, then nothing can be more redemptive."[15]

Step 3: In the holiness code in Leviticus, we are commanded, "You shall rebuke your fellow and do not bear a sin because of him." The Hebrew word for "bear" as in "bear his sin" is the same as that for "lift up." Consequently, a rebuke must be delivered in the context of lifting up the rebuked.

The thirteenth-century Spanish rabbi Yonah Gerondi discussed how this insight can be operationalized. One should not, he wrote, tell a wrongdoer, "Now look, you are a horrible sinner and will pay for your sins." Instead, the rebuker should say, "Now, I think that you are a wonderful fellow; you are a pious man but you don't know it. Of course you have weaknesses but a man of your stature will certainly overcome them."[16] The rebuker must tell the rebuked that he is good—so good that he can reach remarkable heights if only he improves in this specific way.

This guide by no means suggests that it is easy, or ever has been, to live in a world of rebuke. The process of rebuking is not a formula that is easy to administer, will be met by a compliant or even predictable response, or even has a good chance of working. One of the rabbis from the aforementioned Seder at Bnei Brak, Rabbi Tarfon, says in the Talmud, "I would be surprised if there is anyone in this generation who can receive rebuke." His Bnei Brak Sedermate Rabbi Elazar ben Azariah responds, "I would be surprised if there is anyone in this generation who can give rebuke."[17]

Still, we must try—as the father of the wicked son does.

The narrator of the Haggadah begins, "Therefore, set his teeth on edge [or blunt his teeth]." This statement, just through its words, articulates a deeply important message to the father. Every letter in Hebrew corresponds with a number, so words are the sum of the numbers of the letters that create them. *Rasha* (wicked) is 570; *shinav* (his teeth) is 366. When one takes his teeth away from the *rasha*—when 366 is subtracted from 570—the result is 204. And 204 is the number for *tsaddik*—the righteous man.[18] The Haggadah's message for the father is—yes, the process that follows will be difficult. But the reward is great. Your wicked child has the potential to emerge as a righteous man. Now let's try to make that happen.

How could the first step in the process of rebuking a son be hitting him in the mouth? It is not. King Solomon says in Proverbs 13:24, "He who spares the rod hates his son. But he who loves him disciplines him promptly." This just illustrates the Jewish belief that parental love requires rebuke and discipline. It was never meant to be taken literally. The Torah is full of family dysfunction, but there is no case where a parent hits his child. And by the time the Haggadah was written, corporal punishment in Jewish education was forbidden.[19]

So what could this passage mean? As is often the case with biblical passages, the key to understanding this is seeing the context where the passage was similarly used. There are two other references in the Bible to teeth being set on edge—Jeremiah 31:28–29 and Ezekiel 18:2. Both refer to parents eating sour grapes and thus causing their children's teeth to be set on edge. The parent is conceding that the son is flawed because of something that the parent did.

In the Midrash, the third-century Rav Huna (in the name of Rabbi Yochanan) tells of the parable of a man who opened a perfumery shop for his son in a neighborhood of prostitutes. The son "fell into evil ways," and the father got very angry. But a friend of the father says to him, "You were the cause of this youth's corruption, and you shout at him? You set aside all other professions and have taught him only to be a perfumer; you skipped over all other districts and opened a shop for him just in the street where harlots dwell."[20]

In the spirit of Rav Huna, the father of the wicked son begins by rebuking himself. The rebuke is not the perfunctory kind: "If I offended you in any way, I'm sorry." It is the most substantive type—that which reveals self-awareness, vulnerability, and a desire to change. As an example, this self-rebuke just might inspire the wicked son (and perhaps anyone at the Seder) to consider the same process of self-rebuke for himself.

This self-rebuke guides us to ask: Why would the wicked son want nothing to do with Judaism? A child could be drawn to Judaism through textual study or exuberant song, by prayer or by tzedakah, by love of the Land or the joy of communal activity. He might find his Jewish self in religious, national, communal, or intellectual manifestations. He might connect with the blessing of the children on Shabbat, the wedding chuppah, the cleansing of Yom Kippur, celebrating with family and friends at the Seder table, meals in the sukkah, the Hanukkah candles, Purim costumes, or a hundred other things. If the child finds *nothing* in Judaism that moves him, the likely suspect is a lack of exposure or a dearth of love and enthusiasm accompanying any exposure. Those are the sour grapes that the father fed the son.

The self-rebuke is complete. Now for opening with love. The father continues, "It is because of *this* that Hashem did so for me when I went out of Egypt."

Because of this. These might be the three most important words that the father will ever say. The father is telling the wicked son: Thank you for your question! It is *because of this*—because of your question, *it is because of you*—that God made me free! God made me free so that I could learn myself, teach you, and, in the process, build a relationship between us and come closer to God together.

And what does the father learn? That a wicked son could not only become wise, but also righteous. That he, the father, has the power to help make it happen. That personal transformation is possible and accessible to *his* family. That words can enable the most broken relationship to begin again.

The father is essentially thanking the son for teaching him the meaning of freedom and giving its expression a purpose! This is the epitome of Jewish respect, appreciation—and love.

Because of this!

The wicked son is likely not expecting his father to credit him, on Pesach night, with the parent's freedom! How would the son react upon hearing this? If Jacob could open the young men of Haran to rebuke by calling them "brothers," the father at the Seder would have a chance to open his wicked son to rebuke by calling him to reason for his freedom. At the very least, the wicked son will be interested and curious.

The first two steps of the rebuke are complete: The father has rebuked himself and opened the conversation with love and generosity. Now the son is ready for the final step. The father continues, "'For me,' but not for him—had he been there, he would not have been redeemed."

There is a glaring omission in this part of the answer. There is no *you*. In this absence he is telling the son that had the sharp-toothed guy been in Egypt, the guy who found nothing to appreciate in Judaism, the guy who found no place in the community, he would not have been redeemed. But the sharp-toothed guy—the sullen guy, the nihilist, the rude guy, *the wicked son*—that's not you! You have such an important place in the Jewish community, you have so many consequential things to contribute, that it is worthy of my life to help you find them. So let's get out of Egypt together—and really *together*, because only then can each of us be redeemed.

WHO IS THE IDEAL HUSBAND? CONSIDERING THE SIMPLE SON

The simple son is often portrayed visually in Haggadot and at the Seder discussions generally as stupid.[1] As we have discussed and seen, the Haggadah is full of instances where multiple interpretations of the same thing can be true, instructive, and fruitful. But this does not mean that every interpretation is valid. The simple son is not stupid.

The Hebrew word for *simple*—as used in *simple son*—is *tam*. It is used dozens of times in the Bible as *tam* or *tamim*, and figuring out its unifying meaning will help us understand the second son in the Haggadah and at our Seder.

In Genesis 17:1, God appears to Abraham and offers him the most meaningful, ambitious, and inspiring directive possible: "I am the Almighty God; walk before me and be *tamim*." God is not telling Abraham to be stupid.

We are introduced to Abraham's grandson Jacob, with God referring to him as an *ish tam*—a simple man. Jacob is, like every developed biblical figure, full of virtues and flaws. He also seems to have understood genetic engineering millennia before Gregor Mendel "discovered" it. The "simple" person, therefore, can be a genius—and also highly complex.

In the Pesach sequence in Exodus, God tells Moses that the sacrificial lamb—which the Israelites are to consume during their last meal in Egypt—must be *tamim*. In Deuteronomy, there are two uses of *tam* that are deeply instructive for these purposes. God calls *himself tamim*—and explains what he means: "The deeds of the Rock are *tamim*, for all His ways are just; a faithful God, without injustice, He is righteous and upright." And God commands us, "Be *tamim* with God."

Achievement of *tamim* has long been the spiritual ambition of the Jew. It is, Rabbi Isaac says in the Talmud, the attitude a person needs when he does a mitzvah. It is, the great nineteenth-century Hasidic master Rav Nachman of Breslov said, the quality he devotes his entire life trying to achieve. It is, the seventeenth-century Israeli rabbi Yeshayahu Halevi Horowitz (known by his best known work, *Sh'lah HaKodosh*) determined, the most noble of traits.[2]

It is *wholeheartedness*. And this quality is personified at the Seder by our *tam*—the child who is really our "wholehearted son."

The wholehearted son in the Haggadah asks *only*, "What is this?" He is concerned only about the essence of the Pesach experience. He respects his brother who asked about the testimonies, decrees, and ordinances—but that is not the kind of question he would ask. He is not going to perseverate over distinctions and their existential significance. He loves God, loves his faith, is comfortable with the ideas that he learned long ago from his grandparents, and is appreciative of paternal reminding and clarification.

The wholehearted son is the kibbutznik who loves exploring the Land, delights in his family, and is always ready to drop everything to defend his people and his country. He is the volunteer firefighter who leads the welcoming committee at his church, coaches his kids in Little League baseball, roots for the local teams, and hosts the town's Labor Day barbecue that the local kids look forward to all summer. He is the neighbor whom you can leave your kids with at a moment's notice with the surety that the kids will return with muddy clothes, bellies full of pizza, and an excited recounting of the fun they had.

A question for the parents (and their children) at the Seder: Who would you want your daughter to marry—the wise son or the simple/wholehearted son?

As a father of two girls (and two boys), I choose for my daughters—wholeheartedly—the wholehearted son.

WHAT SHOULD WE BE ASKING? CONSIDERING THE SON WHO DOES NOT KNOW HOW TO ASK

When considering the son who is unable to ask, some Seder participants might assume that this is a very young child. God willing, there will be such young children at the Seder. But that child is not going to learn from anything discussed. His experience will be of the music he hears, the food he eats, and the love he feels. No parent would give his non-question a multifaceted "answer" like the one he provides to this question.

Who, then, is unable to ask a question but can learn from an answer?

A lot of people. There are those who are mystical, musical, mechanical, and those with special needs—people who simply do not express themselves intellectually. And there are those who can express themselves intellectually but have a broken heart or a collapsed sense of self and just can't really participate this year. And there is a third kind of person, who will be introduced at the end of this chapter.

This is the only response in the Four Questions provided in the feminine voice, suggesting that it is either provided by the child's mother or by her father calling forth his feminine aspects. It is also the only response where the parent is told *how* to answer. The Hebrew language shows the relationship between these two seemingly disparate unique characteristics. The Hebrew word for compassion, *rechem,* derives from the word for womb. Compassion, as the quintessential feminine quality, defines the voice with which this instruction is issued.

The parent is instructed, "You must *open* [the subject] for him." This notion of "opening" is simple, but it has a profound Jewish resonance that the instruction guides us to explore. Rabbi Jonathan Sacks draws the relationship between this opening and that in the fundamental prayer of Judaism—the Shema. He cites the Kotzker Rebbe, who wondered why the Shema says, "And these words shall be *on* your heart." Why *on* instead of *in* your heart? Because while the words might be right there, we must be open to them. We must let them in. And the words will only enter if we open the heart in a spirit of compassion.[1]

The imperative of opening explains, according to the Kotzker Rebbe, the presence of God. Perhaps the fundamental religious question is: Where is God? One might respond: He is everywhere. Perhaps the Kotzker Rebbe essentially responded when asked this question, "God lives where we let Him in."[2]

The implications are awesome: God could be everywhere. We just have to open ourselves to him, and he will be there.

There is one other kind of person who could be the son who does not know how to ask. This could be someone with plenty of intellectual interest and aptitude. Elie Wiesel cites Rav Levi Yitzchak of Berditchev—the great Hasidic rabbi who lived in the eighteenth century in Ukraine, Belarus, and Poland. Rav Levi Yitzchak used to stop for a long period at this point in the Seder and pray, "God of Abraham, Isaac, and Jacob, the fourth son, he who does not even know how to ask a question, that is me, Levi Yitzchak. If I only knew how to ask questions, I would ask you these questions. Read them in my heart, Almighty God, they are waiting there for you."[3]

Who, in the spirit of Rav Levi, is this type of son who does not know how to ask? It is he who is not sure that he is approaching his personal and professional relationships correctly. It is he who is not sure that he is spending his time with the right people, in the right ways, doing the right things. It is he who is not sure that he knows the pain of those close to him and is equally unsure that he is doing everything possible to help alleviate it. It is he who is not sure that he is exposing each of the children, specifically, to the right people, the right opportunities, the right ideas, and in the right way. It is he who is not sure that he is living wholeheartedly with the specific plan that God has for him and is executing accordingly.

It is he who knows that he could be doing all those things better, if only he had the right questions for the right people. It was Rav Levi Yitzchak of Berditchev. It should be each of us.

FINDING THE IMAGE OF GOD
(IT'S NOT HARD)

Originally, our ancestors were idol worshippers.

We started telling the story by referring to our origin as slaves. Here is where we begin again, referencing our origin as idol worshippers. Seder-goers may ordinarily go quickly through this section of the Haggadah because of how we conceive of idolatry. We might associate idol worship with praying before graven objects, and take comfort in that we don't do that. We might think that we are over idolatry.

There are two problems with that.

First, idolatry is the most frequently prohibited activity in the Torah. The Talmud says that the denial of idolatry is akin to accepting the entire Torah—a belief echoed by Maimonides, who writes, "Whosoever denies idolatry admits the whole Torah, all of the prophets and all in that which the prophets were instructed since Adam even till the end of time. Thus it is the most outstanding commandment of them all."[1] Since the Torah is our eternal guidebook, the most frequently prohibited activity—the one practice considered akin to accepting the whole of it—must still be relevant.

Second, the Haggadah says that originally our ancestors were idol worshippers but now God has "brought us nearer to His service." "Nearer" is a tantalizing word. It clearly suggests that we are not there yet. It seems, then, that there is a continuum from idolatry to service to God. We might be "nearer" to God than our idol worshipping ancestors were, but how much closer? The Haggadah does not say.

If idolatry is a persistent problem and is not a matter of worshipping wooden icons, what is it? It is defined, perhaps best, in the Second Commandment: "Thou shalt have no other gods before me." A created icon is only one kind of god a person can place before God. If serving God is the ultimate end that all other rules and goals serve, then any other ultimate goal—anything "before me"—is an idol.

An idol can therefore be recognition or money, social approval or physical beauty, bodily pleasure or even, as we'll see, one's Judaism. This does not suggest that everything beautiful is an idol. The same thing can be, depending on how it is considered and used, a holy object or an idol. One can love making money in order to alleviate the suffering of God's most vulnerable children. Another can love making money to accumulate the stuff that it can buy. The same thing can, depending on the perspective and use of the person controlling it, be idolatrous or sacred.

Even if we can identify idolatry, a fundamental question remains: What is so bad about it? There are a lot of ways to reject God. There are atheism and agnosticism, but neither is even mentioned in the Torah or the Haggadah. What is it about idolatry that makes it uniquely condemned?

There are at least two possibilities. We have discussed that we banish chametz on Pesach to focus on permanent things. One of the great teachings of Judaism is that the genuinely permanent things are invisible. These include love and justice, truth and empathy, knowledge and wisdom, spiritual hunger and existential need—and God. The worst conceivable affront to the Jewish insistence on the primacy of the invisible is idolatry—which promotes a physical "deity" over an invisible God.

There is a second reason.

In Numbers 5, God instructs Moses to tell the people: "A man or woman who wrongs another in any way, and so commits treachery *toward Hashem,* must confess the sin they have committed. They must make full restitution for the wrong they have done."

Who is the victim of the sin? Clearly: the "another" who was wronged and is due the restitution. But if he were the only victim, why would the Torah say that the wrongdoer commits "treachery toward Hashem"? Because a sin against another person always involves another victim: God.

It is because God identifies so intimately with people that he hates idolatry. As the twentieth-century rabbi Abraham Joshua Heschel explains the strict and enduring prohibition on idolatry, "It is precisely because

God has an image that idols are forbidden. You are the image of God. Every human being is God's image."[2]

There are so many images of God in the world that no one can possibly treat every one of them with the reverence that such sacred creations deserve. That is a tragic reality that our practical God in history must understand. But to compound the problem by manufacturing images (or anything else) ourselves and giving them primacy over the images of God that are so ubiquitous! This is what is so infuriating to God! It is by rejecting idolatry, and therefore accepting our responsibility to the real images of God all around us, that we (per Maimonides) are en route to having accepted the entire Torah.

IDENTIFY ENEMIES—
AND ALSO FRIENDS

It is this that has stood by our fathers and us.
For not only one has risen against us to annihilate us,
but in every generation.

This passage seems to come right from one of the earliest moments in the Torah following the Exodus from Egypt. The newly liberated Jews are wandering through the desert—angry, complaining, and contemplating assassinating Moses. The Jews are at their weakest, threatening no one except for ourselves. It is at this moment when the Amalekites attack. The Jews, with God's direct assistance, win the battle, and Moses says, "There shall be a war for the Lord against Amalek from generation to generation."[1]

The Haggadah tells us similarly, "In every generation they rise against us to annihilate us. And the Holy One, Blessed is He, rescues us from their hand."

This statement might seem anachronistic, discordant, or just harsh. Consequently, some Haggadot omit it altogether. This is a problem for two reasons. One pertains to the vertical conversation we are having with our ancestors, and the other pertains to the horizontal conversation we are having with Jews today who do not enjoy security.

First, the vertical conversation. Pesach was, for many generations before ours, not the night of ideas, conversation, food, song, and celebration that it is for us now. It was a night of terror.

The historian Larry Domnitch explains, "When Passover arrived, Jews celebrated with extreme caution and fear, unsure of the violence that could be unleashed against them." Everyone who has been to a Seder knows how central red wine is to this (and almost every other) Jewish event. The seventeenth-century rabbi David HaLevi Segal of Poland issued a ruling requiring Jews to use white instead of red wine at the Seder so that gentiles would not think that they were drinking the blood of Christian children. This might have saved some people—but not two of his sons, who were killed in a pogrom in 1654.[2]

Accusations that Jews killed gentile children to use their blood in matzah or wine (known as *blood libel*) circulated in England, France, Spain, Poland, Germany, Greece, Hungary, Slovakia, Iran, Ukraine, Damascus, Chicago, New York (the New York blood libel, which was unique in that it ended in a quick and sincere apology from those perpetuating the lie, was in 1928), and recently in the West Bank, Lebanon, Jordan, and the Gaza Strip. Even when religious authorities condemned blood libel as heretical, the belief persisted among large numbers of people.

If most Jews today are unfamiliar with or unfazed by accusations of blood libel, it is because it became much less socially acceptable to express such ideas after the Holocaust. But the Haggadah, paraphrasing the Torah, says that there will be Amalek "in every generation." There will always be people who will attempt to harm and even annihilate us, even when we are not remotely a threat.

If we can't readily identify who it is in this generation, is that because there is no one? Or is it because we are lacking in knowledge or are deficient in honest analysis? Jews in Miami, Sydney, and Toronto might be safe and secure where we are, but the Haggadah reminds us that the most important thing about being a Jew is our participation in the community. When we consider this passage, we should ask: is everyone in the global Jewish community safe and secure? It is doubtful that many Seders in Israel, where half the global Jewish population lives and where genocidal threats from Hamas, Hezbollah, and Iran are a material reality, omit this section of the Haggadah. It is doubtful that Jews in Tehran, Pittsburgh, Poway, on the Gaza border, or Paris omit this section of the Haggadah either.

If there is a problem with acting as if this passage says less than it does, there is another problem with acting as if it says more than it does. The Haggadah only says that in every generation there will be people who want to annihilate us. It does not say that *everyone* will want to do so. In fact, the Torah suggests the opposite.

While the Jews in the Torah have gentile enemies such as Amalek and Balaam, they are far from unchallenged. The biblical Abraham, as the scholar Judy Klitsner shows, is at his lowest point after he gives his wife to the Pharaoh and accepts money for it. He subsequently discovers that his estranged nephew Lot has been taken captive (along with all the goods and food) from the city of Sodom, where he had been living. Abraham takes a small force of 318 men and executes a daring nighttime operation that rescues Lot, the other captives, and all the possessions of Sodom and Gomorrah. King Bera of Sodom (literally: King Evil of Sodom) comes out to meet Abraham. King Bera would surely want this remarkable military leader to join his people and would offer much to consummate this deal. What would Abraham, who had previously sold his wife to another evil king, do?[3]

Out of nowhere, and with no context, comes a gentile king—King Melchizedek (literally: King of Righteousness). This monarch says, in Genesis 14:19, "Blessed be Abraham by God Most High / Creator of heaven and earth / And praise be to God Most High / who delivered your enemies in your hand."

What is this gentile monarch, who has no other role in the biblical story, doing here? He has one function: to remind Abraham that it was God who was responsible for his successes and that he has a special relationship with God—and in so doing to equip Abraham to resist King Bera and continue on God's journey. Strengthened by this mysterious gentile mentor, Abraham adopts King Melchizedek's unique name for God (God Most High) and tells King Bera that he will take nothing from him—"not even a thread or shoelace."

The story of the emerging Jewish family continues in Genesis 37–38. Joseph is thrown into the pit by his brothers and taken by a passing tribe to slavery in Egypt. One of the brothers, Judah, is disgusted by this event (and probably by his own complicity in it) and goes into self-imposed exile. It is there where he forms the only relationship in the Torah described as a "friendship"—with a gentile, Hiram. It is in the midst of this friendship that Judah ends up being the first person in the Torah to concede a mistake, accept blame, and transform himself. These qualities eventually lead Jacob to select Judah as the leader of what would become the Jewish people—who are named for him.

Genesis ends and Exodus begins. The Pharaoh decrees, in an instruction to the gentile midwives Shifra and Puah, that all Jewish baby boys be killed. But, we are told in Exodus 1:17, that they ". . . feared God and did not do what the king of Egypt had told them to do; they let the boys live."

With this action, these women contravened the direct order to them from the most powerful man in the world. In so doing, they saved the Jewish future and invented civil disobedience—the principled refusal to obey a law out of duty to a higher moral authority. Their invention of civil disobedience would be deployed in service of freedom by the American founders, Mahatma Gandhi, Reverend Dr. Martin Luther King Jr., the Confessing Church in Germany in the 1930s, the participants in the Singing Revolution in several Soviet republics, and many others.

Exodus continues, and the Jews cross the Red Sea into the desert. Moses is beginning to establish the governing structure of the emerging nation when his gentile father-in-law, Yitro, comes for a visit. Yitro observes Moses for a day and sees that his son-in-law is hearing disputes "from morning until evening." Yitro tells Moses that this practice is "no good," and will burn him out. Yitro advises Moses to instead create a system of intermediate judges. Moses, the Torah tells us, "listened to his father-in-law and did everything he said." As with the advice that the gentile King Melchizedek gives to Abraham, the wisdom that the gentile Yitro gives to Moses enables the Jewish people to survive a crucial challenge and continue on God's journey. This contribution by a gentile is immortalized in that we name the *parsha,* where we received the Torah from God, after this great gentile—it is Parshat Yitro.

Two years pass, and it is time for the Jews to go to the Promised Land. Moses, for reasons that continue to confound commentators, insists on sending twelve scouts (or spies) first to investigate the Land. Ten scouts come back with a report saying that the inhabitants are too large, strong, and numerous for the Israelites to conquer. This report completely demoralizes the people. There is one scout who, against the other scouts and the masses of people who had been whipped into a frenzy of fear and rebellion, objects to this negative report. This is Caleb, who is twice identified in the Bible as "the son of Jeppunah the Kenizzite." The Kenizzites were a pre-Abrahamic people who are first mentioned in Genesis 15:19. Caleb, thus, is a gentile.

Caleb says, "We should go up and take possession of the Land, for we can certainly do it!" His Jewish comrade Joshua joins him and insists that

God is with them, they should not fear and should allow the Lord to lead them to the "Land flowing with milk and honey."

The Torah practice of learning from gentiles is manifested throughout Jewish teaching and prayer. The Midrash says, "If a person tells you there is wisdom among the [gentile] nations, believe him."[4] This is amplified in a blessing we offer upon an encounter with a wise gentile, "Blessed are You, God, our Lord, King of the universe, who has given from His wisdom to flesh and blood."[5]

This is not the most familiar blessing—that distinction goes to "Baruch Hashem" ("Blessed be He"). When an observant Jew asks another how she is doing, a positive response would be: "I'm doing well, Baruch Hashem." The blessing originates in the Torah, where it appears six times. *All six* expressions are from gentiles: Noah, Melchizedek, Abimelech, Eliezer, Laban, and Yitro.[6]

On March 2, 1961, Rebbe Menachem Mendel Schneerson gave a speech to thousands of his followers. It was Purim, but the memorable part of his speech was not about Haman, Mordecai, or Esther. It was about what "the newspapers reported yesterday and today"—the establishment of the Peace Corps. Summarizing President John F. Kennedy's speech, the Rebbe spoke the language that the Torah uses to describe Abraham's mission. "The [Peace Corps] volunteers will leave their homes, their birthplaces and their families, and set out for a remote region in an undeveloped country . . . to help the people to develop and progress and help them improve their standard of living."

He described President Kennedy's program in detail and told his followers that they should be similarly inspired to leave comforts such as easily accessible kosher food to bring Judaism to Jews in places that would otherwise be deprived of it. "May God grant that with 'light, joy, gladness and honor' Jews will choose to fulfill their mission which God is reminding them through the President."[7]

God is reminding them through the president! Why did the greatest Jewish religious leader of the twentieth century tell the Jews that God was speaking to them through a gentile? Why did the Rebbe instruct his followers that listening to a Christian leader about a secular subject would make them better Jews? He was just applying the lesson of Baruch Hashem.

As we consider the passage in the twenty-first century, which historical example should guide us—those of the centuries when Pesach was a time of terror? Or the Rebbe imploring his followers to learn how to be better Jews from a Catholic president? I think neither.

Jews, who excel at nearly every intellectual endeavor, went without a historian for 1,500 years.[8] This is no accident. Maimonides specifically condemned "historical works" that "do not have any wisdom or physical benefit, except for wasting time."[9] The prevailing Jewish view of history has changed since then, but the Jewish rejection of history as a productive (rather than just interesting) guide to living in the present has a sustaining point. History has continuities and discontinuities—it moves slowly and quickly, backward, and sometimes forward with a gigantic leap. Its volatility makes its predictive value marginal or in some cases negative, while the facts at hand are often easily interpreted on their own. The Jewish–gentile relationship of mutual respect, admiration, teaching, and love that was modeled in the Torah has been tragically absent for most of Jewish history. But starting at approximately the dawn of the third millennium, something changed—and keeps changing.

On the eve of Rosh Hashanah in 2018, the Christian Broadcasting Network ran a live webcast to "celebrate Rosh Hashanah." It included Pat and Gordon Robertson (the founder and CEO of CBN, respectively), musical guests, a shofarist—and the email inviting people to tune in explained Rosh Hashanah and concluded, "This is a wonderful time to see the Lord, repent for wrongdoing, and consecrate ourselves to God, thanking Him for His work in our lives." CBN sends similar messages on all major, and even some minor, Jewish holidays.[10]

Another Christian group, Eagles' Wings, sent out an email at the same time proclaiming a twenty-one-day fast "beginning this Sunday evening as we enter into Rosh Hashanah and we prepare to ascend the hill of the Lord in Jerusalem. It is an Isaiah 2 moment!" *We* enter into Rosh Hashanah: from a large Christian organization! The same email invitation reported on "The Great Buffalo Jewbilee"—the "very first annual Jewish Heritage Festival in Buffalo, NY!" Christians and Jews came together, with a "Shofar Symphony," in "unwavering support and solidarity of the Jewish people and the State of Israel."[11]

In 2019, the Church of God in Christ, a Black church denomination with more members than there are Jews in the United States, created a new position. This is the "Bishop of Israel." Bishop Glenn Plummer, a former chairman and CEO of the National Religious Broadcasters, holds this role, and spreads his church's message ("I stand for Israel—the state, the Land and the people"[12]) throughout the world.

The Catholic Church has had a long and tortured relationship with Judaism and the Jewish people. Yet in 2012, the archbishop of Philadelphia, Charles Chaput, visited Yeshiva University in New York City. He reflected on his experience in an essay in the journal *First Things*.

> Scripture is a romance. It's the story of God's love for humanity. When we give our hearts entirely to seeking God in the richness of his Word, we begin to discover and experience that same kind of electricity. I saw this in the students at Yeshiva [University] . . . I saw in the lives of those Jewish students the incredible durability of God's promises and God's Word. Despite centuries of persecution, exile, dispersion and even apostasy, the Jewish people continue to exist because their covenant with God is alive and permanent. . . . My point is this: What I saw at Yeshiva should apply to every Christian believer, but especially to those of us who are priests and bishops.[13]

There are, literally, *countless* more examples to illustrate the deep, new, and growing Christian love of Jews, Judaism, and Israel. Jews have never had anything like the friends we have in the twenty-first century, especially, but not exclusively, among Evangelical Christians. The political, social, and religious implications of this extraordinary relationship are unfolding along with the friendship.

We may not know what it all means, but we are certainly in the early stages of living the dream of Deuteronomy 32:43: "The nations will sing praises for His people!"

This passage from the Haggadah, which provides an opportunity to consider who wants to annihilate us and who wants to strengthen us, can lead to a discussion of our national relationships. Who are our enemies? Who are our friends? How should we relate to both in the coming year?

THE JEWISH WAY OF LEARNING

*Go and learn what Laban the Aramean attempted
to do to our father Jacob!*

If a parent wants to teach her child something, she will almost certainly use the word *come*—as in "Come here, and let's go over this together." And one would think that the authors of the Haggadah, for whom Torah learning is so fundamental would also have used "come." It would have been the easy, obvious, and logical choice.

Instead, the authors of the Haggadah selected another word. This word choice does not reflect a linguistic preference, but a philosophical orientation and a moral direction. It is "go." The Haggadah tells us that if we want to understand complex biblical characters, especially wily and devious people like Laban, we must "go" into the world. Of course we must also learn through coming. We have to know the story of Laban and Jacob, from *coming*, if we are to deepen our understanding of them by *going*. But it is this deep understanding, the kind that can guide us through the challenges and opportunities that daily living presents, that the Haggadah is guiding us to seek. This means learning about Laban from Labanesque characters we identify in the world, bringing that learning back to Torah study, and carrying the enriched Torah understanding back into the world.

As the Haggadah is designed to guide us through all aspects of life, the instruction to learn about Laban by "going" is intended to be broadly applied—and is firmly rooted in Jewish teaching and practice. One of the most well-known commandments in the Torah concerns Shabbat:

"Six days you shall work, but on the seventh you shall rest." We typically focus on the seventh day—as we contemplate why we should rest,
and what it means to do so. But the resting component covers less than
15 percent of the commandment! The remainder is a requirement to
work—to go out and learn from the world, and to use those learnings
to repair it.

Correspondingly, our greatest rabbis were goers. They had professions
that they practiced regularly. They were sometimes granted allowances and
exemptions by their communities to allow them to study, but none that interrupted with working at their professions. Rabbi Yochanan (who inspired
Resh Lakish to give up being a gladiator and to devote his "strength" to
Torah) was a sandal maker, Rabbi Jose was a tanner, Rav Huna was a water
carrier, Rabbi Joshua was a blacksmith, Rabbi Akiva was a shepherd, and
Hillel the Elder was a woodcutter.[1]

The practice of rabbis having a conventional profession lasted for many
centuries. Maimonides, Nachmanides, and Judah Halevi were physicians,
Don Isaac Abravanel was a financier and statesman, and Rashi was a wine
merchant. The reason all these rabbis had regular jobs was not economic.
It was also philosophical and even religious—reflecting the imperative of
"going" that the authors of the Haggadah share. The first-century sage
Rabban Gamaliel, as quoted in Pirkei Avot, said: "Excellent is the study of
the Law together with worldly occupation, for toil in both of them puts sin
out of mind. But [study of the] Torah which is not combined with a worldly
occupation, in the end comes to be neglected and becomes the cause of sin."
A hundred years later, Rabbi Judah bemoaned that the de-emphasis some
of his colleagues were placing on their occupations resulted in them being
failed professionals and bad rabbis.[2]

The dispositive qualification for service on the Sanhedrin was not
how well versed a potential judge was in the Torah and associated laws—
although those were important. It concerned whether one had children.
One could not serve on the Sanhedrin if he were old (and, hence, was not
raising children), castrated, or had no children. Maimonides explains: "A
man who is advanced in years or who is childless must not be appointed
member of any Sanhedrin, since he is required to be compassionate."[3]

Given that the Jews are the "people of the book," it is especially instructive that seemingly all our greatest authorities have—at seemingly every opportunity—counseled the limits of book learning. From serving as a judge to knowing how to deal with characters like Laban, seemingly every Jewish authority has the one-word message as in our Haggadah passage: Go.

DESTINY'S INGREDIENTS: FAMILY AND DREAMS

For Pharaoh decreed only against the males,
and Laban attempted to uproot everything.

In Genesis 29, Laban identifies the potential of his exiled nephew Jacob as soon as they meet. Jacob, Laban realizes, could make him a lot of money. And Laban has leverage in his beautiful daughter Rachel, whom Jacob desperately wants to marry. In an effort to keep Jacob close to him, he makes Jacob work for seven years to marry Rachel. When the time comes, Laban tricks Jacob into marrying his daughter Leah and makes him work another seven years to also marry Rachel. Laban does everything he can to keep Jacob and the whole family around for as long as possible.

No doubt, Laban is selfish, greedy, and manipulative. But he also allows Jacob to marry both his daughters and keeps the extended family close to him forever. The Pharaoh, on the other hand, brutally enslaves the Jewish people.

And Laban is worse than the Pharaoh? According to the authors of the Haggadah, yes. Such a mysterious and bold claim naturally leads us to ask: *Why?* And two very instructive reasons emerge.

First, Laban's manipulation is a direct attack on the fundamental unit of what the authors of the Haggadah tell us is the essential principle of Judaism—the Jewish community. The Pharaoh wages a war against the Jewish nation, but Laban does so against the Jewish family. It is now a cliché to say how important family is, but that is by no means inevitable.

It is not at all obvious that the fundamental unit of society should be the family—and not the individual, the tribe, the nation, or something else. It is because of the lessons from the Torah that we are able to identify that Laban's assault on the Jewish family qualifies him, in the eyes of the authors of the Haggadah, as even worse than the Pharaoh.

Throughout the Bible, God and Moses emphasize the significance of God's name. When Moses asks God for his name—when he asks God to define God's essence—God refuses to do so. In Exodus, Leviticus, and Deuteronomy, we are instructed not to take the name of the Lord in vain or to swear falsely by his name.

One might think, then, that writing God's name on a scroll and putting it in "bitter waters" to be "erased" would be a serious and even unthinkable offense. And it probably was—to man. However, in Numbers 5, God instructs that his name be dissolved in water, in order to save a marriage. If erasing my name, he effectively says, would help to save a marriage—then, no question, put it in the bitter waters.

The first-century sage Rabbi Meir, inspired by God's example, engineered a situation where he would be publicly spat at for the same purpose: to save a marriage.[1] This model, set by God and exemplified by Rabbi Meir, was to be sustained forever. The nineteenth-century rabbi Samson Raphael Hirsch summarized the role of the family in the Jewish story:

> For the fate of men, their success or failure, is decided neither in the chambers of rulers nor on the battlefield. It is not decided in business concerns, in colleges and institutes of arts and sciences or in houses of worship. It is sealed only in one place—in the parental home.[2]

Every decent parent has one aspiration in common: that their children love and support one another. The universality of this desire can be explained by evolutionary psychology. We parents want to provide our children with safety and security in a complicated, rough, and sometimes unforgiving world. We also want to predecease our children. After we die, who will fill our role as protectors, as sounding boards, as watchmen, as the endlessly generative source of love and trust for our children?

Their spouses, ideally. But they might not have spouses. And even if they do, the marital unhappiness rate (high in the Torah, high today, and proba-bly high always) makes the spousal relationship an undependable substitute for the stability that parents offer. But our other children, their brothers and sisters—they can be the rock; they can be the watchmen.

Laban, for his own purposes, acts to subvert the all-important sibling relationship. His manipulations lead, predictably and inevitably, to jeal-ousy and enmity between his daughters. This tension lasts throughout Genesis, as the sons of Leah hate the son of Rachel so much that they try to kill him. Rachel's son, Joseph, and his brothers reconcile—but the effects of this disunity wrought by Laban continue. The attempted fratricide leads to Joseph and then the family going to Egypt, ultimately placing the Jewish people under the control of a Pharaoh who, we are ominously warned in Genesis 1:8, "knew not Joseph." It is Laban's assault on the institution of the family that becomes the root cause of the hundreds of years of slavery for the entire Jewish people.

The Pharaoh, on the other hand, imposes extremely harsh slavery on the Jews. He decrees that all Jewish baby boys be killed. The Jews, through courage, faith, and the help of righteous gentiles, survive and even manage to thrive in captivity. Perhaps, the authors of the Haggadah are telling us, the Jews can withstand external assaults. But an assault against the Jewish family—for that we have no defense, no strategy, no prayer, no chance.

Second, Laban's assault against the Jewish future is not even limited to familial destructiveness. When Jacob leaves his parents' home in exile en route to meet his uncle Laban in Haran, he stops in Bethel. He puts a rock under his head and falls asleep. He dreams of a ladder connecting heaven and earth, with angels starting on earth and ascending. As Rabbi Shlomo Riskin says, Jacob is dreaming the great Jewish dream—of uniting heaven and earth.[3]

After two decades with Laban, Jacob has another dream. It is of a spot-ted, speckled, and mottled sheep. He is dreaming of wealth disconnected from how he would serve God with his bounty. Rabbi Adin Steinsaltz imag-ines Jacob saying, "When I left the Land, I dreamed of angels ascending and descending from heaven. If I have begun dreaming of goats and sheep, it is a sign that I must return to the Land."[4] It is at this point that God tells Jacob that he must leave.

A person's destiny, the authors of the Haggadah are teaching, is determined by his dreams. Whoever governs one's dreams—whether a parent, a sacred text, a leader, a peer, or someone or something else—largely determines who that person will become. The Pharaoh, despite his brutal enslavement, could never control our dreams. The more he afflicted us, the Torah says, the "more the Israelites multiplied and spread." But Laban, who is fond enough of Jacob to marry him to both of his daughters, is able to change his dream. And for that, the authors of the Haggadah deem him worse than the Pharaoh.

IMAGINATION: THE MOST IMPORTANT PART OF REALITY

An Aramean attempted to destroy my father.
Then he descended to Egypt, and sojourned there.

The authors of the Haggadah are (finally!) ready for us to tell the story of the Exodus itself.

There is an obvious biblical source for the Haggadah—the second book of the Torah: Exodus. The entire story of the Exodus from Egypt—which the Haggadah is supposed to *tell*—is there.

However, the authors of the Haggadah do not choose to tell the story of the Exodus through the second book of the Torah. They tell the story by going all the way to Deuteronomy 26, near the conclusion of the Torah. And the protagonist in the story of the Exodus relayed in the Haggadah is not Moses, Miriam, Aaron, or Joshua. In fact, the protagonist had not even been conceived by the Exodus. He is a farmer who lives far in the future. We tell the story, in other words, through an imaginary man. Even more, we tell the story through an imaginary man conducting an imaginary ceremony in an imaginary temple in a Land of Moses's imagination.[1]

Practical people, or just most adults, sometimes associate the imagination with things that are not real and are, consequently, not serious. These associations may be of a child dreaming of a fantasy world, a marketer trying to convince us to buy a product, or a storyteller entertaining us with a diversion. But such a characterization of the imagination would not explain why the authors of the Haggadah chose to tell the story of the

Exodus through it. And it would not explain Albert Einstein—who, as perhaps the greatest discoverer of realities, said, "Imagination is more important than knowledge."[2]

Why might the imagination be so important to very different geniuses from the authors of the Haggadah to Albert Einstein?

As ever, the Torah is there to clarify and to guide.

We know nothing of Moses's father and little about his mother. The Torah tells us only this about the origin of the man who would be the greatest in history: "A man went from the house of Levi and he took a daughter of Levi." We are not told their names (Amram and Jochebed) until later in the Torah.[3]

Rabbi Shlomo Riskin points out that while we do not know much about his parents, we know about his grandparents. His paternal grandparents named their son Amram, which means "Exalted nation." His maternal grandparents named their daughter Jochebed, which means "Glory be to God."[4]

When they named their children, Moses's grandparents were living in a cauldron of enslavement, oppression, and suffering. In spite of this condition, they maintained an imagination so rich that they were able to see in their children an exalted nation and the glory of God!

After the Exodus, the Israelites went into the desert and proved themselves unprepared for the rigors of freedom in the Promised Land. When confronted with adversity or even insecurity, they often ask to "go back to Egypt." Why would the Jews want to go back to the most brutal slavery the world had known? Because, as Rabbi David Fohrman explains, of their imagination.[5] Although they have only recently escaped Egypt, they are imagining it as a very different place from what it was. In so doing, they are exercising a choice. They could imagine themselves conquering and settling the Land, en route to creating a kingdom of priests and a holy nation in accordance with the divine imperative. Or they could imagine a better past and seek to return to a place that never was. The one thing *they have to do* is to imagine. The imagination, for these ancient people and all those who came after them (especially us), is inescapable.

In fact, every dream, goal, and ambition *requires* imagination. The Torah's vision for us is, as discussed, that we should become a kingdom of priests and a holy nation. How can we achieve it? We can only work toward this sacred goal *after we imagine* what such a society could be like.

The imagination is determinative in almost all human decisions and relationships. Can one change himself? Yes, but after imagining what his life would be like as that improved person. Should one grant forgiveness? Yes, if we *imagine* that the other person, if put in a similar situation, will act differently.

Should a voter pull the lever for this candidate or his opponent? It depends on how the voter imagines the polity under the leadership of each person. How can one person help another through a difficult time? By imagining what the other person is experiencing and imagining again what words and deeds will make the difficult situation better. Should one regret not taking that path rather than the one he did? No—he is just imagining how life would have been on that path, which will be as accurate and productive as those in the Exodus generation imagining life back in Egypt.

A person's biography is written in the language of the imagination.

A child enters fifth grade. Should she devote more practice to basketball or chess or violin? It depends on how she imagines her enjoyment and progress with each of them. Her parents take her to a new restaurant to celebrate her hard work at her chosen activity. Will she order the pizza or the pasta? It depends on which she imagines she will enjoy more.

A decade later, she must decide: Should I choose this career or that one? It depends on how she imagines her happiness and fulfillment across a variety of criteria—each of whose relative importance in the future she must also imagine.

Some time thereafter, she will decide: Should I marry my boyfriend? It depends on how she imagines her life with and without him. She says "Yes" to him or, subsequently, to someone else. She has two children. Should she have another child? It depends on how she imagines her life financially, emotionally, and socially in the near term and in the long term with and without that child. Should she send that child to this or that school? It depends how she imagines her child in each environment, accounting for imagining how each school community *and* her child might change over time.

So *of course* the authors of the Haggadah had us tell our freedom story through the imagination. The imagination enables us to determine what possibilities might exist, where we want to go, who we want to be, what we want to know, what we should do, what we can expect of others and of ourselves. It is the exercise of the imagination that will determine how we will live the following year. And it is our appreciation of the imagination that will enable us to conceive the visions and make the choices that will enable us to live our best lives.

JUDAISM: A RELIGION OF CHARACTER

The imagination, per Albert Einstein, might be more important than knowledge. But *important* does not mean *good*. We can, of course, imagine ourselves doing all kinds of things and being all sorts of people.

Who does Moses imagine the man of the future, who represents everyone in how he tells what became the Pesach story, to be? Who is the imaginary man through whom we tell the story at Pesach? What, in other words, is Moses's vision of the ideal Jew? This ideal Jew, introduced to us in Deuteronomy 26, is the person through whom the authors of the Haggadah choose to tell the Jewish story on Seder night—and so deserves our consideration.

The first thing we learn about Moses's ideal Jew is that he is a regular guy. He is someone that everyone can identify with and that anyone can be. He is not a king or a prophet, a scholar or a warrior—he is, in the words of Rabbi David Fohrman, "a little old farmer."[1]

The second thing we learn about the ideal Jew is that he loves God and has a deeply personal relationship with him. He acknowledges that God has given him the Land, that God has given him his fruits, that it is God to whom the story should be attributed that God took the Jews out of Egypt, and that it is God who is deserving of our offerings and our prayers.

The third thing we learn about the ideal Jew is that he has a *Jewish* memory. The farmer says of his forefather, "*He* descended to Egypt," and a few words later says, "The Egyptians mistreated *us* and afflicted *us*." There is no "them"—only us. Jewish memory is the farmer's Jewish reality and presents in how he sees himself and tells the story of our liberation from Egypt.

The fourth thing we learn about the farmer is that he is a Zionist. The farmer's full communion with his memory demonstrates the observation of the historian Yosef Hayim Yerushalmi, "Only in Israel and nowhere else is the injunction to remember felt as a religious imperative to an entire people."[2] The farmer thanks God for having "brought us to this place, and . . . this Land, a Land flowing with milk and honey."

And we know what all this does for him emotionally and practically. First, emotionally. The farmer, who has traveled to Jerusalem to offer "the first of every fruit of the ground," is awash in gratitude. He is grateful that he is in the Land, he is grateful that the harvest succeeded, he is grateful that he has a special place to provide a welcome offering, he is grateful to God for enabling everything.

Gratitude, the authors of the Haggadah teach us by telling the story through the farmer, is not just a feeling. It is to be the driving idea in our life, the way we should relate to everything and everyone in the world. When observant Jews wake up in the morning, the first thing we say is: "Modeh Ani"—"Grateful am I." Why not the more straightforward "I am grateful"? Because, as Rabbi Shai Held writes, the strange locution is used "as if to suggest that there is no self without gratitude, that I do not become fully human unless and until I convey my gratitude to the One who created the gift that I am, and the even greater gift that I inhabit."[3]

Gratitude is, as Rabbi Held says, where the name *Jew* comes from. Leah, the first daughter of Laban, whom her father tricks Jacob into marrying, always feels unloved—indeed, per Genesis 29:31, "hated." She tries to win her husband's affection by deploying a doomed, tragic, and apparently ancient technique: She gets pregnant. She has three sons, hoping with the first two that her husband will love her and with the third that he will become attached to her. Love proves elusive, as does even attachment. She has a fourth son and names him Judah, saying, "This time I will praise the Lord." Leah's naming of her son articulates the essence of being a Jew: the ability to be grateful *even* in one's disappointment.

Jewish teaching holds that the coming of the Messiah will obviate the need for prayer and sacrifice except for one kind—that of thanksgiving. The theory behind this teaching is reflected every day in the central prayer of Jewish practice: the Amidah. During the recitation of the Amidah, the congregation fulfills its duty by having the chazzan (the cantor) repeat the prayers out loud. There is only one exception that demands the congregation also say the prayer. That is when the leader expresses his gratitude to God. Gratitude, the disposition with which we are to greet the new year and each new day, must be personally experienced and lived by everyone.

Gratitude might sound like an end state—a kind of Jewish nirvana. But Moses, in imagining the farmer, is just getting started. He decrees the expression that will define the way we experience gratitude.

"You shall *rejoice* with all the goodness that Hashem, your God, has given you and your household." The Torah does not say that the farmer is permitted joy, is encouraged to be joyous—but that he *shall* (he must!) be joyous. This conception of joy as a religious requirement starts in the Torah and will be reiterated *everywhere*: in the books of Psalms, Proverbs, Prophets, and elsewhere.

It applies within the experiences one is having. The eighteenth-century Polish rabbi and founder of Hasidic Judaism, the Baal Shem Tov, writes, "The ability to be joyous, by discerning the good and joyous within every experience, is considered as a biblical command."[4]

This applies to the plans one makes for the future. Rabbi Chizkiyah, as recorded in the Talmud, instructs, "In the future, a person will give a judgment and an accounting of everything [permissible] that his eye saw and he did not eat."[5] More than a millennium and a half later, Rabbi Samson Raphael Hirsch showed how at least he acted in response. As an old man, he went on a difficult trip to the Swiss Alps. His students asked him why. He replied, "I may only have a few years left, and when I stand before the Almighty on Judgment Day, I don't want Him to ask me, 'Shimshon, why didn't you see My Alps?'"[6]

And most of all, the religious obligation of joy applies to doing mitzvot—good deeds. In Deuteronomy 28, Moses sums up the Torah in part by listing the behaviors that will bring on curses. One of them is "because you did not serve Hashem, your God, amid joy and goodness of heart." Therefore, serving God—but doing it without joy—is accursed. Why?

This commandment guides us to the heart of a common question. What is the best way to gravitate to things we should do and avoid things we shouldn't? One common answer is: Identify the things you shouldn't do, and call upon your willpower to resist them. However, this is a surprisingly difficult task, even conceptually. The exercise of willpower depends on the successful application of several difficult tasks. The most important is what economists call "temporal discounting"—which is the phenomenon whereby we value the same thing more in the present than we do in the future. The exercise of willpower relies on the assumption that the temporal discounting rate is very low—i.e., that the benefits we will enjoy from having lost weight in the future will be sufficiently high to warrant our eating in accordance with our diet now. That diets almost always fail is a testament to the chance that willpower has against its challengers.

The science writer Brian Resnick reviewed the recent social science literature on willpower. As he reports in *Vox,* a 2011 German study published in the *Journal of Psychology and Social Psychology* had participants report throughout the day their desires, the severity of their desires, and their success in resisting those desires they wanted to rebuff. This, and a subsequent and similar study by Professor Marina Milyavskaya of McGill University, had the same findings. The people who are best at resisting temptations do not have more willpower or more ability to exercise it. They arrange to have fewer temptations and avoid a battle that their willpower is likely to lose.

How did the successful people in these experiments arrange to have fewer temptations? It is not as though they would have enjoyed the temptations less. They just find alternatives that they like as much or more, and thus don't have to call upon their willpower. As Professor Milyavskaya says, "'Want to' goals are more likely to be obtained than 'have to' goals. 'Want to' goals lead to experiences of fewer temptations."[7] This, perhaps, explains the success of the book *Eat This, Not That*—and why Moses commands us to *enjoy* our good deeds. If we *enjoy* doing mitzvot, we will want to do more of them—and will invariably perform them more frequently and better.

Another reason for the commandment to rejoice derives from the fact that joy, unlike happiness, is *always* expressed socially. Moses imagines the farmer, full of gratitude, rejoicing with seemingly everyone—the Levites, the foreigners, and his household. Rav Nachman of Breslov, perhaps channeling this vision, says, "Gratitude rejoices with her sister joy and is always ready to light a candle and have a party."[8] This "party" is literal and is expressed through the Jewish custom of *seudat hoda'ah* (thanksgiving feast). From ancient times until the present, we have a *seudat hoda'ah* when one survives a danger, after a birth, and at other moments when we burst with gratitude and respond with joy.

Moses imagines that this combination of gratitude and joy will have extensive moral implications as well. The genuinely grateful person always asks the source of his gratitude the same question: What can I do for you? And the farmer, who has such a close relationship with God, knows exactly what his divine partner wants. God wants what every parent wants. He wants the farmer to express his gratitude by taking care of God's children who need help—specifically, "the foreigner, the orphan, and the widow."[9]

His relationship with God is about to ascend to a new and higher level. This farmer through whom we tell the Pesach story will now ask God for blessings. And God, Moses imagines, will respond by commanding the farmer to "follow these decrees and statutes." That is easily comprehensible: As with any covenant or even partnership, each party has obligations. Then God's instruction gets very interesting.

God tells the farmer (and, correspondingly, all Jews who follow him) to perform his duties "with all your heart and all your soul." If we do that—if we perform our obligations with all our heart and soul—God will consider us to have walked "in his ways." It is then when we will become his "treasured people" and "holy" to him.

This sequence is deeply instructive, and is reminiscent of the aforementioned commandment to perform mitzvot with joy. Of course, any agreement involves mutual obligations. It is important to all concerned that each party fulfill his obligations completely and well. But does it matter how they *feel* when doing so? If a citizen pays his taxes in full accordance with the law, does it matter if he does so happily or begrudgingly?

Maybe not. But to God, as concerns his Torah, our attitude matters enormously—as we must do so with all our heart and all our soul. In fact, our becoming "a treasured people" to him depends on it.

This sequence reinforces a crucial idea that surfaces throughout Moses's relationship with God. It does not *only* matter to Moses that the farmer offers the first fruits to God. It matters that the farmer does so with gratitude and joy. It does not *only* matter to God that we discharge obligations to the neighbor and the stranger. It matters that we "love" these people.

The Torah's insistence that we fulfill the law with "all our heart and soul" and that we "love" the stranger leads to a fundamental question: If I do the right thing, why does it matter what I think and feel?

A consideration of the Jewish answer to this question can begin with a consideration of the Ten Commandments. They are generally about action—one should honor parents, not steal, not murder, not commit adultery, and so on. But then we have the Tenth Commandment: "Thou shalt not covet." Coveting is not an action. The Tenth Commandment—the one to which the other commandments lead, and into which they culminate—is a feeling, an attitude, a disposition, a character trait. But the Tenth Commandment—the one into which the others culminate—is, "Thou shalt not covet." The subject of the ultimate commandment—the one to which all the others lead—is not an action but a feeling, an attitude, a disposition.

Shortly after God gives us the Ten Commandments, which prohibit idolatry, we construct the golden calf and worship it. God decides to destroy us. The twentieth-century rabbi Nosson Tzvi Finkel observes that God's anger, as expressed in his criticism, is not directed at the idolatry—our action. Instead, God decides to destroy us for being a "stiff-necked people"—for our character. Fortunately, Moses is able to convince God to spare us.

This emphasis on the importance of thoughts and feelings, as distinct from actions, might seem discordant—as it is often said that Judaism is a religion of deed and not creed. This is true, but mainly in that God (as the prophets emphasize) hates ritual observance unaccompanied by sufficient concern for other people—and that people of all faiths can enjoy a close and sacred relationship with God. Yet the Bible is clear, as we see in 1 Samuel 16:7—that God "looks upon the heart." The farmer shows us why.

First, the distinction between a person's character and his actions is not always sharp. It is after the farmer feels gratitude and joy that he is so generous to the foreigner, the orphan, and the widow. One who feels happy about doing something—one who enjoys a task—will do more of it than someone who is only complying dutifully.

Second, the farmer is a regular person. As such, he has a *yetzer tov* (a good inclination) and a *yetzer hara* (an evil inclination). As discussed, these forces are always at battle. If the person's character is good—if he is full of gratitude, love, and openness—then the *yetzer tov* will fight its enemy on more advantageous ground.

Third, the farmer is given many instructions. He is told when to approach God, with what to approach God, and how to approach God, among others. But Moses does not imagine that every challenge or question (or anything close to it) will be covered by a divine instruction. Indeed, Moses says when summing up the Torah in Deuteronomy, "Do what is right and good in the sight of the Lord." Why, given the enormous number of rules, laws, and lessons produced by the Torah, would Moses need what lawyers today might call a catchall phrase? Because he wants the Torah to be a guidebook for all circumstances, and knows that every dynamic society will produce more moral decisions that any system of laws can account for. Therefore, good decision making, on an individual or a societal level, will depend largely on character. A good society depends on people doing the right thing not because they have to but because they want to. And one of the functions of the rules and lessons from the Torah is to teach people how to act and think in their absence.

Fourth, the function of good character is not *only* to encourage good actions on behalf of the singular individual. As discussed with reference to the wicked son, Jewish teaching has always emphasized the importance of associating with people who are positive influences. It is just as important to be that positive influence for others.

This, the Torah shows, is how good societies are constructed. In Genesis 19, God is willing to save Sodom if there are ten righteous people there. Ten people might have had a chance to influence enough others to redeem the city, but not fewer. Numbers matter. The greater the number of morally elevating people in a society, the greater the chances are that a random person will be positively influenced. A good society is constructed through a virtuous cycle drawn by people of character.

This, perhaps, is why the authors of the Haggadah choose to tell the story through one man who is distinguished for only one thing—his character. The ramifications for each of us and, Judaism teaches, perhaps the world, are profound. Rabbi Yisrael Salanter said,

When I was a young man, I wanted to change the world. When I could not change the world, I tried to change my nation. When I could not change my nation, I tried to change my city. When I could not change my city, I tried to change my household. When I could not change my household, I tried to change myself. Then, I realized that if I change myself then I can change my household. If I can change my household then I can change my city. If I can change my city then I can change my nation. If I can change my nation, I can change the world.[10]

This is inspiring: the most systemic change can begin by just chang-ing ourselves. But this by no means implies that changing oneself is easy. Changing one character trait, Rabbi Salanter says in another context, is harder than learning the entire Talmud by heart.[11]

That being said, there are no grounds for despair—only optimism. Every-thing important is difficult, including changing our character. If the farmer illustrates the importance of character, the Pharaoh (as we'll see) shows us how to change ours. And if we can change our character—which we can—we can change the world.

YOU ARE IN THE STORY

With seventy persons, your forefathers descended to Egypt.

Seven. Rabbi Eliyahu Safran of the Orthodox Union calls it "the perfect number. More than that, it is Judaism's most sacred number."[1]

Much of time, he cites Rabbi Shraga Simmons as saying, occurs as natural phenomena. This is true of the month, the day and the night, and even the seasons. These are regulated by rotations of the earth and the phases of the moon. But the days of the week? God ordains the seven-day week, and people implement it. It is the most ubiquitous use of seven, but it is far from the only one.

Jews sit shiva for seven days. The goal of repentence is to "return," to our proper state, and the word *shuv* (return) appears seven times in Parshat Nitzavim, which is read on Rosh Hashanah. A Jewish bride circles her groom seven times, and afterward, seven distinguished guests each recite a blessing. The great symbol of Judaism, the menorah (as distinct from the Hanukiah, which is something different), has seven branches.

Leviticus 23:15, which refers to the time between Pesach and Shavuot, states, "You shall count for yourselves . . . seven weeks; they shall be complete." In Numbers 11:16, God helps Moses to handle a crisis by telling him to appoint seventy elders as advisers. Deuteronomy 8:8 enumerates the *seven* species in the Land of Israel: grapes, wheat, pomegranates, figs, barley, olive oil, and dates. There are, according to the Mishnah, seventy holy days in the Torah— fifty-two Sabbaths, seven days of Pesach, eight days of Sukkot, the Day of Loud Blasts (Rosh Hashanah), Yom Kippur, and Shavuot.[2] The gematria for wine (the Hebrew word is *yayin*), the sacred Jewish beverage, is seventy.

So it is fitting, and perhaps even predictable, that the Haggadah tells us that "with seventy persons, your forefathers descended to Egypt."

Except there is a problem. There are only sixty-nine people, per Genesis 46:26, who descend to Egypt.[3]

Who is number seventy?

Each participant at the Seder. As we will see, the Haggadah instructs that we are still in the process of emerging from slavery and idolatry, and participation in this great Jewish New Year experience of contemplation and commitment, refreshment, and renewal is one of the key moments in that process. If one generation stops, the work of the hundreds of generations who came before us—including the sixty-nine—is for naught. The perpetuation of the story and the continuation of the Jewish people depend on each one of us. We are neither historians nor observers, we are neither commentators nor celebrants. We are participants.

Each of us is number seventy.

This is not a magical or mystical notion. It is within the essence of what it means to be a Jew, and in a way, that is core to the Pesach celebration. The acknowledgment of each person as number seventy ratifies the purpose of Pesach—to assimilate history into memory, to relive the Exodus, to establish every Jew as a member of a community that stretches across generations and across geographies as one.

STARS

*Now Hashem, your God, has made you
as numerous as the stars of heaven.*

We started as seventy. But now we are "as numerous as the stars of heaven"—and, the Haggadah continues, great and mighty. This Haggadah passage derives from Deuteronomy 10:22, which explains how God made us like the stars of heaven. He did so "for abundance." Jews have been called a lot of things, good and bad, but abundant? We have been around for several thousand years and now number approximately 15 million. It only took the Mormons 150 years to get the same number of people. The Pentecostal denomination of Protestant Christianity, which was founded in the early twentieth century, now has approximately 300 million adherents.

Did the Torah and the Haggadah get it wrong?

These questions can be approached through a lens provided by Maimonides. He says that given that the Torah is true and that a scientific fact is true, they can't conflict. If they appear to conflict, the fault must be in our interpretation of the Torah.[1]

And as often happens, a (or the) correct way to interpret the Torah is found in the Torah itself. In Deuteronomy, Moses says, "The Lord did not set his love upon you, nor choose you, because you were more in number than any people; for you were the fewest of people."[2]

So in one part of the Torah, we are as "numerous as the stars in the sky." In another part of the Torah, we are "the fewest of people." The key to understanding each passage just might be the other.

These two concepts can be harmonized when the numbers are considered on a relative basis. The first known archaeological reference to Jews is from the Merneptah Stele, which is an Egyptian artifact from the thirteenth-century B.C.E. It says: "Israel is laid waste, its seed is no more." This would have been a very good prediction. There are dozens of peoples mentioned in the Bible, including the Jews, and there is not a trace of any of the others. How are there any Jews? The Catholic historian Paul Johnson notes, "Above all, that the Jews should still survive when all those other ancient peoples were transmuted or vanished into the oubliettes of history, was wholly predictable. How could it be otherwise? Providence decreed it and the Jews obeyed."[3]

It is a fact against all odds that there are any Jews at all. The difference between the expected (a hard zero) and the actual number of Jews in the world (fifteen million) is *numerous*. For anyone who loves or even appreciates Jews and/or Judaism, the existence of any Jews or anything Jewish constitutes a miracle. For anyone who doesn't, it is a cosmic misfortune. For everyone, it is a lot.

Numerosity as explained relative to what would have been rationally predicted is one explanation. As we have seen, the Torah and Haggadah are full of examples where different explanations of the same thing can simultaneously be true and instructive. This is another such case.

In Exodus 30, God tells Moses to take a census of the children of Israel. However, this census must be conducted *without* counting the people. Instead, each individual must contribute a half shekel. The coins are counted. This might seem like a roundabout way of doing what should be a simple task. You want to know how many people there are? One, two, three—just count them! But that would create two problems, both of which are solved by counting the half shekels.

First, the conventional way of counting people obliterates the uniqueness and significance of each individual. The recognition of God's uniqueness is so central to Jewish religiosity that Maimonides lists it as the second principle of Jewish faith—right after the belief in one God. "I believe with complete faith that the Creator, blessed be His name, is unique and there is no likeness like Him in any way."[4] And as people created in his image, each person is also unique.

Second, as Rabbi Jonathan Sacks notes, nations take censuses "to establish their strength: military, economic or simply demographic. The assumption underlying every census is: there is strength in numbers. The more numerous a people, the stronger it is."[5] Attribute this logic to Jews,

Rabbi Sacks writes, and "the Jewish people would long ago have given way to despair."

How could we be small in number—and also as numerous as the stars? There are two ways. The first is identified by Rabbi Sacks. "Ask Jews to give, and then count their contributions." This insight changes the question aroused by the stars. It is not: How many Jews are there? It is: What are the contributions of the Jews?

The second is revealed in Leviticus 26:8. It reads, "Five of you shall give chase to a hundred, and a hundred of you shall give chase to ten thousand." If, in the first instance, it takes five to chase a hundred, why would it take only a hundred to chase ten thousand in the second? If the ratio required for a successful chase were 1:20, the second numerator should be five hundred—not one hundred. Yet, somehow, the author of the Torah determined that an individual in a group of one hundred could be five times as productive than if he were in a group of five.

The mathematician Alex Klein, in an analysis of this Torah passage, explains, "The ratio between the number of people comprising the society and the relations between them is not linear."[6] When people form relationships and alliances, their power grows geometrically even as their numbers expand arithmetically. For example, three people of equal capacity do not gain in intelligence or strength *individually* when they decide to work together. But they will likely be able to accomplish a lot more as a group than three times what each could do on his own. The leverage they will derive as a team is a function of the closeness of the team. A loosely affiliated group that is more like a collection of individuals will not receive the five times the leverage experienced by the tightly aligned group described in Leviticus.

This is not just theoretical network economics. One of the great sources of Jewish history is the Cairo Geniza—the storeroom of the Great Ezra Synagogue in Egypt where tens of thousands of documents from around a thousand years of early Jewish life were discovered in the nineteenth century. One of the remarkable finds was a check—from, probably, two hundred years before the deployment of paper money. The check, written by a Jew in Baghdad to a Jew in Cairo circa the tenth century, read: "Please give Joseph, the bearer of this check, a hundred coins." The entire basis of this check, and the financial system that it represented, was the existence of a global Jewish community and the trust that existed throughout it. A couple of hundred years later, a Christian merchant in London remarked, "As long as Isaac of York trusted his brother Jacob of Marseilles, and both of them trusted their cousin Joseph of Jerusalem, all three stood to make a profit."[7] With a community like that, activated from London to Baghdad, a small number of people could perform as if their numbers were as great as the stars.

The Haggadah could have used other metaphors for size and taught those same lessons. For instance, God tells Abraham in Genesis 22:17 that his descendants would be as numerous as the stars in the sky *and* the sand on the seashore. Why might the authors of the Haggadah have used stars—or only stars?

The defining fact of each star is its uniqueness. Every star has a different size, brightness, and motion. This fact was known in the ancient world. Isaiah 40:26, quoted in Psalm 147, states, "He counts the numbers of stars, he calls them all by name." The Cornell University astronomer David Kornreich estimates that there are 1 septillion stars in the universe.[8] This number is too large to really understand, and the ancients knew that. Despite their cosmic quantity, God knows each of the stars by name.

We, like the stars, are many individuals in a large system. Which counts—the individual or the community? The answer, according to Isaiah: both. The fundamental principle of Judaism, as we learn from the response to the wicked son, is the strength of the community. The goodness of the community, as we learn from the farmer, is a function of the character of its individual inhabitants. And the character of its individual inhabitants, as we learn from the stars, will be determined to the extent that each person realizes that his sacred uniqueness is appreciated by God.

The contemplation of stars leads us to another conclusion—one made by the *Sfas Emes*. He wrote that while there are a lot of stars, there is still a lot of sky. When we look at the stars, we see their light and are reminded of our purpose as Jews: to bring light unto the darkness. It is our job to be to the world what the stars are to the sky. Rabbi Shai Held, building on the *Sfas Emes*, writes that the stars do not eliminate the darkness. They do not turn the sky into a "palace of light," but they do brighten places that would otherwise be completely dark.[9] In this lies one of the primary Jewish responsibilities, articulated in the first-century by Rabbi Tarfon: "It is not your responsibility to finish the work, but you are not free to desist from it either."[10]

Stars served another purpose in ancient times. This is stellar navigation, which was the only way for ancient people to travel at night. As all stars except for the sun appear to the naked eye to be fixed, stellar navigation is an ancient, well-known, and reliable method. In the Book of Job, celestial navigation was used to prove the mastery of God: "Can you bind the chains of the Pleiades? Can you loosen Orion's belt? Can you bring forth the constellations in their seasons?"[11]

Does celestial navigation work? The U.S. Navy discontinued teaching it only after GPS became ubiquitous in 1997—and reinstituted it almost twenty years later when threats to GPS systems became ubiquitous.[12] The U.S. Merchant Marine Academy has always taught it, with mastery required to join the Coast Guard. It is also still taught in the Israel Defense Forces.

God enabled celestial navigation to work physically. The stars analogy in the Haggadah reminds us that God wants us to enable it to work existentially. The prophet Isaiah, in one of the most soaring statements in religion, said: "I will make you a light unto the nations, so My salvation will reach the ends of the earth . . . nations will walk by your light, kings by your shining radiance." That is the single greatest moral cry to the Jews, something that our New Year celebration would have to include—as it does right here.

RISKING CONGRATULATIONS

Numerous—as it says: I made you as numerous as the plants of the field; you grew and developed, and became charming, beautiful of figure; your hair grown long; but you were naked and bare. And I passed over you and saw you downtrodden in your blood and I said to you: "Through your blood shall you live!"

Everything about the passage that goes by the name *two bloods* is jarring. It comes from Ezekiel, a biblical book written long after the conclusion of the Torah, and has nothing to do with the story of the Exodus. It is hard to imagine that anyone assigned to review all Jewish thought to tell the story of the Exodus would have selected this. This passage, which the Talmud calls "the chapter of rebuke,"[1] is revolting, embarrassing, and simply hideous.

First, the story. Ezekiel 16 tells the story of Jerusalem—portrayed as an infant in the land of the Canaanites whose father is an Amorite and whose mother is a Hittite. God observes this infant on the day of her birth, noting that her cord is not cut, nor is she washed, rubbed in salt, or wrapped in cloth—a direct result, we are told in the text, of no one having "pity or compassion enough to do any of these things for you. Rather, you were thrown into the open field, for on the day you were born you were despised."

The infant, Jerusalem, is abandoned to die.

God comes to the rescue. He sees her "kicking about in your blood and as you lay there in your blood I said to you, with your blood, 'Live!'" And she lives. God makes her grow "like a plant of the field." She develops to where "your breasts had formed and your hair had grown."

The young woman gets older, specifically to where she is "old enough for love." The relationship of God as the father to this surrogate daughter changes. He gives her his "solemn oath" and takes her as his wife. He gives her magnificent clothing of leather, linen, silk, and cloth to wear and jewelry for her hands, neck, nose, ears, and head. She has become "royalty."

Now as the daughter and spouse of God—a woman of beauty, wealth, and renown—she has it all. What does she do? She uses her "beauty and . . . fame" to become a prostitute. She engages in prostitution with her Egyptian "neighbors," who are distinguished by their "giant genitals." Unsatisfied by the Egyptians, she gives herself to the Philistines and the Babylonians as well.

Then—she murders her children and sacrifices them to idols.

But in the end, God says she will atone and seems resigned to forgive her—as he had made a "covenant," a promise that cannot be broken. Lest the daughter/spouse think that she will not suffer for her actions, she shall "remember and be ashamed" forever.

So why would the authors of the Haggadah have included this story in the guidebook that we use to tell the story of the Exodus to our children?

For two reasons. First, to help us understand the nature of freedom. And second, to help us evaluate the moments in our lives.

On Seder night, we relive our transition from slavery to freedom. We were slaves, but due to God's grace, we are now free! It seems like a great triumph, the ultimate cause for celebration. Into that celebration comes Ezekiel 16 with a powerful reminder of one of the salient themes of the Pesach story. We can, like Jerusalem in Ezekiel 16, be given the ultimate freedom and all the opportunities that it provides. And we could respond by directing that freedom toward the most unholy, selfish, and destructive ends.

This instruction leads us to focus on how and why freedom is described as it is in the Pesach sequence in the Torah. We are reminded that God never just says, "Let my people go"—but always follows it with a version of "so that they might serve me." God does not free us from Egypt so that we can do whatever we want so long as we don't hurt anyone. He frees us, as he explains in Exodus 13:9, "so that Hashem's Torah will be in your mouth." Freedom, properly exercised, is not an accomplishment to be celebrated. It is an opportunity that *needs* a purpose. Per the eighteenth-century British political philosopher Edmund Burke, "The effect of liberty to individuals is that they might do what they please. We ought to see what it will please them to do before we risk congratulations."[2]

With the Haggadah providing clarity regarding the importance of distinguishing between an opportunity and an accomplishment—and the ease with which they can be confused—we are guided to another question. Where else in our lives, aside from the consideration of freedom, might we need to be careful about risking congratulations? Where might we make the strategic mistake of saying "Mission Accomplished" when the task is just beginning? Upon consideration, everywhere.

On October 12, 1979, the great Los Angeles Lakers center Kareem Abdul-Jabbar hit a hook shot at the buzzer to win the first game of the NBA season for the Lakers over the San Diego Clippers. The veteran all-star, who had been a heralded champion since his high school days at Power Memorial Academy in the 1960s, headed to the bench. Abdul-Jabbar's twenty-year-old rookie teammate, Magic Johnson, intercepted his center to hug him as though, the television commentator said, "he had just won the NCAA championship."[3] The *Los Angeles Times* reported Abdul-Jabbar's reaction: It was "perhaps the first time in years he had laughed on a basketball court."[4] It was ironic laughter, the response of the man of experience observing a rookie celebrate at a laughably premature stage in a long process.

Magic Johnson was fortunate to have the mentorship of a captain who, perhaps by having led a NBA championship team himself, knew what it took to earn congratulations and deserve celebration. One does not need to be a NBA champion to be confronted with this challenge. What are weddings about? Two people who *aspire* to be a happily married couple—an endeavor with challenges and responsibilities to come, and a success rate that hovers well below even. What are fiftieth anniversaries about? Generally, two people who have merged into one, created a multigenerational family, and experienced love, struggle, loss, and triumph together to emerge stronger than ever. Do our modes of celebrating each accurately reflect these realities?

The same set of questions applies to every celebration—especially our Pesach celebration. We discussed earlier how perhaps the best way to understand a people is to observe how they celebrate. Why do we celebrate our Festival of Freedom by taking such an encompassing, comprehensive, and sometimes difficult moral inventory? To remind ourselves, perhaps, of the lesson being taught by the "chapter of rebuke." Being given freedom, as God provides "Jerusalem" in Ezekiel and us in the Exodus, is nothing to celebrate. The question of whether we deserve a celebration depends on what we do with the freedom. In dreams, the poet William Butler Yeats said, *begins* responsibility. Our Pesach celebration helps us identify those responsibilities and provides us with the infrastructure to fulfill them in accordance with our ideals and our potential. Our genuine freedom is the ability to make it worthy of celebration.

WHY DID GOD WAIT?
WHEN BAD THINGS HAPPEN
TO GOOD PEOPLE

The Egyptians did evil to us and afflicted us.

The slave experience endured for more than a hundred years. It was, as this passage from the Haggadah and the previously discussed historical account demonstrate, extremely brutal. And contemplating it, especially on Seder evening when we recognize God's power and majesty, leads us inevitably to one question.

Why did God allow this experience to endure for so long? Or more fundamentally: Why does God, who is omnipotent and as our God in history cares about everything in our lives, permit evil?

God granted people free will, and this inevitably means that people will act in and out of accordance with God. God could not have both granted free will and prevented its usage. That would violate the laws of logic, which he also gave us. Either we have free will or we don't. This dynamic is not a reflection of God's lack of power, but of his omnipotence. One way to exercise omnipotence is to relinquish some power, never to be able to capture it again. This is what God did when he granted people free will.

Human suffering, thus, is the inevitable casualty of free will. This possibility might explain the Pharaoh enslaving the Jews. But it does not explain a child who dies of cancer, a pit bull that mauls an elderly couple taking a walk, or the Indian Ocean earthquake and tsunami of 2004 that killed 225,000 people across a dozen countries.

Why might such acts, that have nothing to do with free will, happen in a world governed by an omnipotent and benevolent God? Why do bad things happen to good people?

One way to approach this question is through the fact that the Hebrew language has two words that describe why: *lama* and *madua*. Their meanings are entirely different.

Madua seeks to explain what the *Hebrew Language Detective* calls "the cause of a past occurrence," as in: "*Why* did the item dropped from the table fall to the ground?"[1] *Lama* seeks to explain "toward what end," as in: "*Why* did you behave that way?"

The English language might (perhaps unfortunately) have only "why"—but we have two meanings as well. In fact, they explain our most familiar joke. When the questioner asks, "Why did the chicken cross the road?" he is asking a *madua* question—but receives a *lama* answer. The result of this confusion is funny.

But the distinction does not usually lead to laughs. When Moses is on the mountain with God, receiving the Ten Commandments, the people create an idol (a golden calf) and worship it in what is probably an orgy. God is furious, and Moses asks him why he is so angry. It would make no sense for Moses to use the scientific *why*. Why (*madua*) is God angry? Uh—because you are gone for a few weeks, and the people respond by creating an idol and having an orgiastic worship experience around it.

But that isn't the question. Moses is asking the *lama* question. To what end, he asks God, is your anger directed? It is this question that causes God to realize that his anger does not serve any purpose, and in fact he needs the Jewish people to accomplish his goals.[2]

Why does God keep the Jews enslaved for so long? Or, more broadly, why do bad things happen to good people? Attempts to answer this question from the perspective of *madua* are often simply hideous. They usually involve a commentator identifying something about the victim that he finds objectionable—sometimes even related to the religiosity of the victim. The commentator then says that God either directed or permitted the suffering of the victim as punishment.

How could a putatively intelligent or religious person think that he knows God so well that he can precisely identify what God considers a crime and a punishment? It starts with the fact, as Nassim Taleb has demonstrated, that human beings crave explanations and thus prefer non-sensical ones to none.[3] The kind of nonsense that purports to explain why God would have allowed a horrible event to happen migrates to a confusion of *madua* and *lama*. We can scientifically explain why a ball thrown in the air comes down, but not why a bad thing happened to a good person. But asking the *lama* question—asking to what end something bad happened—presents an opportunity.

Those who ask *lama* don't ask the reason that something like an earthquake happened. They create the reason, and in doing teach us—by doing—the meaning of another Hebrew word. This is *mashber*, which means both "crisis" and "birthing chair." We see *lama* in action when the parent of a child who died of cancer works to cure that cancer or comfort families in similar situations, when a famous athlete writes about his depression to make it socially acceptable for others suffering from mental illness to acknowledge theirs, and when Holocaust survivors exited the worst Jewish experience in history and in only a few years helped create the greatest Jewish achievement since God gave Moses the Torah at Mount Sinai.

This logic should not imply that there is anything acceptable or redemptive about suffering. The *lama* question is only available to a heroic person in a conducive circumstance. The distinction between the scientific and the existential *why* is, and should be, no solace to the boys forced to rape their mothers in the Congo, the pregnant Jewish women who in the Chmelensky Massacre in mid-seventeenth-century Poland had their babies cut from their stomachs and replaced by living cats after the women's hands were cut off so they could not remove the animals, the Yazidi women who were made sex slaves by Islamist terrorists, the Jews who were gassed in Nazi concentration camps, or to all those who have lost loved ones to plague, earthquakes, tsunamis, and hurricanes.

There is a well-known Hebrew expression: "Gam Zu Letova"—"This, too, is for the good." Jews say this after a misfortune to encourage the sufferer (who may be oneself) to realize that there could be something good, even if unforeseen, to come from her pain. This sentiment has its place, as it can help the sufferer to ask the *lama* question. But sometimes the situation is so bad that saying that it is for the good is worse than deeply insensitive: It is hideous. Some situations are irredeemably bad and should be recognized as such.

How, then, should we look at the long Egyptian slavery? Or how should we look at tragedies, whether or not they are the result of man's evil, in our world? Once again, the Torah has the guidance we need. In Leviticus 10:1, Aaron's sons Nadav and Abihu are killed after bringing a "strange fire" to the altar. Moses tries to console his brother—but Aaron, we are told, "was silent." From that story we learn the first response to offer a victim. In the words of Maimonides, "We do not relate teachings of Torah law or homiletic insights in the home of a mourner. Instead, we sit in grief."[4]

Maimonides is right. One cannot, as Moses learned, productively tell a sufferer that what happened is all for the good—let alone that she should create something positive from her agony. Sometime later, a *lama* answer can emerge. But only, possibly, later.

How, in the spirit of *lama*, can we understand why God allowed the slavery in Egypt to last for hundreds of years? Perhaps so that we could forever testify to the evil of slavery, so that we could treasure freedom and experience it with gratitude, so that we could develop a philosophy of freedom that would inspire the world, so that we would learn to prioritize education and allow its fruits to benefit the Jewish people and eventually all mankind.

Still, there are limits. A Jew can, and perhaps must, ask whether God could have taught the same lessons through something other than centuries of brutal slavery. And perhaps no response to that challenge will suffice. Sometimes, perhaps, the distinction between *lama* and *madua* just will not, and should not, help in the wake of the suffering. In those cases, Rabbi Milton Steinberg provides a perspective: "The believer has to account for the existence of unjust suffering. The atheist has to account for everything else."[5]

JEW HATRED, EXPLAINED

The Egyptians did evil to us—as it says: Let us deal
with them wisely lest they multiply and, if we happen to
be at war they might join our enemies and fight against us.
And they afflicted us—as it says: They set taskmasters over
them in order to oppress them with their burdens; and they
built Pithom and Raamses as treasure cities for Pharaoh.

They imposed hard labor upon us.

Anti-Semitism is often called "the world's oldest hatred." There are two questions about it that have plagued the many people who have tried to understand and repel it. Why do Jew haters hate us, and what can we do about it? The answer to both questions is in this Haggadah passage, inclusive of the three verses that immediately precede it.

In Exodus 1:7–12, the narrator tells us that the

Children of Israel were fruitful, teemed, increased, and became strong. A new king arose over Egypt, who did not know of Joseph. He said to his people, Behold! The people, the Children of Israel, are far more numerous and stronger than we. Come, let us outsmart them lest they become numerous and it may be that if a war will occur, they, too, might join our enemies, and will wage war against us and go up from the land. . . . But as much as [the Egyptians] would afflict them [the Jews], so they [the Jews] increased and spread out; and they [the Egyptians] became disgusted because of the Children of Israel.

A comprehensive understanding of Jew hatred is revealed by unpacking this passage.

The first thing to note is the observation, made independently by Rabbis Adin Steinsaltz and Meir Schweiger, that frames the discussion. This moment is the first time that the Jews are identified, by a person, as a people. Before the Pharaoh identified us as the "Children of Israel," we were a fractured and dysfunctional family. By calling us the "Children of Israel," our first enemy made us a people.[1]

It might seem curious that we proudly became a people and adopted our name (Children of Israel) as a result of a designation made by an enemy. This practice, however, became common. The term *queer* was coined as an insult in the late nineteenth century and was later adopted with pride by the LGBTQ community. The term *neoconservative* was designated by the socialist Michael Harrington and was immediately embraced by those in the group.

The first characterization of the Children of Israel is as "fruitful"—a seemingly positive association with God's directive in Genesis 1:28 to be "fruitful and multiply." But this positive sense is immediately overridden with the term *teemed* (or *swarmed*). This term is always associated with the lowest animals. The Torah in Leviticus 11:29 speaks of the "swarming things that swarm on the ground"—identified as a mole rat, lizards of various kinds, and mice—as not only being unkosher to eat but being forbidden to even touch. Even an article of clothing or wood that touches such a creature is considered unclean.

This is how the Pharaoh thinks of the Jews. The Pharaoh's characterization of Jews as swarming animals would become a standard expression of Jew haters. The 1940 Nazi propaganda film *The Eternal Jew* portrays Jews as rats. In 2018, Louis Farrakhan tweeted, "I'm not an anti-Semite. I'm anti-termite." This association has been further adapted by haters including the Hutus who called the Tutsis "cockroaches" in the run-up to the 1994 Rwandan genocide and the Europeans who put a rat on the shoulder of the caricatured Jew in the 2018 Aalst Carnival.[2]

The Pharaoh immediately moves from the most direct form of Jew hatred to another that has become just as prevalent. He says that the Jews are capable of, and at least potentially desirous of, overthrowing his regime. The text gives us no indication that the Jews, a group that was not even a people before the Pharaoh declares it so, have any political or military capabilities—let alone the wherewithal to threaten the most powerful regime in the world. Thus, the Pharaoh, in one breath, invents the Jews as a people and the paranoid notion of the inexplicably powerful and nefarious Jew.

Modern manifestations of this idea proliferate in accusations of Jews controlling the global finance system, the media, and even governments. In 1922, the German general Erich Ludendorff attributed the defeat of Germany in the Great War to "the supreme government of the Jewish people [which] was working hand in hand with France and England. Perhaps it was leading them." In 2003, Malaysian prime minister Mahathir Mohamad gave a speech at the Organization of the Islamic Conference, stating, "The Jews rule the world by proxy." Henry Ford's 1920s era pamphlet *The International Jew* combined both elements of Jew hatred in saying, "If there is one quality that attracts Jews, it is power. Wherever the seat of power may be, thither they swarm obsequiously."[3]

The Pharaoh's statement in the Torah, quoted in the Haggadah, also reveals a common tactic of the Jew hater. The Pharaoh says in Exodus 1:10, "Let us outsmart them"—and therefore does not command the extermination of the Jews immediately. He starts a slave system that gradually becomes more brutal, specifically dictates that the Jewish girls should live (as he commands the death of the boys), and co-opts Jews into being the foremen to enforce their compatriots' servitude.

Indeed, the system of slavery the Pharaoh constructed could have fooled people into concluding that he was not a Jew hater but an ambitious builder who is, like other rulers of his day, using the slave labor available to him. But he later has the Jews find straw for their bricks from all over Egypt. The slaves, predictably, are much less productive. If the Pharaoh is primarily interested in building, he would supply the Jews with the raw materials so that they could work with maximum efficiency. But as his primary interest is Jew hatred, he sacrifices this efficiency to increase Jewish suffering.

The Pharaoh regards the increased suffering of the Jews as a good thing itself—and, like every good thing, worth sacrificing something for (in this case, efficiency). The increased suffering of the Jews has another benefit for him. The more the Jews suffer, the more the Egyptians "became disgusted because of the Children of Israel." The increased disgust, therefore, leads to intensification of the slavery. Fired with "disgust," we learn in Exodus 1:13, the Egyptians enslave the Children of Israel with "crushing hardness." That phrase—"crushing hardness"—is used again in the immediately following verse, suggesting that the disgust is really an inspiration for the Egyptians to apply "crushing hardness" as often and obsessively as they could.

One might think that Jewish weakness (as exacerbated by the "crushing hardness") would diminish the Egyptian hatred of the Jews. It certainly removes any reason for it, as a weakened, enslaved Jewish people could not plausibly threaten the strongest regime in the world. But the Jew hatred intensifies as the Jews become weaker. It is by making the Jews noticeably weak that the Pharaoh primes the Egyptian society to join in his Jew hatred, and the plans that come with it—particularly, per Exodus 1:16, the drowning of all Jewish boys as they are born.

If we are surprised by this—if we think that weakness invites compassion and sympathy—it is only because we have internalized the Torah commandments to love the stranger and care for the foreigner, the orphan, and the widow. It is not the natural or normal way that feelings go, but rather the Torah's redirection of them.

The Pharaoh's system of Jew hatred unfolds steadily but gradually, in accordance with his early recognition that he has to be "smart" about it. We know from the existence of the "mixed multitude" who join us in the desert that not everyone in Egypt wanted to eliminate the Jews at all costs. If the Pharaoh had rushed into the final solution—slavery of "crushing hardness," the murder of all Jewish baby boys—he would have risked an internal revolt. He needed to diminish the conviction and influence of those people in order for him to be safely able to go as far as he did, and he was able to accomplish that by creating more Jewish weakness.

The tactic of the Jew hater to operate slowly, methodically, and thus subtly would become widely adopted. Hitler declared his genocidal intentions in *Mein Kampf* (1925) and slowly readied the German people for the Final Solution, which was hatched seventeen years later. Today, Jew haters with any sophistication say that they are fine with Jews, speak warmly of Jewish friends, and even drop a phrase in Hebrew—and work to delegitimize, weaken, or destroy the country where more than half of the world's Jews live and where the Jewish dream is being lived. The intelligence of the go-slow strategy is exemplified by how it allows people and nations to inflict maximal harm on the Jewish people while enabling them to plausibly claim that they abhor Jew hatred.

The Pharaoh's intense hatred of the Jews, even when we are demonstrably weak, arouses one to ask a fundamental question that has often been asked of Jew haters: Why do they hate us? The answer is provided in Exodus 1:9. In literally the same breath, the Pharaoh identifies the Jews as a people and invents the hatred of Jews. The Jewish people started at the very same moment as Jew hatred.

Why do Jew haters despise us? There is no right or wrong answer because there is no answer. It is like asking the rabbi at a New York synagogue why he lets the Knicks go so many years without a title. *Jew hatred has nothing to do with Jews.* We did not even exist as a people before the Pharaoh declared his Jew hatred. And the fact that the Jews have nothing to do with causing Jew hatred answers another persistent question. How can Jew haters have despised us for being regime threats, regime enablers, Christ killers, rootless cosmopolitans, parochial nationalists, heartless capitalists, subversive socialists, atheists, religious fanatics, racially impure, racists, and colonialists?

Although these seem like a diverse and mutually exclusive collection of accusations, they have a unifying consistency. It is revealed in this Torah passage. The Pharaoh is able to become a Jew hater by associating the Jew with the destruction of the thing most precious to him: the preservation of his regime. In seemingly every case of Jew hatred since, the Jew hater has also associated the Jew with the opposite of the thing most sacred to him.[4]

The most important thing for the Pharaoh was the preservation of his regime, so he said that the Jews wanted to overthrow him. In the Middle Ages, the host (the body of Jesus Christ, manifest in bread) was considered the most holy object for Christians, so they routinely massacred Jews they accused of desecrating the host.[5] Voltaire was the quintessential intellectual, so he called Jews "plagiarists in everything."[6] Karl Marx was a Communist, so he wrote of the Jews, "What is his worldly God? Money . . . Money is the jealous God of Israel, in the face of which no other god may exist. . . . The chimerical nationality of the Jew is the nationality of the merchant, of the man of money in general."[7] Hitler was a racist and a national socialist, so he accused Jews of being a "parasitic race" that worshipped money.

Today, those who consider human rights or anti-colonialism to be their defining ideology often single out for condemnation the Jewish state.[8] Those who consider white nationalism to be their defining characteristic invariably end up chanting things like, "The Jews will not replace us."[9] *Out* magazine called Tel Aviv "the gay capital of the Middle East," and *The Boston Globe* declared Tel Aviv more gay-friendly than San Francisco, Berlin, or Amsterdam.[10] Yet organizers of the Chicago Dyke March, like their counterparts in Madrid, forbid pro-Israel Jewish groups from marching, alleging that the Israeli flag is a symbol of something called "pink-washing."[11]

Is the idea of pink-washing incomprehensible? Sure—in the same way that the Pharaoh's concern that the Israelites were plotting to topple him is incomprehensible. As we will discuss with reference to the plagues, people are capable of believing practically anything to confirm their beliefs. The Jew hater is similarly capable of believing anything about the people who represents the opposite of his most sacred belief.

If Jew hatred existed for as long as the Jewish people and if it fulfills a need of the hater independent of the Jew, there are several profound implications for contemporary philo-Semites. First, there is no point in trying to talk a Jew hater out of his loathing. A lover of the Jews will achieve nothing by explaining to a Marxist that Jews care about more than money, to a BDS activist that Israeli companies have a lot of women on their boards, or to a white nationalist that Jews don't want to have anything to do with him (let alone replace him).

Jew hatred is structurally indifferent to any realities that can be clarified, facts that can be taught, and certainly to any concessions that can be made. This is because it is not about facts, realities, or anything else to do with the Jews. As the historian Barbara Tuchman concluded toward the end of her long career, "Anti-Semitism is independent of its logic. What Jews do or fail to do is not the determinant. The impetus comes out of the needs of the persecutors and a particular political climate."[12]

This story of the Pharaoh's attitude towards Jews in the beginning of Exodus not only diagnoses Jew hatred but also describes how we should fight it. As discussed, the sight of weak Jews encourages and enables the Pharaoh to increase his oppression. We learn from the Pharaoh that Jew hatred increases commensurate with its success. The weaker the Jews are, the more virulent Jew haters become. Barbara Tuchman again: "The rule of human behavior here is that yielding to an enemy's demands does not satisfy them but, by exhibiting a position of weakness, augments them. It does not terminate hostility but excites it."[13]

The implications for those who want to fight Jew hatred are as relevant now as they have been at any point since the Exodus story was first read. This passage from Exodus 1 suggests three ways to fight Jew hatred and one way not to. Jews often respond to Jew hatred by asserting our status as victims, past or present.[14] This, as the Torah teaches us, completely misreads the psychology of the Jew hater. To fight Jew hatred, the Jew should be strong, proud, and powerful.

This is not a phenomenon unique to Jews. It is a staple of human psychology. In the classic eighteenth-century book of parental advice *Chesterfield's Letters,* the British lord tells his son, "There is nothing people will bear more impatiently, or forgive less, than contempt."[15] And from the Pharaoh to those chronicled by Chesterfield, people have responded to weakness with contempt.

How should the Jew avoid contempt and become strong, proud, and powerful? The answer to this question suggests the first of three ways to fight Jew hatred that derive from the Exodus story. We should refuse on principle to engage a Jew hater on his terms, work to strengthen the Jewish state, raise proudly Jewish children, build Jewish institutions, and engage in the world in an effort to be a light unto the nations. After all this, the Jew hater will still despise the Jew. But he will be robbed of the contemptuousness that makes his hatred more contagious, virulent, and dangerous.

Second, we can learn from the previously discussed story of Shifra and Puah—the Egyptian midwives who disobey the Pharaoh's orders to kill all the baby boys. Their technique is telling. They tell the Pharaoh that they are trying to kill the boys but the Jewish women give birth too quickly in the fields. This triggers the Pharaoh's association of Jews with animals, and so he believes them. The insight behind their tactic: Accept that the Jew hater will try to be smart, but realize that Jew hatred is so fundamentally ridiculous that the hater's argument will always have some glaring stupidity that can be used to thwart its execution.

Third, the Jew can combine another lesson from Shifra and Puah with the learning derived from the Haggadah's statement, "All who are needy." There is no meaningful notion of human independence. There will never be enough Jews to address those who would destroy us. But as long as there are enough gentile friends and allies with whom we can become interdependent, we will be fine.

Moses is the greatest Jew, God's indispensable partner in liberating the Jews from Egypt. He needs God to overcome the Pharaoh's Jew-hating regime. He also needs gentiles. There would, of course, be no Jews, no Judaism, and no Torah without Moses. Moses survives only because he is adopted by the Pharaoh's daughter. Many of his male contemporaries who survive infancy and are around for the Exodus owe their lives to the righteousness and courage of Shifra and Puah. And Moses thrives as a leader only because of the advice and love of his gentile mentor and father-in-law, Yitro.

Jew hatred is, as it always has been, rampant—in places expected and surprising, articulated crudely and with cleverness. Is Jew hatred now (or at any point) rising or falling? It has always been ubiquitous and resistant to measurement, so we don't know. But one thing about it is knowable. It is the worst time in history to be a Jew hater. The Jews have a remarkable nation-state. Almost every Jew in the world is free to practice his faith. We have boundless opportunities to learn, develop, and build great Jewish institutions and communities. We have, for the first time, tens of millions of deeply devoted gentile allies and potential allies—a number that is growing fast and therefore may be understated. This is the best time in history to be a Jew, and the worst to be our enemy.

THE PRAYER

We cried out to Hashem, the God of our fathers—as it says:
It happened in the course of those many days that the king of
Egypt died; and the Children of Israel groaned because of their
servitude and cried; their cry because of the servitude rose
up to God. Hashem heard our cry.

This passage from the Haggadah comes from Exodus 2:23. And the introduction, "We cried out to Hashem, the God of our fathers," makes it very clear what this is. It is a prayer. And just two words in this prayer—"we cried"—articulate the specific and even peculiar way in which Jews pray and what, in turn, that way reveals about the Jewish heart.

The prayer, we learn in the Haggadah, is delivered through "a cry"—a description that is repeated in this short passage *six times*. The insistence on emphasizing how the prayer was offered speaks to the importance of its delivery mechanism. Rabbi Yose ben Chalafta, as recorded in the Talmud, ruled that the Shema must be said in a voice at least loud enough for the one praying to hear his words.[1] The two great Jewish law compilers, Maimonides (twelfth-century Spain/Egypt/Morocco) and Joseph Karo (sixteenth-century Israel), disagreed on the primary purpose of prayer. But they used almost the same language to describe how prayer must be offered. In the words of Joseph Karo, "One should not solely pray in his heart, but rather one must enunciate the words with his lips and make it heard with his own ears."[2]

It might seem curious, then, that the central prayer in the Jewish service is the "Silent Amidah." In fact, this is the prayer that Maimonides and Joseph Karo refer to in their aforementioned rulings. The "Silent Amidah" in

Judaism is really a prayer said quietly so that others can *hear* themselves pray it. This notion is reinforced with the word that is often used to describe Jews at prayer—*davening. Daven* is a Yiddish word that derives from the Hebrew *dovaiv,* which means "to move the lips."

The reason that Judaism insists on spoken prayer cuts to the core of the Jewish vision for man's relationship with God—in three ways. First, a silent prayer risks being a purely spiritual moment. This is a problem. The body, and the physical life it represents, is our indispensable mechanism for doing God's work in the world—from its powers to speak, procreate, and move. It must be elevated and its activities made sacred. Hence, prayer must involve the physical as well as the spiritual.

Second, the imperative to pray audibly is also revealed through a consideration of thoughts in general. Our thoughts, even when we try to focus, roam through unrelated subjects, take strange detours, and are easily interrupted by a signal from any of our senses. It is by speaking that we apply a coherence to otherwise chaotic thoughts and thus genuinely evaluate ourselves as we stand before God. This discipline leads us to dismiss things we realize are unworthy or even wrong, emphasize things that we realize are important, and prioritize what we really want and need.

Third, every human relationship is sculpted and determined by one thing: audible communication. Silence can be part of a relationship, but only after people have gotten to know each other well by frequently speaking with each other. By speaking our prayers, we vivify the notion that one should speak with God as she would with anyone who is sitting beside her.

The relational purpose of always speaking our prayers leads to the question that has interested, concerned, and even vexed people struggling with faith: What is the purpose of prayer? This passage reveals two.

One purpose is that of petition—of asking for God's intervention. In this passage in the Haggadah, the Jews cry to God for freedom and he immediately remembers (and we'll soon consider the significance of this word). In one breath, the prayer is asked and answered. This prayer works so fast and so efficiently that it jars the reader into responding, "Wait! That's not how prayer works!"

That's right. The Haggadah and the Torah are not history books and do not tell everything that happened to the people they discuss. The Jews, like all ancient peoples, were religious. They had been enslaved for hundreds of years and had presumably prayed before. Why does this prayer, unlike previous prayers, trigger God's remembering?

We don't know. We can empathize with our ancestors, who must have thought that their prayers were not being heard and that their suffering was not being even acknowledged by God. They must have felt abandoned by God. And we can even be angry with God for not answering their prayers and forcing them to remain enslaved. But we cannot know why God did not respond until he did. However, the question of why God did not respond until he did teaches us several things about him.

When we question why God did not respond until he did to the cry of our ancestors, we are acknowledging that *he did respond*. In other words, prayer works. That we know prayer works but not when, where, or how yields another revelation about God. God is not an ATM whose bounty can be unlocked with the right code, a pharmacist who can dispense a drug that will make the problem all better, or a DJ who will play a request if asked nicely. This could never be the case. People often pray for contradictory things, with good people and laudable intentions on both sides of the prayer. After all, if two fine young men pray that the same young woman will return their affections, what is God to do? God may have plans for the future that we don't know about—and which may make a current prayer impossible to answer now. God is not, and never could be, *transactional*. If God is not transactional, he must be only one thing. He must be *relational*.

But there is a seeming disconnect. Our understanding of God is so limited that we have no idea when, why, or how he responds to our prayers. That God is far beyond our understanding can be intimidating and creates a distance from him. How, we might ask, can we have a meaningful relationship with someone about whom there is so much we will never understand?

The answer to this question prepares us for *all* our other relationships, even the one we have with ourselves. The answer might come by contemplating the nature of surprise. We are surprised by the unexpected. Say you walk into your home and you hear a voice scream from behind a corner. Will you be surprised? It depends on whether you *knew* that your daughter was going to hide there and try to scare you.

Given how often we are surprised by public figures, friends, colleagues, family, our children, and even ourselves (as is evidenced in the expression "I didn't know I had it within me," even as "it" was always within!), a realization emerges: We *really know* very few (if any) people. So what? We still have fulfilling and loving relationships. While a relationship requires the predictability and stability that come from knowledge, it thrives on the mystery and dynamism that come from lack of knowledge. If we expect and even welcome this tension in our relationships with other people, we can do so with God as well. And if we can do so with God, we can do so with other people.

The relational purpose of prayer is reflected in the name of God used in this Haggadah passage. God has several names in the Torah. The name used in this passage, Hashem, is used to describe an intimacy between God and his people. For instance, many prayers are introduced with "Baruch Ata Hashem"—our way, in the words of Rabbi Steven Weil, "of addressing God as 'you' in the very familiar Second Person."[3] This "you," per Rabbi David Wolpe, is only used to address someone who is "right there."[4] When we speak to God in this way, we are addressing someone who is physically right beside us—connoting a familiarity and an intimacy that can only be experienced in the context of a committed relationship.

The deeply relational purpose of communicating with God is evidenced by the fact that there is no Hebrew word for *prayer*. The English word *prayer* derives from the Latin word *precari,* which means "to beg or ask." Hebrew has no equivalent word because the acts of begging and asking are exclusively *transactional*—and this is only a part of the fundamentally *relational* Jewish prayer experience. The closest Hebrew word to *prayer* is *tefila. Tefila* derives from two roots. One is *tafal,* which means to connect or bind. When we do *tefila,* therefore, we are connecting with God.

And we are doing so in a very particular way. The word *tefila* also derives from the word *palel,* which means "to judge or to analyze." The act of doing *tefila* is described using a reflexive verb: *lehitpalel.* A reflexive verb describes what one does to himself. For instance, "She taught herself how to ski" involves a reflexive verb.

The English *pray* is not a reflexive verb. When one *prays,* he is petitioning God. He is not necessarily doing anything to himself. When a Jew engages in *tefila,* he is judging and/or analyzing himself. Why would we need to analyze ourselves en route to deepening our connection to God? A consideration of how we interact with powerful people is instructive.

Before engaging with an interviewer for a job, the parents of a new girlfriend, or the audience in front of whom we are speaking, we analyze everything from how we should look to what we should emphasize about ourselves. It is in the gap between our understanding of who we are and who we need to be for a particular encounter where preparation operates. If we prepare with such thought and concern for human relationships, how much more so with God and his world? For that, we have *tefila*.

The fundamentally relational purpose of Jewish worship is not contrary to the petitionary purpose. It encompasses it. Every relationship with a power dynamic involves petition—or what, in the English language, is called *prayer*. Children ask their parents for money, employees ask their bosses for promotions, sick people ask doctors to heal them, accused people ask lawyers to vindicate them, students ask their teachers for knowledge, and lawyers ask judges to award their clients' money in the section of the legal document called a "prayer." Petition is certainly a part of *tefila*—it is just not the whole thing.

If petition is only a part of the Jewish worship experience, what should the rest of our communication with God be about? Our own experience can guide us. A wife does not want every conversation with her husband to be about religious truth, a child does not want every conversation with his parents to be about their dreams for posterity, a friend does not want every conversation with her friend to be about their relationship, and God does not want every communication with us to be about world peace. A parent wants to hear everything about and from her child, and would never tell a child that something is insufficiently important or interesting to discuss. Our God in history wants an intimate relationship, which involves the sharing of *all* kinds of thoughts, concerns, and dreams.

The scholar Nehemia Gordon describes his quintessentially Jewish prayer experience:

Sometimes I will be praying and I will be asking God for help with my issues, my problems and my petty situations. And I wonder at times: Does the Creator of the universe—is this too small for Him to deal with? But our God is that big and powerful and amazing that He can hear your issues and your problems and your situations and He hears and He responds. He could have just said—I know the pain of my people in Egypt; I know everything! But He didn't say that. He said Shemati: I've heard. It really does have a power for the Creator of the Universe to hear and respond. That excites me![5]

If the six uses of "crying out" in this Haggadah passage indicate the importance of the *tefila* being spoken, there are four times when another easily overlooked word is used very meaningfully. This is "we" or "our"—as in, "*We* cried out to Hashem . . ." The *tefila* is offered audibly. It is also offered collectively.

Most Jews will recognize this requirement of the collective as the basis for a minyan—which is the quorum of ten Jewish adults needed for a religious service. The Torah never requires a minyan, but the rabbis of the Talmud analyzed verses of Leviticus in conjunction with verses in Numbers to generate the rule. Consequently, Jews today generally practice in according with the principle articulated by Judah Halevi. He writes, "A prayer, in order to be heard, must be recited for a multitude, or in a multitude or for an individual who could take the place of a multitude."[6] What kind of individual could take the place of a multitude—and thus be able to pray alone? "None such," Judah Halevi writes, "is to be found in our age."[7]

The need for communal prayer, even in the absence of an explicit Torah directive, is another instance where Maimonides and Joseph Karo agreed. Maimonides writes, "A person should . . . never recite his prayers in private when he is able to pray with the congregation. . . . Whoever has a synagogue in his town and does not worship there is called a bad neighbor."[8] Joseph Karo held that if a person could not pray with a congregation, he should pray when the congregation is praying—and if he cannot pray when the congregation is praying, he should go to synagogue and pray alone.[9]

Why is Judaism so insistent that prayer must be offered collectively? There are at least three reasons.

First, we worship better when we do so together. The thirteenth-century Catalan rabbi Menachem Meiri said that communal prayer enables the proper "concentration of the heart."[10] One's ability to focus is greater among others who are also praying, and in a place that is designed to be conducive to it. If distraction is one problem of worshipping alone, asking God for the wrong things is another. Left alone, Judah Halevi wrote, one might pray for harm to befall another member of the community. One is far less likely to offer such a petition in the community, particularly as the prayer has to be articulated out loud, than one who worships in solitude.

The second reason we pray together will be familiar to any parent. Does a parent of several young children derive more pleasure watching them play by themselves apart, or together? If a parent has several older children who all live in apartments near one another, would she prefer that they each have Shabbat dinner alone, together, or not care? Every parent will answer the same. As we are created in God's image, we can understand why God wants us to pray together. The least we can do for God is to give him pleasure!

The third reason is illustrated through what Judaism means by *together*. Abba Binyamin, a third-century rabbi, said that if two people enter a synagogue to pray and one leaves before the other, the one who left gets "his prayer thrown back in his face."[11] Multiple people worshipping at the same time, in the same place, are not necessarily doing so together. The prayers must be done genuinely together because of what happens when people come together to do something they all believe is meaningful.

Two people may enjoy going to the movies together every Thursday, but their relationship will likely be much deeper, richer, and more dependable if they instead devote that time to working together to accomplish something in accordance with a principle they share. Similarly, the insistence that people worship together creates bonds that strengthen what the Haggadah tells us, in the response to the wicked son, is the "fundamental principle" of Judaism—the Jewish community.

The community-building function that accrues to worshipping together is present in a controversy that more than occasionally riles Orthodox synagogues—that of the "Kiddush Club." This club "meets" in the middle of the service—when a large group of usually men get up during the haftarah to drink scotch together! Most rabbis hate this, as it is disruptive to the service and disrespectful to whomever is chanting the Torah or haftarah. But why do they tolerate it? And how can anyone—let alone large groups of people in many synagogues—think that this is remotely okay? Because it is a community-building exercise—a sacred consequence of worshipping together. And everyone who appreciates Judaism has to respect that, even if they quite reasonably would prefer it be accomplished other than through a Kiddush Club that meets in the middle of services.

Whether or not a synagogue has a Kiddush Club, the requirement that Jews worship together provokes the challenge that seems to emerge in any discussion of Jewish community. We discussed the challenges that a wicked son can pose to the Seder, and how the parents' response accounts for the fact that he could disrupt the sacred gathering and corrupt his age-mates. Of course, the archetype of the wicked son does not only emerge at the Seder. He and the challenges he poses are often present—especially for a religion so oriented around community. What should be done about a worship service's equivalent of the wicked son?

Rav Hana bar Bizna, quoting Rabbi Shimon Hasida, addressed this question in the Talmud. He notes that galbanum, which was considered foul-smelling, is included in the incense offered in the Tabernacle. He deduces that "sinners" *especially* should be welcomed in synagogue.[12] The great early Zionist rabbi Abraham Isaac Kook observed that the word *tzibur* (community) is an acronym of *tzaddik, beinoni,* and *ve-rasha* (righteous, intermediate, and the wicked).[13] The wicked, Rav Kook deduces, must be welcomed in the Jewish worship community—as they are members of the community, and could be positively influenced by others. The Torah, as we have previously discussed Rabbi Joseph Soloveichik saying, requires Jews to sacrifice personal purity in order to elevate others. The communal prayer space is an ideal place to experience that.

WHAT IT MEANS TO KNOW

God remembered His covenant with Abraham, with Isaac, and with Jacob. God saw the Children of Israel and God knew.

God remembered? God knew? What could this mean? Could God have *forgotten* that the Jews to whom he had given the covenant of Land, children, and blessings were enslaved in Egypt? Simply, no. Whatever one's conception of God, that is not possible.

This is far from the only time in the Torah when we are told that "God remembered." God "remembered" Noah in the flood, Joseph in the prison, and Rachel trying to conceive. There could have been no "forgetting" in any of those stories, either.

The Torah deploys the same dynamic with the word most similar to remember—*know*. We are told in the Torah that Adam "knew" his wife and then had a child, that the cupbearer who Joseph saved in prison "forgot" him and that the subsequent Pharaoh "knew not Joseph." Perhaps most of all, God tells Moses that not even the forefathers knew him by the name he was about to reveal even though they had all called him by it.

What, then, could *remember* and *know* mean?

The Haggadah guides us to the answer. This section of the Haggadah, where the intriguing "remember" and "know" appear, immediately precedes the plagues. This follows the biblical narrative and the lesson it instructs. God remembers and knows, we see, immediately before his most spectacular actions. It is not that he was ever ignorant or forgetful. It is just that he does not dignify purely cognitive awareness with acknowledgment. Knowledge, in divine terms, is always tied to action.

This concept manifests throughout some of the most important lessons the Torah teaches, even when terms like "knowledge" and "remember" are not specifically mentioned. For instance, God states in Numbers 5 that a sinner must confess and make restitution. There is an alternative: The sinner could feel guilty about the sin, ask God for forgiveness, and resolve to do better in the future. But that possibility is not even acknowledged.

Internal knowledge—in this case, that one sinned—*compels* external action: confession and restitution. "Repentance," regardless of how strongly it is "felt," does not exist without confession and restitution. If one knows something but does not act accordingly, it is as if he was never aware of it.

God remembered! We are soon to see what that meant for him, for the slaves, for the world—and for us. But there is one very important subject to address first.

THE UNFINISHED:
THE JEWISH WAY OF
LIFE AND DEATH

He brought us to this place, and He gave us this Land,
a Land flowing with milk and honey.
—This is not in the Haggadah (Let's see why!)

The Farmer's Declaration in the Torah, which extends from "An Aramean attempted to destroy my father" to "Hashem took us out of Egypt with a mighty hand and an outstretched arm" in Deuteronomy 26, is the longest continuous quotation from the Torah in the Haggadah.

That is not surprising, as it is through the Farmer's Declaration that we tell the story of the Exodus from Egypt. What is surprising, as Rabbi Shai Held notes, is that it is not just a little longer.

The passage starts with Deuteronomy 26:5 and goes through 26:8, omitting . . . the destination! Deuteronomy 26:9 says: "He brought us to this place, and He gave us this Land, a Land flowing with milk and honey."[1] This omission is so striking that it practically begs us to wonder: Why would the authors of the Haggadah, in recounting the Farmer's Declaration, end the passage before its culmination one line later?

Nothing in the Haggadah will answer that question. Instead, other passages in the Haggadah will arouse the question again. For instance, we read in the Haggadah of the covenant that God made with Abraham in Genesis 15:13–14: "Know well that your offspring shall be strangers in a land not theirs, and they shall be enslaved and oppressed for four hundred years. But I will execute judgment on the nation they shall serve, and in the end they shall go free with great wealth." But the Haggadah omits the subsequent passage "your descendants will return here to this Land."

Forty is the Jewish number of transition. Noah is in the ark for forty days, Moses is on the mountain for forty days, and women are pregnant for forty weeks. It is predictable, therefore, that this number would have a major presence as we usher in the Jewish New Year. And it does. There are Four Questions, Four Sons, and four cups of wine. These correspond with the four expressions of redemption in Exodus 6:6–7: "I will bring you out from under the yoke of the Egyptians and free you from their slavery. I will deliver you with a demonstration of My power and with great acts of judgment. I will take you to Me as a nation."[2]

There is, as Rabbi Jonathan Sacks points out, a problem. That passage from Exodus actually has *five* expressions of redemption. The four expressions of redemption referenced in the Haggadah are from Exodus 6:6–7. But Exodus 6:8 contains another: "And I will bring you to the Land I swore."

At seemingly every opportunity—removing the crucial passage that concludes a Torah sequence, truncating the covenant to leave out the destination, basing the Seder around the expressions of redemption but excluding the ultimate one—the authors of the Haggadah insist on doing something very curious.

They are *determined* to make the story incomplete.

In this, they are following God in his existential moment of self-definition. In Exodus 3:13, God appears to Moses at the burning bush. Moses asks God what he should say if the Israelites ask about God's name. God replies, "I will be what I will be."

This is astonishing. God, who is both eternal and perfect, is saying that even he will be something different in the future. God is saying that he is still learning, developing, evolving, and growing! If God is saying that he is unfinished and always will be, the implications for us are clear and existential. The Torah illustrates what this means for us, through its characterization of the best and worst Jews in the Torah.

In Genesis 12:2, God promises Abraham the ultimate blessing of descendants and a great nation. As Abraham nears death, he has one son who is banished and another whose eldest grandchild is completely ill-equipped for the responsibility of transmission. The only territory he has in the Land is a grave. Yet it is at this moment when the Torah characterizes Abraham as one who "has everything." *Abraham* has everything? Yes! Completion was never going to happen. Abraham had gotten the Jewish journey started—while providing the next generation with what it needed to continue his work. That is, in Jewish terms, everything.

If Moses is the most well-regarded Jew in the Torah, Korach is the least. Korach leads a rebellion against Moses, but it is hardly the only revolt against Moses in the desert. So why is Korach uniquely reviled in the Jewish religious tradition?

The answer lies in his complaint against Moses. Korach does not, like other rebels, grumble about the lack of provisions or worship an idol. Instead, he says in Numbers 16:3, "All the community are holy. . . . Why then do you raise yourself above the Lord's congregation?"

What is so bad about that? Why does saying that everyone is holy make Korach a bad guy at all, let alone the worst Jew in the Torah? After all, God often issues a variant of the same instructions: "You shall be holy, for I, the Lord, am holy." Isn't Korach identifying with this great statement of Jewish aspiration?

The difference between the statement of Korach ("All the community are holy") and that of Moses ("You shall be holy") is one word. And that word—*shall* instead of *are*—is what constitutes the gulf between the greatest and the worst Jews in the Torah. The twentieth-century philosopher Martin Buber explains: "Both Moses and Korach desired the people to be the people of YHWH [God], the holy people. But for Moses, this was the goal. . . . For Korach, the people, as being the people of YHWH, were already holy."[3]

The sin—the great, unforgivable, eternal sin—is in saying that the Jewish people are *complete*.

The latter four books of the Torah (from Exodus to Deuteronomy) are generally about Moses working to bring his people to the Promised Land. Moses's great ambition is to lead his people into, and in, the Promised Land. Yet God tells Moses that he will die without ever entering. God, responding to Moses's prayer to be able to enter, allows him to view the Land from afar—but that's it.

Why does God prohibit Moses from entering the Promised Land? To be sure, Moses, like every giant in the Torah, had significant flaws and made commensurate mistakes that disappointed God. Countless commentators have opined about what Moses did to make himself ineligible.[4] But what does God say? The final words of the Torah are from God: "Never again has there arisen in Israel a prophet like Moses. . . . No one has shown the mighty power or performed the awesome deeds that Moses did in the sight of all of Israel."[5]

So God is happy with Moses at the very end—so happy that he says that there will never be as great a man as him. So why not let Moses lead the people to the Promised Land, rather than a lesser person? It is not that the great man had physically reached the end. Moses is not Willie Mays with the Mets or Michael Jordan with the Wizards. Even at 120, the Torah tells us, Moses's "eyes were undimmed and his vigor unabated."[6]

Moses could not continue because his was the greatest Jewish story—and Jewish stories don't have happy endings. In fact, they don't have endings at all.

This insistence on not having endings goes against everything we expect from stories and always has. Aristotle wrote that a "whole story has a beginning, a middle and an end." Professor Troy Troftgruben writes that there is a "consensus" among scholars that five works "represent the ancient novel in its classic, Greek form." They all conclude with a reunion of lovers who had been separated.[7] From Heliodorus to Harry Potter, readers have always expected and received satisfying endings.

Though the Torah and the Haggadah are great literature, this is a reminder of what we discussed earlier: To understand a book, a reader must first correctly identify its genre. And these great Jewish texts are not primarily literature. They are guidebooks. So why do the Torah and the Haggadah guide us away from endings?

There are at least three reasons.

First, the Pesach (and, by extension, the Jewish) experience is oriented toward turning ancient experience into contemporary memory. The authors of the Torah and the Haggadah wanted to overcome the inevitable forgetting that comes with there being so much history. They also wanted us to learn from every word and sometimes every letter in these texts. They apparently knew what modern social science has recently discovered: endings would have rendered those existential goals impossible to achieve.

In their book *The Power of Moments: Why Certain Experiences Have Extraordinary Impact,* Professors Chip and Dan Heath write, "What's indisputable is that when we assess our experiences, we don't average our minute to minute sensations."[8] Instead, we recall the peak (the most intense) and/or the ending of the experience. Its manifestations are everywhere. A Swedish study, for instance, showed that the level of pain that women recall from giving birth is often correlated with their assessment of how they considered the childbirth experience to have concluded.[9]

This phenomenon, known as peak-end theory, was identified by the Nobel Prize–winning psychologist Daniel Kahneman at the turn of this millennium. Professor Kahneman notes that memory, like everything else related to evolution, is adapted to help us survive. Consequently our memories do not need to be good at measuring "ongoing happiness or total suffering." They are optimized for telling us how good or bad experiences were, and how they ended.[10]

This psychological phenomenon presents a problem for Judaism. Memory, for Jews, is not only about surviving. It is about living. A memory that emphasizes the peak and the end of an experience does not enable the Jewish imperative, which is to absorb the full experiences of the past into the present. A way of telling a story that emphasizes one part of it would not work for the Jews, who insist that every word in the Torah is important and instructive— and that the same passage can yield multiple learnings.

The second problem with endings is illustrated by Aristotle's characterization of an effective ending. An ending should be, he says, "surprising, but inevitable."[11] A story, in other words, should have exciting plot twists and end in a way that leads the reader to conclude that it was inevitable.

The problem: In real life, no ending is inevitable.

For instance, let's imagine a close presidential election. One candidate emerges victorious as a result of winning several important states by small margins. It is a surety that analyses will immediately follow and continue for years explaining the sociological dynamics that the president triggered in the electorate, the incompetence of his opponent as a candidate, the failure of the media in its predictions, the doubling down on "what worked" in the winner's party, and the soul-searching in the loser's party.

But the fact is the result could have easily gone the other way. If it did, analyses reflecting *the opposite* would have been authoritatively pronounced. But if a different outcome that could have easily happened can lead to fundamentally different analyses, then there must be no truth to the analyses. The success of the Torah and the Haggadah depends on our deriving guidance from their stories and laws for every aspect of our lives—an enterprise too rich and too important to risk the interpretive distortions imposed by endings.

The third, and greatest, problem with endings is revealed through the feeling that they produce. When one completes a school year, a work project, or a meal, one feels satisfied. The resulting serenity, for many religions and philosophies, is a wonderful feeling—perhaps the crown of sentiments and even the ultimate state. Judaism hates it. Rabbi Adin Steinsaltz, surveying the widespread rabbinic criticism of the biblical Jacob for wanting to "dwell," concludes, "God bestows many favors and gifts upon the righteous . . . but tranquility is not one of them."[12]

There are two reasons that tranquility is inaccessible to the righteous.

The first is explained through a question asked in the seminal book of Jewish ethics, Pirkei Avot: "Who is the rich one?" The answer: "He who is satisfied with his lot."[13] The crucial words there are *his lot*—meaning only his material possessions. It is by being satisfied with one's material state that one is able to genuinely understand the moral nature of satisfaction and dissatisfaction— and to be appropriately dissatisfied. "A pious Jew," Rabbi Yisrael Salanter says, "is not one who worries about his fellow man's soul and his own stomach; a pious Jew worries about his own soul and his fellow man's stomach."[14]

A Jew is called to always be distressed by the material well-being of others in need and with his lack of progress in alleviating enough of it. He knows that the world is full of hunger and loneliness, oppression, and deprivation. The consequences are that real people, whom he at least loves as the stranger, are suffering. And he is always acutely aware that God gave him the ability to do something—not everything but something—about it. This awareness exists in a particular psychological state, one articulated by Israel's founding father and later president Shimon Peres.

President Peres lived a long life as a champion of Jewish innovation and inventiveness. When he was asked to identify "the greatest Jewish contribution to humanity," he had a lot to choose from. He also had an answer at hand: "Dissatisfaction."[15] It is this dissatisfaction that keeps the Jew always aware of the problems that need to be alleviated and the urgency for him to do so.

The second reason that satisfaction is a forbidden emotion is explained by the name of Moses's chief Jewish antagoinist—Korach, and helps to explain why Korach is widely considered the worst Jew in the Torah. The word *Korach* derives from the words meaning "baldness" and "ice." These have one thing in common: They are both places where nothing grows.[16] And when nothing grows, the thing is complete—it is done; it is what it is.

When a person considers himself complete, he will be led in one of two directions—both of which are morally catastrophic. Let's say that a person sets a New Year's resolution to quit smoking. A month later, he lights up. If he thinks of himself as complete, he will conclude that he is weak, that he is a hypocrite, that he is a failure. With a diminished self-conception, he will keep smoking. Alternatively, he could conclude that he is not complete— but someone who made a one-time mistake in the process of conquering a difficult habit. In that case, he should resume the process of quitting. Which should he do?

The answer is obvious, and the fundamental reason is provided in the dominant expression of the relationship that God wants with us. Abraham walks ahead of God, Noah walks with God, God tells us that we should walk in his ways and that our greatest reward is that he will walk among us.[17] When it comes to interacting with or like God, there is no mention of either stopping or arriving. It is only walking—which always includes the possibility of slipping, falling, getting lost, or discovering something serendipitiously.[18]

Judaism offers two archetypes for death. One is that of Methuselah, who enjoyed the greatest longevity of anyone in the Torah 969 years. Yet, as Rabbi Gerald Wolpe pointed out, we do not know what he wanted to change, whom he wanted to influence, what his dreams and aspirations were.[19] It is entirely possible that his name never surfaced at a Seder and quite certain that no one *ever* blessed a child to be like Methuselah.

This is not a commentary on the Jewish philosophy of longevity. One of the rare areas of universal agreement around Torah commentary concerns Leviticus 18:5, where we are commanded to "live by these commandments." Everyone acknowledges that *live by* is distinguished from *dying from.* Thus, the opportunity to save a life supersedes almost every other commandment at all times. One of the most famous statements of Judaism is from the Talmud—"Whomever saves one life, it is as if he has saved an entire world."[20] So the lack of regard for Methuselah is in spite of the Jewish yearning for long life.

As important as longevity is, there is something even more consequential. It is illustrated through the Torah's treatment of Sarah and Jacob.

There is a parsha named for Sarah, Chaye Sarah ("Life of Sarah"). And there is one named for Jacob, Vayechi ("And he [Jacob] lived"). There is one problem. Chaye Sarah starts with her death, and Vayechi is all about Jacob's death. Why would the parshas about their deaths be titled about their lives? Because, the author of the Torah is teaching us, the definition of a worthy Jewish life is one that, like Rabbi Schneur Zalman's Seder, does not end. The Talmud uses the same word, *kever*, in reference to both a womb and a grave. When someone who has lived a meaningful life dies, she gets a new life—in the world that is created by the people she inspired and by the good deeds whose impact will reverberate far into the future.[21] Meaningful lives, therefore, never end. They just begin again.

Many cultures and religions have a notion of life after death, from mummification to reincarnation to a heaven/purgatory/hell dynamic. The Torah has none of that. Instead, we have Methuselah, Sarah, and Jacob. Unlike Methuselah, we know just how Sarah and Jacob lived lives of deep purpose and profound moral ambition. They devoted themselves, with tribulation and sacrifice, with triumphs and mistakes, toward making the world a dwelling place for God. They each had the goal of creating a people that would reside in the Promised Land as ethical monotheists setting a moral example for the world.

It is an awesome goal that they do not come close to achieving. Yet they leave behind the people, the memories, the lessons, and the values that enable the work toward their goals to continue. Every Shabbat, we bless our girls that they should be like Sarah. The most popular male name for each year in the first decade of the twenty-first century was Jacob, and we call ourselves the Children of Israel.[22] And on Shabbat, we bless our boys that they should be like Jacob's grandsons—Ephraim and Manasseh.

The insistence on non-endings throughout the Haggadah leads us to ask and enables us to answer what might be *the* fundamental Jewish question. What is a full Jewish life? It is one that does not end. And how does one secure that non-ending? In the same way that Sarah, Jacob, and Moses do—by setting, and insistently working toward, a goal that cannot be achieved in one's lifetime.

WHY JEWISH BOYS EMERGE FROM THE WOMB UNCIRCUMCISED

Take this staff in your hand, that you may perform miracles with it.

The plagues are about to begin. Before they begin, though, God has a seemingly prosaic instruction for Moses in Exodus 7:9: "Take your staff." This is the first appearance of a staff in Exodus. Moses and Aaron will use it many times subsequently—to turn water to blood in the first plague, to make Egypt teem with frogs, to part the Red Sea, to win the battle against the Amalekites, and against God's wishes to strike the rock rather than speak to it.

The use of a staff might seem unremarkable until we consider that *God* commands its use. Why would God need a piece of used equipment in the hand of a man to accomplish his goals? God has the ability to create the world in six days. He has the ability to part the Red Sea at exactly the right time to enable the Jewish slaves to cross and the Egyptian army to drown. He doesn't need equipment to accomplish either.

Now he needs a staff? Yes—to guide us in two distinct and important ways.

The first function of the staff is foreshadowed in Genesis 1:26 when God says: "Let us make man." Who is the *us*? Some commentators suggest angels, but there is another interpretation that every mother who has sung a song to her unborn child will understand. He is talking with the humanity he is about to birth. Why is he talking with the not yet existent humanity? Because he is anticipating something with such enthusiasm that he is relating to it already.

God wants Jewish boys to be circumcised, but has the father either perform the circumcision or delegate it.[1] God wants the Jews freed from Egypt, and he has Moses and Aaron intercede with the Pharaoh to make it happen. After Moses smashes the Ten Commandments on the tablets that *God* wrote for him at Sinai, God allows his prophet to begin again by instructing *Moses* to inscribe the tablets.[2] God wants no chametz on Pesach, and he tells people to get rid of it.[3] God wants the poor, widowed, orphaned, and converted to be taken care of, and he directs people to provide for them.[4] God wants the Jews to create a kingdom of priests and a holy nation, and we have to fight for, settle, and work it.[5] Our most blessed food is bread, which (according to Rabbi Joseph Soloveitchik) achieves that status because it only exists when God provides the raw material (the wheat) and people do considerable work to make the final product.[6]

In this context, the source of God's anticipation becomes apparent. It is for a partnership with people. He will provide the vision and will always be there to help. But he will work in partnership with people, who have the ability to make even the most mundane objects holy agents of God's will. Hence: the staff.

Why would God, who is omnipotent and has so many hopes for his world, insist on acting with human partners? A question about why God would do something is always fraught. But it is also, to those who seek him, irresistible.

There are at least three reasons why God insists on working with a partner.

The first reason is revealed immediately after we cross the Red Sea. Soon after the miraculous liberation, the people start complaining. Indeed, our complaints become so fierce that Moses fears for his life. The putative reason for this complaining is lack of water—but they let the real reason slip: "Is the Lord among us or not?"[7]

It was a reasonable question. Up to that point, the Jews only experienced the power God—he who parted the sea and rained forth manna from the heavens. Acts of awesome power were not enough to sustain the relationship, even for a brief time, following the event. The people needed to know, in a way that displays of power could not articulate, that God was close to them. An abiding relationship requires, God and Moses learn, strength *and* intimacy. This combination of strength and intimacy—of capability and closeness—can be best achieved by the constant togetherness that defines a genuine partnership.

The second reason why God needs a partnership is that it is only through such a relationship that the loyalty and steadfastness that he needs for the Jews to become his kingdom of priests and a holy nation can be secured forever. We discussed earlier how, when all our provisions were provided by God in the desert following the Exodus, we "craved a craving." We dream of five food items from Egypt, all of which require people to cultivate. And we respond to the manna (the perfect food) that God gave us in the desert by grinding, pounding, and cooking it—by working on it. The result of being given everything: the people complain, yearn for Egypt, and weep in their family groups. Moses becomes completely exasperated, and God is furious.

Why is being given everything we need such a disaster? Rav Kahana, the ancient sage of the Talmud, observed that a person prefers a *kav* (a measure of grain) of his own produce to nine *kav* of another person's. This view was confirmed by his contemporary Ben Hai-Hai, who said, "According to the effort is the reward."[8] In the twenty-first century, social scientists have identified this phenomenon as the *IKEA effect*.

The social scientists from Harvard, Yale, and Duke who identified the IKEA effect in 2011 describe it in language reminiscent of Rabbi ben Hai-Hai: "The more effort people put into some pursuit, the more they come to value it." Consumers in their study were willing to pay 63 percent more for an item that they constructed than one that was constructed for them. This conclusion was replicated in numerous similar studies and confirmed the results from many more—from baking cakes to making origami cranes to valuing food sources—in humans and even animals.[9]

God's project of freedom would not work if it consisted entirely of him giving us even the things we need. It would only work, he learns, if we invest ourselves in the relationship in a material way. God will only succeed if we become his co-creators—if we become his partners.

The third reason constitutes what Rabbi Adin Steinsaltz identifies as "the basis of Maimonides' ethical theory."[10] In the daytime of our lives, when we are seemingly going from success to success, we modulate our self-estimation by recognizing that our fortune is due in part to the work of our senior partner. In the nighttime, we might feel so lost and broken that we just don't know how we can continue. The Jewish prayer of healing, from Psalm 121:2, has a built-in commentary. The psalm is: "My help is *from with* the Lord"—not "from the Lord" or "with the Lord" but "*from with* the Lord." This strange construction begs us to ask: Does help come from or with the Lord? The answer is clear: the God-man relationship is a partnership, where the help we receive from and with God is so intertwined that grammatical conventions become gladly overriden.

Of course, sustaining and meaningful partnerships don't create themselves or thrive in a vacuum. Whether with other people or with God, their vision requires execution—and their execution involves people with all our vulnerabilities, weaknesses, and challenges. The author of the Torah uses the staff—this staff that is in the Haggadah—to show us how to create one. In Exodus 17:6, God wants water to come from a rock and tells Moses to strike it.

The lesson for us is in the language he uses to deliver the message, in Exodus 17:5. "Pass before the people and take with you some of the elders of Israel; and take in your hand *your staff* with which you struck the Nile [to create blood with the first plague]." The next reference to the staff comes only four verses later when Moses tells the people how they are going to win the battle against the attacking Amalekites: "Tomorrow I will stand on top of the hill with *the staff of God* in my hands."

So whose staff is it? When Moses speaks, he says that it is God's. When God speaks, he says that it is Moses's.

The relationship is so close and the contributions are so linked that the partners are like one, inseparable and unseverable. A story of the twentieth-century Jerusalem rabbi Aryeh Levin and his wife, Tzipora, is often told to engaged couples as an example of the kind of partnership they should want to achieve. Rabbi Levin took his wife to a physician and said, "Doctor, my wife's foot is hurting *us*."[11] In the best partnerships, there is no notion of singular destiny or individual ownership.

There are, theoretically, lots of tools that God could have used to symbolize this partnership—even if God wanted something with which Moses could simultaneously point, strike, and use for balance. As in English, there are several Hebrew words for *stick*. There is *makel,* which is used to keep sheep and cattle in line. There is *mishennet,* a cane that is used for support. And there is *mateh,* the staff. The nineteenth-century Ukrainian master Rabbi Meir Leibush ben Yehiel Michel Wisser (known as the Malbim) considers Exodus 4:2, which says, "What is this in your hand?" God knows, of course, what is in Moses's hand. God, the Malbim suggests, wants to see what kind of stick Moses thinks it is.

In his answer, *mateh,* Moses is declaring what kind of leader he intends on being. Rabbi Norman Lamm points out that the word *mateh* derives from the word *natoh*—which means to "stretch forth the hand, to point to new horizons, to new and higher goals."[12] That is the ambition, which the staff is capable of helping to fulfill. But what will the staff actually enable Moses to do? The first thing that the staff does in Moses's hand, a moment after he receives it, is to produce a snake. This reptile, which had been the enemy of man since Adam and Eve, causes Moses to scurry from it in fear.

What is Moses, or we, supposed to make of this tool that has such glorious potential—and yet produces a snake in its first use? Don Isaac Abravanel offers a resolution. The next appearance of the staff is in Exodus 4:17, when God tells Moses that he shall perform the signs [to the Pharaoh] with the "staff you shall take in your hand." Four verses later, God again refers to the signs Moses would perform. This time, however, God says, "See all the wonders I have put in your hand and perform them before Pharaoh."[13]

What happens to the staff? It is there in 4:17, but seemingly disappears four verses later. But of course Moses does not lose it. Its career is just getting started in the Torah, and it is with us in the Haggadah. God is just emphasizing that it was never the change agent itself. Those were always God's wonders and Moses's hand.

Abravanel's understanding of the staff can also be seen in its composition. The staff would be used, as God tells Moses, "to perform miracles." Yet the Torah does not describe it with any kind of grandeur. It is not bejeweled, blessed, or otherwise distinctive. It is just a simple piece of used equipment.

And it is the simplicity of the biblical staff that enables it to keep on guiding us through the Torah. Following the failure of Korach's rebellion, Moses gives each of the tribal leaders a staff, and lays them in the Tabernacle. The next day, Moses comes back and the staff of Aaron has blossomed—with a flower bud and ripened almonds. Rabbi YY Jacobson, drawing from Rebbe Menachem Mendel Schneerson, notes that this exercise could not have been to reestablish Aaron's priesthood. That had just been done, and Aaron's priestly authority was not in doubt. The purpose of this strange exercise is not to show who the leader is, but to establish what a leader does.

"The primary quality . . . of a man of God," Rabbi Jacobson writes, "is his or her ability to transform lifeless sticks into orchards. . . . The Jewish high priest perceives even in a dead stick the potential for rejuvenation."[14]

The Rebbe took the lesson that he learned from the blossoming staff and applied it in a way that is profoundly relevant to the question of how to treat the wicked son or the sinning congregant. Rabbi Berel Baumgarten asked the Rebbe if he should expel a student who continually smoked on Shabbat and was corrupting others. The Rebbe's response, as summarized by Rabbi Jacobson:

> Love him to pieces. Embrace him with every fiber of your being, open your heart to him, cherish him and shower him with warmth and affection. Appreciate him, respect him and let him feel that you really care for him. See in him that which he or she may not be able to see in themselves at the moment. View him as a great human being, and you know what? He will become just that.

This, Rabbi Jacobson says, "is the sign of a true leader: Where others might have seen a spiritually arid staff, a Rebbe saw the potential or the creation of the most beautiful and inspiring garden."

The consistent prominence of this piece of used equipment at many of the pivotal moments in the Torah guides us to one of the fundamental principles of Judaism. Many religions and philosophies reflect the belief that this world is an unsavory passageway to a better world of purely spiritual existence. Thus, the holy people are those who are detached from the activities of the world and live in selfless and perhaps solitary communion with God. Judaism says the opposite. Our staffs—the ordinary things that we use to do our work right here on earth—can be instruments of divine will. Everything—our staffs and our food, our computers and our phones, our credit cards and our relationships—can be used to help even the seemingly lifeless blossom into something magnificent and sacred. Or they can be thrown to the ground, used to create something that even Moses will flee from.

This lesson from Moses's staff extends well beyond material things and scary animals. Indeed, everything in the world other than God is Moses's staff. Love can either lead parents to provide the finest moral education for their children, or it can cause them to cheat their children into college.

Religion can lead its adherents to contract Ebola while providing medical care to strangers, or it can lead people to hijack airplanes and fly them into buildings.[15] Jewish teaching makes it clear that this dynamic applies even, and perhaps especially, to our sacred text. The third-century rabbi Joshua ben Levi said that the Torah can be an "elixir of life" or a "deadly poison."[16] The tool, no matter how awesome its potential, can only be sacred in our hands, used properly.

WHY ANY PLAGUES?

The plagues are, for many, the most familiar part of the Seder. All repeat Seder-goers will be familiar with blood, frogs, cattle disease, and slaying of the firstborn. This is because of what Rabbi David Fohrman calls the *lullaby effect*.[1] Parents sing "Rock-a-Bye Baby" to their children, not realizing that it is a song about the violent death of an infant. In Pesach terms, synagogue gift shops carry gifts like the "Adorable Set of Ten Plush Passover Plague Representations, with Convenient Carrying Drawstring Bag,"[2] despite each plague being about mass suffering or death. It might be best to start the consideration of the plagues anew.

The fundamental question about the plagues is why they exist at all. Ask an adult why God produced the plagues and she will likely answer: Their purpose was to pressure the Pharaoh into letting the Jews go. In other words—sufficiently torture the Pharaoh, and he will do what God and Moses want.

Alternatively, give a five-year-old a thought experiment. Tell her, "You are God and have unlimited power and ability. Your goal is what your parent just said—to free the Jews from slavery. You will do so by getting them from Egypt to the desert. Getting from the desert to the Promised Land will come later—for now, your goal is to get the Jews from Egypt to the desert. You are God, so be very creative! The only technique unavailable to you, for reasons that will be discussed shortly, is changing the Pharaoh's mind. What would you do?"

The five-year-old might suggest a flying vehicle, a giant waterslide that starts in Egypt and ends in the desert, supersonic foot speed that kicks in when the Egyptians are sleeping and lasts for just enough time for the Jews to get to the desert, or a drink that puts the Egyptians to sleep for enough time for the Jews to escape.

She is unlikely to suggest anything like the plague sequence in Exodus.

The deployment of anything like the plagues, she would intuit, would take a lot of time, involve continual uncertainty, and inflict significant pain on lots of innocent people (including the Jews). At the very least, she would effectively suggest, the plagues are a highly inefficient way to free the Jews.

The five-year-old would be right. And there is no way that the plagues were all God can think of—he could, of course, conceive of anything that anybody, including our hypothetical five-year-old child, could. The purpose of the plagues must have been something other than freeing the Jews.

Indeed, God clearly articulates the purpose of the plagues before they begin. In Exodus 5, Moses asks the Pharaoh to let the Jews go for a three-day journey. The Pharaoh replies, "Who is Hashem that I should heed His voice to send out Israel? I do not know Hashem."

God accepts the challenge, saying in Exodus 7:5, "Egypt shall know that I am Hashem." The plagues start thereafter.

God chooses the cumbersome, difficult, painful, and inefficient mechanism of the plagues to free the Jews because he is really trying to do something else. He is attempting to win an argument. If he can convince the Egyptians, the most powerful regime in the ancient world, that he is the one true God, then he would win the world. The polytheistic regime, whose logic culminates in slavery and child murder, would lose. The monotheistic vision, whose logic is universal love and ubiquitous concern, would triumph.

It is through the plagues that God seeks to win that argument and in the process reveal himself.

FIRST, HARMLESS MAGIC

Immediately after announcing his intention to educate the Egyptians that he is God, God makes a tactical move. God resolves to begin the educational process in a language the Pharaoh can understand. God says in Exodus 7:9: "When Pharaoh speaks to you and says, 'Produce your marvel,' you shall tell Aaron . . ." God knows the Pharaoh, and that the monarch's religious commitments would revolve around magic—the supposed triumph over the laws of nature. This is not, as Moses and the other Jews will soon find out, God's way—but God is willing to prove himself on the Pharaoh's turf.

"We can start there," God effectively says. His first instruction to Moses and Aaron does not involve a plague. It is to perform a magic trick. He tells Moses to instruct Aaron to cast his staff down before the Pharaoh, at which point it would turn into a serpent. Aaron does so, and the trick works. The Pharaoh calls in his magicians and matches it.

The Pharaoh would have appreciated this apparent victory. As the Christian scholar Dave Livingston writes, the serpent was a sign of a ruler's power. The Pharaoh's crown featured a cobra ready for battle, as did the throne of the most famous Pharaoh, King Tut. To overcome the cobra symbol is to overcome the power of the Pharaoh.[1]

Still, the test was not very impressive. Snake tricks were common in ancient Egypt, and are now easily understood. The Egyptian cobra can be immobilized but not killed by squeezing its neck at a particular place. It could then be placed into a rod. When the rod is thrown to the ground, the snake comes out.[2] Another ancient technique involves cooling the snake and pressuring its head, leading the snake to believe that it is being crushed by a predator. The snake then freezes in place and looks like a rod. The "magician" then throws the snake to the ground, where it slithers away. This is, according to the traveler Tahir Shah, the "oldest illusion on record" and is still practiced today.[3] The Pharaoh's trick seems to have been a variation on one of these tricks.

Why would God pick a test that the Egyptians could easily emulate, especially as the Pharaoh could have interpreted it as vindicating his god? Because of what comes next. The staffs of both the Jews and the Egyptians become snakes. But then Aaron's staff swallows the Egyptian staffs. This was different. The Egyptian magicians were accustomed to staffs swallowing snakes, but not other staffs.

Defeated in the magic contest, the Pharaoh and his men do not seem to care. In fact, we are told that the Pharaoh "strengthens his heart." God's attempt at a peaceful display of his mastery over Egyptian religion—the magic trick—may have succeeded technically. But it fails strategically.

God needs to try something else.

RATIONALITY: FIGHTING BLOOD, FROGS, AND LICE WITH . . . MORE BLOOD, FROGS, AND LICE

It is Exodus 7, and God orders the first plague. The Nile River, the life source of Egypt, will turn to blood. God tells Moses to tell Aaron to take his staff and strike the Nile. Aaron does so as the Pharaoh watches. The Nile turns to blood. The fish die. The water becomes undrinkable—and it overflows everywhere, in accordance with God's description that it would be, per Exodus 7:19, "even in vessels of wood and stone."

As Rabbi David Fohrman says, there is a certain poetic justice to the first plague.[1] The Pharaoh had, at the time of Moses's birth, ordered all Jewish infant boys to be thrown into the river. He had turned the Nile into an execution chamber, transforming his source of life into a killing field.

How does the Nile seem in the morning after the boys are drowned in it during the evening? Still. Quiet, as though nothing had happened. Now the God in history intervenes and shows the Pharaoh what he had made it: literally, a bloodbath.[2]

And the Pharaoh's response? He could, presumably, have asked his magicians to turn the blood back to water. The Pharaoh has another idea. *He has his magicians turn more water into more blood.* And they do so with a predictable result. When they are done, there is no water that any Egyptian can drink.

The first plague does not convince the Pharaoh of anything. But God, per Exodus 8:2, is ready. "I will plague your whole country with frogs. The Nile shall swarm with frogs and they shall come up and enter your palace, your bedchamber and your bed, the houses of your courtiers and your people and your ovens and your kneading bowls."

This is apparently not enough, because then God promises to deliver the frogs to another place. "The frogs shall come *into* you and your people and your courtiers."[3] How will the frogs get *into* the Egyptians? They are too big to enter the ear, mouth, or nose. What is the only other possibility? Ask the young children where the frogs must have entered the Egyptians—and they will get it right and remember it.

Frogs are literally jumping everywhere. But good news for the Pharaoh: He has magicians. He can instruct them to make the frogs disappear. Instead, he tells them to make more frogs.

God is ready with the third plague—gnats. There are so many of this quintessentially annoying creature that "all the dust of the land became gnats." The Pharaoh's magicians respond by . . . attempting to produce more gnats. But when it comes to making the smallest creature, the magicians of this culture that values hugeness fail.

One could easily assess the situation and say, "Pharaoh: Your water sources are turned to blood and are flooding the land—and you respond by creating more blood. Your every structure becomes filled with frogs—and you respond by creating more frogs. Your land becomes filled with gnats—and you try to make more of them. Why don't you use your power to, for instance, try to turn the blood back into water and make the frogs disappear?"[4]

Because he is a Jew hater.

As we have previously shown, the Pharaoh had already established himself as the first Jew hater. He shows us that the existence of Jew hatred has nothing to do with Jews and that it increases in the face of Jewish weakness. In the first plague, he teaches us another rule of Jew hating.

Many people, to this day, have said that the Jew hater won't do this or that because the consequences would be painful to him. The term often used is "rational"—as in the Jew hater might *think* a lot of things, but there are limits to what he will *do* because he is "rational."[5] But rationality asks only whether the amount of effort is commensurate with the value of the expected result *to the person making the calculation.* The Pharaoh, as previously discussed, has already commanded the Jews to make the same amount of bricks while refusing to provide straw—a decision that cost him economically but paid off in the increased suffering of the Jews. Here, the Pharaoh, intent on enslaving the Jews and defeating their God, *thoughtfully and purposefully* increases the amount of blood and frogs that are defiling and destroying Egypt. It is just a price the Egyptians are willing to pay to afflict the Jews and their God.

How has history validated or invalidated the Torah's judgment about the rationality of Jew haters? In the second half of 1944, it was clear that the Germans were losing the war and needed to husband all resources for the war effort. Yet Germany directed its resources toward the systematic murder of Hungarian Jews and succeeded in killing more than 550,000 of the 800,000 Jews in Hungary. Iranian President Akbar Rafsanjani said on Jerusalem Day in 2001, "If one day the Islamic world is equipped with weapons like those Israel possesses now, then the imperialist strategy will reach a standstill because even the use of one nuclear bomb within Israel will destroy everything. However, it will only harm the Islamic world. *It is not irrational to contemplate such an eventuality.*"[6]

President Rafsanjani was right about one thing. From the perspective of the Jew hater, it is not irrational to contemplate such an eventuality. The Pharaoh established that. Rafsanjani just adapted it.

At least one major question is still aroused by the structure of the first three plagues. Rashi observes that God tells Moses *to tell Aaron* to strike either the water or the earth to produce each of these three plagues. These are the only three plagues where God issues this seemingly in-efficient instruction.[7] Why would God have chosen such a roundabout tactic with these three?

God, Rashi says, would not have asked Moses to strike the water or the earth because the waters of the Nile carried him to safety as a baby, and the earth accepted the corpse of the Egyptian man he killed in defense of the Jewish man whom the Egyptian was attacking. Thus, God does not ask Moses to strike the water or the ground out of gratitude to the inanimate things that saved him. If Moses owes gratitude to the inanimate, imagine the gratitude that Moses (and all those who come after him) owes to the living beings around us. Gratitude, God demonstrates, should become such a part of who we are that we think, feel, and act in the language of gratitude—and experience it everywhere, even with inanimate objects.

HABITS: HOW THE PHARAOH TEACHES US TO LIVE FREELY

Before discussing the subsequent plagues, it is important to discuss the difference in the Pharaoh's attitude toward the first five and the second five. At the end of each of the plagues, we are told that the Pharaoh's heart is hardened. The great question arising from this is: Who does the hardening? In the first five plagues, the Torah tells us that either the Pharaoh's heart became hard or "Pharaoh hardened his own heart." The dynamic changes in the second half of the plague sequence, when God hardens the Pharaoh's heart in four of them.

That God hardens the Pharaoh's heart in the initial plagues has vexed Torah commentators for millennia. Why would God want to "win" an argument with the Pharaoh by hardening his heart—and thus controlling his mind? What guidance could God possibly be providing us about how to live as free people by changing the Pharaoh's mind . . . for the worse?

None. It would be neither sensible, instructive, nor just for God to change the Pharaoh's mind. Although it seems like God does so anyway—after all, the Torah says that God "hardened" the Pharaoh's heart—we should treat God like any other suspect. Is this, conceivably, the kind of thing that he might do? And, related, what might be his motive? Is there another way to consider all this heart hardening?

The Pharaoh is hardly the first person or the last person to infuriate and/or disappoint God. In response to other offenses, God drowns most of the world in a flood,[1] destroys two cities with brimstone and fire,[2] forces people to drink gold powder,[3] and has a band of rebels swallowed by the earth.[4] But God never changes anyone's mind or even suggests that he might do so.

Why not? One who is omnipotent would have the ability to be able to relinquish power—as relinquishing power is an act of power itself. So perhaps God relinquished the power to change minds when he created free will. Or perhaps he retained that power but never uses it.

All we really know is that God must have decided that man's free will is inviolable, even to him. He is infinitely complex and multifaceted, but the reader of the Torah is never surprised by anything he does. God is consistent.

If God's hardening of the Pharaoh's heart is not meant to change his mind, what could it have been about? There are two distinct explanations, which are consistent with the God we know from the Torah, consistent with each other, and (most importantly) consistent with the Torah's function as a guidebook.

The first explanation is provided by Nachmanides, the thirteenth-century master. He argues that God hardens the Pharaoh's heart to *preserve* his free will.[5] Several times during the plagues, the Pharaoh agrees to let the Jews go. But as soon as the plague is alleviated, the Pharaoh changes his mind. These plagues, Nachmanides concludes, do not change the Pharaoh. They just torture him. The Pharaoh says he would free the Jews because (like most people) he would have said anything to end the torture. But as soon as the torture is over, the Pharaoh "hardened his heart," reverting to what he really believes and keeping the Jews enslaved.

Now more plagues are coming. They would, logically, have to be more punishing than the first set. Is it possible that the Pharaoh would, because of the torture of the plagues, just give in and free the Jews? Sure, he had almost done so previously, and a little more torture might make him fold. But God was never trying only to free the Jews.

God's goal is not to free the Jews, but to win an argument. He wants to convince the Pharaoh of the truth of ethical monotheism, and in so doing inspire all the other nations to similarly recognize his truth. A quick escape following a "decision" made under torture would not accomplish that. The Pharaoh would only recognize God as a powerful god who won a battle. So God hardens the Pharaoh's heart, giving him the strength to withstand the torture and decide for himself whether or not to free the Jews.

The second explanation for why God hardened the Pharaoh's heart draws from the order of the hardening. Only *after* the Pharaoh hardens his own heart many times does God harden the Pharaoh's heart at all. The Pharaoh's heart doesn't go back to its original state after he hardens it after each plague because *that is not what hearts do.* Every act of the human heart does something to the heart. Here, the Pharaoh's heart becomes harder every time he hardens it. After five plagues, the Pharaoh's heart became so hard that it is as if God had hardened it. In other words, the Pharaoh's refusal to free the Jews in response to the early plagues became a habit.

That God's hardening of the Pharaoh's heart *followed* the Pharaoh's hardening of his own heart yields a fundamental Jewish teaching. Everyone understands that there is a relationship between thought and action. The common psychological assumption is that we think and then we act—we develop a conviction or a feeling and then act accordingly. But this does not describe the Pharaoh and the plagues. Though the lives of his subjects and the future of his regime are at stake, he violates the first rule of holes and keeps digging. His conduct is better explained by a dictum from the second-century sage Simeon ben Azzai. "One commandment," he says, "draws in another after it. And one sin draws another after it."[6]

This observation turns into moral guidance when placed alongside a story from the Talmud. There is a debate among several leading rabbis over the most important passage in the Torah. Rabbi Akiva, as previously discussed, says that it is "Love your fellow as yourself." Simeon ben Azzai says that it is "Man is created in the image of God."[7] Ben Zoma says that it is "Shema Yisrael"—"Hear, O Israel." The surprising entry into this competition is from Rabbi Shimon ben Pazi. He chooses a seemingly obscure verse from Exodus 29:39: "The first lamb you shall sacrifice in the morning and the second lamb you shall sacrifice in the evening."[8]

The winner: Shimon ben Pazi. Rabbi Doron Perez, the leader of the Mizrachi World Movement, explains Ben Pazi's victory: "It is only through a continuous and consistent commitment, day in and day out, that change in ourselves and the world can truly be evoked. . . . This is Ben Pazi's secret."[9]

Ben Pazi's secret articulates one of the most important psychological truths in Judaism. It is reflected in the order of the words we used to accept the Torah itself, in Exodus 24:7: "We will do and we will hear." First we do, and then we think. We don't act because we think a certain way. We think a certain way because we act as we do. Our thoughts, our characters, our perspectives, our ideas, and consequently our future actions are a product of what we do now. The lesson is clear, profound, and important: If you want to have a certain quality, *act it*—and soon it will be like God instilled it.

We are the product of what we do continually. We are, in other words, the sum of our habits. And this might be the most liberating idea in the world.

Ben Pazi's secret means that we are not products of our environments, our genes, our childhoods, or our emotions, all of which are difficult or impossible to control, interpret, and even identify. We are products of our actions, which are easier to control. As the seventeenth-century master Rabbi Moses Luzzatto says, "The external movement rouses the inner one and certainly the external movement is more in his power than the inner ones. Thus, if he exercises what is in his power to do, this will lead him to also attain what is not in his power."[10]

If we can control our actions, and our actions determine our thoughts, and the combination of actions and thoughts determines who we are, the Jewish answer to the best question—How can I be a better person?—emerges.

The Jewish answer: You can be whoever you choose to be. All you have to do is decide what kind of person you want to be and *act* accordingly.

The nineteenth-century European master Rabbi Yisrael Meir Kagan (known by his great work, *Chofetz Chaim*) was once asked by a young devotee whether it would be better to take a job in the bank cashing checks or taking deposits. The Chofetz Chaim told the young man to cash the checks, because the constant act of giving would make him a giver.[11]

Maimonides, commenting on Rabbi Akiva, says that virtues "do not come to a man according to the quantity of the greatness of the deed, but rather according to the great number of good deeds." It is preferable, therefore, to give many small gifts of charity over one large gift because "the repeated act of generosity" will make the person a giver.[12]

The implications for all of us today are stunning. If you want to be a generous person, don't worry about what latent insecurities may be causing you to donate less than you should. Just give *every* day. If you wish you were friendlier, don't plumb the depths of your childhood to figure out why you are so inwardly focused. Just greet two new people *each* day with a bright hello.

As we contemplate changing ourselves through forming new habits, two questions naturally arise. The first is: How far must I go, *each day*, toward creating a new habit—and thus a new personality trait? The Kotzker Rebbe, speaking about why a Psalm refers to a distance as from east to west, asked his followers, "How far is east to west?" His students would suggest different answers until he told them the correct one: The distance from east to west is one step.[13] Just one step every day will, in time, make you a different person.

The second question: How much time? Time is a crucial element of any future-oriented decision, from investing money to changing character—as it, along with the reward, forms the two determinants of whether a good deal is possible. We do not know precisely how long the plagues lasted. But one analysis, accounting for the length of time a huge swarm of locusts (the eighth plague) would need to consume all the vegetation to when flax and barley ripen in Israel, put it at 20 weeks—and evenly split between the first five and the next five.[14] Thus, it would have taken the Pharaoh thirty-five days to form his habit of insisting that the Jews remain enslaved. No plague, tellingly, could change that.

In the Talmud, Rabbi Yochanan says that it takes thirty days to form a habit.[15] A 2009 study from the *European Journal of Social Psychology* reports that the formation of a habit takes an average of sixty-six days, specifying, "Missing one opportunity to perform the behaviour did not materially affect the habit formation process."[16]

The Jewish philosophy of habit is embodied in the magnificent expression *second nature*. While the idea of one's nature might be complicated (from what it is to how to modify it), one's second nature is very real and not at all complicated. And neither, *thrillingly*, is changing it. One has to choose who he wants to be, select the habits that will make him that kind of person, practice them regularly, and he will soon be acting in accordance with his second nature. And his first nature, whatever it is, will not matter nearly as much as his second nature—which he will have designed and sculpted.

And it all starts with one step taken thoughtfully and performed habitually.

"ALL MY PLAGUES": THE ESSENCE OF GOD, REVEALED IN HAIL

At first glance, the seventh plague seems like a continuation of the preceding ones. Wild animals, cattle disease, boils, and now hail.

But this is not how God sees it. This plague, God tells Moses in Exodus 9:14 to tell the Pharaoh, is equivalent to sending *all My plagues.* Why is it the equivalent of "all My plagues"? Because it will embody the purpose of the plagues—as God explains in Exodus 9:16: "So that My name will be declared throughout the world!"

The Pharaoh is given the opportunity to acknowledge God. If the Pharaoh refuses, this plague will come. This plague would be "a very heavy hail at this time tomorrow, the likes of which have never occurred in Egypt from the day it was founded until now."[1] The severity—the power—is clearly presented. It will be "very heavy," the worst Egypt has ever seen.

But the severity of the plague is not what makes it remarkable. It is the freedom that the Egyptians are given to easily avoid it. "Now, gather in your livestock and all that you have in the field. The hail shall fall on any man or beast that is found in the field and not brought into the house, and they will die."[2] Everyone has the opportunity to avoid the plague. All it requires is acknowledging God and acting accordingly.

We ordinarily think of a warning as something harsh and confrontational. But if one party wants to harm the other party, the first party would not issue a warning. He would just strike. One warns only when he prefers *not* to harm the other. In fact, one who issues a warning sacrifices one of the most important offensive advantages—the element of surprise.

During Israel's 2014 war in Gaza, the Israel Defense Forces deployed a technique known as *roof knocking*. Before destroying a building that was housing terrorists and their weapons, the IDF dropped dummy bombs on the roof. This gave everyone in the building, including terrorists, a chance to leave. The survival of these terrorists would be dangerous, and perhaps lethal, to Israelis. But the IDF still issued a warning. Was the IDF directly employing a lesson from the seventh plague? Certainly—either by design or from having ingrained its teaching.

A warning coming from God would have been completely radical to the Egyptian polytheist. Polytheistic gods were provincial. They had a territory or a people for whom they were responsible, and everyone else was either the enemy or irrelevant. In the Egyptian mind, what kind of God would protect them from a plague? What kind of God would, in the spirit of not wanting them to get hurt, issue a warning?

There is only one possibility: their own God. And that is just what God was announcing: I am your God, too. In fact, I'm everyone's God and there is none other.

Some people heeded the warning. "Whoever feared the word of God among Pharaoh's servants drove his servants and his livestock into the houses." Others did not. "But whoever did not put his heart to the word of God left his servants and his livestock in the field."[3]

The plague is devastating. Exodus 9:25: "Throughout the entire land of Egypt the hail struck all that was in the field, man and beast, all the vegetation of the field, and it broke all the trees of the field."

This arouses a fundamental question. Why didn't the Egyptians just go inside? This wasn't some unproven deity issuing a blustery threat. This was the *seventh* plague! Wouldn't his warning warrant going inside for a few hours?

Rabbi Norman Lamm, in a sermon from 1955, notes how the Torah describes the two classes of Egyptians. There were those who "feared the word of God" and took shelter. And there were those who "did not put his heart to the word of God."[4]

Rabbi Lamm points out that these two are not natural opposites. The natural opposite of one who does not fear God is one who does not believe in God or one who rejects God. There were concepts and words for both of these in ancient Hebrew and available to the author of the Torah. But the Torah rejects those, and instead casts indifference to God as the opposite of fearing him.

The worst attitude, then, that one can have to God is not rejecting or even hating him. Ignorance can be converted into knowledge, and hatred can be transformed into love. If there is nothing there—if there is apathy—there is nothing to even communicate with.

Speaking in the mid-twentieth century in the United States, Rabbi Lamm provides some of the consequences of indifference that he observed. "Medical doctors know that indifference can allow a small growth to develop into something that kills. Marriage counselors know that more marriages are broken by indifference than by differences. The indifference of the Great Powers to the plight of European Jewry resulted in the loss of one-third of our people."[5]

The seventh plague rains down. The Pharaoh, tortured by what he calls in Exodus 9:28 the "overabundance of Godly thunder and hail," agrees to free the Jews. Moses stretches out his hands to God, and the weather catastrophe ends. Then the Pharaoh changes his mind and refuses to let Moses's people go.

The seventh plague fails.

"CAN'T YOU SEE EGYPT IS LOST?": WHEN CHANGE IS HARDER THAN IT SHOULD BE

Seven devastating plagues have passed, and the Pharaoh is no closer to freeing the Jews or recognizing God's sovereignty than he was at the beginning. God and Moses are losing. How does God deal with failure?

First, he recognizes it. God realizes that he has not yet been able to convince the Egyptians of his sovereignty and of the truth of ethical monotheism. He concedes his tactic but not his overall mission.

Instead, he pivots. The plagues will continue, but with a different purpose. They will, per Exodus 10:2, enable, "you [to] relate in the ears of your son and your grandson how I toyed around with the Egyptians and about the miraculous signs which I performed among them—that you may know that I am Hashem." He will not educate the world all at once. He will do so through a specific people.

The coming plague of locusts promises to be vicious. "It will consume everything of yours that remains from the hail, and it will eat all of your trees that grow from the field. They will fill your houses, your servants' houses, and the houses of all the Egyptians, in a way which your fathers and grandfathers have not seen since the day they came onto the earth until today."[1]

After delivering that message, Moses and Aaron leave the Pharaoh. This detail—that they left—is important, as it establishes that the Pharaoh is now alone with his advisers. There are no outsiders whom they have to impress, manipulate, or otherwise be inauthentic in front of. It is just the Pharaoh and his advisers. The servants say in Exodus 10:7, "How long will this one be a stumbling block to us? Let the people go and they will worship their God. Do you not yet know that Egypt is lost?"[2]

Do you not yet know that Egypt is lost? What a question! There could be no greater rhetorical assault on the Pharaoh.

This response is instructive because it establishes the relationship that the Pharaoh has with his servants. The servants are not afraid or intimidated by the Pharaoh. The servants express their opinions, which criticize the Pharaoh's positions, freely and directly to him—and suffer no punishment for it. The Pharaoh is not a totalitarian leader who would torture or execute a servant for expressing a contrary opinion.

It is not just that the Pharaoh tolerates this insubordination. He is convinced by it. The Pharaoh, following the advice of his servants, tells Moses that the Jewish men can go to the desert to "serve Hashem"—for, apparently, a prayer service. But of course Moses does not accept the deal on those terms. Moses insists on everyone. It's all or nothing. The Pharaoh chooses nothing. The locusts come, cover "the surface of the entire land," and consume all the grass and all the fruit that was not already destroyed by the hail.

THE NINTH PLAGUE: WHEN EVEN LIGHTING A CANDLE, TO SAVE MY LIFE, IS IMPOSSIBLE

As Rabbi Ana Bonnheim and Professor Devora Ushpizai have both observed, the plagues increase in severity.[1] It would have to be this way: it would only be logical for God to respond to the Pharaoh's continued intransigence by issuing more punishing plagues. Accordingly, the penultimate plague—darkness—must be, from God's perspective, the worst one aside from the tenth: the slaying of the firstborn. This is a bold claim. If you had the choice to avoid any of the first nine plagues, which would you select? The water supply turning to blood and flooding and filling every crevice of your environment, frogs so ubiquitous that they enter your body, wild beasts menacing you (or worse), hail that is filled with fire and kills your animals (the basis of the economy and food supply), or three days of darkness? There could be a case for most of them—but I suspect that darkness is the one that most people would accept. No one even gets physically hurt or even threatened by it. Yet God selects darkness to be the ninth plague. Why?

As ever, the search begins with the text. This plague is described as a "thick darkness" so powerful that "no person could see his brother, nor could any person rise from his place for three days." The Egyptians had an easy solution. According to the National Candle Association, candles were invented five thousand years ago, millennia before the Exodus—*in Egypt*.[2] The Egyptians could have avoided this plague by lighting a candle.

Why didn't they do so? Each child at the Seder will know the answer. And that answer begins a logical progression that each adult will understand, culminating in why God seems to have considered this the worst plague except for the slaying of the firstborn.

Darkness, as every child who has been afraid of the dark knows, is the province of the unrestrained imagination. It is the environment where anxieties are created, exacerbated, and transformed into dread and danger. This fear, known as *nyctophobia,* is also common among adults. A 2017 British study revealed that most adults wake up twice a month feeling that something scary is in the room, and 20 percent check under their beds and close cupboards and drawers to protect against monsters before retiring.[3]

This fear constitutes an immense Jewish concern. As we have previously discussed, the dictate "do not fear" is—by far—the most frequently mentioned commandment in the Torah. Why would the authors of the Torah and the Haggadah have been so deeply concerned about it? There are at least two reasons. The first is articulated by Rabbi Joseph Soloveitchik's self-description: "I know I am perplexed that my fears are irrational, incoherent. At times I am given over to panic; I am afraid of death . . . I don't know what to fear, what not to fear; I am utterly confused and ignorant. Modern man is, existentially, a slave because he is ignorant and fails to identify his own needs [regarding what to fear]."[4] Fear, this great rabbi said, *enslaves.*

The second is articulated by the Spelman College psychologist Beverly Daniel Tatum. "Fear," Professor Tatum writes, "immobilizes, traps words in our throats and stills our tongues . . . when we are afraid, it seems like we cannot think, we cannot speak, we cannot move."[5]

Enslaved and immobilized, a person in fear regards everyone and everything as potential sources of danger—and can't do anything about it. If everyone is a potential or actual threat, then no one is deserving of the trust needed to form a relationship. This is what the Torah seems to be describing. The darkness, per Exodus 10:22, is so "thick"—the fear is so palpable—that no man could "see his brother." If the problem were just physical darkness, the Torah would have used a broader term. It might have said that no man could see "another." But this darkness produces a fear that is so irrational, consuming, and disorienting that it makes sustaining even the closest relationship impossible. The ninth is a plague against Egyptian relationships.

Professor George Vaillant spent more than thirty years directing the Grant Study at Harvard Medical School. The Grant Study has analyzed the lifetime happiness and wellness of 268 college sophomores from the classes of 1939–44, including John F. Kennedy. With the study now ending,

Professor Vaillant and his colleagues are able to make final conclusions. "When the study started," Professor Vaillant said in 2017, "nobody cared about empathy or attachment." At its near conclusion, he identified the three ingredients for a long and happy life: "Relationships, relationships and relationships."[6]

It took generations of Harvard social scientists to discover what the author of the Torah taught us in the ninth plague: that the determinant of happiness is relationships. This plague against Egyptian relationships caused no man to be able to, per Exodus 10:23, "rise from his place"—get out of bed—for three days. What kind of darkness has these qualities: one that is physically felt, radically isolates each person, and makes any engagement with the world impossible? The kind described by William Styron in his masterpiece *Darkness Visible,* the kind described by Churchill as his "black dog," the kind that Samuel Johnson said that he would trade his right arm to be rid of.

This is psychological depression, judged by the author of the Torah to be worse than blood, hail, locusts, and wild beasts.

PRELUDE TO THE TENTH PLAGUE: MOSES BECOMES A LEADER

The tenth plague is unlike any of the preceding nine. First, there is a long prelude. This prelude is one of the most dramatic moments in literature and religion. As such, it is the quintessential teaching moment, and the author of the Torah will take it to guide us in a variety of important ways as individuals, as Jews, and as children of God.

In Exodus 12:35, Moses tells the Jews to ask the Egyptians for silver, gold, and clothing on their way out. This might seem like an outrageous request, but the Egyptians are happy to comply! The reason for the immediate acceptance of this request is provided in the preceding chapter. Per Exodus 11:3: "The Lord disposed the Egyptians favorably toward the people. Moreover, Moses himself was much esteemed in the land of Egypt, among Pharaoh's courtiers and among the people."

Moses is popular? Moses, who is the human embodiment of nine devastating plagues? Moses, who is taking the slaves out of a slave economy? This Moses is "much esteemed" all throughout the land of Egypt?

Apparently, yes. Why? One thing we will soon see is that there has been no moral reckoning on the part of the Egyptians. Moses, to the Egyptian mind, has a lot of power. And perhaps that, to this people whose theology is based on strength and power, is enough. The Egyptians do not become philo-Semites, but the causes for the contempt they showed earlier are gone. The powerful Jews are doing much better in their relations with the Egyptians than the weak Jews did earlier.

Moses delivers the plague to the Pharaoh in Exodus 11:4:

Toward midnight I will go forth among the Egyptians, and every firstborn in the land of Egypt shall die, from the firstborn of Pharaoh who sits on his throne to the firstborn of the slave girl who is behind the millstones and all the firstborn of the cattle. And there will be a big cry in all the land of Egypt, that there has been none like it and there won't continue to be like it. But not a dog will move its tongue at any of the Children of Israel, from man to animal, so that you'll know that God will distinguish between Egypt and Israel. And all these servants of yours will come down to me, and they'll bow to me, saying: "Go out, you and all the people who are at your feet." And after that, I'll go out![1]

Moses leaves the Pharaoh "in burning anger." This is, in the words of University of Georgia professor Richard Elliott Friedman, "tremendously important, a turning point in Moses' life." Before this point, Moses was only channeling God. Now he is also speaking for himself, telling the Pharaoh that the Egyptian leaders will bow down to him and that he will go out on his terms. Moses is now a confident leader.[2]

The notion that Moses would introduce himself as a leader through anger is instructive. One of the thirteen attributes of God that will be revealed in Exodus 34:6 is that God is "slow to anger." Maimonides explains that anger is an "exceedingly bad quality; one from which it is proper that one distance himself to an extreme." He likens anger to idolatry and states that it causes wisdom to depart from a scholar and the prophetic spirit to depart from a prophet.[3] Anyone who has seen what otherwise nice, thoughtful, and intelligent people can say and do when angry can understand why this quality is uniquely condemned.

And yet Moses introduces himself with *extreme* anger and is not criticized by God or anyone else for it. The reason for his anger must have something to do with why it is justified. Moses has just told the Pharaoh that at about midnight, God will strike down the Egyptian firstborn. How would Moses, as God's greatest prophet, have felt about that? God had shown with his warning at the hail plague that he did not want to harm any Egyptian. Moses, learning from God, wants to achieve his objective without inflicting unnecessary pain upon the Egyptians. It would have been easy for the Pharaoh to relent and avoid all those deaths. But this is not what he chose.

Resh Lakish, the rabbi in the Talmud who was previously a gladiator, imagines Moses slapping the Pharaoh in the face, as if to try to literally knock sense into him—and avoid the killings that are otherwise going to happen.[4]

Moses's anger, whether accompanied by a slap or not, has no effect.

ALLEGIANCES BUILD: THE ARCHITECTURE OF RELATIONSHIPS, THE CONSTITUTION OF SOCIETY

The tenth plague is unique for many reasons. One is that it is the only plague for which there is a break between its announcement and its execution. And quite a break it is. No one except, *maybe,* God knows whether the Jews will be freed—or what anyone will conclude about God from the plague sequence. The Jews have to consider that there is a good chance that the plagues will fail and that they will be consigned to brutal slavery en route to individual and national death. God has to consider that everything he dreamed of since Creation will be for naught and that his future in the world—his role as the God in history—will be finished.

The stakes are as high as they could be. God uses this opportunity to teach. God says, in Exodus 12:3,

> Tell the whole community of Israel that on the tenth day of this month each man is to take a lamb for his family, one for each household. If any household is too small for a whole lamb, they must share one with their nearest neighbor, having taken into account the number of people there are. You are to determine the amount of lamb needed in accordance with what each person will eat. . . . Do not leave any of it until the morning.

We have discussed this passage previously, in the section covering how and why the Seder is done in households. In the Pesach spirit of retelling and reliving, it is worth revisiting this passage now in its chronological context in the Exodus story.

As previously discussed, the "no leftovers" direction in this Torah passage has profound and perpetual implications. It would take at least fifteen people to consume a lamb. No household could do so alone. The first, and fundamental, act of a free people is to give and share—and, in so doing, to create a community.

The Christian author Linda Cox analyzes the Hebrew word *v'natanu*, which means "and they shall give." The word, as in the English transliteration (*natan*), is a palindrome—it reads the same in either direction. She calls it "God's palindrome"[1]—as it indicates that giving is always a two-way activity. The giver always receives.

It is easily understandable that giving is gratifying and therefore that the giver automatically receives at least the pleasure that accompanies gratification. But the author of the Torah, in Exodus 12:3, extends God's palindrome much further—and shows how it forms the basis of the entirely original Jewish conception of how people can best engage socially and commit communally.

The key to this moral invention is the word *each*—as in "each" man is to take a lamb for his household. Individuals may participate differently in this ritual. Some may host and some may attend. But the differences should not detract from the governing principle. Everyone must participate. And this universal participation is structured so that everyone both has and fulfills a need.

The needs are fairly simple. The poor need the rich for the lamb. The rich need the poor to fulfill the obligation to finish the lamb completely that night. The Jewish society would be, as we relive with the invitation "All who are needy, let them come and celebrate Pesach," one of mutual responsibility and universal participation. And the implications are awesome.

As we have previously discussed, the first thing that God says about man is that we are created in his image. This was a radically subversive claim. Ancient peoples generally held that the royal elites were created in the image of their gods, and everyone else existed to serve them. In came the Torah, saying that everyone is created in the image of God. And if everyone is created in the image of God, then everyone shares the most important part of who they are—meaning that, fundamentally, all people are created equal.

But every idea in this world, even one directly from God, needs a hospitable environment in order to flourish. The Jews of Genesis were a feuding family without a land and with only sporadic engagement with the other peoples. Then we were slaves in Egypt. In neither case did we have the opportunity to do much with the idea that all people are created in the image of God.

On the other hand, if the Exodus worked, we would be a free people— first in the desert and then in our own Land. We would have the opportunity to put the metaphysical idea of equality into practice. We would be able to construct a society as God dreamed of—one that would be a dwelling place for him and a light unto the nations. This ambition had never been conceived before. How could such a society be constructed?

With one word—*each*—God provides the seminal instruction about how to create this society. There would be no group of elites with a close relationship to God who would instruct the lesser people. No one will hand out the lambs to everyone else. Each person has the obligation to fulfill God's instruction. As Rabbi Samson Raphael Hirsch writes, the consumption of the lamb was, "at one and the same time, both a communal sacrifice and an individual sacrifice. It was a national act, not performed by national representatives but by each individual Jew."[2] Each person bears the responsibility of the collective, and in that notion democratic citizenship is born.

This act—this individual and national act—contains the logic that will resolve one of the most persistent and vexing questions humans face. It is a question that has been expressed everywhere, with the most widespread political and personal implications. It is the question of what happens when multiple obligations meet limited resources—thus, it is probably the most frequently presented moral question. It is: To whom am I responsible?

We have a variety of social affiliations, often manifested in our attachments to family, to friends, to community, to society, to the nation, and to humankind. We can also be fans of the same team, veterans of the same unit, colleagues at the same company, descendants from the same land, alumni of the same school, participants in the same club, members of the same political party, congregants of the same synagogue, devotees of the same cause, and infinitely more. The result of there being limited resources (of time, money, and attention) and many affiliations is that our responsibilities seem to compete with and crowd each other out.

Consequently, the question *To whom am I responsible?* challenges us to this day and sometimes, seemingly, all day.

This question is answered in Exodus 12 and amplified throughout the rest of the Torah.

All obligation starts with an individual—"each man"—a unique, responsible, full individual created in the image of God. The individual then joins a household. The households, through the commitments they make together on this greatest night in history, form a community. This community exists in tribes, which are named at the end of Genesis and will be important throughout the Torah. And the tribes will form the Jewish nation, which, through its conduct and its interactions, will be a light unto the nations.

Allegiances, the author of the Torah teaches us in Exodus 12, do not require trade-offs. Instead, they build on each other. Strong individuals create good families. Good families provide the bulwark for vibrant communities. Vibrant communities create healthy societies. Healthy societies enable great nations. And great nations inspire the world.

The notion of how allegiances do not trade off but instead build will be present through the rest of the Torah, both subtly and directly. In Numbers 24:5, the gentile seer Balaam observes of the Jews: "How goodly are thy tents, O Jacob, and thy tabernacles, O Israel!"[3] The good tents come first, and are followed by good tabernacles.

In Deuteronomy 15:11, Moses summarizes the obligations of the Torah in part by saying: "Therefore, I command you, saying, you shall surely open your hand to your brother, to your poor one and to your needy one in the Land." The order, as with the hardening of the Pharaoh's heart, is dispositive. One's first obligation is to his family, then to his city, and then to the entire Land. Jewish obligation begins at home, but they do not end there. We are to become good particularists in order to become great universalists. As the writer Cynthia Ozick notes, we blow into the narrow end of the shofar to create a sound that is heard through the wide end.[4]

How did this Torah insight prove itself throughout history? A few thousand years after the events of Exodus 12, the British philosopher and parliamentarian Edmund Burke stated what became one of the most most important ideas in modern political thought: "To be attached to the subdivision, to love the little platoon we belong to in society, is the first principle (the germ as it were) of public affections. *It is the first link in the series by which we proceed towards a love to our country, and to mankind.*"[5] True—and a beautiful restatement or interpretation of what Jews have learned at Pesach from Exodus 12.

We can assess this insight, as well, using twenty-first-century social science. It is obvious that married people, and particularly married people with children, usually have more claims on their time than single people. One might think, thus, that the domestic responsibilities that married people have will make them less able to engage in civic and universalist activities than single people. Yet married people (especially those with children) both volunteer and vote at vastly higher rates than single adults.[6]

Just as married people have obligations that single people do not, religious people have responsibilities that secular people do not. At the very least, this includes supporting faith-based institutions with time and money. Given the financial demands of religious charities, it might not be surprising that religious people give more to charity than do secular people. What is surprising—although perhaps not to the students of Exodus 12—is that religious people give far more to *secular charities* than do secular people.[7] Conditioned and habituated to give in the little platoons, religious people become stronger universalists.

The great observer of the United States Alexis de Tocqueville called America a "nation of joiners." Two centuries later, that designation is still true—although there is significant variance in who joins. People of any religion are likelier to join groups than those who are unaffiliated, and Jews are far likelier to join groups than anyone else.[8]

Still, Jews have a lot to learn from this Exodus sequence. Rabbi Shlomo Carlebach was a frequent guest on American college campuses in the 1960s and '70s. He often asked the students about their faith. He said that if a student said that he was a Catholic, he knew that the student was a Catholic. If a student said that he was a Protestant, he knew that the student was a Protestant. If the student said, "I am a humanist," Rabbi Carlebach knew that he was a Jew.[9]

Similarly, the youth movement of Conservative Jewry voted in 2014 to allow its youth leaders to date gentiles. The main reason given: "the recognition that they [gentiles] were created *B'tzelem Elohim* (in the image of God)."[10]

It is perfectly clear in the Torah that *everyone* is created in the image of God. It is also perfectly clear that Jews who want to marry only Jews can do so in accordance with the highest principles of biblical humanism. For it is by being proud Jews, by building warm and inviting *Jewish* homes, and by participating in a vibrant Jewish community that we can most effectively serve as friends, allies, and colleagues of gentiles.

The most ambitious Jewish vision—*the messianic vision*—involves this kind of Jewish identity along with the similar identities of others. The prophet Isaiah describes what will happen "on that day"—the day when the Messiah comes. The nations of the world—he enumerates Egypt, Israel, and Assyria—will recognize the Lord. The groups will not merge into one universalist entity where anyone will marry anyone, and distinctions and differences are erased. Instead, the Egyptians, Assyrians, and Jews will remain distinct as God says in Isaiah 19:25, "Blessed be Egypt my people, Assyria my handiwork, and Israel my inheritance." The groups, in the presence of the Messiah, will remain separate and independent—but will worship the one God together.

It is by forming strong and distinctive groups (of faith, of nation, of much else) that people can cultivate the values and characteristics that can make us, *simultaneously,* engaged and effective universalists—now and "in that day."

HASTE: THE MORAL IMPERATIVE OF SPEED

The attire is dictated. Exodus 12:11: "This is how you shall eat it: your loins girded, your sandals on your feet, and your staff in your hand; and you shall eat it in haste: it is a Pesach offering to the Lord." It is, perhaps, not as much attire as a uniform. Uniforms are clothing made purposeful—to make the wearer noticeable (a retail worker or a police officer), deindividualized (the Yankees baseball jersey, which has no last name on it), or optimized for a specific activity (a bicycle racer). Here, the uniform is to enable the Jews to leave fast—in the moment and forever, with imagery that will stay with readers of the Torah forever.

The imagery is a literary masterpiece. We, thousands of years later, can *feel* the anticipation and almost join our ancestors at what became the model of the Seder. This literature invites us to live with our ancestors in the liminal space between slavery and freedom. And it certainly enables us to experience the purpose of the uniform. It is Moses telling us how to be prepared for God, an instruction that is issued in Egypt and carries forward until this day.

The existential word from this passage is *haste*. The irony about its importance is that it is, in this passage, unnecessary. When one is instructed to have a meal with shoes on his feet, a staff in his hand, and his loins girded, he does not expect a leisurely dinner. Why, then, does the author of the Torah have to instruct our ancestors to eat in haste? The appearance and continued reappearance of the word *haste*, even when it is not necessary from a literary perspective, can only be in the great guidebook that is the Torah for one reason: to teach us something about haste as an idea and an imperative itself.

What could it be? The first clue: "Haste" does not make its biblical entrance in the Pesach story. In Genesis 18, three strangers appear at Abraham's tent as he is recovering from his circumcision. Abraham tells them that he is going to prepare a meal for them. These strangers are on a journey, and they presumably are not in danger of missing any appointments. Still, Abraham "hurried" to Sarah and tells her, "Quick"—make some cakes. Then Abraham "ran" to pick out a calf and he gives it to a servant, who "hurried" to prepare it.

Abraham is not the only person who "hurried" when the task's performance did not demand immediacy. Many years later, Abraham's unnamed servant goes on a mission to find a wife for Abraham's son Isaac. The servant meets Rebecca, who gives him a drink of water. But she doesn't just "give" him a drink of water. Rebecca, per Genesis 24:18, "quickly lowered" the jug and gives him the drink. When he finishes drinking the water, she says that she has to get water for his camels. "So she *hurried* and emptied her jug into the trough and kept running to the well to draw water . . ."

The servant wasn't going anywhere, and the camels certainly weren't either. So why is Rebecca rushing so much? And why does the Torah, in which every word is significant, tell us how fast she lowers the jug to give to the servant? What's going on with all this rushing—from Abraham, from Rebecca, from God's instruction to the Jews on our most fateful night?

The great eighteenth-century Italian rabbi Moses Luzzatto explains,

> When the time of its performance [that of a good deed] comes, or when it happens to present itself to him, or when the thought of performing it enters his mind, he should hurry and hasten to seize hold of it and perform it, and not allow time to lapse. For there is no danger like its danger. Since, behold each new second that arises can bring with it a new impediment to a good deed . . . It is to be observed that all the deeds of the righteous are done in haste.[1]

If one waits, a seemingly sensible reason not to do the deed will inevitably present itself. There will be a competing priority, a reason that it is really better that performance of the good deed wait, a promise to get to it later when one is less busy. An alliance between rationalization, deprioritization, and forgetfulness is always ready to do battle, often secretly, against the urge to do a good deed—and will usually win. So Abraham, Rebecca, and Moses effectively instruct: Don't give it a chance. When the opportunity to do a good deed presents itself, they say, the pace to do it is "with haste." The time to do it is *now*.

The long prelude is over. It is time for the tenth plague.

THE TENTH PLAGUE:
WHAT IT MEANS THAT THE
JEWS ARE THE CHOSEN PEOPLE

*Toward midnight I will go forth among the Egyptians, and every
firstborn in the land of Egypt shall die, from the firstborn of
Pharaoh who sits on his throne to the firstborn of the slave girl
who is behind the millstones and all the firstborn of the cattle.
And there will be a big cry in all the land of Egypt, that there
has been none like it and there won't continue to be like it.*

The tenth plague: the slaying of the firsrtborn of Egypt. Every Egyptian
home will have a dead child.

The prerequisite to approaching this plague is to consider: Who is the
firstborn? Most people will respond: That is easy: the firstborn is one who
was born ahead of all the others. In other words, the oldest. Why, one might
reasonably ask, are you asking such an obviously answered question?

Because of what we learn in Exodus 4:22, the prelude to the plagues.
God, through Moses, is beginning the process of educating the Pharaoh
about who the Jews are—and who God is. He does so through a curious instruction. "Say to Pharaoh," he tells Moses, "So said Hashem, 'My *firstborn*
son is Israel.'" But the Jews weren't the first people in the Torah—not even
close. Abraham, the first Jew, fought in a war involving *nine* other peoples.
And these don't include some of the other peoples who also precede the Jews:
the Amorites, the Canaanites, the Hittites, the Perritizes, the Jebusites, and
others.

Complicating God's instruction to Moses is the context in which it is

issued. The ancient world was oriented around primogeniture, which accords special privileges and responsibilities to the chronologically firstborn.
And God hates it. Whether Cain v. Abel, Ishmael v. Isaac, Esau v. Jacob,
Leah v. Rachel, Joseph v. his brothers, Peretz and Zerach, Manasseh and
Ephraim, God constantly has a non-chronologically firstborn child receive
the familial privilege—which is usually generational leadership, the ability
to marry first, or primary responsibility for transmitting Judaism into the
future. This subversion of primogeniture is often the cause of severe tension,
which manifests itself in family exile, blinding jealousy, and attempted fratricide and actual fratricide.

Why would God, who subverts the system of primogeniture at every opportunity and at any cost, declare the Jews to be his firstborn? More, God
implies that our status as the firstborn is our defining characteristic, as it is
all he instructs Moses to tell the Pharaoh about us. What is going on here?

This is a quintessential example of what Maimonides (citing the Talmud)
means when he says that the Torah speaks in the language of man.[1] Anyone
in a multichild family can understand the usual role of the firstborn. If the
firstborn tells her younger siblings to violate the rules and ignore the values
of their parents, the result will be an unhappy family that fails to transmit
the values of the parents through the generations. If the firstborn in a family
faithfully guides her siblings toward her parents' deepest moral ambitions,
the family can be happy and have its values effectively transmitted.

The firstborn in the Torah's imagination is, therefore, not about chronol-
ogy. It is about transmission. It is about who is going to most effectively
carry the values of the parent to the other children. In telling Moses to tell
the Pharaoh that the Jews are his firstborn, God wants the Pharaoh to know
who God wants Jews to be. We are to be God's culture carriers, the people
who transmit the message of ethical monotheism to the nations of the world.

This is what it means to be "the chosen people." Being the chosen people
does not mean that God loves us or cares about us more than any of his
other children—any more than a parent loves or favors her first child over all
others. It means that God expects us, through what we say and how we act,
to carry his message to the world—to become, as the prophet Isaiah said,
a light unto the nations. It does not mean having a special status; it means
having a distinctive obligation with commensurate responsibilities.

God makes this abundantly clear in Exodus 19:5. We can only be his "most beloved treasure of all peoples" if we "hearken well to Me and observe my covenant." If we don't? The prophet Amos says, "You only have I singled out of all the families of the earth: therefore I will visit upon you all your iniquities."

Correspondingly, the firstborn in the Egyptian household is no more the eldest child than the Jews are the first people on earth. He is the culture carrier. By ordering the slaying of the Egyptian firstborn, God is decreeing that the culture of Egypt be destroyed. Its chain of transmission will be cut. The culture that brutally enslaved a stranger people, the culture of warring and provincial gods devoid of any morality, the culture that drowned all Jewish baby boys in the Nile would be annihilated.

The Egyptians would receive their message on this fateful night. How about the Jews? The choreography of that evening, as provided in Exodus 12, provides the message. The Jews are to cover our doors in blood, stay up all night in anticipation, and then suddenly rush out into an entirely new world. What does that describe? There is only one possibility. It is a birth scene. The Jews, on this night, are to begin again. The night would become, as President Abraham Lincoln said in 1863 while contemplating a different liberation, a new birth of freedom. And the leader will be a third-born child—Moses.

With the primogeniture of Genesis and the slavery of Exodus gone, the Jews would finally have the opportunity to become God's firstborn. What culture would this potentially firstborn people carry? The qualities are articulated in Exodus 12 right before the final plague: It will be a culture of education, of generosity, of respect for individuals and regard for the community they build, of openness, of being wholehearted with God and with others, and of readiness to serve.

At midnight, Hashem smites the firstborn in every Egyptian household. Every house, the Torah tells us, has a corpse. The Pharaoh calls to Moses and Aaron and tells them that they can leave—the children, the sheep, and the cattle, everyone and everything.

The Pharaoh even asks Moses and Aaron for a blessing.

The Jews rush out, with gold and silver provided by the Egyptians. The Pharaoh had changed his mind so many times before. What is this man of habit likely to do this time? The Jews are in a race against time.

And so the Jews get ready to leave. The Jews are joined (as previously discussed) by a "mixed multitude"—gentiles. This mixed multitude must have been largely Egyptians who had chosen to align themselves with the Jewish people and the Jewish future. There is no textual indication that they converted. We can presume that they maintain their gentile identities while living as friends and allies of the Jews.

And then there were those who did convert. The rules regarding them are clearly dictated in these precious moments. God says in Exodus 12:49,

> When a proselyte sojourns among you he shall make the Pesach-offering for Hashem; each of his males shall be circumcised and then he may draw near to perform it and he shall be like the native of the Land; no uncircumcised male may eat of it. One law shall there be for the native and the proselyte.

From the start, the proselytes are as much a part of the emerging Jewish nation as those who descended directly from Jacob and Joseph.

It is this moment that makes it easy for Maimonides to respond as he does in his famous letter to Obadiah, a convert to Judaism. Obadiah asks whether he should say "God of *our* fathers" and "God who brought *us* out of Egypt." Addressing the man as "the wise and learned proselyte," Maimonides writes, "You should say everything as prescribed. Do not change anything. Rather, you shall bless and pray in the same way that every natural-born Jew blesses and prays, whether as an individual or when leading the congregation."[2]

In other words, as one of God's firstborn.

HOVERING, RESCUING, AND PROTECTING: NO ONE "PASSED OVER" ANYTHING, AND WHY THAT IS IMPORTANT

As mentioned earlier, the term *Passover* is a terrible term for this great holiday. The term "Passover" derives from a mistake concerning the word "Pesach." The mistake is a mistranslation and a misunderstanding that blocks some of the deeply profound guidance that this holiday offers.

In Exodus 12:7, God instructs the Jews to take blood from the sacrificed lamb and to put it on the doorposts and on the lintels of their homes. The blood, God explains six verses later, "shall be a sign for *you* upon the houses where you are. I shall see the blood and *pasach* over you; there shall not be a plague of destruction upon you when I strike in the land of Egypt." It is this *pasach* that is often translated as "Passover"—with the interpretation being that we put blood on our doorposts so that "the destroyer" of Exodus 12:23 (God's agent, who would carry out the plague) would know which homes were Jewish and God would pass over them.

There are four problems with this analysis.

First, several of the plagues exempted the Jews. Yet God does not need any help identifying which homes are Jewish in those instances. He presumably does not lose that capability.

Second, the Jews are commanded to apply blood to the doorposts (the vertical sides of the door) and to the lintel (the upper horizontal side). If God needs to be shown which homes are Jewish, why would he need blood outlining the door in all three places?

Third, if the "destroyer" is destroying, would a Jewish household want

God "passing over" it? No! A Jewish household would want God to come and stay—unless, as we'll see, he is really already there.[1]

Fourth, God specifies very clearly in Exodus 12:13 who the blood is for. "The blood shall be a sign *for you* upon the houses where you are." Not, in other words, for *God*—but for *you*. And "you," of course, is us.

This raises two questions. First, what is the purpose of the blood? Second, what is *pasach*?

We have discussed one purpose of the blood—to show the Jews that the fateful night in Egypt is a birth scene, during which we would be reborn. As Rabbi Norman Lamm said in a 1969 sermon, there is another, complementary, purpose that is revealed by the location of the blood in the home. It is not in the bedroom or the dining room but on the doorpost, which is where people enter and exit their homes. The purpose of the blood is to educate the Jews, forever, regarding how to enter *and* exit *our* homes.

On the most important night in history, God is telling us: You must be a Jew in your comings and your goings. You must be a Jew when you are at home and when you are in the world. When you come home, you are to create a Jewish home—one full of Torah and moral education, one full of joy and support, one full of love and learning. When you go out, you are to do so as Jews—as ambassadors of God, as representatives of your people, and embodying the principles of the great freedom story that reached its culmination on the night our ancestors put the blood on the doorposts.[2]

If Pesach is not "Passover," what is it? To translate words from the Torah, we generally go to other sources that mention the same word. This enables us to ascertain how, by analyzing the context in both cases, the meanings might overlap and the definition can thus reveal itself. The term *Pesach* appears at another place in the Bible—in Isaiah 31:5, in reference to the Assyrian invasion of Israel in the eighth century B.C.E. "Like birds hovering overhead / the Lord Almighty will shield it and deliver it / He will *pasoach* it and will rescue it."

That's it! *Pesach* means "hover over"—with the purpose of *hovering over* being shielding, sparing, protecting, and ultimately delivering and rescuing.[3] When "the destroyer" is doing his work and God is hovering over our homes, he is performing another service that cannot be explained by any notion of "passing over." He is performing a function that, to the enslaved Jews, would have seemed inexplicably absent for too long a time.

He is watching. He is watching over us.

WATCHING: THE EXISTENTIAL EXPERIENCE

After the tenth plague concludes, the biblical author does something unique. He interprets the immediately previous events, encapsulating in one phrase everything that had just happened. In Exodus 12:42, the Torah says simply, "*It is a night of watching* for the Lord, to bring them out of Egypt, so this same night is a night of watching for all the Children of Israel throughout their generations."

Throughout their generations: that is us—you, me, and other Seder-goers in the twenty-first century.

Night of watching. If we were to associate one idea with the Exodus, reasonable choices might include freedom, liberation, community, faith. All those, the author of the Torah would certainly say, are important. But the most important takeaway from the Exodus, the theme of the Pesach story, is something else. It is *watching*.

Watching?

We normally associate watching with activities such as television, sports, and birds. But the Torah's summing up of the Exodus cannot be a call to passive observance. There must be something deeply active and of existential importance about watching.

What could it be?

A slave's fundamental experience is being watched. The slave master is concerned that the slave will reject or resist doing what and going where he is told, and so the slave master watches. He never stops watching.

On the fifteenth of Nisan, the fact that the Jewish people are being watched stays the same. But everything about it is completely different. No longer are the Jews being watched by our Egyptian slave masters. We are now being watched by God, hovering over our homes to protect us.

The idea of watching hits a crescendo in the Exodus, as the responsibility of watching shifts from the Egyptians to God. But it has a long history, as if the author of the Torah were just waiting for the moment when it could be done right. The Torah tells us in Genesis 2:15 that man's role in the Garden of Eden is to "watch over it." Cherubs (angels) are soon assigned to "watch over" the path to the tree of life. Shortly thereafter, Cain murders Abel and says what has become one of the most famous lines in the Torah: "Am I my brother's keeper?" But the word is not really *keeper*—it is *shomer:* "watchman." In his blistering response, God issues his first instruction about human relations: we are to watch over our brethren.

In Genesis 26:5, God gives his divine covenant to Abraham. It is that "all the nations of the earth will be blessed through your seed because Abraham listened to my voice and kept my watch." Watching over God's creation, or watching with God, is what will qualify the world to receive his ultimate blessing.

After the pivotal "night of watching," the Torah continues to use *watching,* per Professor Richard Elliott Friedman, as a "standard expression in the Torah for conveying loyalty to God." We are instructed to watch the Sabbath to sanctify it, watch the commandments, watch the month of spring, watch ourselves lest we forget God, and watch the opening of our mouth.[1] The fundamental purpose of Pesach itself, according to God in Exodus 12:24, is to "watch this matter as a statute for you and your children forever."

So *of course* the Torah names the most important evening in history the "night of watching" and the holiday on which it would be commemorated *Pesach*—after God's hovering over our homes in an act of obvious and active watching.

In the context of the Torah being the ultimate guidebook, what can we learn from all this existential watching?

Perhaps two things—related to watching's two functions: as a mechanism for evaluation, and an expression of caring. The role of evaluation in watching is articulated by the biblical Job: "For His eyes are upon man's ways and He sees all his steps."[2] Evolution has conditioned us for watching and being watched. The human eye, compared with that of other mammels, has the most color contrast (the whites of the eyes against the colored pupils) and the smallest pupils. The evolutionary purpose is to optimize people for "gaze detection"—watching and being watched.[3] This is presumably to enable us to detect a threat in our environment that may come from someone who may be observing us. It also has significant moral consequences. A study by Melissa Bateson and colleagues at Newcastle University shows that just a poster of staring eyes in a university cafeteria reduced littering by fifty percent.[4]

"Watched people," in the words of the psychologist Ara Norenzayan, "are nice people."[5]

There is another way to conceive of the experience of being watched, which also explains why we are conditioned by evolution for it. It helps to maximize the chances for our children's long-term survival. This is the one that is described in one of the most haunting love songs in the American songbook, George and Ira Gershwin's "Someone to Watch over Me": "There is someone I am longing to see / I hope that he turns out to be / Someone to watch over me."

Exactly. That is what love is: a commitment to watch over the beloved, to anticipate their needs and understand their dreams, to always be as ready to act on behalf of the watched as God instructs the Jews to be during the last meal in Egypt. This is what we do for our child when we stand over her crib and just watch her sleep. In a couple of decades, she will decide who she wants to spend her life with. We will want many things for her in that moment, but mostly someone who will watch over her when we are no longer able to. Perhaps the most common words on one's deathbed are: "Promise me that you will watch over your mother (or brother or sister) when I'm gone."

What do we want the person doing the watching (ourselves, our child's spouse, the person we are asking on our deathbed) to watch for? Anything and everything, always and forever—whatever, at any given point, our beloved needs to be shielded, protected, and rescued from.

It is the first experience of freedom and, since the Exodus, the faith of the Jew: God is watching us and watching over us.

WHY POLITICAL ARGUMENTS ARE USUALLY A WASTE OF TIME, OR WORSE

Do the plagues work?

Exodus 14:5: "Now it was told to the king of Egypt that the people had fled and the heart of Pharaoh and his servants was turned against the people; and they said, 'Why have we done this, that we have let Israel go from serving us?'" The Pharaoh then sends "all the chariots of Egypt" to catch the Jews before we make it out of Egypt.

So even after ten plagues, the Pharaoh sends all his chariots to fight the force that had defeated him so catastrophically. They do not go because they have to. As discussed, the direct and contrary feedback from his courtiers after the eighth plague ("Can't you see Egypt is lost?") indicates that he is not a totalitarian figure who kills everyone who disagrees with him. The charioteers go because they, too, want to recapture the Jews. Indeed, Rashi points out that the description of the charioteers' chasing the Jews refers to the Egyptians in the singular (*noseah* instead of *nosiem*).[1] The Egyptian charioteers are riding separately, but they are thinking and acting as one.

Before the plagues started, God had declared their purposes—to show the Egyptians (and through them the world) "that I am the Lord." It would now be a good time for God to evaluate their effectiveness. Ten plagues, including the slaying of the firstborn, are done. The Pharaoh and his charioteer(s) chase the Jews in an attempt to bring us back to Egypt and enslave us again. God gave it his all, but completely failed.

What could God or Moses have done differently or additionally to convince the Pharaoh to free the Jews and/or to embrace ethical monotheism? After having tried everything from a nice request to slaying of the firstborn, it is safe to say: Nothing. Why did the argument, delivered through the words of Moses and the actions of God, fail so completely? It is not because the Pharaoh or his charioteers were special. It is because they were ordinary.

The sixteenth-century statesman Francis Bacon explains in a very different context:

> The human understanding when it has once adopted an opinion (either as being the received opinion or as being agreeable to itself) draws all things else to support and agree with it. And though there be a greater number and weight of instances to be found on the other side, yet these it either neglects and despises or else by some distinction sets aside and rejects.[2]

This description—which could have been of the Pharaoh and his charioteers after ten plagues—has been borne out by modern science. In the 1950s, the psychologist Leon Festinger explored how members of a doomsday cult became more convinced of their apocalyptic views after the fateful time passed.

> A man with a conviction is a hard man to change. Tell him you disagree and he turns away. Show him facts and figures and he questions your sources. Appeal to logic and he fails to see your point. . . . Suppose an individual believes something with his whole heart; suppose further that he has a commitment to this belief and he has taken irrevocable actions because of it; finally, suppose that he is presented with evidence, unequivocal and undeniable evidence, that his belief is wrong: what will happen? The individual will frequently emerge, not only unshaken, but even more convinced of the truth of his beliefs than ever before. Indeed, he may even show a new fervor for convincing and converting other people to his view.[3]

In the twenty-first century, social scientists have used modern capabilities to answer the same question that Professor Festinger asked: How and why do people change their minds? In 2004, Emory University professor Drew Westen put supporters of George Bush and John Kerry under a functional magnetic resonance imaging (fMRI) machine to see how their brains reacted when their candidates contradicted themselves. Professor Westen found that the dorsolateral prefrontal cortex (which is affiliated with reasoning) was not aroused, but the orbitofrontal cortex (which processes emotions), the anterior cingulate cortex (which monitors conflicts), and the posterior cingulate cortex (which is associated with addiction) were.[4] And perhaps most tellingly, once the subjects came to a conclusion, their ventral striatum was aroused. This is the part of the brain that is affiliated with orgasms. As the Pharaoh shows, it is hard to argue with that.

God soon learns that the problem of persuasion is not even limited to opponents. He frees the Jews in a spectacular display so impressive that it would captivate a nation of moviegoers thousands of years later—and follows up by providing for all our needs in the desert and directing us to the Promised Land, where we can fulfill our and his destiny. And yet the Books of Exodus and Numbers are basically chronicles of Jewish intransigence, rebellion, and insecurity that manifest (multiple times) in a stated desire to go back to Egypt! So the plagues don't work with the Egyptians and don't even work when redirected to convince the Jews.

The education that God, and the rest of us with him, receives with the failure of the plagues is one for the ages. It is especially ripe to guide in this era when technology has made attempts at public persuasion so easy to mount. Successful persuasion does not come from sermons, lectures, arguments, singular acts, data, claims, or any other short-term demonstration. It almost always comes as a result of long-term commitment, of genuine compassion (actual "suffering with"), of demonstrated respect and acts of love. It is living far more than telling—it is admiration far more than instruction—that leads people to want to believe what someone else believes. The Exodus, God learns, is just the beginning of the process of showing even the Jews who he is and what it should mean for them. The lesson, as Rabbi David Wolpe says, is that this kind of education would "have to be done in every generation and with every child."[5]

Hence, the Seder.

THE SECRET TO HAPPINESS
AND GOODNESS

*Rabbi Jose the Galilean said: How does one derive that
the Egyptians . . . were struck by fifty plagues and
at the Sea by two hundred and fifty!*

The next section of the Haggadah contains a seemingly obscure and even weird debate between three rabbis: Rabbi Jose the Galilean, Rabbi Eliezer, and Rabbi Akiva. It is about the number of plagues that enabled the Jews to escape from Egypt. The debate goes from 60 to 240 to 300, with Rabbi Akiva arguing for the highest number.

Before discussing why the authors of the Haggadah judge Rabbi Akiva the winner, a more fundamental question emerges. Why does it matter how many plagues some ancient rabbis identify in the Pesach story? How can a plague-counting contest among ancient rabbis help us to live better, fuller, and more meaningful lives today?

First, it is important to define what a plague is. Given that the debate starts at 60, these plagues are obviously not only the ten discussed at the Seder. The rabbis are defining divine interventions (or miracles) as plagues. This debate among the rabbis is an invitation for us to discuss and understand the nature of miracles. And quite a debate it is! There is a 500 percent variation in the number of divine interventions that they identify.

And before understanding what a miracle is (and, thus, how it can be identified), it is important to identify what it is not. The dictionary definition of miracle is, "A surprising and welcome event that is not explicable by natural and scientific laws and is therefore considered to be the work of a divine agency."[1] This definition of *miracle* is essentially the same as that offered by the Egyptians in the third plague. In that plague, God produces gnats, and the Egyptian magicians respond by attempting to produce more gnats. They fail. After they fail—*because* they fail—they say, "This is the finger of God."[2] Because there is a gap in scientific understanding of capability—here, producing gnats—they credit God.

In his 1894 lecture "The Ascent of Man," the Scottish biologist and evangelist Henry Drummond named this theory the *god of the gaps*. Its adherents, Drummond writes, "ceaselessly scan the books of Nature and the fields of Science in search of gaps—gaps they will fill up with God."[3] Drummond contrasts his God—the "immanent God, the God of evolution"—with "the occasional wonder-worker" who exists in ignorance (the gaps) and then disappears with knowledge.

To assess the god of the gaps, we can posit a scenario of three people: Jim, Joan, and Jack.

A. Jim turns fifteen and contracts a disease that is surely fatal. The best doctors in the world consult on his case and tell him that he likely will not make it through the week. He prays and is fine the next morning. His case is studied, as no one can scientifically explain his recovery.

B. Two years later, Joan turns fifteen and contracts the same disease. In the time since Jim got sick, a drug that cures the disease was discovered. Joan takes it and is fine.

C. Jack turns fifteen and never gets the disease.

Where can God be most easily identified? Some people, unwittingly evoking the god of the gaps, will say that God was most present in Jim's case. But why would a pharmaceutical development have the power to suddenly displace God? Why would God be present in ignorance and absent in knowledge? He gave us the ability to learn! Given that Jack is the most fortunate of the three children, wouldn't God be most deserving of recognition in his case?

The Jewish alternative to the "God of the Gaps" is foreshadowed in the prelude to the Exodus story. Moses is tending his flock in the desert when "the angel of the Lord appeared to him in flames of fire from within a bush." This is the opposite of a gap, as bushes burn in the desert all the time. However, Moses identifies a "great sight"—that the bush is on fire but is not consumed. It is Moses's *watching and then noticing* something different and spectacular in an otherwise everyday occurrence that leads God to select this displaced shepherd to lead the Jewish people from slavery to freedom and to introduce God to the world.

It is not only that Moses notices, important as that is. It is that he notices the presence of God in the ordinary. This would be the idea that would guide Jews forever. The Midrash says, "Every day, miracles befall a person as great as the miracles of the Exodus."[4] Observant Jews acknowledge this by praying three times a day: "Your miracles every day with us."[5] These everyday miracles are acknowledged in the one hundred blessings an observant Jew makes every day for occasions that can be scientifically explained, such as waking, relieving oneself, and eating. And these are far from the only type of miracle we appreciate, especially at the Pesach Seder.

In 1911, the great scholar of the Middle East Theodor Nöldeke wrote in the *Encyclopædia Britannica:* "The dream of some Zionists that Hebrew—a would-be Hebrew, that is to say—will again become a living, popular language in Palestine has still less prospect of realization than their vision of a restored Jewish empire in the Holy Land."[6]

This was the standard view of experts (and almost everyone else) at the time. Hebrew had ceased being a spoken language in around 200 CE. In 1882, the world had one native Hebrew speaker—Eliezer Ben-Yehuda's son Ben Zion, who was brought up speaking only the nonfunctional Jewish language that his father was attempting to reestablish. It would have been more reasonable to consider raising a son to speak a language that no one else did child abuse than the beginning of a completely unprecedented national revival. Professor Nöldeke's contemporary Rabbi Simon Bernfeld might have thought so. He wrote in 1912, "To make the Hebrew language a spoken tongue in the usual sense of the word is . . . impossible. It has never occurred in any language of the world. A broken glass can no longer be put back together."[7]

As Rabbi Jason Rubenstein of Yale University observes, Professor Nöldeke and Rabbi Bernfeld were right. The revival of Hebrew violates all the laws and logic that responsible scholars are charged with discovering. If they could have been asked what it would take for there to be strong and vibrant

Jewish state where Hebrew is the language used to debate in the Knesset, order coffee, collaborate on scientific discoveries, cheer on teams, conduct diplomacy, do businesses, sing popular songs, and educate children—they certainly would have said: A miracle. And they would have been right.[8]

If we identify asking and receiving a Hebrew greeting in Israel as a miracle and, like Rabbi Akiva with his 250, can identify miracles everywhere, how will life seem? Rabbi Abraham Joshua Heschel had an answer: radically amazing. It is this "radical amazement," Rabbi Heschel writes, that constitutes "the chief characteristic of the religious man's attitude toward history and nature."[9]

Where else might we, open to being radically amazed, find miracles? Maimonides, who was a physician as well as a rabbi and philosopher, identified one place. "Knowledge of the Divine cannot be attained except through knowledge of natural sciences."[10] There is no conflict between religion and science—quite the contrary: science, according to Maimonides, illustrates and deepens religious faith so profoundly that its cultivation is a religious necessity. The more we understand science, the more we marvel at the God who created its precision, its elegance, and its endlessness. The more we know God, the more we appreciate his wonder that is expressed in science.

In the twenty-first century, we can put Maimonides's claim that the truth of science and its manifestation in nature amplify the love of God to factual tests. We can start with the existence of life itself. According to the magazine *Discover*, "The Universe is unlikely. Very unlikely. Deeply, shockingly unlikely."[11] How unlikely might that be? Scientists consider an event with the chance of one in ten to the fiftieth power of happening to be effectively impossible. The Nobel Prize–winning biologist Francis Crick said that the odds of intelligent life existing on earth being "the result of non-directed processes" are approximately one in ten to the two billionth power. He concluded, "An honest man, armed with all the knowledge available to us now, could only state that in some sense, the origin of life appears at the moment to be almost a miracle, so many are the conditions which would have to be satisfied to get it going."[12]

Other scientists, from a variety of religious and philosophical commitments, have arrived at the same conclusion.

The Nobel Prize–winning chemist Ilya Prigogine wrote, "The statistical probability that organic structures and the most precisely harmonized reactions that typify living organisms would be generated by accident is zero."[13] The Swiss physicist Marcel Golay determined that the odds of the simplest living protein forming by chance are one in ten to the 450th power.[14] How remote is that? There are ten to the 80th power atoms in the observable universe.

The late Sir Fred Hoyle was a British astronomer who formulated the thesis of stellar nucleosynthesis. He calculated the odds of *any* life (not just intelligent human life) emerging from nonliving matter (a process known as abiogenesis) to be one in ten to the 40,000th power.

Professor Hoyle's description of it became known as the "junkyard tornado theory." "The chance that higher life forms might have emerged in this way is comparable with the chance that a tornado sweeping through a junk-yard might assemble a Boeing 747 from the materials therein."[15]

The physicist Michio Kaku, cofounder of string field theory, writes that the earth is in the "Goldilocks Zone region of space"—referring to Goldilocks' porridge: "not too hot, not too cold, but just right." Specifically, Professor Kaku elucidates, "the fundamental parameters of the universe appear to be perfectly 'fine-tuned'"

Perfectly is a bold word coming from a physicist. He explains:

For example, if the nuclear force were any stronger, the sun would have simply burned out billions of years ago, and if it were any weaker the sun wouldn't have ignited to begin with. The Nuclear Force is tuned Just Right. Similarly, if gravity were any stronger, the Universe would have most likely collapsed in on itself in a big crunch; and if it were any weaker, everything would have simply frozen over in a big freeze. The Gravitational Force is Just Right.[16]

If one considers the simultaneous emergence of numerous *essential* and *extremely* low-probability events to be a "miracle" or at least a reason to be "radically amazed," then a discovery emerges. Life itself commands radical amazement. And if life itself is radically amazing, then anything within life is more radically amazing—as the chance of anything happening in the world is less than the chance of the world existing. Consequently, it is very easy to get to a high miracle count—and why Rabbi Akiva wins. It is also easy to see how this philosophy could be applied in our lives.

We awake, we breathe (even while we sleep), we open our eyes and see, we hear the sounds of children downstairs, we immediately recall the tasks for the day: amazing! We relieve ourselves in the bathroom, we walk down the stairs and our legs move as commanded by our brains, we turn on the faucet and clean water comes out, there is food ready to be eaten, we check a device that enables us to easily access all the world's public knowledge, we see our spouse and our children and simultaneously experience love, appreciation, anticipation, insight, memories, and dreams. Unbelievable! Each of these tasks requires the successful operation of a system whose massive number of components we cannot identify and whose coordination we cannot comprehend. Radically amazing, indeed. And we have not even had breakfast yet.

Modern social science is demonstrating just how important this output of counting more miracles is—and in ways that extend even further than one's moral and religious development. Professor Robert Emmons of the University of California at Davis had his subjects spend nine weeks expressing what each one was grateful for. The result was a 25 percent increase in happiness. A wide-ranging study by Professor Emmons of people ages eight to eighty determined that those who practice gratitude exercise more, sleep better, have lower blood pressure, have stronger immune systems, have kidneys that are better able to filter waste, are more alive and awake, experience more joy and pleasure, and are more forgiving, helpful, generous, and compassionate.[17]

These findings have been validated by many other studies, and by simple observation. Let's imagine two people—one who is always grateful for lots of things and one who is rarely grateful for anything. Which person will be more perturbed by life's small indignities, annoyances, and disagreements? Which person is going to more easily imitate God in being, per Exodus 34:6, "slow to anger"? Which person will find what is good and enjoyable in all kinds of situations and people? Which person (everything else aside!) would you prefer your child to marry?

Surely, the kind of person who would win a miracle-counting contest.

"DAYENU": HOW TO
EXPRESS GRATITUDE

The first thing about "Dayenu": It is a magnificent song. We have discussed the intimate connection of music and memory, and "Dayenu" demonstrates it. Its words and its lyrics are among the most recognized parts of any Seder. But it is the familiar things, those that we think we know, that often require the most investigation.

An initial look at the content of "Dayenu" should arouse curiosity. We sing that if God had split the sea but not led us through to dry land, it would have been enough for us. But we would have drowned. We sing that if he had led us through to dry land but not drowned our oppressors, it would have been enough for us. But the Egyptians would have enslaved and/or killed us. We sing that if God had provided for our needs in the desert for forty years but did not feed us manna, it would have been enough for us. But we would have starved.

How does that work? Why are we effectively expressing gratitude for something that would have ended in death?

Read or sung in a vacuum, that dispositive question leads to only one answer: We shouldn't be! However, nothing about "Dayenu" occurs in a vacuum. Instead, it comes immediately after Rabbi Akiva shows us why it is better to count more miracles. Rabbi Akiva *shows* us why we should count many miracles, and "Dayenu" *expresses* how we should do so. The success of gratitude, the defining quality of the Jew, requires *both* the idea and the execution. So the authors of the Haggadah give us the section on miracles followed immediately by "Dayenu."

Just as "Dayenu" emerges in conjunction with what immediately precedes it, each of its verses can only be understood along with all the others. And this realization alone provides the initial education into the expression of gratitude.

Most of what arouses gratitude is multifaceted. Our son gets appendicitis and emerges from the hospital healthy several days later. We are, of course, grateful to the physician who treated him. But the doctor was not operating alone. There was the teacher who pulled the doctor aside thirty years before and told him that if he stopped goofing around, he would realize that he had a real gift for science, the rich uncle who told the doctor to go to medical school without worrying about tuition, the receptionist who slotted in the appointment just before the day concluded, the nurses who had everything set perfectly and watched over him continuously, the custodians who kept the facilities clean, the donors whose funds built the hospital originally, the taxi driver who rushed through traffic to get to the hospital quickly, the mechanic who fixed the brakes on the taxi the day before—and so many more.

Rabbi David Fohrman shows how "Dayenu" is the ancient Jewish expression of the modern scientific discovery of irreducible complexity. This term *irreducible complexity* was invented by Professor Michael Behe, who describes it as "a single system of several interacting parts, and where the removal of any one of the parts causes the system to cease functioning."[1]

Life on earth required God to create the big bang and a perfectly positioned sun, moon, and Jupiter, and lots of other massively improbable events to happen with astonishing precision. If *any* one of them did not happen, there would be no life on earth. We need our parents to conceive us, to care for us in the womb, and provide us with food, shelter, values, and lots of other things in the course of a short childhood. If any one of these things did not happen, the Seder would be at least one person fewer this year. This notion of irreducible complexity applies to most things in our world—from the food in our refrigerator to the car in our garage to the telephone in our hands. In each case, a lot of different things need to work *perfectly* for the system to function at all.

How do we express our gratitude for gifts of irreducible complexity—to our parents for creating and sustaining us or to God for doing the same with that and everything else . . . among other things? In exactly the same way as "Dayenu" instructs. It is by showing appreciation for every component that we express gratitude for the system as a whole.

So does it make sense *outside* of this context to say that if he had split the sea for us but had not led us through to dry land, it would have been enough for us? No, we would have drowned. Inside the concept of irreducible complexity, the answer is different. The splitting of the sea was meaningless by itself. But it was not by itself. It was an indispensable part of the system working. We should be grateful for it as if our lives depended on it—because they did.

Expressing gratitude in the context of irreducible complexity teaches us something else about its best expression. The composer of "Dayenu" could have just given God one big thanks for all he did during the Exodus. Instead, he expresses gratitude in fifteen distinctive ways. Why does the composer of "Dayenu" choose the latter?

The answer is provided in most of the great love songs. This is fitting, as all genuine love involves abundant gratitude—to the beloved, to God, to the others involved in the relationship. The female lover in the Bible's Song of Songs does not tell her beloved that he is attractive; she says, "Pleasing is the fragrance of your perfumes." Her lover does not tell her that she is "gorgeous" but instead says, "Your cheeks are beautiful with earrings, your neck with strings of jewels."

It is the "raspberry beret" that caught Prince's imagination, it is "the way you wear your hat" that aroused Gershwin's fancy, it is the "motor trips and burning lips and burning toast and prunes" that made Sinatra sing, "Thanks for the memory."

Gratitude and love, we see, are always best expressed in the *specific*.

Every Seder participant can appreciate this, and participate accordingly. The morning after the Seder, would a host like to hear from an attendee: "Thank you for a wonderful evening. I loved everything about it"? Sure, it's better than nothing.

But the host would be much more gratified if the attendee instead said: "Thank you for a wonderful evening. First, the chicken was delicious, and your children! Particularly when Yael asked if she could ask a 'fifth question,' and when Steve made the analogy about the irreducible complexity of 'Dayenu' to his basketball team. And I left thinking about what my 'needs' really are and should be—and Jack told me this morning that he is resolved to, as God really meant when he commanded matzah on Pesach, always act without delay, and . . ."

ALWAYS A SECOND CHANCE

When the Jews had been in the wilderness for exactly one year, it was time for the Pesach offering. They make the Pesach offering, per Numbers 9:5, "according to everything that Hashem had commanded Moses."

But there is a problem.

There are men who have been contaminated by a human corpse, which automatically disqualifies them from being able to participate in the Pesach celebration. It does not seem hard to warrant being named in the Bible. According to the *The Jewish Encyclopedia* (1906), there are 15,000 people in the Bible, who share 2,800 names.[1] Yet, the Torah does not tell us the names of these men—signifying that they are ordinary people. They could be anybody in the community.

These men are not okay with this. They ask in Numbers 9:7, "Why should we be diminished by not offering Hashem's offering in the appointed time among the Children of Israel?"

This could not have been a new problem. Due to impurity and other reasons, people presumably missed other holidays that occurred throughout the year. But Pesach is the only holiday that people request to participate in after they have missed it.

There is something about Pesach, and only Pesach, that makes it the only holiday in the Torah where anyone requests a do-over.

Moses has not anticipated this problem. It never came up in any of his discussions about Pesach and its observance with God or anyone else. What is Moses to do? The law is clear: One cannot celebrate in a state of ritual impurity. But he also has a direct line to the boss, and decides to use it.

It is as though God was waiting for the question. He says in Numbers 9:10,

Speak to the Children of Israel, saying: If any man will become contaminated through a human corpse or on a distant road, whether you

or your generations, he shall make the Pesach-offering for Hashem. In the second month, on the fourteenth day, in the afternoon, shall they make it; with matzah and bitter herbs shall they eat it.

God's response to Moses is to add another holiday, what we call *Pesach Sheni*: the Second Pesach. A careful look at God's answer reveals something remarkable. Moses had asked only about those who were "contaminated by a corpse." God *expands* the question to include those "on a distant road." More, there is an accent over *distant road*, indicating that the beneficiaries of this holiday are not just those who are physically distant.[2] It includes those who are at the steps of the celebration and, for whatever reason, cannot bring themselves to join.

God, in response to an argument from several ordinary men, changes the laws of Pesach and the Torah itself.

What might have inspired God to realize that these men were right? What might have caused the Almighty to conclude that these nameless men were correct that his rules did not sufficiently reflect the principles and potential of Pesach? What had these men identified that God neglected, and was reason not only to accept but to enlarge their complaint?

It is not usually possible to say that there is one purpose for a holiday. But Pesach Sheni is unique in many ways, including this one. It has one purpose. It is the holiday that recognizes and celebrates second chances. It is the holiday that teaches us, per the Lubavitcher Rebbe Yosef Yitzchak Schneerson (known as "The Previous Rebbe"), that "Nothing is ever lost; it's never too late! Our conduct can always be rectified. Even someone who was impure, was far away and *desired to be so,* can still correct himself."[3]

The lesson of Pesach Sheni is that every Jew, regardless of how far he is from God and from Judaism, can be redeemed. And redemption does not imply that *teshuvah*—return—requires that he must change everything immediately. Pesach Sheni, unlike the holiday a month before, is a one-day affair. The beneficiary of Pesach Sheni must eat matzah and maror, but he does not have to cleanse his home of chametz, and he can enjoy bread for the rest of the week. God enthusiastically issues a second chance to anyone who desires to return, welcomes them with creative openness, and is practical in what he requires and expects of them.

Pesach, like everything else meaningfully Jewish, is never finished.

NOTES

AUTHOR'S NOTE

1. Genesis 12:11.

2. Lipka, Michael. "Seder and American Jews." Pew Research Center, April 14, 2014. http://www.pewresearch.org/fact-tank/2014/04/14/attending-a-seder-is-common-practice-for-american-jews/.

3. Genesis 2:18.

THE METHODOLOGY

1. Hess, J. M. "Johann David Michaelis and the Colonial Imaginary: Orientalism and the Emergence of Racial Antisemitism in Eighteenth-Century Germany." *Jewish Social Studies* 6, no. 2 (2000): 56–101. doi:10.1353/jss.2000.0003.

THE REAL JEWISH NEW YEAR

1. Maimonides, Mishneh Torah, Laws of Human Dispositions 2:3.

2. Lipka, Michael. "Seder and American Jews." Pew Research Center, April 14, 2014. https://www.pewresearch.org/fact-tank/2014/04/14/attending-a-seder-is-common-practice-for-american-jews/.

3. "How the Biblical Exodus Influenced America's Independence." Patterns of Evidence, July 19, 2019. https://patternsofevidence.com/2019/07/06/exodus-influenced-americas-independence/.

4. Soloveichik, Rabbi Meir. "Sacred Time, Ep 2: Rosh Hashanah—Creation and Parenthood." YouTube, September 7, 2018. https://www.youtube.com/watch?v=-0EDRGKuTm0&t=0s&list=PL6oZLDbtGHeUpRDFIGhcyxwh7rxRnmoH1&index=4.

5. Gordon, Nehemia. "How Yom Teruah Became Rosh Hashanah." Nehemia's Wall, September 22, 2019. https://www.nehemiaswall.com/yom-teruah-day-shouting-became-rosh-hashanah.

6. The one mention, according to Rabbi Israel Drazin, is in Ezekiel (a prophetic work). Ezekiel, Rabbi Drazin notes, identifies Rosh Hashanah around the time of Pesach. Israel Drazin, "Rosh Hashanah Is Not a Biblical Holiday," *Times of Israel,* September 17, 2017, https://blogs.timesofisrael.com/rosh-hashanah-is-not-a-biblical-holiday/.

7. Van Dyke, Henry. *Fisherman's Luck and Some Other Uncertain Things.* New York: Charles Scribner's Sons, 1920. Pg. 95.

8. Posner, Menachem. "How Does the Spring Equinox Relate to the Timing of Passover?—About the Jewish Leap Year." Chabad.org, March 26, 2007. https://www.chabad.org/holidays/passover/pesach_cdo/aid/495531/jewish/How-Does-the-Spring-Equinox-Relate-to-the-Timing-of-Passover.html.

9. Spring is nature's instruction that from darkness comes light and that the ability to re-create is as much a part of the world as the seasons. If it's the Jewish New Year, it's time to renew and re-create—and to contemplate and celebrate both. https://www.timesofisrael.com/why-israel-is-a-pilgrimage-site-for-birds-and-birdwatchers/.

10. "How Many People Are Needed to Eat a Korban Pesach in One Night?" Mi Yodeya, May 16, 2016. https://judaism.stackexchange.com/questions/71335/how-many-people-are-needed-to-eat-a-korban-pesach-in-one-night.

HAGGADAH: WHEN A GREAT BOOK IS NOT MEANT TO BE READ

1. Pirkei Avot 5:21.

2. BT Menachot 43b.

3. Parker, Arthur Alexander. "Re-Reading Nabokov." WAG, February 1, 2003. http://www.thewag.net/books/nabokov2.html.

   See also: Wolpe, Rabbi David. "Yitro: Standing Again at Sinai." Sinai Temple, February 2, 2013. https://www.sinaitemple.org/worship/sermons/yitro-standing-sinai.

GOD'S BUSINESS CARD

1. "Making the Most of Toronto," *The Economist*, July 28, 2008, https://www.economist.com/gulliver/2008/07/28/making-the-most-of-toronto.

2. Maimonides, *Guide for the Perplexed*, Chapter 26: "The Torah speaks according to the language of man, that is to say, expressions, which can easily be comprehended and understood by all, are applied to the Creator."

3. Hope, Kibuye. "Solar Installation at Kibuye Through ITEC." *Vimeo*, October 9, 2019. https://vimeo.com/365301530.

4. Gellman, Marc. "What Are You Looking For?" First Things, March 1, 1997. https://www.firstthings.com/article/1997/03/002-what-are-you-looking-for.

5. Ibid.

6. This references the Pesach Sheni story in Numbers 9 and the Daughters of Zelophehad story in Numbers 27.

THE CRAZIEST DREAM COMES TRUE: WHY WE LIVE IN MOSES'S WORLD

1. Romey, Kristin. "Exclusive: Ancient Mass Child Sacrifice May Be World's Largest." *National Geographic*, April 26, 2018. https://www.nationalgeographic.com/news/2018/04/mass-child-human-animal-sacrifice-peru-chimu-science/.

2. "'Children Should Be Seen and Not Heard'—the Meaning and Origin of This Phrase." Phrasefinder, n.d. https://www.phrases.org.uk/meanings/children-should-be-seen-and-not-heard.html.

3. Merrifield, Mary. "On Children's Dresses." *The Englishwoman's Domestic Magazine*, vol. 5–6, May 1856. Pp. 313–14.

4. BT Shabbat 119b.

5. Esther Rabbah 9:4.

6. "Returning the Hearts of the Fathers." Chabad.org, n.d. https://www.chabad.org/therebbe/livingtorah/player_cdo/aid/2289712/jewish/Returning-the-Hearts-of-the-Fathers.htm.

Margolin, Dovid. "Podcast: Dovid Margolin on the Rebbe's Campaign for a Moment of Silence." Tikvah Fund, May 1, 2019. https://tikvahfund.org/library/podcast-dovid-margolin-on-the-rebbes-campaign-for-a-moment-of-silence/.

7. Exodus 12:30.

8. Havlidis, Dimitris Romeo. "Medieval Education in Europe: Schools & Universities." Lost Kingdom, March 21, 2015. https://www.lostkingdom.net/medieval-education-in-europe/.

9. Moynahan, Brian. *God's Bestseller: William Tyndale, Thomas More, and the Writing of the English Bible: A Story of Martyrdom and Betrayal.* New York: St. Martin's Press, 2003. Pg. 72.

10. Daniell, David. *William Tyndale: A Biography.* New Haven, CT: Yale University Press, 2001. Pg. 120.

11. Lawson, Steven. "William Tyndale's Final Words." Ligonier Ministries, February 18, 2015. https://www.ligonier.org/blog/william-tyndales-final-words/.

12. British Broadcasting Corporation. The Top 100 Great Britons, December 4, 2002. https://web.archive.org/web/20021204214727/http://www.bbc.co.uk/history/programmes/greatbritons/list.shtml/.

13. Roser, Max, and Esteban Ortiz-Ospina. "Literacy." Our World in Data, September 20, 2018. https://ourworldindata.org/literacy.

14. Sacks, Jonathan. *A Letter in the Scroll: Understanding Our Jewish Identity and Exploring the Legacy of the World's Oldest Religion.* New York: Free Press, 2009. Pg. 133.

15. Pirkei Avot 5:21.

16. Jonquière, Tessel M. *Prayer in Josephus.* Leiden, Netherlands: Brill, 2007. Pg. 104.

17. BT Menachot 29b.

18. Sacks, Jonathan. "Parshat Matot: Judaism Believes That Children Are the Future." Algemeiner, July 29, 2019. https://www.algemeiner.com/2019/07/29/parshat-matot-judaism-believes-that-children-are-the-future/.

Pařík, Arno. "Jewish Education." Jewish Museum in Prague, December 3, 2006. https://www.jewishmuseum.cz/en/program-and-education/exhibits/archive-exhibits/328/.

BT Bava Batra 21a.

19. Freeman, Tzvi. "Eight Great Things About Jewish Mothers. Really.—How Jewish Mothers Were the Early Adopters of Health, Education and Everything Else That's Good for the World." Chabad.org, n.d. https://www.chabad.org/library/article_cdo/aid/3976582/jewish/Eight-Great-Things-About-Jewish-Mothers-Really.htm.

20. Smalley, Beryl. *The Study of the Bible in the Middle Ages.* Notre Dame, IN: University of Notre Dame Press, 1964. Pg. 78.

21. Neusner, Jacob. *Understanding Jewish Theology: Classical Issues and Modern Perspectives.* Binghamton, NY: Global Publications, 2001. Pg. 57.

Zborowski, Mark, and Elizabeth Herzog. *Life Is with People: The Culture of the Shtetl.* New York: Schocken, 1988. Pg. 294.

22. Jacobson, Rabbi Y. Y. "How to Address the Four Sons in Our Own Homes & Communities." TheYeshiva.net, April 14, 2016. https://www.theyeshiva.net/jewish/2763.

23. "Literacy Rates Continue to Rise from One Generation to the Next." UNESCO, September 2017. http://uis.unesco.org/sites/default/files/documents/fs45-literacy-rates-continue-rise-generation-to-next-en-2017_0.pdf.

24. Mietkiewicz, Mark. "Nobel Prize and the Jews." Canadian Jewish News, December 11, 2018. https://www.cjnews.com/living-jewish/nobel-prize-and-the-jews.

25. Curtin, John. "What's With the Jews?" CBCnews, n.d. https://www.cbc.ca/documentarychannel/docs/whats-with-the-jews1.

GETTING READY: WHEN THE PREPARATION IS PART OF THE EVENT

1. Exodus 12:1–20.

2. Sefer Kuzari 3.

3. Sacks, Rabbi Jonathan. "Seven Principles of Jewish Leadership." Rabbi Sacks, June 14, 2012. http://rabbisacks.org/seven-principles-of-jewish-leadership-written-for-the-adam-science-foundation-leadership-programme/.

4. An Internet search on "Passover Relief Fund" will yield many opportunities.

"Ma'ot Chitim—'Wheat Money': Donate to Your Local Passover Charity Fund!" Chabad.org, n.d. https://www.chabad.org/holidays/passover/pesach_cdo/aid/1170218/jewish/Maot-Chitim-Wheat-Money.htm.

One such example: In March 1865, an editorial in *The Jewish Messenger* (a southern Jewish publication) read: "An appeal has been made through Mr. N. J. Brady, now at Savannah, on behalf of the Jewish residents of that city. It is desired to procure for them about five thousand pounds of *matzot*. Many of the inhabitants, formerly wealthy, are in extremely straitened circumstances, and besides, have lost entirely the means of baking for the ensuing Passover." The editorial urged support, noting the generosity of Savannah Jewry in the past: "The Israelites of Savannah as a community here, in former years, have been prompt and generous in response to calls for aid."

By Pesach, six weeks later, northern Jewish communities had generously donated, enabling their Southern brethren to conduct Seders and creating a moment of unity during the time of the nation's greatest division. Source: Domnitch, Larry. "Passover After the Civil War." My Jewish Learning, n.d. https://www.myjewishlearning.com/article/passover-after-the-civil-war/.

5. See Shulchan Aruch, Yoreh De'ah 248:1, Talmud Bava Batra 9a, and Numbers 18:28.

6. Numbers 10:31.

7. Heinricher, Mary. "OHSU." *OHSU* (blog), January 25, 2013. https://blogs.ohsu.edu/brain/2013/01/25/emotional-distress-similar-to-physical-pain-in-brain/.

8. BT Berachot 5b.

9. Malachi 3:23–24.

10. "First to Forgive: Story of Joseph's Brothers." https://www.ifcj.org/learn/holy-land-moments/daily-devotionals/first-to-forgive/.

11. Tzemach Tzedek, Ohr HaTorah, Leviticus Vol 3, Pg. 856.

Jacobson, Rabbi Y. Y. "How to Get Over Grudges and Resentment." TheYeshiva.net,

October 9, 2016. https://www.theyeshiva.net/jewish/7171/lecture-yehudi-conference-how-to-get-over-grudges-and-resentment.

12. For a modern explanation of *right versus right,* see Kidder, Rushworth M. "How Good People Make Tough Choices: Resolving the Dilemmas of Ethical Living." Institute for Global Ethics, n.d. https://www.cusd200.org/cms/lib7/IL01001538/Centricity/Domain/352/ethicspercent20book.pdf. (Professor Kidder may have been the first to use the term *right versus right.*)

13. Mishneh Torah, Laws of Chanukah 4:14.

14. A characteristically excellent discussion from YY Jacobson is "Why We Forgive." Yehudi, October 21, 2016. YouTube video. https://www.youtube.com/watch?v=tlCL_R2V7Y4&feature=youtu.be.

15. Brooks, Alison Wood, Hengchen E. Dai, and Maurice E. Schweitzer. "I'm Sorry About the Rain! Superfluous Apologies Demonstrate Empathic Concern and Increase Trust." *Social Psychological and Personality Science* 5, no. 4 (September 26, 2013): 467–74. https://doi.org/10.1177/1948550613506122.

16. Tanya, Likkutei Amarim, chapter 5.

17. BT Pesachim 29b, BT Chullin 98 a-b.

18. Cohen, Rabbi Dovid. "Doing Business Involving Non-Kosher Food." Chicago Rabbinical Council, January 2008. http://www.crcweb.org/kosher_articles/business_involving_non_kosher.php.

19. Soloveichik, Rabbi Meir. "Sacred Time, Ep 9: Passover—The Four Freedoms." YouTube, April 10, 2019. https://www.youtube.com/watch?v=hUs1HpjTJp8.

20. Nikolov, Vassil. "The Prehistoric Salt-Production and Urban Center of Provadia-Solnitsata, Northeastern Bulgaria." *Méditerranée,* no. 126 (January 2016): 71–78. https://doi.org/10.4000/mediterranee.8246.

   Jarvis, Cynthia A., and E. Elizabeth Johnson. *A Feasting on the Word Commentary: Feasting on the Gospels.* Louisville, KY: Westminster John Knox Press, 2015. Pg. 82.

   "Salt." Marblehead Salt Co., n.d. http://www.marblchcadsalt.com/shop-1.

21. Wenham, Gordon J. *The Book of Leviticus.* Grand Rapids, MI: Eerdmans, 1979. Pg. 71.

22. Leviticus 2:13.

   Numbers 18:19.

   2 Chronicles 13:5.

23. Wenham, *The Book of Leviticus.* Pg. 71.

24. "Salt." Red Star Yeast, n.d. https://redstaryeast.com/yeast-baking-lessons/common-baking-ingredients/salt/.

25. Shulchan Aruch, Orach Chayim, 431:1.

26. BT Pesachim 8a.

27. Shulchan Aruch, Orach Chayim 431:1.

28. Avodas Yisroel, Shabbat Hagadol. Pg. 30.

29. Jacobson, Rabbi Y. Y. "Your Stress-Free Pesach Seder." TheYeshiva.net, April 6, 2017. https://www.theyeshiva.net/jewish/4183/your-stress-free-pesach-seder.

A., Rabbi Ben. "The Feather, the Spoon and the Candle." Chabad.org, n.d. https://www.chabad
.org/library/article_cdo/aid/1172862/jewish/The-Feather-the-Spoon-and-the-Candle.htm.

30. Berger, Micha. "Kallah XIV: Internalizing Torah." Mussar Institute, n.d. https://
mussarinstitute.org/Yashar/2016-06/kallah.php.

31. Numbers 27:16.

32. Torath Kohanim 16:61, BT Yoma 12b.

33. Lamm, Norman. "Something Different for a Change (Sermon)." New York: The Jewish
Center, April 28, 1973. https://archives.yu.edu/gsdl/collect/lammserm/index/assoc/HASH8eb6
.dir/doc.pdf.

34. "'Sticks and Stones May Break My Bones'—the Meaning and Origin of This Phrase." Phrasefinder, n.d. https://www.phrases.org.uk/meanings/sticks-and-stones-may-break-my-bones.html.

35. "Nirtzah-Acceptance." Chabad.org, n.d. https://www.chabad.org/holidays/passover/pesach
_cdo/aid/269921/jewish/Nirtzah.htm.

36. Quoted in: Simmons, Shraga. "Midot Series #1: The Art of Character Perfection," December
19, 2015. https://www.aish.com/sp/pg/The-Art-of-Character-Perfection.html.

SINGING THE TABLE OF CONTENTS: WHY HIGHLY RELIGIOUS MARRIED WOMEN ARE SO SEXUALLY SATISFIED

1. Genesis 6:1–2.

2. Genesis 6:5–8.

3. A terrific discussion of order and freedom at the Seder is in: Brown, Erica. *Seder Talk: The
Conversational Haggada: Eight Essays for the Eight Days of Pessaḥ.* Jerusalem: Maggid Books and
OU Press, 2015.

See also: Jacobson, Rabbi Y. Y. "I Am a Thief." TheYeshiva.net, April 9, 2019. https://www
.theyeshiva.net/jewish/6287.

4. As told to: Gordon, Devin. "John Wooden: First, How to Put on Your Socks." *Newsweek,*
October 24, 1999. https://www.newsweek.com/john-wooden-first-how-put-your-socks-167942.

D'Amelio, Tony. "Bill Walton: Learning to Lace My Shoes Was a John Wooden Success Lesson." D'Amelio Network, July 11, 2017. http://blog.damelionetwork.com/sports-motivational
-speaker-bill-walton-learning-to-tie-shoes-was-john-wooden-success-lesson-for-life.

5. Balboni, Michael J., and John R. Peteet, eds. *Spirituality and Religion Within the Culture of
Medicine: From Evidence to Practice.* New York: Oxford University Press, 2017. Pg. 358.

VanderWeele, T. J. "Religion and Health: A Synthesis." In: M. J. Balboni and J. R. Peteet
(eds.). *Spirituality and Religion Within the Culture of Medicine: From Evidence to Practice.* New
York: Oxford University Press, 2017. Pp. 1–2.

6. "Marriage and Men's Health." Harvard Health, July 2010. https://www.health.harvard.edu
/mens-health/marriage-and-mens-health.

7. Krongrad, Arnon A., et al. "Marriage and Mortality in Prostate Cancer." *Journal of Urology*
156, no. 5 (November 1996): 1696–700. https://doi.org/10.1097/00005392-199611000-00041.

"Bladder Cancer: Men at Risk." Harvard Health, April 2011. https://www.health.harvard
.edu/mens-health/bladder-cancer-men-at-risk.

8. "Marriage and Men's Health."

Ikeda, Ai, et al. "Marital Status and Mortality Among Japanese Men and Women: The Japan Collaborative Cohort Study." *BMC Public Health* 7, no. 1 (July 2007). https://doi.org/10.1186/1471-2458-7-73.

9. Salamon, Maureen. "11 Interesting Effects of Oxytocin." LiveScience, May 30, 2013. https://www.livescience.com/35219-11-effects-of-oxytocin.html.

10. Liu, Hui, et al. "Is Sex Good for Your Health? A National Study on Partnered Sexuality and Cardiovascular Risk Among Older Men and Women." *Journal of Health and Social Behavior* 57, no. 3 (September 6, 2016): 276–96. https://doi.org/10.1177/0022146516661597.

Also see: "Marriage and Men's Health."

Stritof, Sheri. "The Benefits of Having Sex More Often." Verywell Mind, June 23, 2019. https://www.verywellmind.com/why-to-have-sex-more-often-2300937.

11. Burton, Natasha. "Marriage Sex: The Truth About Sex After Marriage." *HuffPost,* April 18, 2012. https://www.huffpost.com/entry/marriage-sex_n_1422644.

12. Yau, Nathan. "Married People Have More Sex." FlowingData, December 30, 2017. https://flowingdata.com/2017/07/03/married-people-sex/.

13. Wilcox, W. Bradford, Laurie DeRose, and Jason S. Carroll. "The Ties That Bind: Is Faith a Global Force for Good or Ill in the Family?" Institute for Family Studies, May 18, 2019. https://ifstudies.org/ifs-admin/resources/reports/worldfamilymap-2019-051819final.pdf. Pg. 22–24.

Wilcox, W. Bradford, Jason S. Carroll, and Laurie DeRose. "Religious Men Can Be Devoted Dads, Too." *New York Times,* May 18, 2019. https://www.nytimes.com/2019/05/18/opinion/sunday/happy-marriages.html.

MUSIC AND FOOD: THE THEOLOGY AND SCIENCE OF REMEMBERING

1. Keeler, Jason R., et al. "The Neurochemistry and Social Flow of Singing: Bonding and Oxytocin." *Frontiers in Human Neuroscience* 9, no. 518 (September 23, 2015). https://doi.org/10.3389/fnhum.2015.00518.

Griffin, Michael. "Want to Build Empathy Within Your Staff? Sing Together." *Learning Strategies for Musical Success* (blog), June 29, 2014. https://mdgriffin63.wordpress.com/2014/06/29/sing-together-and-connect-oxytocin/.

2. Dymoke, Ned. "Study: Memories of Music Cannot Be Lost to Alzheimer's and Dementia." Big Think, April 29, 2018. https://bigthink.com/news/ever-get-the-tingles-from-listening-to-good-music-that-part-of-your-brain-will-never-get-lost-to-alzheimers.

3. "Young Adults Reminisce About Music from Before Their Time." ScienceDaily, September 9, 2013. https://www.sciencedaily.com/releases/2013/09/130909093120.htm.

4. Benhamou, Rebecca. "Jewish Children Hidden Twice over by the Church." *Times of Israel,* May 27, 2013. https://www.timesofisrael.com/jewish-children-hidden-twice-over-by-the-church/.

Simmons, Rabbi Shraga. "Shema Yisrael." Aish.com, n.d. https://www.aish.com/jl/m/pb/48954656.html.

Mock, Robert. "How Rabbi Yosef Shlomo Kahaneman Saved Jewish Orphans in Catholic Orphanages After the Holocaust." *Destination Yisra'el* (blog), October 16, 2012. https://destination-yisrael.biblesearchers.com/destination-yisrael/2012/10/how-rabbi-yosef-shlomo-kahaneman-saved-jewish-orphans-in-catholic-orphanages-after-the-holocaust.html.

5. Allen, John Scott. *The Omnivorous Mind: Our Evolving Relationship with Food.* Cambridge, MA: Harvard University Press, 2012. Pp. 154–61.

WHAT WE CAN LEARN FROM AN EGG: THE LOGIC OF THE SEDER PLATE

1. Shurpin, Yehuda. "Why the Egg (Beitza) on the Passover Seder Plate?" Chabad.org, n.d. https://www.chabad.org/holidays/passover/pesach_cdo/aid/3295864/jewish/Why-the-Egg -Beitza-on-the-Passover-Seder-Plate.htm. And Rabbi Yaakov Leiner, *Seder Haggadah Shel Pesach im Sefer Hazmanim,* Pg. 55.

2. Ibid., Shurpin

3. Rabbi Yisroel Baal Shem Tov, Keser Shem Tov, vol. 3. Pg. 94.

Ibn Ezra on Exodus 8:22: "Eggs." Jewish Virtual Library, n.d. https://www.jewishvirtuallibrary .org/eggs.

Rama on Shulchan Aruch, Orach Chayim 560:2.

4. Rashi on BT Shabbat 87a.

5. Alpert, Joan. "The Sweet Story of Charoset." *Moment,* March 25, 2013. https://momentmag .com/the-sweet-story-of-charoset/.

6. BT Pesachim 116a.

7. Maimonides, Mishneh Torah, Laws of Leavened and Unleavened Bread 7:11.

8. Bamidbar Rabbah 13:16.

9. Kaunfer, Elie. "Mah Nishtanah: The Freedom of Multiple Meanings." Hadar, June 5, 2017. https://www.hadar.org/torah-resource/mah-nishtanah-freedom-multiple-meanings.

INVITE *THAT* SELF

1. Mishnah Zevachim 5:8.

2. Mishnah Bava Metziah 4:10.

3. Kaufman, Lilly. "The Golden Crown of Parenting." Jewish Theological Seminary, February 28, 2020. http://www.jtsa.edu/the-golden-crown-of-parenting.

4. Rashi on Deuteronomy 34:12.

5. BT Berachot 35b.

6. Fohrman, Rabbi David. "What Does the Torah Teach About Parenting?: A Guide to Parenting." Aleph Beta, n.d. https://www.alephbeta.org/playlist/a-guide-to-parenting.

7. Hammond, Darin L. "11 Reasons Why You Need to Be More Independent." Lifehack, November 26, 2013. https://www.lifehack.org/articles/productivity/11-reasons-why-you-need -more-independent.html.

Brown, Joel. "8 Important Reasons Why You Should Be More Independent." Addicted 2 Success, June 17, 2013. https://addicted2success.com/life/8-important-reasons-why-you-should -be-more-independent/.

8. A magnificent discussion of this is provided by Rabbi Y. Y. Jacobson at: Jacobson, Rabbi Y. Y. "To Cook or to Roast—That Is the Question." TheYeshiva.net, March 22, 2013. https://www .theyeshiva.net/jewish/105/to-cook-or-to-roast-that-is-the-question.

9. Pogrebin, Abigail. "Does God Love Us?" Forward, September 5, 2020. https://forward.com/life/453815/does-god-love-us/.

10. Jacobson, "To Cook or to Roast—That Is the Question."

11. Solomon, Eric. "Despite a Rise in Hate, This Hanukkah Choose Hope." News Observer. *Raleigh News & Observer*, December 12, 2017. https://www.newsobserver.com/opinion/op-ed/article189427734.html.

12. Jung, C. G. *Modern Man in Search of a Soul*. Eastford, CT: Martino Fine Books, 2017. Pg. 234.

13. Frankl, Viktor E. *Man's Search for Meaning: An Introduction to Logotherapy*. Boston: Beacon Press, 2006. Pg. 126.

THE GREATEST PRINCIPLE OF THE TORAH

1. Jarus, Owen. "Who Were the Barbarians?" LiveScience, April 27, 2018. https://www.livescience.com/45297-barbarians.html.

2. Fallon, April E., and Paul Rozin. "The Psychological Bases of Food Rejections by Humans." *Ecology of Food and Nutrition* 13, no. 1 (1983): 15–26. https://doi.org/10.1080/03670244.1983.9990728.

3. Smith, Adam. *The Theory of Moral Sentiments*. Los Angeles: Logos Books, 2018. Pg. 121.

4. JT Nedarim 30b.

5. Firestone, Reuven. "The Commandment to Love and Help the Stranger." ReformJudaism.org, September 24, 2016. https://reformjudaism.org/learning/torah-study/torah-commentary/commandment-love-and-help-stranger.

6. Held, Rabbi Shai. "Turning Memory into Empathy." Hadar, n.d. https://www.hadar.org/torah-resource/turning-memory-empathy.

7. Held, Rabbi Shai. "The Faces of Guests as the Face of God." Hadar, podcast audio, https://www.hadar.org/torah-resource/face-guests-face-god.

    Held, Rabbi Shai. "Turning Memory into Empathy." Hadar, podcast audio, https://www.hadar.org/torah-resource/turning-memory-empathy.

8. "Love: Definition of Love by Oxford Dictionary on Lexico.com. Also Meaning of Love." Lexico Dictionaries: English. Accessed June 4, 2020. https://www.lexico.com/en/definition/love.

9. "'Why Do I Love My Abuser?'" National Domestic Violence Hotline, September 21, 2016. https://www.thehotline.org/2016/09/21/why-do-i-love-my-abuser/.

10. Wolpe, David. "Vayikra—The Meaning of Sacrifice." Sinai Temple. Accessed March 28, 2020. https://www.sinaitemple.org/worship/sermons/.

11. Matthew 5:43.

12. Fohrman, David. "How to Love Your Neighbor as Yourself: What Does It Really Mean?" Aleph Beta. Accessed June 4, 2020. https://www.alephbeta.org/playlist/love-your-neighbor-meaning.

13. Branson, Richard. Twitter post. November 13, 2012, 11:35am. https://twitter.com/richardbranson/status/268391549048610817.

14. Parrott-Sheffer, Chelsey. "16th Street Baptist Church Bombing." *Encyclopædia Britannica*, June 26, 2020. https://www.britannica.com/event/16th-Street-Baptist-Church-bombing.

15. "Nazi Sex Slave Story Finally Told at Camp." thelocal.de, February 28, 2009. https://www.thelocal.de/20090228/17711.

16. Charen, Mona. "Don't Forget How Butcher of Baghdad Earned the Name." *Baltimore Sun*, December 7, 2018. https://www.baltimoresun.com/news/bs-xpm-2003-03-10-0303100303-story. html.

17. The expression, "love the sinner and hate the sin," derives from St. Augustine's Letter 211 ("With love for mankind and hatred of sins") and is articulated as currently understood in Mahatma Gandhi's autobiography.

Psalm 97 is widely attributed to King David (for instance, by the Latin Vulgate and the Septuagint) but the author is unnamed. Interesting analyses of this idea of hatred are:

Boteach, Rabbi Shmuley. "And Hate the Sinner Too." *HuffPost*, June 21, 2013, www.huff-post.com/entry/and-hate-the-sinner-too_b_3129324.

Tauber, Yanki. War. March 7, 2003. www.chabad/org/library/article_cdo/aid/72365/jewish /War.htm.

18. Yalkut Shimoni, I Samuel, Chapter 121.

JUST WHO ARE YOU CALLING A STRANGER?

1. Sarma, Nahum M. *Exploring Exodus: The Origins of Biblical Israel*. New York: Schocken Books, 1996. Pg. 23.

2. Breggin, Peter Roger. *Beyond Conflict: From Self-Help and Psychotherapy to Peacemaking*. New York: St. Martin's Press, 1992. Pg. 105.

"Learned Helplessness: Examples, Symptoms, and Treatment." What Is Learned Help-lessness? Medical News Today, May 31, 2019. https://www.medicalnewstoday.com/articles /325355.

3. Nachmani, Tovah Leah. "5780-Bo: What Our Stories Tell About Us." Elmad, January 27, 2020. https://elmad.pardes.org/2020/01/5780-bo-what-our-stories-tell-about-us/.

LOVE AND RESPONSIBILITY: ISRAEL

1. Blessings: Genesis 12:2–3.

Descendants: Genesis 15:5.

The Land of Israel: Genesis 15:18–21.

The repeat of the promise to Isaac: Genesis 26:3–4.

The repeat of the promise to Jacob: Genesis 27:13–15.

2. Wouk, Herman. *The Will to Live On: This Is Our Heritage*. HarperCollins ebooks. Pg. 13.

3. "How Many of the 613 Mitzvos Can We Do Only in Israel?" Mi Yodeya, November 1, 2011. https://judaism.stackexchange.com/questions/11044/how-many-of-the-613-mitzvos-can-we-do -only-in-israel.

4. Gordon, Nehemia, and Shannon Davis. "God Is a Zionist—Hebrew Voices." Nehemia's Wall, May 8, 2019. https://www.nehemiaswall.com/god-zionist. Biblical references to being instructed to act with our hearts and souls include Deuteronomy 4:29, 4:39, 6:5–6, 10:12, 11:13, 11:18, 13:4, 26:16, and 30:2.

5. Isaiah 40:2, Isaiah 66:11.

Psalms 137:5–6.

The translation "heart-Jerusalem" comes from Shlomo Riskin's "Torah Lights: Devarim:

Legacy, History and Covenant." Riskin, Shlomo. *Torah Lights: Devarim*. Efrat: Ohr Torah Stone, 2014.

JUDAISM IN A WORD: *NEWNESS*

1. Geary, James. "Guest Post: James Geary on Metaphor, a Taxonomy." *New York Times,* February 8, 2011. https://schott.blogs.nytimes.com/2011/02/08/guest-post-james-geary-on-metaphor-a-taxonomy/.

2. Weiss, Rabbi Andrea L. "Exploring the Multiple Metaphors for God in Shirat Haazinu." TheTorah.com., n.d. https://www.thetorah.com/article/exploring-the-multiple-metaphors-for-god-in-shirat-haazinu.

3. Black, Max. "Proceedings of the Aristotelian Society." London: Blackwell Publishing on behalf of the Aristotelian Society, May 23, 1955.

4. Holtzen, William Curtis. *The God Who Trusts: A Relational Theology of Divine Faith, Hope, and Love*. Downers Grove, IL: IVP Academic, 2019. Pg. 27.

5. Numbers 16:14.

6. Sinensky, Tzvi. "Jewish Sources on Slavery." Sefaria, n.d. https://www.sefaria.org/sheets/5722?lang=bi.

7. Gould, J. J. "Slavery's Global Comeback." *Atlantic*, December 12, 2012. https://www.theatlantic.com/international/archive/2012/12/slaverys-global-comeback/266354/.

8. Campbell, Scott. "Siddharth Kara Warns That Slavery Is Most Profitable Now." *Daily Mail Online,* July 31, 2017. https://www.dailymail.co.uk/news/article-4745938/Slavery-profitable-experts-warn.html.

  Walkfreefoundation.org.

  Many other easily accessible sources testify to the ubiquity of modern slavery.

  Also: "Trafficking in Persons Report 2018." U.S. Department of State, n.d. https://www.state.gov/j/tip/rls/tiprpt/2018/index.htm.

9. Sforno on Exodus 12:2.

10. Mishnah Rosh Hashanah 2:7.

11. The eighteenth-century German poet Heinrich Heine called the Torah the "portable homeland of the Jew": Sacks, Rabbi Jonathan. "The Heart, the Home, the Text." Chabad.org, n.d. https://www.chabad.org/parshah/article_cdo/aid/1942768/jewish/The-Heart-the-Home-the-Text.htm.

12. Rabbi Gedalyahu HaLevi Schorr, Ohr Gedalyahu, Bo:1.

13. Prero, Rabbi Yehudah. "Bar/Bat Mitzvah: A Re-Enactment of 'Kabolas Hatorah.'" Torah.org, n.d. https://torah.org/learning/lifecycles-mitzvah-barmitzvah2/.

14. Rashi on Deuteronomy 6:6.

15. James, William. *The Principles of Psychology*. New York: Henry Holt, 1918. Pg. 625.

16. Arstila, Valtteri. "Time Slows Down During Accidents." Frontiers in Psychology. Frontiers Research Foundation, June 27, 2012. https://www.ncbi.nlm.nih.gov/pmc/articles/PMC3384265/.

17. James, William. *The Principles of Psychology*. Pg. 625.

18. Cooper, Belle Beth. "The Science of Time Perception: Stop It Slipping Away by Doing New Things." Buffer, July 2, 2013. https://buffer.com/resources/the-science-of-time-perception-how-to-make-your-days-longer.

19. Choi, Janet. "How to Slow Down Time: The Science Behind Stopping Life from Passing You By." *I Done This* (blog), August 30, 2019. http://blog.idonethis.com/science-of-slowing-down-time/.

20. Ulrich, Rolf, and Karin M. Bausenhart. "The Temporal Oddball Effect and Related Phenomena: Cognitive Mechanisms and Experimental Approaches." *The Illusions of Time*, September 2019, 71–89. https://doi.org/10.1007/978-3-030-22048-8_5.

21. Taylor, Steve. "Why Time Seems to Pass at Different Speeds (Part 2)." *Psychology Today*, July 7, 2011. https://www.psychologytoday.com/us/blog/out-the-darkness/201107/why-time-seems-pass-different-speeds-part-2-1.

22. King, Martin Luther, Jr. "I've Been to the Mountaintop." Martin Luther King, Jr. Research and Education Institute, n.d. https://kinginstitute.stanford.edu/encyclopedia/ive-been-mountaintop.

23. Greenberg, Dov. "Do Not Fear Which Verse Appears Most Often in the Torah?" Jewish Gems. Chabad. Accessed June 4, 2020. https://www.chabad.org/multimedia/video_cdo/aid/1916012/jewish/Do-Not-Fear.htm.

THERE IS SUCH A THING AS A BAD QUESTION—AND SOMETIMES A GOOD REASON FOR IT

1. BT Pesachim 109a.

2. Maimonides, Mishneh Torah, Laws of Leavened and Unleavened Bread 7:3.

3. Hoffman, Lawrence A., and David Arnow. *My People's Passover Haggadah: Traditional Texts, Modern Commentaries*. Vol. 1. Woodstock, VT: Jewish Lights Publishing, 2008. Pg. 42.

4. Levinson, Matt. "The Coaching Model." Edutopia, April 8, 2015. https://www.edutopia.org/blog/the-coaching-model-matt-levinson.

"Teachers Talking." UNICEF, n.d. https://www.unicef.org/teachers/learner/paths.htm.

Collett, Johnny W. "Rethinking Special Education." U.S. Department of Education, September 20, 2018. https://sites.ed.gov/osers/2018/09/rethinking-special-education/.

5 Pirkei Avot 2:5.

6. Klein-Halevi, Yossi. "On the Transformation of Israeli Music." The Tikvah, podcast audio, March 25, 2020. https://podcasts.apple.com/us/podcast/yossi-klein-halevi-on-the-transformation-of-israeli-music/id921756215?i=1000469500198.

7. Canfield, Jack, and Victor Hansen. *Chicken Soup for the Soul: Stories to Open the Heart and Rekindle the Spirit*. Google Books. Accessed June 4, 2020. https://books.google.com/books?id=XI0F7jSjg44C%2Ccollege+professor.

8. Weinreb, Rabbi Tzvi Hersh. "Talk to Yourself." Chabad.org, n.d. https://www.chabad.org/therebbe/article_cdo/aid/2235925/jewish/Talk-to-Yourself.htm.

THE GREAT JEWISH PERMISSION

1. Mishnah Pesachim 10:4.

2. Schweiger, Meir. "5767—Pesach: The Maggid." Elmad, March 28, 2010. https://elmad.pardes.org/2010/03/5767-pesach-the-maggid-2/.

3. Aristotle, *Poetics* 1450 b27.

4. Wiesel, Elie. *Messengers of God: Biblical Portraits and Legends.* New York: Simon and Schuster, 2005. Pg. 32.

Wiesel, Elie. "Seth in the Bible." Biblical Archaeology Society, December 8, 2019. https://www.biblicalarchaeology.org/daily/people-cultures-in-the-bible/people-in-the-bible/seth-in-the-bible/.

Gerson, Mark. "The Rabbi's Husband with Mark Gerson, Interview with Rabbi Moshe Scheiner." 2020, podcast. https://podcasts.apple.com/us/podcast/joseph-reconciles-his-brothers-rabbi-moshe-scheiner/id1510424100?i=1000484568346.

5. Genesis 32:29.

6. Wolpe, Rabbi David." Off the Pulpit." Sinai Temple, May 14, 2015. https://www.sinaitemple.org/learning_with_the_rabbis/writings/2015/051415Self-Transformation.pdf.

7. "Arbor Day Around the World." Arbor Day Foundation, n.d. https://www.arborday.org/celebrate/world-dates.cfm.

8. Beit HaBechirah, Rosh Hashanah 1:1.

9. Isaiah 57:19.

10. BT Berachot 34b, BT Sanhedrin 99a.

11. Tanya, Likkutei Amarim, Chapter 7.

12. Fohrman, Rabbi David. "Why Did Jonah Run? If Jonah Never Really Repented, Why Do We Read His Story on Yom Kippur?" Aleph Beta, n.d. https://www.alephbeta.org/playlist/story-of-jonah.

THE GREATEST SEDER OF ALL

1. Walzer, Michael. *Exodus and Revolution.* New York: Basic Books, 1998. Pp. 3–4.

2. Tocqueville, Alexis de. *Democracy in America.* Edited by Bruce Frohnen. Washington, DC: Regnery, 2002. Pg. 245.

3. Fahmy, Dalia. "Americans Are Far More Religious Than Adults in Other Wealthy Nations." Pew Research Center, July 31, 2018. https://www.pewresearch.org/fact-tank/2018/07/31/americans-are-far-more-religious-than-adults-in-other-wealthy-nations/.

4. On the description of the chosen people and the reference to the Pharaoh, see: Feiler, Bruce S. *America's Prophet: How the Story of Moses Shaped America.* New York: HarperPerennial, 2010.

William Bradford's words: Kamrath, Angela E. "Why the Pilgrims Identified with the Israelites." Founding, May 12, 2017. https://thefounding.net/pilgrims-identified-israelites/.

The Bradford quote referencing Moses and the Israelites leaving Egypt: Feiler, *America's Prophet*, Pg. 8.

The Red Sea reference: Freund, Michael. "How the Exodus Story Created America." Michael Freund, March 29, 2013. http://www.michaelfreund.org/13124/exodus-america.

Mayflower Compact reference: Powell, Scott S. "Thanksgiving: The First and Essential American Holiday." *American Spectator,* November 22, 2018. https://spectator.org/thanksgiving-the-first-and-essential-american-holiday/.

Kamrath, Angela E. "The Pilgrims' Mayflower Compact as Covenant." The Founding, May 25, 2017. https://thefounding.net/the-pilgrims-mayflower-compact-was-a-covenant/.

5. Paine, Thomas. "Thomas Paine: Common Sense." UShistory.org. Accessed February 19, 2020. http://www.ushistory.org/paine/commonsense/sense4.htm.

6. "Proposal for the Great Seal of the United States, [before 14 August 1776]." Founders Online. National Archives and Records Administration. Accessed July 23, 2020. https://founders.archives.gov/documents/Franklin/01-22-02-0330.

7. "Benjamin Franklin's Great Seal Design." Great Seal, n.d. https://greatseal.com/committees/firstcomm/reverse.html.

8. Hay, Robert P. "George Washington: American Moses." *American Quarterly* 21, no. 4 (1969): 780–91. https://doi.org/10.2307/2711609.

9. Feiler, Bruce. "How Moses Shaped America." *Time,* October 12, 2009. http://content.time.com/time/subscriber/article/0,33009,1927303-2,00.html.

10. Marbury, Herbert Robinson. *Pillars of Cloud and Fire: The Politics of Exodus in African American Biblical Interpretation.* New York: New York University Press, 2015. Pg. 23.

11. Ibid.

Also: Jones, Absalom. "A Thanksgiving Sermon." Project Canterbury, n.d. http://anglicanhistory.org/usa/ajones/thanksgiving1808.html.

12. Smith, Yolanda Y. "The Bible in Song: Reclaiming African American Spirituals." Yale University, 2008. https://reflections.yale.edu/article/between-babel-and-beatitude/bible-song-reclaiming-african-american-spirituals.

13. "Harriet Tubman, the Moses of Her People." Harriet Tubman, n.d. http://www.harriet-tubman.org/moses-underground-railroad/.

14. Douglass, Frederick. *The Life and Times of Frederick Douglass.* New York: Literary Classics of the United States, 1994.

15. Langston, Scott M. "The Exodus in American History and Culture." Society of Biblical Literature, n.d. https://www.sbl-site.org/assets/pdfs/TB6_Exodus_SL.pdf.

16. Kaminer, Michael. "How Abraham Lincoln Became America's Moses." *Forward*, April 13. 2015. https://forward.com/schmooze/218274/how-abraham-lincoln-became-americas-moses/.

17. Hodes, Martha Elizabeth. *Mourning Lincoln.* New Haven, CT: Yale University Press, 2015. Pg. 111.

18. Coffin, Charles Carleton. *Abraham Lincoln.* New York: Harper and Brothers, 1893. Pg. 534.

19. Arrington, Todd. "Exodusters." National Parks Service, April 10, 2015. https://www.nps.gov/home/learn/historyculture/exodusters.htm.

20. Boyd, Melba Joyce. "Frances E. W. Harper & the Evolution of Radical Culture." Solidarity, n.d. https://solidarity-us.org/atc/55/p2840/.

21. Marbury, *Pillars of Cloud and Fire,* Pg. 52.

22. King, Martin Luther, Jr. "The Death of Evil upon the Seashore." Stanford University, May 17, 1956. http://okra.stanford.edu/transcription/document_images/Vol03Scans/256_17-May-1956_The%20Death%20of%20Evil%20upon%20the%20Seashore.pdf.

23. Selby, Gary S. *Martin Luther King and the Rhetoric of Freedom: The Exodus Narrative in America's Struggle for Civil Rights.* Waco, TX: Baylor University Press, 2008.

24. Cleage, Albert B., and George Bell. *Black Christian Nationalism: New Directions for the Black Church*. Luxor Publishers of the Pan-African Orthodox Christian Church, 1987, Pg. 7.

25. "About Relief Portrait Plaques of Lawgivers." Architect of the Capitol, n.d. https://www.aoc.gov/art/relief-portrait-plaques-lawgivers/about-relief-portrait-plaques-lawgivers.

26. Weiss, Marshall. "A Sanctuary out of the Exodus." *Haaretz*, December 12, 2013. https://www.haaretz.com/israel-news/culture/1.4785759.

27. Presley, Cecilia DeMille, and Mark A. Vieira. *Cecil B. DeMille: The Art of the Hollywood Epic*. Philadelphia: Running Press, 2014. Pg. 110.

28. The monologue, called by Cecil B. DeMille, "a short introduction," is here: https://www.youtube.com/watch?v=o8iNvzzak5U.

29. "All-Time Box Office Top 100." Filmsite, n.d. https://www.filmsite.org/boxoffice.html.

"He Himself Was 'Colossal.'" *Montreal Gazette*, January 22, 1959. https://news.google.com/newspapers?nid=1946&dat=19590122&id=6IoxAAAAIBAJ&sjid=aKgFAAAAIBAJ&pg=1891,3704755.

30. The parallels with the Moses story are stunning. Moses was, of course, saved from sure destruction (the Pharaoh's order that all Jewish baby boys be killed) by being put on a transportation vehicle (an "ark") and sent to the vast nowhere. Moses, like Superman, manages to land safely—in his case, thanks to the courage of the Pharaoh's daughter, who notices a crying baby floating in the river. Moses, too, grows up devoted to principles that would not be far from "Truth, justice, and the American way"!

31. Siker, Jeffrey "President Bush, Biblical Faith, and the Politics of Religion." Society of Biblical Literature, n.d. https://www.sbl-site.org/publications/article.aspx?ArticleId=151.

32. "Barack Obama: Selma Voting Rights March Commemoration Speech." Civil Rights Issues. March 4, 2007. https://www.c-span.org/video/?196942-1/barack-obama-remarks-selma-2007

FEELING GOD'S PLEASURE

1. BT Chagigae 3a.

2. Ibn Ezra on Deuteronomy 5:18.

3. Numbers 15:38–39.

See also: Sacks, Rabbi Jonathan. "Assembling Reminders (Shelach Lecha 5775)." Rabbi Sacks, June 10, 2015. http://rabbisacks.org/assembling-reminders-shelach-lecha-5775/.

Also: Feuer, Mike. "Shemot 5779: The Trigger for Redemption." Elmad, December 23, 2018. https://elmad.pardes.org/2018/12/shemot-5779-the-trigger-for-redemption/.

4. BT Menachot 44a.

5. Numbers 15:38–41.

6. BT Menachot 44a.

7. Duhaime, Erik P. "Is the Call to Prayer a Call to Cooperate? A Field Experiment on the Impact of Religious Salience on Prosocial Behavior." *Judgment and Decision Making* 10, no. 6 (November 2015): 593–96. http://journal.sjdm.org/15/15623/jdm15623.html.

With thanks to Anna Philipps for bringing this up in Torah study on the Torah portion of Schlach, which has this mention of tzitzit.

8. Malhotra, Deepak. "(When) Are Religious People Nicer? Religious Salience and the 'Sunday Effect' on Pro-Social Behavior." *Judgment and Decision Making* 5, no. 2 (April 2010): 138–43. http://journal.sjdm.org/10/10216/jdm10216.html.

9. BT Chagigah 9b.

10. Berman, Alison E. "Technology Feels Like It's Accelerating—Because It Actually Is." *Singularity Hub*, July 10, 2019. https://singularityhub.com/2016/03/22/technology-feels-like-its-accelerating-because-it-actually-is/.

11. McPharlin, Mike. "God Made Me Fast." YouTube, April 19, 2016. https://www.youtube.com/watch?v=ile5PD34SS0.

The movie might not have been accurate in its description of Jenny Liddell's position on her brother running in the Olympics. "Jennie Liddell." IMDb. Accessed June 4, 2020. https://www.imdb.com/name/nm0509171/.

THE STORY IS YOURS: WHERE ARE MOSES, JOSEPH, AND THE WOMEN OF THE EXODUS?

1. Ecclesiastes 5:1.

LIVING BY PRINCIPLES

1. BT Pesachim 108a.

2. BT Bava Metzia 31a.

3. Lapin, Rabbi Daniel. "Do You Hear Me?" Rabbi Daniel Lapin, September 10, 2013. https://rabbidaniellapin.com/do-you-hear-me/.

4. Shulchan Aruch, Yoreh De'ah 240:25.

Rabbi Abraham Hirsch ben Jacob Eisenstadt of Byelostok, Pischei Teshuva, Yoreh Deah 240:22.

Rama on Shulchan Aruch, Yoreh De'ah 240:25.

Based on God's command for Abraham to leave his father's house and settle in Israel (Genesis 11:32) and Rabbi Assi leaving his mother to live in Israel (Tractate Kiddushin 31b).

Shulchan Aruch, Yoreh De'ah 240:15.

HUMILITY CAN BE A SIN

1. JT Berachot 32b.

Other Talmudic sources make him eighteen years old.

2. Shahbandeh, M. "Size of the Anti-Aging Market Worldwide 2018-2023." Statista, May 15, 2020. https://www.statista.com/statistics/509679/value-of-the-global-anti-aging-market/.

3. Hochstein, Avital. "Chayyei Sarah: When Did Humanity Begin to Age and What Is the Value of Aging?" Shalom Hartman Institute, November 17, 2019. https://www.hartman.org.il/chayyei-sarah-when-did-humanity-begin-to-age-and-what-is-the-value-of-aging/

4. Lewis, C. S., *Mere Christianity* (C. S. Lewis Signature Classics). HarperCollins ebooks. Pg. 128.

5. Scheiner, Rabbi Moshe. "Is Life a Gift or a Loan?" YouTube, March 6, 2019. https://www.youtube.com/watch?v=SQjORQLTQAI&ab_channel=PalmBeachSynagogue.

See also: Pirkei Avot 3:16.

6. BT Shavuot 39a.

7. "Parshat Nitzavim In-Depth." Chabad.org, n.d. https://www.chabad.org/parshah/in-depth/default_cdo/aid/58283/jewish/Nitzavim-In-Depth.htm.

8. Twerski, Abraham. "Building Self-Esteem in Children." Aish, August 7, 2004. https://www.aish.com/f/p/48960876.html.

9. Fohrman, Rabbi David. "What Sarah's Character Teaches Us About Living Our Best Life." Aleph Beta. Accessed June 4, 2020. https://www.alephbeta.org/playlist/life-lessons-from-sarahs-character.

WHEN TO FIND GOD

1. Jong, Jonathan, Jamin Halberstadt, and Matthias Bluemke. "Foxhole Atheism, Revisited: The Effects of Mortality Salience on Explicit and Implicit Religious Belief." *Journal of Experimental Social Psychology* 48, no. 5 (September 2012): 983–89. https://doi.org/10.1016/j.jesp.2012.03.005.

2. "Terror Management Theory." Ernest Becker Foundation, n.d. https://ernestbecker.org/resources/terror-management-theory/.

3. Castle, Tyler. "Does Wealth Make Us Less Religious?" Initiative on Faith and Public Life, March 26, 2015. https://faithandpubliclife.com/does-wealth-make-us-less-religious/.

4. Gecewicz, Claire. "'New Age' Beliefs Common Among Both Religious and Nonreligious Americans." Pew Research Center, October 1, 2018. https://www.pewresearch.org/fact-tank/2018/10/01/new-age-beliefs-common-among-both-religious-and-nonreligious-americans/.

5. Banerjee, Neela. "Wiccans Keep the Faith with a Religion Under Wraps." *New York Times*, May 16, 2007. https://www.nytimes.com/2007/05/16/us/16wiccan.html.

6. "When Man Ceases to Worship God." Society of Gilbert Keith Chesterton, April 29, 2012. https://www.chesterton.org/ceases-to-worship/.

7. Deuteronomy 26: 11–12.

COMMITMENT

1. Simmons, Rabbi Shraga. "Bnei Brak Wise Men." Aish.com, April 2, 2003. https://www.aish.com/h/pes/h/Bnei-Brak-Wise-Men.html.

THE JEWISH SECRET OF PARENTING

1. Deuteronomy 6:4, Zacharia 14:9, Job 13:3.

2. Rabinowitz, Louis. "TORAH MIN HA-SHAMAYIM." *Tradition: A Journal of Orthodox Jewish Thought* 7, no. 1 (1964): 34–45. Accessed June 4, 2020. www.jstor.org/stable/23255980. Pg. 39.

3. Blech, Rabbi Benjamin. "The Oscar Nominated Film About the Four Sons at the Seder." Aish.com, March 24, 2018. https://www.aish.com/h/pes/h/The-Oscar-Nominated-Film-about-the-Four-Sons-at-the-Seder.html.

HOW INTELLECTUAL INQUIRY IS OF LIMITED VALUE: CONSIDERING THE WISE SON

1. Mishnah Berakhot 9:5.

2. Bereshit Rabbah 9:7.

3. BT Shabbat 156a.

4. JT Tractate Terumot 47a.

5. Jacobson, Y. Y. "The Insanity of the Human Psyche." The Yeshiva, May 19, 2016. https://www.theyeshiva.net/jewish/2800.

6. BT Tamid 32a.

   See also: Pirkei Avot 2:9.

7. Siegel, Danny, Neal Gold, and Joseph Telushkin. *Radiance: Creative Mitzvah Living.* Lincoln, NE: Jewish Publication Society, 2020. Pg. xv.

8. Kristol, Irving. "On the Political Stupidity of the Jews." Tikvah Fund, 1999. https://tikvahfund.org/uncategorized/on-the-political-stupidity-of-the-jews/.

9. Johnson, Paul. *The History of the Jews.* New York: Harper Perennial, 1988. Pp. 341.

10. BT Keddushin 40b.

11. Pirkei Avot 3:17.

THE FUNDAMENTAL PRINCIPLE OF JUDAISM: CONSIDERING THE WICKED SON

1. Maimonides, Mishneh Torah, Laws of Human Dispositions 6:1.

2. Selikow, Terry-Ann, Nazeema Ahmed, Alan J. Flisher, Catherine Mathews, and Wanjiru Mukoma. "I Am Not "umqwayito": A Qualitative Study of Peer Pressure and Sexual Risk Behaviour Among Young Adolescents in Cape Town, South Africa." *Scandinavian Journal of Public Health* 37, no. 2 suppl. (June 2009): 107–12. doi:10.1177/1403494809103903; "Peer Pressure." U.S. Department of Health and Human Services, March 25, 2019. https://www.hhs.gov/ash/oah/adolescent-development/healthy-relationships/healthy-friendships/peer-pressure/index.html; Wang, Shirley S. "Peer Pressure for Teens Paves the Path to Adulthood." *Wall Street Journal,* June 17, 2013. https://www.wsj.com/articles/SB10001424127887324520904578551462766909232. National Center for Education Statistics, June 1997. https://nces.ed.gov/pubs97/web/97055.asp.

3. Riskin, Rabbi Shlomo. "Rabbi Riskin on Parshat Chukat—Torah Lights 5772." YouTube, June 24, 2012. https://www.youtube.com/watch?v=uIrpGyJeEYE.

4. Updike, John. "Hub Fans Bid Kid Adieu." *New Yorker,* October 22, 1960. https://www.newyorker.com/magazine/1960/10/22/hub-fans-bid-kid-adieu.

5. Feigenbaum, Rabbi Shimon. "Seder Thoughts." Torah from Dixie, n.d. http://www.tfdixie.com/holidays/passover/009.htm.

6. https://www.heschel.org/the-heschel-experience/pluralism.

7. Derech Eretz Zuta 9:2.

8. Mishnah Rosh Hashanah 2:8, 2:9.

   Issacson, Chaim. "The Jewish Month." *Jewish Magazine,* February 2000. http://www.jewishmag.com/29mag/moon/moon.htm.

9. Midrash Tanhuma Buber Nitzavim 4.

10. "Kedoshim In Depth—A Condensation of the Weekly Torah Portion Alongside Select Commentaries Culled from the Midrash, Talmud, Chassidic Masters, and the Broad Corpus of Jewish Scholarship." Chabad. Accessed June 4, 2020. https://www.chabad.org/parshah/in-depth /default_cdo/aid/75895/jewish/In-Depth.htm.

11. Telushkin, Joseph, *A Code of Jewish Ethics: Volume 1: You Shall Be Holy* (Deckle Edge 2006), Pg. 84.

12. Scheiner, Rabbi Moshe. "Conduit = Can Do It." YouTube, May 16, 2019. https://youtu.be /QvMHmA14D7Y.

Schneerson, Rabbi Menachem M. "Shalom Aleichem–Aleichem Shalom." Chabad.org, n.d. https://www.chabad.org/therebbe/article_cdo/aid/2513936/jewish/Shalom-Aleichem-Aleichem -Shalom.htm.

13. Bereshit Rabba 54:3.

14. Bereshit Rabbah 54:3.

15. King, Martin Luther, Jr. "Address at the Freedom Rally in Cobo Hall." Martin Luther King, Jr., Research and Education Institute, June 23, 1963. https://kinginstitute.stanford.edu/king -papers/documents/address-freedom-rally-cobo-hall.

16. Lamm, Rabbi Norman. "What Makes a Jewish Song Jewish." Yeshiva University, February 9, 1952. https://archives.yu.edu/gsdl/collect/lammserm/index/assoc/HASH01f2.dir/doc.pdf.

17. BT Arachin 16b.

18. Moss, Aron. "The Wicked Son." Chabad.org, n.d. https://www.chabad.org/holidays /passover/pesach_cdo/aid/660998/jewish/The-Wicked-Son.htm.

See also the discussion of the wicked son, especially for the parental responsibility: Sacks, Jonathan. *Rabbi Jonathan Sacks's Haggadah: Hebrew and English Text with New Essays and Commentary.* New York: Continuum, 2007.

The gematria for teeth is also attributed to the eighteenth-century rabbi the Vilna Gaon: Herczeg, Yisrael Isser Zvi. *Vilna Gaon Haggadah: The Passover Haggadah with Commentaries.* Brooklyn: Mesorah, 1999.

19. BT Bava Batra 21a.

20. "Parshat Ki Tisa In-Depth." Chabad.org, n.d. https://www.chabad.org/parshah/in-depth /default_cdo/aid/39522/jewish/Ki-Tisa-In-Depth.htm.

WHO IS THE IDEAL HUSBAND? CONSIDERING THE SIMPLE SON

1. The characterization of this son as "stupid" seems to derive from the third son being identified as "stupid" in: JT Pesachim 70b.

2. Rabinowitz, Shmuel. "Parshat Shoftim: The Power of Wholeheartedness." *Jerusalem Post,* August 8, 2013. https://www.jpost.com/Opinion/Columnists/Parshat-Shoftim-The-power-of -wholeheartedness-322519.

Held, Rabbi Shai. "Against Half-Heartedness." Hadar, November 2013. https://www.hadar .org/torah-resource/against-half-heartedness#source-418.

Pearce, Rabbi Stephen S. "Finding Wholeheartedness in Your Life." ReformJudaism.org, September 21, 2017. https://reformjudaism.org/learning/torah-study/noach/finding-wholeheartedness -your-life.

Bronstein, Rabbi Yisrael. "Shirat Devorah." *Shirat Devorah* (blog), November 2, 2010. http://shiratdevorah.blogspot.com/2010/11/most-noble-trait.html.

WHAT SHOULD WE BE ASKING? CONSIDERING THE SON WHO DOES NOT KNOW HOW TO ASK

1. Sacks, Rabbi Jonathan. *Rabbi Jonathan Sacks's Haggadah: Hebrew and English Text with New Essays and Commentary.* New York: Continuum, 2006. Pg. 226.

2. Emrani, Afshine. "The Kotzker Rebbe: Angels, Miracles and Broken Hearts." *Jewish Journal,* March 2, 2020. https://jewishjournal.com/mobile_20111212/154886/the-kotzker-rebbe-angels -miracles-and-broken-hearts/.

3. Wiesel, Elie. *A Passover Haggadah as Commented upon by Elie Wiesel.* New York: Simon and Schuster, 1993. Pg. 35.

FINDING THE IMAGE OF GOD (IT'S NOT HARD)

1. BT Chullin 5a, Sanhedrin 100b, and Maimonides, Mishneh Torah, Foreign Worship and Customs of the Nations 2:5.

2. Green, Arthur. *Judaism's Ten Best Ideas.* Woodstock, VT: Jewish Lights Publishing, 2014. Pg. 12.

IDENTIFY ENEMIES—AND ALSO FRIENDS

1. Exodus 17:16.

2. Domnitch, Larry. *Jewish Holidays: A Journey Through History.* Northvale, NJ: Jason Aronson, 2000. Pg. 19.

3. Klitsner, Judy. "Inside-Outside Biblical Leaders and Their Non-Jewish Mentors." May 12, 2017, podcast. https://podcast.occsp.org/wp/category/klitsner_judy/.

4. Eichah Rabbah 2:13.

5. BT Berachot 58a.

6. Wolpe, Rabbi David. "'Baruch HaShem,' Indeed." *Times of Israel,* August 23, 2017. https://blogs.timesofisrael.com/baruch-hashem-indeed/.

"When Did the Jews Adopt the Custom of Saying 'Baruch Hashem'?" Mi Yodeya, March 3, 2016. https://judaism.stackexchange.com/questions/68837/when-did-jews-adopt-the-custom-of -saying-baruch-hashem.

Melchizedek's formulation was slightly different but substantively the same. It was Baruch El Elyon: "Blessed Be the Most High God."

7. Schneerson, Rabbi Menachem Mendel. "Ask Not What G-d Can Do for You . . ." Chabad .org, March 2, 1961. https://www.chabad.org/therebbe/livingtorah/player_cdo/aid/878371 /jewish/Ask-Not-What-G-d-Can-Do-For-You.htm.

8. Yerushalmi, Yosef Hayim. *Zakhor Jewish History and Jewish Memory.* Seattle: University of Washington Press, 2002. Pg. 16.

9. Maimonides Commentary on Mishnah Sanhedrin 10:1.

10. "Ground-Breaking Israel Films." CBN Israel, n.d. https://www.cbn.com/giving/special /israeldvds.aspx.

11. The Great Buffalo Jewbilee: https://eagleswings.org/the-great-buffalo-jewbilee/.

12. Plummer, Dr. Glenn R. "Dr. Glenn R. Plummer." YouTube, May 27, 2015. https://www
.youtube.com/watch?v=hrMMilD89Lw.

13. Chaput, Charles J. "Yeshiva Lessons." First Things, August 2012. https://www.firstthings
.com/article/2012/08/yeshiva-lessons.

THE JEWISH WAY OF LEARNING

1. Singer, Isidore, Cyrus Adler, and Susan Rothchild. *The Jewish Encyclopedia: A Descriptive Record of the History, Religion, Literature, and Customs of the Jewish People from the Earliest Times.* Prepared under the direction of Cyrus Adler. Isidore Singer, Project and Managing Editor, Assisted by American and Foreign Boards of Consulting Editors. New York: Ktav, 1964. Pg. 295.

2. Pirkei Avot 2:2.

3. BT Sanhedrin 36b and Maimonides, Mishneh Torah, The Sanhedrin and the Penalties Within Their Jurisdiction 2:3.

DESTINY'S INGREDIENTS: FAMILY AND DREAMS

1. JT Sotah 5a–b.

2. Hirsch, Samson Raphael. *The Hirsch Haggadah.* 2nd ed. Nanuet, NY: Feldheim, 1994. Pg. 14.

3. Riskin, Shlomo. *The Passover Haggadah: With a Traditional and Contemporary Commentary.* Brooklyn, NY: Ktav, 1983. Pg. 74.

4. Steinsaltz, Rabbi Adin Even-Israel. *Talks on the Parasha.* Jerusalem: Koren, 2015. Pg. 310.

IMAGINATION: THE MOST IMPORTANT PART OF REALITY

1. See Rabbi David Wolpe's magnificent sermon on the farmer and the imagination: Wolpe, Rabbi David. "Ki Tavo—Imagination." Sinai Temple, September 24, 2016. https://www.sinaitemple
.org/worship/sermons/ki-tavo-reward-mitzvah/.

2. From a 1929 interview that Professor Einstein had with the *Saturday Evening Post.* Nilsson, Jeff, and Nicholas Gilmore. "Albert Einstein: 'Imagination Is More Important Than Knowledge': The Saturday Evening Post." *Saturday Evening Post* comments, March 20, 2010. https://www
.saturdayeveningpost.com/2010/03/imagination-important-knowledge/.

3. Exodus 2:1, Exodus 6:20.

4. Riskin, Rabbi Shlomo. "Parshat Shmot: An Ode to Grandparenthood." *Jerusalem Post,* January 8, 2015. https://www.jpost.com/Not-Just-News/Parshat-Shmot-An-ode-to-grandparenthood-387128.

5. Fohrman, Rabbi David. "Optimism vs. Pessimism: The Danger of Blurring Imagination and Reality." Aleph Beta, n.d. https://www.alephbeta.org/playlist/parshat-shelach-is-hope-irrational.

JUDAISM: A RELIGION OF CHARACTER

1. Fohrman, David. "Bikkurim: The Historical Significance of the First Fruits Offering." Aleph Beta. Accessed June 4, 2020. https://www.alephbeta.org/playlist/parshat-ki-tavo-your-place-in
-jewish-history.

2. Yerushalmi, Yosef Hayim. *Zakhor: Jewish History and Jewish Memory.* Seattle, WA: University of Washington Press, 2002, Pg. 9.

3. Held, Rabbi Shai. "Can We Be Grateful and Disappointed at the Same Time?" Hadar.org, July 29, 2014. https://www.hadar.org/torah-resource/can-we-be-grateful-and-disappointed-same -time.

4. Keter Shem Tov, appendix 169.

5. JT Kiddushin 48b.

6. Goldson, Rabbi Yonason. "Ethics of the Fathers, 3:9 Direct Line to the Heaves." Aish.com, Nov. 11, 2006. https://www.aish.com/sp/pg/48909322.html.

7. Resnick, Brian. "Why Willpower Is Overrated." *Vox*, January 15, 2018. https://www.vox.com /science-and-health/2018/1/15/16863374/willpower-overrated-self-control-psychology.

8. Morinis, Alan. "Path of the Soul #3: Gratitude." Aish.com. Accessed June 4, 2020. https:// www.aish.com/sp/pg/48906987.html.

9. Deuteronomy 10:18.

10. Goldstein, Justin. "Ha'Shofar, the Newsletter of Congregation Beth Israel," May 2019.

11. Quoted in: Linzer, Dov, "Change? Yes We can." YC Torah, December 24, 2015. https:// library.yctorah.org/2015/12/change-yes-we-can/.

Widely cited, including: "Personal Growth in Judaism II: Making It Happen." OLAMI Re-sources, n.d. http://nleresources.com/wp-content/uploads/2012/07/Personal-Growth-in-Judaism -II.pdf.

YOU ARE IN THE STORY

1. Safran, Rabbi Eliyahu. "Seven: The Power of Numbers." OU Torah, n.d. https://www.ou.org /torah/parsha/parsha-from-ou/seven-the-power-of-numbers/.

2. Bamidbar Rabbah 14:12.

3. Rashi identifies that there were only 69 people—Rashi on Genesis 46:26.

STARS

1. "Torah versus Science." Aish.com, n.d. https://www.aish.com/atr/Torah_versus_Science.html.

2. Deuteronomy 7:7.

3. Johnson, Paul. *A History of the Jews.* London: Weidenfeld and Nicolson, 1987. Epilogue.

4. Maimonides, Commentary on Mishnah, Sanhedrin 10:1.

5. Sacks, Rabbi Jonathan. "Ki Tissa (5770)—Counting the Contributions." Rabbi Sacks, March 6, 2010. http://rabbisacks.org/covenant-conversation-5770-ki-tissa-counting-the-contributions/.

6. Sela, Shlomo. "Parashat Behar-Behukotai." Lectures on the Torah Reading by the faculty of Bar-Ilan University, Ramat, Gan, Israel, June 1998. https://www.biu.ac.il/JH/Parasha/eng/bahar /kle.html.

7. Wein, Berel. "How the Jews Invented Checks." Jewish History Blog, February 20, 2010. https://www.jewishhistory.org/how-the-jews-invented-checks/.

8. Howell, Elizabeth. "How Many Stars Are in the Universe?" Space.com, May 18, 2017. https:// www.space.com/26078-how-many-stars-are-there.html.

9. Sfas Emes, Exodus, 5632.

Held, Rabbi Shai. "Lighting Up the Darkness: Hanukkah as a Spiritual Practice." *HuffPost,* May 25, 2011. https://www.huffingtonpost.com/rabbi-shai-held/lighting-up-the-darkness-_b_791649.html.

10. Pirkei Avot 2:16.

11. Job 38:31.

12. Brumfiel, Geoff. "U.S. Navy Brings Back Navigation by the Stars for Officers." NPR, February 22, 2016. https://www.npr.org/2016/02/22/467210492/u-s-navy-brings-back-navigation-by-the-stars-for-officers.

Mollman, Steve. "The US Navy Is Reinstating the Ancient Art of Celestial Navigation to Fight a Very Modern Threat." Quartz, October 15, 2015. https://qz.com/524795/the-us-navy-is-reinstating-the-ancient-art-of-celestial-navigation-to-fight-a-very-modern-threat/.

Ahronheim, Anna. "IDF Teaches Cadets the Language Needed to Win the Next War." *Jerusalem Post,* May 26, 2020. https://www.jpost.com/israel-news/learning-the-same-language-to-win-the-next-war-629336.

RISKING CONGRATULATIONS

1. BT Shabbat 129b.

2. Burke, Edmund. *Reflections on the Revolution in France.* North Chelmsford, MA: Courier Corporation, 2012. Pg. 6.

3. "Earvin 'Magic' Johnson's 1st NBA Game," YouTube, February 5, 2010, https://www.youtube.com/watch?v=uv4Yy6aAWgw.

4. Ostler, Scott. "Here's a Big Hug for Kareem, Other Assorted Awards." *Los Angeles Times,* June 11, 1985. https://articles.latimes.com/1985-06-11/sports/sp-10469_1_boa-constrictor.

WHY DID GOD WAIT? WHEN BAD THINGS HAPPEN TO GOOD PEOPLE

1. Balashon. "Lama and Madua." Balashon, May 9, 2016. http://www.balashon.com/2016/05/lama-and-madua.html; Fohrman, David. "Can Prayer Change God's Will? How Moses' Bravery Influenced God's Actions." Aleph Beta. Accessed June 4, 2020. https://www.alephbeta.org/playlist/can-we-change-gods-will.

2. "Lama and Madua." *Balashon,* May 9, 2016. https://www.balashon.com/2016/05/lama-and-madua.html.

3. Taleb, Nassim Nicholas. "Learning to Expect the Unexpected." https://www.edge.org/3rd_culture/taleb04/taleb_indexx.html.

4. Maimonides, Mishneh Torah, Laws of Mourning 13:9 and 13:3.

5. Prager, Dennis. *The Rational Bible: Exodus: God, Slavery, and Freedom.* Washington, DC: Regnery Faith, 2018. Pg. 30.

JEW HATRED, EXPLAINED

1. Wolpe, Rabbi David. "Shemot—Becoming a People." Sinai Temple, January 2, 2016. https://www.sinaitemple.org/worship/sermons/shemot-becoming-people/.

Schweiger, Meir. "5780—Shemot: Who Are You—What Is Your Name?" Elmad, January 12, 2020. https://elmad.pardes.org/2020/01/5780-shemot-who-are-you-what-is-your-name/.

2. O'Grady, Siobhán. "Rwandan Who Called Tutsis 'Cockroaches' in 1992 Gets Life Sentence." *Foreign Policy*, April 19, 2016. https://foreignpolicy.com/2016/04/15/rwandan-who-called-tutsis -cockroaches-in-1992-gets-life-sentence/; Drury, Colin. "Antisemitic Carnival Float Had Cari-catures of Smiling Jews, Sacks of Money and a Rat." *Independent*, March 7, 2019. https://www .independent.co.uk/news/world/europe/antisemitism-belgium-carnival-jewish-aalst-money -a8809736.html.

3. Kellogg, Michael. *The Russian Roots of Nazism: White Émigrés and the Making of National Socialism, 1917–1945*. Cambridge: Cambridge University Press, 2005. Pg. 128.

"Malaysia Defends Speech on Jews." BBC News, October 17, 2003. http://news.bbc.co.uk/2 /hi/asia-pacific/3196234.stm.

Heller, Kevin Jon. "Henry Ford—Not Such a Good Role Model." Opinio Juris, April 3, 2012. http://opiniojuris.org/2012/04/03/henry-ford-not-such-a-good-role-model/.

4. I owe this insight to a discussion I had with Michael Oren in Tel Aviv. Michael remarked on how he was attacked as a boy growing up in New Jersey for being a "Christ killer." Jewish kids in New Jersey are not now being attacked as "Christ killers," because the insult no longer speaks to a dominant belief of the anti-Semites. Instead, students at high schools and colleges are being attacked for being affiliated with the racist and colonialist Jewish state—as anti-racism and anti-colonialism are the dominant beliefs of these anti-Semites.

See also: Sacks, Rabbi Jonathan. "The Mutating Virus: Understanding Antisemitism." Rabbi Sacks, September 27, 2016. http://rabbisacks.org/mutating-virus-understanding-antisemitism/.

5. "Desecration of Host." Jewish Virtual Library, n.d. https://www.jewishvirtuallibrary.org/host -desecration-of.

6. Poliakov, Léon. *The History of Anti-Semitism: Volume 3: From Voltaire to Wagner*. Philadel-phia: University of Pennsylvania Press, 2003. Pg. 89.

7. Marx, Karl. *On the Jewish Question*. Proofed and Corrected: by Andy Blunden, Matthew Grant and Matthew Carmody, 2008/9. https://www.marxists.org/archive/marx/works/1844 /jewish-question/.

8. Marks, Jonathan. "At Williams College, Zionists Need Not Apply." *Commentary*, May 2, 2019. https://www.commentarymagazine.com/anti-semitism/at-williams-college-zionists-need-not-apply/.

9. Dvorak, Petula. "White Supremacists Are Recruiting White Teens Online. Parents Must Stop Them." *Washington Post*, August 15, 2019. https://www.washingtonpost.com/local/white -supremacists-are-recruiting-white-teens-online-parents-must-stop-them/2019/08/15/5169c192 -bf69-11e9-b873-63ace636af08_story.html.

10. Muther, Christopher. "Welcome to Tel Aviv, the Gayest City on Earth." *Boston Globe*, March 17, 2016. https://www.bostonglobe.com/lifestyle/travel/2016/03/17/welcome-tel-aviv-gayest-city -earth/y9V15VazXhtSjXVSo9gT9K/story.html.

11. "After Banning Jewish Flags Last Year, Chicago Dyke March Displays Palestinian Flags." Jewish Telegraphic Agency, June 25, 2018. https://www.jta.org/2018/06/25/united-states/banning- jewish-flags-last-year-chicago-dyke-march-displays-palestinian-flags.

12. Moskovitz, Daniel J. "Pharaoh Didn't Know Joseph." My Jewish Learning, n.d. https://www .myjewishlearning.com/article/Pharaoh-didnt-know-joseph-and-perhaps-we-forgot-him-too/.

13. Ibid. Reston, James. "Who Are the Friends of Israel?; WASHINGTON." *New York Times,* January 31, 1975. https://www.nytimes.com/1975/01/31/archives/who-are-the-friends-of-israel -washington.html.

14. In 2018, the Williams College Council was presented with the opportunity to vote up or down on accepting the Williams Initiative for Israel—when every club that had been proposed over the past ten years had been easily accepted. The anti-Semites opposed the Williams Initiative for Israel for predictable reasons. Some of the Jewish students responded by saying that they were victims too. The anti-Semites responded by saying that they would not allow invocation of the Holocaust to diminish Palestinian suffering. The anti-Semites won, 13–8, making the Williams Initiative for Israel the first group voted down by the council in ten years.

15. Chesterfield, Philip Dormer Stanhope, and David Roberts. *Lord Chesterfield's Letters.* Oxford: Oxford University Press, 2008. Pg. 15.

THE PRAYER

1. Shulchan Aruch, Orach Chayim 101:2, Mishneh Torah, Prayer and the Priestly Blessing 5:9, Mishnah Berachot 2:3.

2. Shulchan Aruch, Orach Chayim 101:2.

3. Weil, Rabbi Steven. "Tefillah: A Unique Method of Communicating with God." Jewish Action, 2010. https://jewishaction.com/from-the-desk-of-rabbi-steven-weil/tefillah_a_unique _method_of_communicating_with_god/.

4. Wolpe, Rabbi David. "Vayikra: The Meaning of Sacrifice." Sermon given on March 28, 2020. https://www.sinaitemple.org/worship/sermons/.

5. Gordon, Nehemia. "Torah Pearls #13—Shemot (Exodus 1:1–6:1)." Nehemia's Wall, January 13, 2020. https://www.nehemiaswall.com/torah-pearls-shemot.

6. BT Berakhot 21b.

7. Sefer Kuzari 3.
   BT Berakhot 21a.
   BT Megilla 23b.

8. Maimonides, Mishneh Torah, Prayer and the Priestly Blessing 8:1.

9. Shulchan Aruch, Orach Chayim 90:9.

10. Jacobs, Louis. "Demythologising the Rabbinic Aggadah: Menahem Meiri." Seforim Blog, June 30, 2014. https://seforimblog.com/2014/06/demythologising-rabbinic-aggada/.

11. BT Berakhot 5b.

12. BT Keritot 6b.

13. Pinner, Daniel. "Be an Etrog!" Israel National News. Accessed June 4, 2020. http://www .israelnationalnews.com/Articles/Article.aspx/13845.

THE UNFINISHED: THE JEWISH WAY OF LIFE AND DEATH

1. Held, Rabbi Shai. "The Journey and the (Elusive) Destination." Hadar, n.d. https://www .hadar.org/torah-resource/journey-and-elusive-destination.

2. Sacks, Rabbi Jonathan. "The Missing Fifth—an Extract from Rabbi Sacks' Haggada."

Rabbi Sacks, March 28, 2015. http://rabbisacks.org/the-missing-fifth-an-extract-from-rabbi-sacks-haggada/.

JT Pesachim 10:1, is the source that the four cups respond to the four expressions.

Kaplan, Rabbi Mendel. "Four Expressions of Redemption: How to Study Torah—Va'eira." Chabad.org, n.d. https://www.chabad.org/multimedia/video_cdo/aid/1731266/jewish/Four-Expressions-of-Redemption.htm.

3. Kahn, Yoel H. "What's Your Problem?" ReformJudaism.org, June 7, 2010. https://reformjudaism.org/learning/torah-study/torah-commentary/whats-your-problem.

4. Seventeen theories are listed here: Kasher, Rabbi David. "EIGHTEEN ANSWERS—Parshat Chukat." ParshaNut, n.d. https://parshanut.com/post/122430845981/eighteen-answers-parshat-chukat.

5. Deuteronomy 34:10–12.

6. Deuteronomy 34:7.

7. Troftgruben, Troy M. *A Conclusion Unhindered: A Study of the Ending of Acts Within Its Literary Environment*. Tübingen: Mohr Siebeck, 2010. Pg. 62.

8. Heath, Chip, and Dan Heath. *The Power of Moments: Why Certain Experiences Have Extraordinary Impact*. New York: Simon and Schuster, 2017. Pg. 9.

9. Collingwood, Jane. "Childbirth Experience Determines Memory of Pain." Psych Central, October 8, 2018. https://psychcentral.com/lib/childbirth-experience-determines-memory-of-pain/.

10. Kahneman, Daniel. "Daniel Kahneman on Misery, Memory, and Our Understanding of the Mind." NPR. March 13, 2018. https://www.npr.org/transcripts/592986190.

11. Aristotle, *Poetics* 1452a.

12. Steinsaltz, Rabbi Adin Even-Israel. *Talks on the Parasha*. Jerusalem: Koren, 2015. Pg. 74.

13. Pirkei Avot 4:1.

14. Fuchs, Rabbi Raphael. "The View from the Beis Medrash." JewishPress.com, February 6, 2013. https://www.jewishpress.com/sections/community/the-view-from-the-beis-medrash/my-machberes-55/2013/02/06/2/.

15. Peres, Shimon. "The Dissatisfied Nation." *The Peoplehood Papers: The Collective Jewish Conversation: Its Role, Purpose and Place in the 21st Century* 9 (November 2012): 8–10. https://www.jpeoplehood.org/wp-content/uploads/2012/11/Peoplehood9final.pdf.

Peres, Shimon, and David Landau. *Ben-Gurion: A Political Life*. New York: Nextbook/Schocken, 2011. Pg. 14.

16. Azolai, Rabbi Menachem. "Parsha Korach." Translated by Dov Elias. Light of Emuna, June 23, 2012. http://tloe.mmny.net/wp-content/uploads/2013/11/TLOE-2012-0623-Korach-5772.pdf.

Parsons, John J. "The Madness of Korach: Further Thoughts on Parsha Korach." Hebrew for Christians, n.d. https://www.hebrew4christians.com/Scripture/Parashah/Summaries/Korach/Madness/madness.html.

17. Genesis 6:9.

18. Rabbi David Wolpe has spoken of the imperative of walking many times in this context—and always magnificently. For instance: Wolpe, David. "Emor—Who's a Hypocrite?" Sinai Temple, May 21, 2016. https://www.sinaitemple.org/worship/sermons/emor-whos-hypocrite/.

19. Wolpe, Rabbi David. "Methuselah and Me." Sinai Temple, November 27, 2017. https://www.sinaitemple.org/learn/off-the-pulpit/methuselah-and-me/.

Lawson, Wayne. "Methuselah: What Are You Living For." Bedford Presbyterian Church, n.d. https://www.bedfordpresbyva.org/docs/People_To_Know_Series/2015-4-19_Methusalah-What_Are_You_Living_For.pdf.

20. Mishnah Sanhedrin 4:5.

21. BT Niddah 21a.

22. https://www.ssa.gov/oact/babynames/top5names.html.

WHY JEWISH BOYS EMERGE FROM THE WOMB UNCIRCUMCISED

1. Leviticus 12:3.

2. Exodus 34:1.

3. Exodus 12:15.

4. Exodus 22:22.

5. Exodus 19:6.

6. Riskin, Rabbi Shlomo. "'What's So Special About Bread?'" Torahplace, n.d. http://www.torahplace.com/whats-so-special-about-bread/. The reference to Jews coming out of the womb uncircumcised comes from a discussion that the Roman governor Tyrannus Rufus the Evil had with Rabbi Akiva, as reported in Midrash Tanchuma, Tazria 5.

7. Exodus 17:7.

8. Pirkei Avot 5:23.

9. Norton, Michael I., Daniel Mochon, and Dan Ariely. "The 'IKEA Effect': When Labor Leads to Love." Harvard Business School, 2011. https://www.hbs.edu/faculty/Pages/item.aspx?num=41121.

10. Steinsaltz, Adin Even-Israel. "Let My People Know." Aleph Society, June 13, 2018. https://steinsaltz.org/essay/goldenmean/.

11. Ullman, Rabbi Yirmiyahu. "Love." Ohr Somayach, July 19, 2003. https://ohr.edu/explore_judaism/ask_the_rabbi/ask_the_rabbi/1118.

12. Lamm, Rabbi Norman. "The Staff of Moses: Three Views on Leadership." Yeshiva University, January 7, 1961. https://archives.yu.edu/gsdl/collect/lammserm/index/assoc/HASH36b2.dir/doc.pdf.

13. Abravanel on Exodus 4:18.

14. Jacobson, Y. Y. "Let There Be Life!" The Yeshiva, June 18, 2015. https://www.theyeshiva.net/jewish/2486.

15. "Facing Darkness (Film)." Samaritan's Purse. Accessed June 4, 2020. https://www.samaritanspurse.org/our-ministry/facing-darkness/.

16. BT Yoma 72b.

WHY ANY PLAGUES?

1. Fohrman, Rabbi David. "Serpents of Desire: Good and Evil in the Garden of Eden." Jewish World Review, October 15, 2004. http://www.jewishworldreview.com/1004/fohrman1.php3.

2. "Adorable Set of Ten Plush Passover Plagues Representations, with Convenient Carrying Drawstring Bag." Amazon, n.d. https://www.amazon.com/Adorable-Passover-Representations-Convenient-Drawstring/dp/B00BI1N8N6.

FIRST, HARMLESS MAGIC

1. Livingston, David. "The Plagues and the Exodus." Ancient Days, n.d. http://davelivingston.com/plagues.htm.

2. Butt, Kyle. "Egyptian Magicians, Snakes, and Rods." Apologetics Press, n.d. https://www.apologeticspress.org/apcontent.aspx?category=11&article=1704.

3. Shah, Tahir. *Sorcerer's Apprentice*. London: Secretum Mundi, 2013. Pp. 134–5.

Other ancient snake tricks are reported by: Korem, Danny. *Powers: Testing the Psychic and Supernatural*. Westmont, IL: InterVarsity Press, 1988. Pg. 176.

RATIONALITY: FIGHTING BLOOD, FROGS, AND LICE WITH . . . MORE BLOOD, FROGS, AND LICE

1. Aleph Beta used to have an outstanding series of videos on the plagues on its site. The video on the first plague is no longer there. There are still remarkable discussions of the plagues, among other topics, on alephbeta.com.

2. Fohrman, Rabbi David. "The Three Great Lies of the Exodus: Understanding the Miraculous Signs God Showed Moses." Aleph Beta, n.d. https://www.alephbeta.org/playlist/three-miracles-of-moses.

3. Exodus 7:29.

4. The point that the Pharaoh could have attempted to turn the blood back into water is from Rabbi Samson Raphael Hirsch.

See: Weiss, Rabbi Avi. "Charlatans Can't Fool People Forever." *South Florida Sun-Sentinel*. January 21, 2020. https://www.sun-sentinel.com/florida-jewish-journal/devar-torah/fl-jj-torah-weiss-va-eira-20200122-20200121-dy2d2oj65jc2zloze6elszhx6q-story.html. Accessed February 27, 2020.

5. For instance, the former chairman of the Joint Chiefs of Staff, General Martin Dempsey, said that Iran was a "rational" power in his assessment of the Iranian nuclear threat.

6. Hashemi-Rafsanjani, Akbar. "Qods Day Speech (Jerusalem Day)." GlobalSecurity.org. December 4, 2001. https://www.globalsecurity.org/wmd/library/news/iran/2001/011214-text.html.

7. Rashi on Exodus 7:19 and 8:12.

HABITS: HOW THE PHARAOH TEACHES US TO LIVE FREELY

1. Genesis 7:6–24.

2. Genesis 19:24–25.

3. Exodus 32:20.

4. Numbers 16:31–33.

5. Nachmanides on Exodus 7:3.

This interpretation is also that of the masters: Rabbi Joseph Albo, Book of Roots IV:25, and Sforno on Exodus 7:3.

6. Pirkei Avot 4:2.

7. JT Nedarim 30b.

8. Rabbi Jacob ibn Habib, Ein Yaakov, Introduction.

See also: Herman, Rabbi Ben. "The Most Important Verse in Torah." Meet Rabbi Herman, April 2, 2018. https://rabbibenherman.com/2018/04/02/the-most-important-verse-in-torah1/.

9. Perez, Rabbi Doron. "The Most Important Passuk in the Torah." World Mizrachi, n.d. https://mizrachi.org/the-most-important-passuk-in-the-torah/.

Rabbi Moshe Gitler points out that this idea comes from: Rabbi Yaakov Ibn Chaviv, Netivot Olam, Netiv Ahavat Reia 1:4.

10. Rabbi Moses Luzzatto, *The Path of the Just*. Northvale, NJ: Jason Aronson, 1996. Chapter 7.

11. Ben-Avie, Michael, Yossi Ives, and Kate Loewenthal. *Applied Jewish Values in Social Sciences and Psychology*, Cham, Switzerland: Springer International, 2015. Pg. 135.

12. Maimonides, Commentary on Mishnah, Pirkei Avot 3:15.

13. Simmons, Rabbi Shraga. "Middot Series #1—the Art of Character Perfection." Aish.com, December 19, 2015. https://www.aish.com/sp/pg/The-Art-of-Character-Perfection.html.

Bogomilsky, Moshe. "Questions and Answers on the Torah Reading of the First Day of Shavuot." Chabad.org, n.d. https://www.chabad.org/library/article_cdo/aid/2836589/jewish/Torah-Reading-of-the-First-Day-of-Shavuot.htm.

14. "How Long Did the 10 Plagues of Egypt Last?" JesusAlive. Accessed June 4, 2020. https://jesusalive.cc/ques219.htm.

15. JT Taanit 2b.

16. Lally, Phillippa, Cornelia H. M. van Jaarsveld, Henry W. W. Potts, and Jane Wardle. "How Are Habits Formed: Modelling Habit Formation in the Real World." Wiley Online Library. John Wiley and Sons, July 16, 2009. https://onlinelibrary.wiley.com/doi/abs/10.1002/ejsp.674.

"ALL MY PLAGUES": THE ESSENCE OF GOD, REVEALED IN HAIL

1. Exodus 9:18.

2. Exodus 9:19.

3. Exodus 9:20–21.

4. Lamm, Rabbi Norman. "On Having a Heart." Yeshiva University, January 22, 1955. https://archives.yu.edu/gsdl/collect/lammserm/index/assoc/HASH01fa.dir/doc.pdf.

5. Ibid.

"CAN'T YOU SEE EGYPT IS LOST?": WHEN CHANGE IS HARDER THAN IT SHOULD BE

1. Exodus 10:6.

2. Exodus 10:7.

THE NINTH PLAGUE: WHEN EVEN LIGHTING A CANDLE, TO SAVE MY LIFE, IS IMPOSSIBLE

1. Bonnheim, Ana. "The True Purpose of the Plagues." ReformJudaism.org, January 24, 2017. https://reformjudaism.org/learning/torah-study/torah-commentary/true-purpose-plagues; Ushpizai, Devora. "The Plague of Darkness—Social Aspects." Bar Ilan University, April 16, 2019. https://www1.biu.ac.il/indexE.php?id=14535.

2. "History." National Candle Association, n.d. http://candles.org/history/.

3. "A Surprising Number of Adults Are Still Scared of the Dark and Check for Monsters Under Their Bed." *Mirror,* November 14, 2017. https://www.mirror.co.uk/news/weird-news/surprising -number-adults-still-scared-11520336.

4. Soloveitchik, Rabbi Joseph B. "Redemption, Prayer, Talmud Torah." *Tradition: A Journal of Orthodox Jewish Thought* 17, no. 2 (1978): 55–72. https://traditiononline.org/redemption-prayer -talmud-torah/.

5. Beverly Daniel Tatum, *Why Are All the Black Kids Sitting Together in the Cafeteria.* New York: Basic Books, 2017. Pg. 331.

6. Mineo, Liz. "Good Genes Are Nice, but Joy Is Better." *Harvard Gazette,* April 11, 2017. https://news.harvard.edu/gazette/story/2017/04/over-nearly-80-years-harvard-study-has-been -showing-how-to-live-a-healthy-and-happy-life/.

PRELUDE TO THE TENTH PLAGUE: MOSES BECOMES A LEADER

1. Exodus 11:4–8.

2. Friedman, Richard Elliott. *Commentary on the Torah.* New York: HarperCollins, 2012. Loc. 15622 (Kindle).

See also: Rodman, Rabbi Peretz. "Moses and His Flare of Anger." *New York Jewish Week,* December 31, 2013. https://jewishweek.timesofisrael.com/moses-and-his-flare-of-anger/.

3. Maimonides, Mishneh Torah, Laws of Human Dispositions 2:3.

See also: Tractate Nedarim 22b and Tractate Pesachim 66b.

And: Rosenfeld, Rabbi Dovid. "Chapter 2, Law 3©—Anger and Self-Worship." Torah.org, n.d. https://torah.org/learning/mlife-ch2law3c/.

4. BT Zevachim 102a.

ALLEGIANCES BUILD: THE ARCHITECTURE OF RELATIONSHIPS, THE CONSTITUTION OF SOCIETY

1. Cox, Linda. "God's Palindrome." Kathy Harris Books, April 21, 2013. https://kathyharrisbooks .com/gods-palindrome/.

2. Hirsch, Samson Raphael. *The Hirsch Haggadah.* 2nd ed. Nanuet, NY: Feldheim, 2014. Pg. 12.

3. Numbers 24:5.

4. Merwin, Ted. "Horns of Plenty." *New York Jewish Week,* July 25, 2017. https://jewishweek .timesofisrael.com/horns-of-plenty/.

5. Burke, Edmund. *Reflections on the Revolution in France.* North Chelmsford, MA: Courier Corporation, 2012. Pg. 44.

6. "Volunteering in the United States, 2015." U.S. Bureau of Labor Statistics, February 25, 2016. https://www.bls.gov/news.release/volun.nr0.htm.

7. Zinsmeister, Karl. "Are People of Faith More Charitable? The Evidence Points to 'Yes.'" PennLive, January 5, 2019. https://www.pennlive.com/opinion/2017/11/are_people_of_faith _more_chari.html.

"New Report Finds Religious People Are More Likely to Donate." Philanthropy Daily, October 25, 2017. https://www.philanthropydaily.com/religious-philanthropy-faith/.

8. Sandstrom, Aleksandra, and Becka A. Alper. "Americans with Higher Education and Income Are More Likely to Be Involved in Community Groups." Pew Research Center, February 22, 2019. https://www.pewresearch.org/fact-tank/2019/02/22/americans-with-higher-education -and-income-are-more-likely-to-be-involved-in-community-groups/.

9. Aron, Lewis, and Karen E. Starr. *A Psychotherapy for the People: Toward a Progressive Psychoanalysis*. New York: Routledge, 2013. Pg. 342.

10. Heilman, Uriel. "USY Drops Ban on Interdating." Jewish Telegraphic Agency, September 26, 2017. https://www.jta.org/2014/12/23/united-states/usy-drops-ban-against-interdating-1.

HASTE: THE MORAL IMPERATIVE OF SPEED

1. Luzzatto, Moshe Ḥayyim. *The Path of the Just*. Northvale, NJ: Jason Aronson, 1996. Chapter 7.

THE TENTH PLAGUE: WHAT IT MEANS THAT THE JEWS ARE THE CHOSEN PEOPLE

1. BT Nedarim 3a.

2. Exodus 12:48.

3. Gray, Alyssa. "Maimonides' Letter to a Man Named Ovadyah." Jerusalem, 1995. http://huc.edu/sites/default/files/Academics/Learn/Gray.VideoPodcast.TextMaimonides.pdf.

HOVERING, RESCUING, AND PROTECTING: NO ONE "PASSED OVER" ANYTHING, AND WHY THAT IS IMPORTANT

1. A comprehensive analysis by Dr. Barry Dov Walfish, the Judaica specialist at the University of Toronto Libraries, can be found here: Walfish, Barry Dov. "Why 'Passover'? On the True Meaning of Pesah." TheTorah.com, n.d. https://thetorah.com/why-passover-on-the-true-meaning-of -pesah/.

2. Mechilta D'Rabbi Ishmael on Exodus 12:13.

Lamm, Rabbi Norman. "Neither Thy Honey Nor Thy Sting." Yeshiva University, January 25, 1969. https://archives.yu.edu/gsdl/collect/lammserm/index/assoc/HASH083c.dir/doc.pdf.

3. No ancient Aramaic translations use *Passover*. They all used *spare* or *protect*. See: Flashman, Alan. "How Pesach Became Passover." TheTorah.com, n.d. https://thetorah.com/how-pesach -became-passover/.

WATCHING: THE EXISTENTIAL EXPERIENCE

1. Friedman, Richard Elliott. *Commentary on the Torah*. New York: HarperCollins, 2012. Loc. 7023 (Kindle).

See also: Genesis 2:15, 22:18, 28:15, 28:20, 4:9; Leviticus 18:30, 22:9; Deuteronomy 4:9, 4:23, 6:12; Joshua 23:11; 2 Chronicles 23:6; Ezekiel 44:8, 44:16, 48:11; Habakkuk 2:1; and Zechariah 3:7—and the Priestly Blessing.

Deuteronomy 6:17.

Deuteronomy 16:1.

Deuteronomy 8:11.

Proverbs 21:23.

2. Job 34:21.

3. Perry, Philip. "Why Is It You Can Sense When Someone's Staring at You?" Big Think, August 20, 2017. https://bigthink.com/philip-perry/why-is-it-you-can-sense-when-someones-staring-at-you.

4. Bateson, Melissa, et al. "Do Images of 'Watching Eyes' Induce Behaviour That Is More Pro-Social or More Normative? A Field Experiment on Littering." *PLOS One* 8, no. 12 (December 5, 2013). https://doi.org/10.1371/journal.pone.0082055.

5. Doane, Michael. "An Outline of Norenzayan's 'Big Gods.'" Religious Studies Project, March 5, 2014. https://www.religiousstudiesproject.com/2014/03/05/an-outline-of-norenzayans-big-gods-by-michael-doane/.

WHY POLITICAL ARGUMENTS ARE USUALLY A WASTE OF TIME, OR WORSE

1. Rashi on Exodus 14:10.

2. Bacon, Francis. *The New Organon or True Directions Concerning the Interpretation of Nature.* n.p.: Createspace, 2014. XLVI.

3. Festinger, Leon, Henry W. Riecken, and Stanley Schachter. *When Prophecy Fails: A Social and Psychological Study of a Modern Group That Predicted the Destruction of the World.* New York: Harper & Row, 1964. Pg. 3.

4. Westen, Drew, et al. "Neural Bases of Motivated Reasoning: An fMRI Study of Emotional Constraints on Partisan Political Judgment in the 2004 U.S. Presidential Election." *Journal of Cognitive Neuroscience* 18, no. 11 (November 18, 2006): 1947–58. https://doi.org/10.1162/jocn.2006.18.11.1947.

Brewer, Judson, Kathleen Garrison, and Susan Whitfield Gabrieli. "What About the 'Self' Is Processed in the Posterior Cingulate Cortex?" *Frontiers in Human Neuroscience* (October 2, 2013). https://www.frontiersin.org/articles/10.3389/fnhum.2013.00647/full.

Shermer, Michael. "The Political Brain." *Scientific American*, July 1, 2006. https://www.scientificamerican.com/article/the-political-brain/.

5. Wolpe, Rabbi David. "Vaera: Fail Better." Sinai Temple, January 21, 2012. https://www.sinaitemple.org/worship/sermons/vaera-fail-better/.

THE SECRET TO HAPPINESS AND GOODNESS

1. https://www.oxfordreference.com/view/10.1093/oi/authority.20110803100200612

2. Exodus: 8:19.

3. Drummond, Henry. "The Ascent of Man," 1894. https://doi.org/10.1017/cbo9780511692857.

4. Tanna D'vei Eliyahu 2.

5. The Modim prayer in the Silent Amidah Prayer.

6. Rubenstein, Rabbi Jason. "Do You Believe in Miracles?: The Subjectivity of the Miraculous." Hadar, n.d. https://www.hadar.org/torah-resource/do-you-believe-miracles.

"1911 Encyclopaedia Britannica/Semitic Languages." Wikisource, March 5, 2018. https://en.wikisource.org/wiki/1911_Encyclopedia_britannica/Semitic_Languages.

7. Blau, Joshua. *The Renaissance of Modern Hebrew and Modern Standard Arabic: Parallels and Differences in the Revival of Two Semitic Languages.* Vol 18. Los Angeles: University of California Press, 1981, Pg. 4.

Rubenstein, "Do You Believe in Miracles?"

8. Rubenstein, "Do You Believe in Miracles?"

9. Heschel, Abraham Joshua. *Between God and Man: An Interpretation of Judaism.* Edited by Fritz A. Rothschild. New York: Free Press, 1997. Pg. 41.

10. Maimonides, Moses. *The Guide for the Perplexed*, preface. Cited in Kaveh, Moshe, "Torah and Science." https://www.biu.ac.il/JH/Parasha/eng/bereshit/kavet.html.

11. Lemley, Brad. "Why Is There Life?" Discover, November 1, 2000.

12. Crick, Francis, *Life Itself: Its Original and Its Nature.* New York: Simon & Schuster, 1981. Pg. 88.

13. Prigogine, Ilya, Gregoire Nicolis, and Agnes Babloyantz. "Thermodynamics of Evolution." *Physics Today* 25, no 11 (November 1, 1972): 23.

14. Braden, Greg, *The Science of Self-Empowerment.* Carlsbad, California: Hayhouse, 2017. Pg. 92.

15. "Hoyle on Evolution," *Nature*, Vol. 294. November 12, 1981, Pg. 105

16. Kaku, Michio, "The Paradox of Multiple Goldilocks Zones or 'Did the Universe Know We Were Coming?'" BigThink, May 20, 2011. https://bigthink.com/dr-kakus-universe/the-paradox-of-multiple-goldilocks-zones-or-did-the-universe-know-we-were-coming.

17. Emmons, Robert A. "Why Gratitude Is Good." *Daily Good*, June 20, 2011. Also UC Davis Health, "Gratitude is Good Medicine," November 25, 2015.

"DAYENU": HOW TO EXPRESS GRATITUDE

1. Fohrman, Rabbi David. "The Meaning Behind Passover's Most Famous Song: Dayeinu: Would It Really Have Been Enough?" Aleph Beta, n.d. https://www.alephbeta.org/playlist/meaning-of-dayeinu-song-lyrics.

ALWAYS A SECOND CHANCE

1. http://www.jewishencyclopedia.com/articles/6352-freudline.

2. Rabbi Eliezer and Rabbi Yose both say "far-off" steps on the Temple steps. Rashi agreed. Mishnah Pesachim 9:2.

3. Greengrass, Rabbi Rachel. "Pesach Sheni and Second Chances: A Reading for Your Passover Seder." Religious Action Center of Reform Judaism, n.d. https://rac.org/sites/default/files/NCJW%20Florida-RAC%202nd%20Chances%20Seder%20reading.pdf.

Tauber, Yanki. "Never Too Late." Chabad.org, n.d. https://www.chabad.org/library/article_cdo/aid/2900/jewish/Never-Too-Late.htm.

Touger, Eli, trans. "Pesach Sheni: A Second Chance for Spiritual Progress." Chabad.org, n.d. https://www.chabad.org/therebbe/article_cdo/aid/154182/jewish/Pesach-Sheni.htm.

ABOUT THE AUTHOR

Michael Gerson

MARK GERSON, an entrepreneur and philanthropist, is the co-founder of Gerson Lehrman Group, African Mission Healthcare, and United Hatzalah of Israel.

A graduate of Williams College and Yale Law School, Mark is the author of books on intellectual history and education. His articles and essays on subjects ranging from Frank Sinatra to the biblical Jonah have been published in *The New Republic, Commentary, The Wall Street Journal,* and *USA Today.* He hosts the popular podcast *The Rabbi's Husband* and writes a weekly Torah column for the Christian Broadcasting Network. Mark is married to Rabbi Erica Gerson. They and their four children live in New York City.